# INTERVENTION IN THE AGING PROCESS

## Part A
## Quantitation, Epidemiology, and Clinical Research

## MODERN AGING RESEARCH

*Series Editors*

Richard C. Adelman
Jay Roberts

George T. Baker III
Vincent J. Cristofalo

**Volume 1: Neural Regulatory Mechanisms During Aging,** Richard C. Adelman, Jay Roberts, George T. Baker III, Steven I. Baskin, and Vincent J. Cristofalo, *Editors*

**Volume 2: Aging and Human Visual Function,** Robert Sekuler, Donald Kline, and Key Dismukes, *Editors*

**Volume 3: Intervention in the Aging Process,** William Regelson and F. Marott Sinex, *Editors.* Published in two volumes. Part A: Quantitation, Epidemiology, and Clinical Research. Part B: Basic Research and Preclinical Screening.

# INTERVENTION IN THE AGING PROCESS

## Part A

## Quantitation, Epidemiology, and Clinical Research

Proceedings of The Fund for Integrative
Biomedical Research (FIBER) Symposium
held in Boston, Massachusetts
November 5 and 6, 1982

### Editors

### William Regelson

Fund for Integrative Biomedical Research
Washington, D.C.
Department of Medicine
Medical College of Virginia
Richmond, Virginia

### F. Marott Sinex

Section on Bio-Medical Gerontology
Boston University School of Medicine
Boston, Massachusetts

## Alan R. Liss, Inc., New York

**Address all Inquiries to the Publisher**
**Alan R. Liss, Inc., 150 Fifth Avenue, New York, NY 10011**

**Copyright © 1983 Alan R. Liss, Inc.**

**Printed in the United States of America.**

**Library of Congress Cataloging in Publication Data**

International Symposium on Intervention in the Aging
   Process (1982: Boston, Mass.)
   Intervention in the aging process.

   (Modern aging research; v. 3)
   Includes index.
   Contents:  pt. A. Quantitation, epidemiology, and
clinical research.—  pt. B. Basic research and preclinical
screening.
    1. Aging—Congresses.  2. Aging—Prevention—Congresses.
3. Geriatrics—Congresses.  I. Regelson, William.
II. Sinex, F. Marott.  III. Title.  IV. Series.
[DNLM:  1. Aging—Congresses.  2. Longevity—Congresses.
3. Research—Congresses.  W1 MO117 v.3 / WT 104 I61i 1982]
QP86.I57  1982     618.97       83-19958
ISBN 0-8451-2302-5 (pt. A)
ISBN 0-8451-2303-3 (pt. B)
ISBN 0-8451-2399-8 (two-volume set)

# Contents

# Contributors to Part A

**Michael A. Aiken,** Section on Biochemical Pharmacology, National Heart, Lung, and Blood Institute, Building 10, Room 7N262, Bethesda, MD 20205 **[215]**

**Gary A. Borkan,** Normative Aging Study, Veterans Administration Outpatient Clinic, 17 Court Street, Boston, MA 02108 **[99]**

**Arthur Cherkin,** Geriatric Research, Education, and Clinical Center (GRECC), Veterans Administration Medical Center, Sepulveda, CA 91343 **[225]**

**James F. Flood,** Geriatric Research, Education, and Clinical Center (GRECC), Veterans Administration Medical Center, Sepulveda, CA 91343 **[225]**

**Karl Folkers,** Institute for Biomedical Research, University of Texas at Austin, Austin, TX 78712 **[199]**

**A.L. Goldstein,** Department of Biochemistry, George Washington University School of Medicine, 2300 Eye Street, N.W., Washington, DC 20037 **[169]**

**Joseph W. Goldzieher,** Department of Obstetrics and Gynecology, Baylor College of Medicine, 6720 Bertner Avenue, Houston, TX 77030 **[247]**

**N. Hall,** Department of Biochemistry, George Washington University School of Medicine, 2300 Eye Street, N.W., Washington, DC 20037 **[169]**

**Richard Hochschild,** Hoch Company, 2915 Pebble Drive, Corona del Mar, CA 92625 **[113]**

**Robert A. Levine,** Section on Biochemical Pharmacology, National Heart, Lung, and Blood Institute, Building 10, Room 7N262, Bethesda, MD 20205 **[215]**

**Peter LeWitt,** Experimental Therapeutic Branch, National Institute of Neurological and Communicative Disorders and Stroke, Building 10, Room 3D12, Bethesda, MD 20205 **[215]**

**Walter Lovenberg,** Section on Biochemical Pharmacology, National Heart, Lung, and Blood Institute, Building 10, Room 7N262, Bethesda, MD 20205 **[215]**

**T.L.K. Low,** Department of Biochemistry, George Washington University School of Medicine, 2300 Eye Street, N.W., Washington, DC 20037 **[169]**

**Leonard Miller,** Section on Biochemical Pharmacology, National Heart, Lung, and Blood Institute, Building 10, Room 7N262, Bethesda, MD 20205 **[215]**

**P.H. Naylor,** Department of Biochemistry, George Washington University School of Medicine, 2300 Eye Street, N.W., Washington, DC 20037 **[169]**

**Laura L. Pashko,** Fels Research Institute, Temple University Medical School, Philadelphia, PA 19140 **[267]**

The number in brackets indicates the opening page of the contributor's article.

Robert H. Purdy, Department of Organic Chemistry, Southwest Foundation for Research and Education, San Antonio, TX 78284 [247]

William Regelson, Fund for Integrative Biomedical Research, National Council on the Aging, 600 Maryland Avenue, S.W., Washington, DC 20024 [xiii,3]

Arthur G. Schwartz, Fels Research Institute, Temple University Medical School, Philadelphia, PA 19140 [267]

Mildred S. Seelig, Medical Department, Goldwater Memorial Hospital, Roosevelt Island, New York, NY 10044 [279]

F. Marott Sinex, Section on Bio-Medical Gerontology, Boston University School of Medicine, 80 East Concord Street, Boston, MA 02118 [xiii,129]

David A. Snowdon, Schools of Health and Medicine, Loma Linda University, Loma Linda, CA 92350 [141]

Robert H. Tannen, Fels Research Institute, Temple University Medical School, Philadelphia, PA 19140 [267]

Dorothy B. Villee, Harvard Medical School, Children's Hospital Medical Center, 300 Longwood Avenue, Boston, MA 02115 [151]

Janet P. Wallace, Adult Fitness Program, Department of Physical Education, San Diego State University, San Diego, CA 92182 [307]

M.M. Zatz, Department of Biochemistry, George Washington University School of Medicine, 2300 Eye Street, N.W., Washington, DC 20037 [169]

# Contents of Part B

# Contributors to Part B

Jonathan R. Archer, The Jackson Laboratory, Bar Harbor, ME 04609

Clinton M. Astle, The Jackson Laboratory, Bar Harbor, ME 04609

Helmut Bertrand, Departments of Biology and Chemistry, University of Regina, Regina, Saskatchewan, Canada S4S 0A2

Vincent J. Cristofalo, The Wistar Institute, 36th Street at Spruce, Philadelphia, PA 19104

Richard G. Cutler, Gerontology Research Center, National Institute on Aging, Baltimore City Hospital, Baltimore, MD 21224

Cathy A. Finlay, The Wistar Institute, 36th Street at Spruce, Philadelphia, PA 19104

William J. Freed, Adult Psychiatry Branch, National Institute of Mental Health, St. Elizabeth's Hospital, Washington, DC 20032

Scott D. Gorman, The Wistar Institute, 36th Street at Spruce, Philadelphia, PA 19104

David E. Harrison, The Jackson Laboratory, Bar Harbor, ME 04609

D.S. Heron, Department of Isotope Research, The Weizmann Institute of Science, Rehovot 76100, Israel

Thomas E. Johnson, Department of Molecular Biology and Biochemistry, University of California at Irvine, Irvine, CA 92717

J.A. Joseph, American Cyanamid Company, Lederle Laboratories, CNS-Biology, Pearl River, NY 10965

Hans Laufer, Biological Sciences, University of Connecticut, Storrs, CT 06268

Kristin Lindseth, Department of Psychology, San Jose State University, San Jose, CA 95192

Philip D. Lipetz, General Molecular Applications, Inc., 1834 Elmwood Avenue, Columbus, OH 43212

M. Lyte, Department of Membrane Research, The Weizmann Institute of Science, Rehovot 76100, Israel

Jaime Miquel, Biomedical Research Division, NASA Ames Research Center, Moffett Field, CA 94035

Paul D. Phillips, The Wistar Institute, 36th Street at Spruce, Philadelphia, PA 19104

William Regelson, Fund for Integrative Biomedical Research, National Council on the Aging, 600 Maryland Avenue, S.W., Washington, DC 20024

G.S. Roth, Gerontology Research Center, National Institute on Aging, Baltimore City Hospitals, Baltimore, MD 21224

D. Samuel, Department of Isotope Research, The Weizmann Institute of Science, Rehovot 76100, Israel

M. Shinitzky, Department of Membrane Research, The Weizmann Institute of Science, Rehovot 76100, Israel

J. Smith-Sonneborn, Departments of Zoology and Physiology, University of Wyoming, Laramie, WY 82071

**Ralph E. Stephens,** Department of Radiology, Ohio State University, Columbus, OH 43210

**Roy L. Walford,** Department of Pathology, UCLA School of Medicine, University of California, Los Angeles, CA 90024

**J.R. Whitaker,** Gerontology Research Center, National Institute on Aging, Baltimore City Hospitals, Baltimore, MD 21224

**Jerry R. Williams,** Department of Radiology, George Washington University School of Medicine, 2300 Eye Street, N.W., Washington, DC 20037

**Richard Jed Wyatt,** Adult Psychiatry Branch, National Institute of Mental Health, St. Elizabeth's Hospital, Washington, DC 20032

**Bert M. Zuckerman,** Laboratory of Experimental Biology, University of Massachusetts, East Wareham, MA 02538

# Preface

The Fund for Integrative Biomedical Research (FIBER) believes that aging is a process that can be modulated to improve the quality of human life. The scientific community and the public should understand that aging is a programmed event and is not just the cumulative result of a random collection of degenerative diseases.

FIBER, a private, nonprofit organization, was organized four years ago with assistance from Senator Alan Cranston because of our concern for the gap in the transfer of basic and preclinical scientific information into clinical studies. This is of particular concern because of the social and economic problems related to the debility and dependency of the aged and the increasing size of our elderly population.

FIBER acts as a catalyst to bring basic aging research information to more rapid clinical realization with the goal of improving the quality of human survival within our life time.

FIBER functions by providing seed and travel money for innovative research. FIBER also helps by seeking to identify larger sources of funding for investigators and holds workshops and conferences highlighting important areas of aging research. Since we opened our doors in February 1980, we have held the following FIBER supported or sponsored conferences which gives one an idea of the range of our interests in the aging field:

> Biomarkers in Aging; New Approaches to Acute and Chronic Ischemia; Juvenile Hormone and Retinoic Acid: Their Possible Role in Aging; The Role of Mitochondria in Aging; Dehydroepiandrosterone Workshop; Role of Pyrophosphates in Metabolic Control.

We have supported the following symposia:

> Aging, Cardiorespiratory Fitness and Cognitive Performance with North American Society for Psychology of Sports and Physical Activity; Neuroendocrine Control of Immunity with the University of Kentucky; Science Writers Seminar on Intervention in Aging with Rockefeller University.

This text on Intervention in Aging is the result of a FIBER conference held in conjunction with the postgraduate medical education program of Boston University, November 5 and 6, 1982. This program and its text are divided into four major sections of research and review concerned with intervention in the aging process.

## Part A

1. Biomarkers of Aging: The need to quantitate the aging process for the results of intervention to be evaluable.
2. Epidemiological and clinical research data and discussion of potentially clinically useful anti-aging drugs and programs.

## Part B

3. Discussion of basic research data defining aging as a distinct syndrome.
4. Anti-aging screening programs of scientific validity, clinical predictability and cost effectiveness.

Before one can evaluate programs of intervention in aging, one must be able to quantitatively measure aging in clinical study. Because of this need, a section on Biomarkers in Aging occupies a major chapter of the first volume. This section catalogues many of the observations that have been made about aging in human subjects and animal models.

Until methods and centers for bioquantitation of aging are developed, we cannot expect the effective entry of the pharmaceutical industry into the search for anti-aging drugs because of the cost, time and uncertainty involved.

We feel that centers of excellence for the bioquantitation of aging should be a primary goal of the National Institute on Aging. University or medical centers should be encouraged to develop programs for quantitative studies of physiologic age. Aspects of these programs should be modeled on the longitudinal study of the National Institute on Aging in Baltimore, which is celebrating the 25th anniversary of its founding.

Clinical groups with a strong interest in this area are those in cardiovascular rehabilitation, sports medicine, Alzheimer's disease study and diabetic control where performance and pathophysiology are age related. Bioquantitation and intervention will, undoubtedly, be developed first as profit-making ventures for cardiac rehabilitation and improvement of athletic performance.

The insurance industry should recognize that the efficient use of age-quantitated biomarkers will revolutionize the character of their actuarial risk pool that governs current insurance programs. The public should be aware that efforts to accurately quantitate aging is the first step in programs that can be developed to prevent debility and dependency, which often accompany a longer life expectancy.

This volume identifies a number of drugs and programs that are currently ready for clinical application to age-related disease problems or study of the aging process itself.

We feel that nutritional and exercise programs could be placed on a more rational basis if observations of combined modalities are made in model systems, as we feel that it is naive to assume that a single agent will solve all the problems of aging.

While we are suspicious of beneficial claims for high dose multivitamin, antioxidant or nutritional programs that have not been tested in validated model systems, studies of nutritional emphasis should be encouraged.

Discussed in this volume, as an agent that may modify the aging process, is the native hormone dehydroepiandrosterone (DHEA), which declines with age and is of potential promise in diabetes and cancer prevention and treatment. Another such compound is tetrahydrobiopterin ($BH_4$), which is an enzymatic cofactor of importance to neurotransmitter function in Parkinson's disease and the depression of aging. Unfortunately, $BH_4$ is an orphan drug because of patent and production problems despite a population in need that numbers in the multimillions. What is needed is a concerted, coordinated effort on the part of the National Institutes of Health and the pharmaceutical industry to make $BH_4$ or analogues available for major clinical testing.

While it is not popular, at this time, to clinically test drug combinations, we feel that the paper of Arthur Cherkin and James Flood on "Remarkable Potentiation Among Memory-Enhancing Cholinergic Drugs in Mice" summarizes the need for studies of drug combinations based on results in a model system. Such drug combinations must be looked at in man and encouraged by an enlightened F.D.A. attitude toward the need to find new approaches to the debility of aging. Drug combinations in aging are necessary, both for the convenience of patient acceptability and for the reason that single agents are not sufficient to solve the multifactorial problems that aging represents.

The first volume of our text on Intervention in Aging presents the evidence that aging is quantifiable and there may be drugs or hormones available that are worthy of clinical trial.

This text emphasizes FIBER's search for quality in a lengthened life. Intervention in aging is possible if preclinical and clinical studies are conducted in a manner that is rational, comparative and quantitative.

Without the help of the following individuals, this conference would not have been possible.

Mr. Miles Rubin, Senator Alan Cranston, Dan Perry, Paul Glenn, Harvey Silbert, Dr. Marcus Rabwin, Don Yarborough, Ms. Joyce Fordham, Mrs. Eva Gross, Ms. Donna Marcy, and Althea Roach Thomas.

We wish to thank Johnson and Johnson and Hoffmann-La Roche pharmaceutical companies for their generous financial support.

**William Regelson and F. Marott Sinex**
FIBER, National Council on the Aging,
600 Maryland Avenue, S.W.,
Washington, D.C. 20024

# QUANTITATION OF HUMAN AGING

Intervention in the Aging Process, Part A: Quantitation, Epidemiology, and
Clinical Research, pages 3–98
© 1983 Alan R. Liss, Inc., 150 Fifth Avenue, New York, NY 10011

BIOMARKERS IN AGING

William Regelson, M.D.
Professor of Medicine, Medical College of Virginia
Richmond, Virginia; Scientific Director, Fund for
Integrative Biomedical Research, Washington, D. C.

I.    INTRODUCTION

It is becoming more apparent that aging is a distinct
syndrome of defined biochemical and physiologic identity
rather than the cumulative effect of individual chronic
diseases.  The concept of aging, as a biologic syndrome, is
important if we are to avoid the high cost of chronic care.
We must mobilize our resources to avoid age related debility
and dependency before it becomes clinically evident.

The future is hopeful in that animal models have demonstrated our capability of delaying or modulating the aging
process in terms of both median and absolute survival.
However, to go from model systems to man, we must develop
clinical programs that have the biochemical and physiological markers that will permit us to monitor changes to conveniently determine if clinical manipulations can slow or
reverse the aging process.

Currently, aging assessment is primarily concentrated
on the elderly, but for it to become an adjunct to clinical
intervention, assessment of physiologic age must be made
periodically throughout adult life to enable us to act
prophylacticaly to improve the quality of our survival as we
age.  Clinical evaluation of biochemical or physiological
age must go beyond nutritional assessment or evaluation of
the chronically ill (Palgi et al., 1981), but must include
quantitation of broad aspects of the aging syndrome.

The development of protozoal (paramecia), fungal
(neurospora), and tissue culture screens, as well as more

sophisticated studies in nematodes, fruit flies and rodents will permit the economic preclinical screening of single and combined agents for eventual clinical development. For these screening programs to be meaningful, measurement of functional age is critical, as with clinical biomarkers in place, we will be able to measure age changes in months rather than in decades. This will place us in the same preclinical screening position that has led to progress in infectious disease and cancer chemotherapy.

The clinical problems of intervention are complicated because there are distinct differences in patterns of response to drugs or programs, depending on the particular portion of the subjects life cycle they are administered. As an example, enforced exercise can maintain muscle function when applied early enough in the life cycle (Smith, 1980) but it increases free radical formation and (Davies et al., 1982) can also decrease survival in rodents, depending upon the age at the time of enforced activity (Steinhagen-Thiessen et al., 1980/1981; Debes and Samorajski, 1980). Circadian rhythms can also be a factor in age related responses to drug administration (Scheving et al., 1974) which may have a bearing on age related drug studies.

As discussed at this conference, we have agents or programs which alter aging in animal models and which are readily available. Apart from dietary restriction and exercise, these include; anti-oxidants; magnesium; dehydro-epiandrosterone (DHEA); L-dopa; tetrahydrobiopterin, ubiqui-none, cholinergics and "active lipid". To evaluate these agents in man requires functional assays of physiologic age.

The first FIBER conference dealt with "Biomarkers in Aging" (April, 1979). This has been followed by an extremely effective conference organized by the National Institute of Aging on June 1-2, 1982 (Reff and Schneider, 1982). Lists of physiologic tests that may be pertinent to aging have been discussed by Heron and Chown (1967) Ries (1974) Rockstein et al. (1974) Bourliere (1978) Dietz and Marcum (1979) and by Comfort (1979) and Kenney (1982) and have been discussed in this text by Borkan, Miquel, Lindseth and Harrison.

In regard to other reviews of biomarkers in aging, the reader is referred to the many papers of N. W. Shock and others beginning in 1960 and reported in the National Insti-tute of Aging's longitudinal studies. Shock (1960) listed nerve conduction velocity, standard cell water content,

cardiac index, glomerular filtration (inulin clearance)
vital capacity, maximal breathing capacity and standard
renal plasma flow (Diodrast) as correlating with clinical
aging.  The following are texts with good general reviews of
the physiologic quantitation of aging:  Palmore, 1970;
Timiras, 1972; Anderson, 1976; Everitt, 1976, 1981; Finch
and Hayflick, 1977; Bourliere, 1978; Cape, 1978; Frolkis,
1979; Goldman, 1979; Rossman, 1979; Kanungo, 1980; Jacobs,
1981; Smith and Serfass, (1981); Vernadakis and Timiras,
1982; and, of course, the CRC Handbooks on:  Physiology
(Masoro et al., 1981), Immunology (Kay and Makinodan,
1981); and the Biochemistry (Florini et al., 1981), of
aging.

Manuals have been developed consisting of a series of
simple functional tests by Morgan (1981).  Most importantly,
Hochschild has contributed a chapter to this text which
discusses instrumentation (the H-Scan) which provides twelve
rapid, convenient tests that can be self administered to
quantitate physiologic age.

We feel that the following physiologic and biochemical
parameters might well be applied in organized programs for
quantitating human age.  Some are available for immediate
use and others require development directed toward validation
and improvement in cost effectiveness or adaptation from
animal models to clinical application.


II.  PHYSIOLOGIC PARAMETERS

A.  Respiratory:  Forced Vital Capacity (FVC)

Reddan (1980) has provided an excellent review of
respiratory decline with age which is associated with changes
in chest wall and lung parenchyma.

We feel that currently the most important measurable
index of aging that summates physical changes is the evaluation of forced vital capacity (Kannel and Hubert, 1982).  In
this regard, the importance of pulmonary changes with age
have been demonstrated by the Framingham Heart Study which
showed, in their twenty year mortality study, that death
related predictably to biennially measured vital capacity.
Excess mortality at low vital capacity was noted in the
elderly as well as the young in both sexes and in non-
smokers as well as smokers.  This relationship was independent

of obesity and persisted despite exclusion of subjects with
pulmonary disease, asthma or chest deformity.

Vital capacity predicted for both long and short term
mortality. Excess deaths from all major causes occurred at
low vital capacities although deaths from cardiovascular
disease were predominant. Vital capacity was one of the
strongest predictors of premature mortality, second only to
age itself, even when compared to the major cardiovascular
risk factors.

One major correlate of forced vital capacity is hand
grip strength. This is not surprising as the effect of age
on vital capacity is thought to relate to compliance or
recoil factors in the chest (Mittman et al., 1965; Reddan,
1981), and age changes in respiratory capacity may be due to
the loss of muscle power or a stiffer, less compliant chest
wall or diaphram. If this is true, then vital capacity
changes may be the respiratory equivalent of the senile gait
with its implication of Parkinson equivalency. In support
of this, Sastry and Owens (1980) have reported a decline in
the response of the aging isolated rat hemidiaphragm to
acetylcholine or electrical stimulation.

L-dopa dietary administration in mice, beginning at 8
weeks, increased average survival as well as maintenance of
spontaneous motor activity with aging (Papavasilou et al.,
1982). We have to ask if L-dopa enhancement of spontaneous
motor activity seen in aging animals could effect respiratory
exchange as it does locomotor activity. We need data regarding forced vital capacity of Parkinson victims to see if
this can be increased by dopaminergic treatment or by tetrahydrobiopterin ($BH_4$) administration as discussed at this
meeting (see chapters by Lovenberg, and Levine and Folkers
in this text).

Of interest to intervention, at this meeting, Wilson
has discussed the San Diego State Long Term Exercise Program
where regular aerobic exercise delays the decline in vital
capacity seen with aging. Similar results have been shown
by Dill et al., (1982) and by Reddan (1981). While Cunningham et al. (1982) showed that self selected walking gaits on
a treadmill were age correlated with $VO_2$ max and the aerobic
fitness of the individual independent of age. Bourliere
(1978), in his discussion of the ecology of human senescence,
finds that cardiac and respiratory fitness relates to the
regular intensity of physical activity. People, as remote

from each other as mountain dwellers in the Ethiopian Highlands and the Himalayas, preserve their respiratory capacity even in advanced age.

Apart from direct measurement of vital capacity, the new ausculatory technology that determines air exchange by electronic ascultation with measurement of changing vibratory frequencies may be of value in clinically quantitating pulmonary alterations as a function of age (Hardin and Patterson, 1979).

The respiratory area should include efforts at quantitating laryngeal function, as with age the vocal cords bow which causes the voice to break or drop in pitch.

B.   Cardiac Function:

A fall in resting cardiac output with age has been known for many years (Brandfonbrener et al., 1955) and alterations in cardiac function with aging have most recently been discussed by Lakatta (1982) in animal models and by Gerstenblith (1982) and Sheppard (1981) in their discussions of cardiovascular aging in man.

Age changes in cardiac function range from increased muscle stiffness, delayed and prolonged relaxation due to calcium flux abnormalities or to decreased responses to catecholamines and ouabain.  Of practical importance is the high incidence of coronary sclerosis with increased risk of coronary occlusion and failure to recover from ischemic injury with increasing age.

Postmortem studies have indicated the development of significant coronary artery disease with increasing age. Significant coronary vascular disease is present in over 50% of men age 60 years or more (White et al., 1950).  While routine history and resting electrocardiograms correctly identify about one-half of those individuals with significant coronary problems, the recent development of stress thallium scans (Melin et al., 1981) has made available a more sensitive and specific technique for the diagnosis of coronary insufficiency.  As mentioned by Gerstenblith (1982), the association of both a positive stress electrocardiogram and stress thallium scan have a predictive accuracy of nearly 100% in populations which have both a high and low prevelance of coronary disease (Melin, 1981).

Echocardiography also represents one of the most accessible and simplest methods for quantitating age related cardiac function (Gerstenblith et al., 1977; Gerstenblith, 1982; Gardin et al., 1977; Derman, 1977). The echocardiograph combined with gated nuclear cardiac scans (Port et al., 1980) gives us both an estimate of ventricular related age changes as well as information regarding problems of coronary insufficiency. Of significant importance to exercise programs, gated nuclear cardiac scans can measure changes with age on exercise.

As an outpatient procedure, the stress test i.e., the Master and Oppenheimer (1979) two step test, can establish the maximum number of foot-pounds of work accomplished with return of pulse and systolic blood to control levels as a time related correlate with chronologic age (Dehn and Bruce, 1972). However, the best measurement of overall cardiovascular performance with stress is the measurement of maximum oxygen consumption (Powell, 1974) which declines above age 40 at a constant rate independent of the age related loss of total muscle mass (Petrofski and Lind, 1975).

With age, the ability of the heart to respond to catecholamines during stress declines. There is decreased ability to increase heart rate with exercise or to an infusion of isoproternol (Yin et al., 1970). Decreased cardiac response is not surprising as with psychosocial stress, catecholamine urinary levels are lower in an older population and do not return toward baseline as rapidly following removal of a stressful event (Faucheux et al., 1981).

There are laboratory studies which relate chronic digoxin induced bradycardia to increases in mouse absolute and average survival (Coburn et al., 1971) but how this relates to the above clinical responses, is unknown.

Invasive studies have indicated that stroke volume and cardiac output are decreased with increasing age. This is associated with an increase in total peripheral vascular resistance which occurs both with rest and exercise (Gerstenblith, 1982). As discussed earlier, the value of measurements of left ventricular filling rates with two-dimensional echocardiography or gated cardiac blood pool scans should provide enough information to quantitate cardiac or coronary status (Strashun et al., 1981).

The above, when combined with dilution techniques for cardiac output and maximum oxygen uptake, could provide quantitative data for evaluation of the usefulness of anti-aging drugs or aerobic exercise programs (Smith and Serfass, 1980). Alternatively, if the value of cardiac impedance technology (Kubicek et al., 1974) as a non-interfering measurement of cardiac function becomes more generally accepted, it could provide a simple screen to quantitate age related cardiac changes. Support for its value, in a comparison with isotopic indicator dilution methods, has been reported by Williams and Caird (1980). In this regard, currently, Folkers is studying the clinical effects of the mitochondrial respiratory cofactor ubiquinone, (Q10), with cardiac impedance measurement of cardiac output. Cardiac response to ubiquinone is being evaluated in hypertension, myocardial failure, ischemic injury and anthracycline toxicology (Folkers and Yamamura, 1981). Q10 is being used in Japan as a primary agent for the treatment of hypertension and the failing heart (Folkers et al., 1981), and Q10 should be clinically studied using accepted cardiovascular functional techniques to see if it alters age related cardiac functional changes. In addition, Q10 may have broad application as it apparently also stimulates immune responsiveness and increases the average survival of mice (Bliznikov, 1981).

Another agent which could effect cardiac function in an aging population, which is available in Europe but not available in this country, is carnitine (Shug, 1979). This mitochondrial cofactor involved in fatty acid utilization is a key factor in muscle and fat metabolism and is a dietary requirement of the newborn. Carnitine has been shown to protect the ischemic heart (Shug, 1979, Thomsen et al., 1979) and restore functional capacity in the failing heart in clinical studies at the University of Wisconsin.

C.    Peripheral Vascular Response:

What is needed to make vascular responses a biomarker for aging are simple assays of changes in peripheral and capillary flow since loss of blood flow, in the microcircula-tion, is a major factor that fails with progressive age. In aging, the number of capillaries per unit of tissue is decreased, with capillary fibrosis, thickening of basement membrane and capillary constriction (Rosenthal, 1981). Capillary growth is defective in wound healing (Yamaura and Matsuzawa, 1980).

Infrared camera surveying could provide an age related profile of tissue blood flow as a function of age. Howell (1981) has developed quantitative data regarding direct temperature gradient readouts in decubital areas and the lower limbs of elderly women.

In a plethysmographic study of postural changes in the elderly, 3/4 of subjects showed pathologic peripheral circulatory responses to beta-adrenergic stimulators. The vasodilating effects of beta-adrenergic stimulation is more compromised with age than vasoconstriction (Strozzi et al., 1979).

For larger vessels, Doppler ultrasound technique can be useful in peripheral blood flow measurement as well as assay of carotid changes that can reflect on the risk of stroke (Lewis et al., 1979). Techniques for noninvasive evaluation of peripheral arterial disease has been reviewed by Lee et al. (1980). These include arterial and photoplethysmography and electromagnetic flowmetry.

Most recently, Sigel et al. (1982) have used ultrasound echogenecity in flowing blood of large abdominal veins to produce patterns which correlate with red cell aggregation, tributary mixing and the colloid state of plasma.

Within blood itself, in aging rabbits, Frolkis et al. (1980) have reported that kallikreinogen content in blood was decreased with kallikrein and kininase activity increased. There were associated rises in the level of 5' nucleotidase and adenosine deaminase in the blood and myocardium of older animals. The latter is important because it relates to changes associated with cellular function where 5' nucleotidase rises with age and where adenosine increases can block lymphocyte response. Adenosine may have a local circulatory role with adenosine increases in older animals modifying local blood flow.

The action of the kallikrein system on blood clotting and vascular reactivity is something that requires study in aging patients. In addition, studies of blood viscosity should be made as there is evidence that fibrinogen levels rise with age and this can have effects on blood flow and oxygen diffusion. This is reviewed in an excellent article by Rai (1981).

D.    Renal Function:

One major functional defect with age that can be measured is the decline in glomerular filtration rate.  Progressive changes in the renal handling of creatinine or inulin have resulted in age adjusted normative standards developed by the NIA Gerontology Research Center (Rowe, 1982).  Functional changes correlate with glomerular sclerosis and the thickening of all capillary basement membranes in aging rats (Bolton and Sturgill, 1979; Johnson, 1979).

The decline in clinical renal function, as seen in 24 hour endogenous creatinine clearance studies, begins in the middle of the fourth decade.  It is hoped that better imaging techniques could give us insight into the functional changes of the kidney based on simple screening methods as although biopsy can be meaningful, it is not a procedure for routine use.

Of importance, mouse aging research studies, by Johnson and Cutler, (1980), have demonstrated that hypophysectomy can result in disappearance of age related basement membrane glomerular capillary changes which indicates that the renal changes of aging may be a reversible phenomena.

E.    Bone Loss:

Age related bone loss is a significant problem leading to skeletal collapse and fracture and is a leading cause of disability in elderly women.  Heaney (1982), at the NIA's Biomarker Review, speaks of a variety of techniques that are clinically applicable to quantitate this problem as do Smith et al. (1981) in their excellent review and several texts on this subject (DeLuca et al., 1981; Cohn, 1981).

Heaney lists radiogrammetry, single or dual photon absorptiometry (photodensometry); total and partial body neutron activation analysis; computed tomography; Compton-scanner; biopsy and calcium balance, as techniques to measure patterns of skeletal change in the aged.

The vitamin K dependent amino acid, gamma-carboxyglutamic acid (GLA) is responsible for bone matrix integrity. GLA is acomponent of osteocalcin and its excretion is increased in osteoporosis, which is a disease of age.  Gundberg and Gallop (1981) have developed a sensitive immunoassay for osteocalcin which should be looked at as a biomarker.

Macek et al. (1980) suggest that gamma carboxyglutamic acid should be examined in connective tissue. GLA rises with age in bone matrix and it may be a factor in soft tissue calcification.

The need for biomarkers is seen in the fact that it took Hoffman-La Roche eight years of clinical study before its efficacy claims for D3 in osteoporosis were accepted by the F.D.A. In terms of techniques available for measuring age related bone changes, computer tomography may currently be our best available tool, but are not suitable for major outpatient programs. Currently, bone densitometers designed for office use are what is needed to provide screening technology at reasonable cost, i.e., Norland, Ft. Atkinson, Wisconsin. The problem of prevention or reversal of bone loss in the aged requires readily applied routine techniques for patient evaluation.

There is evidence that parathyroid hormone (PTH) levels increase in the elderly (Insogna et al., 1981) and assays for PTH should be developed along with $1,25 \ (OH)_2D \ (D_3)$ and calcium levels correlated with bone changes.

Apart from parathyroid, vitamin $D_3$ and calcium intake relationships, we feel that the bone loss of aging should be looked at carefully in association with growth hormone production and somatomedin levels. Age related bone changes are similar to those seen with acromegaly: hypercalciuria, increased hydroxyproline excretion and increased serum calcium levels (Linfoot, 1981).

F.   Finger Nail Growth:

Orentreich et al. (1979) has developed a simple, inexpensive, non-invasive technology for measurement of nail growth. They have found that the rate of finger nail growth measured over one year, can give quantifiable information that correlates with age. Linear nail growth decreases 50% over the life span of humans and dogs and techniques have been developed that allows this information to be obtained as part of a simple outpatient clinical evaluation.

Nail samples, like hair, can provide us with samples for trace metal and biochemical analysis.

G.   Skin Retraction and Cutaneous Wound Healing:

Skin extensability and elasticity, as a declining

factor of aging, has been reviewed by Cape (1981). This has been measured by strain gauges, suction devices and disc torsion instruments. Measurement of elastic retraction of human skin has provided an age related correlate (Stell, 1979).

Du Nöuy (1916) demonstrated that in epithelial wounds of equal size, the rate of healing varied in inverse ratio to age. This was correlated, in aged rats, with the strength of the wound and the speed of fibroplasia by Howes and Harvey (1932) . Cutaneous wound healing depends on both epithelialization and contracture and the latter is significantly delayed in older rabbits (Billingham and Russel, 1956).

Carrel and Ebling (1923) found antagonistic factors to the growth of fibroblasts in the wounds of old as compared to young chickens. The Orentreich Foundation for the Advancement of Science (1982) have reconfirmed this data and found similar correlates in man. Most importantly, this group has reported that fibroblasts obtained from human skin biopsies are stimulated to grow at faster rates in the pooled serum of young in contrast to old donors.

We feel it is feasible to study wound repair in simple punch biopsy sites which, apart from providing material for tissue culture, could provide an opportunity to measure the rate of healing and its modulation in respect to age and aging intervention.

A simpler technique could be provided by the intra-cutaneous *in vitro* injection of the fluorescent dye, dansyl chloride, which has been used as a biomarker for aging. Measuring the length of time dye coloration disappears from a fully stained stratum corneum (Grove and Kligman, 1979) relates to age. Techniques of this kind could be adapted to the measure of capillary growth which is defective in wound repair of older animals (Yamaura, Matsuzawa, 1980).

A simple application of dermatological clinical measurement is to measure the decline in skin thickness which occurs with age (Hall et al., 1981) where a sharp fall is seen beginning at age 60. Changes in skin thickness have been related to a decline in the quantity of cutaneous vitamin D precursors.

Aging decreases the capacity of human skin to synthesize vitamin $D_3$ despite solar ultraviolet radiation (Holick and MacLaughlin, 1981).

Mast cell levels decline in the gingiva of aging mice (Cullen and Tonna, 1979), and study of mast cell population in gum or skin biopsies of man should be done to see if this cell population, important to immunity, atherosclerosis and angiogenesis, alters with aging.

H.   Autonomic Nervous System Function:

Plasma catecholamine levels respond to a variety of events: posture, blood volume, exercise, stress and drug administration.   There is evidence for a plasma noradrenaline increase in aging humans (Halter and Pfeiffer, 1982; Rowe and Troeni, 1980; Ziegler et al., 1976) which has recently been reviewed by Halter and Pfeiffer (1982).

The sensitivity of our capacity to measure norepinephrine and epinephrine in human plasma makes this a quantitative measure that can be used as a biomarker for aging (Galbo et al., 1975; Halter and Pfeiffer, 1982; Rowe and Troen, 1980; Ziegler et al., 1976).   In support of this, norepinephrine release stimulated by exercise and upright posture and stress are greater in the elderly (Halter and Pfeiffer 1982).

In relation to the above, increases in monoamine oxidase (MAO) activity has been shown to be elevated in plasma, brain tissue and platelets of older as compared to younger individuals (Bridge, 1979, 1981).   In platelets, the decade of age 50-59 shows an increase in MAO activity which is also associated with increased thermolability of the enzyme.   Platelets can be readily obtained for catechol and other assays as a potential biomarker to quantitate age.

Methods to assess autonomic activity that reflect on sympathetic tone include pupillometry (Pfeiffer et al., 1982) and nocturnal penile tumesence.   Also included are response to positional changes and response to environmental stress (Collins et al., 1980).

Although pulse rate is not always definitive as an autonomic peripheral event or an end organ effect related to the sensitivity of the myocardium (Pfeiffer et al., 1980), it can be used as an autonomic biomarker.   There is an age related increase in the resting heart rate and a decline in its variability to exercise.

Measurement of cholinergic and other autonomic responses to the growing number of neurotransmitters deserves development and specific research encouragement. The most exciting observation relates to the change in the level of tyrosine/tryptophane hydroxylase, an enzyme effecting serotonin, catecholamine and dopamine neurotransmitter levels which are modulated by tetrahydrobiopterin ($BH_4$). This has been discussed in this volume by Lovenberg and Levine and Folkers.

There is a loss of beta adrenergic receptors in lymphocytes with aging and these cells provide a readily obtainable cell population for biomarker assay (Schocken and Ross, 1977). It will be of interest to see if lymphocyte autonomic receptor changes with age reflect on increases in catechol amine, monoamine oxidase or cell membrane rigidity changes that are associated with aging.

    I.   Sensory:

    1.  The ear and auditory function:

The external ear progressively changes with age with continued growth of the ear lobe and increased hairiness of the tragus. Whether this could constitute a biomarker is less important than the functional impairment to hearing seen with progressive age.

Age changes in hearing ability are referred to as "presbycusis" which has been defined as: impairment of pure tone thresholds; frequency discrimination, auditory temporal discrimination and sound localization ability; impairment of speech discrimination and ability to recall long sentences.

In terms of pure-tone hearing loss, presbycusis represents one of the major sensory changes occurring with clinical aging. This topic has been reviewed recently by Corso (1982) and Olsho et al. (1982). Approximately 80% of individuals with hearing problems are over 45 years of age and significant hearing loss is seen in 55% of those over 65 years. Hearing problems are present in 75% of individuals between 75 and 79 years.

Of interest, hearing is effected not only by changes in the middle and inner ear, but it might be possible to quantify aging by examining the character of the ear canal which is collapsed in 37% of nursing home residents between 65 and 79 and 51% of those aged 80 or over (Schow and Goldbaum, 1980). Techniques for measuring external auditory

canal compliance might provide an effective summation of
cartilagenous and bone changes that could quantify age. The
above is also associated with changes in the quantity and
character of cerumen.

With aging, the function of the middle ear is altered
by ossification of the tympanic ring and replacement of
elastic tissue by collagen. There is also thinning and
calcification of the ossicular joints. Quantitation of
these changes, as age related, is needed and tympanometry
and measurement of the acoustic reflex may eventually provide
useful age indicators related to the above.

The most exploitable area for quantitative measurement
of hearing loss rests in the inner ear where most investigators feel that age changes relate to loss of hair cells or
to disturbances in inner ear metabolism. Loss of hair cells
or increased rigidity of the basilar membrane of the inner
ear results in inner ear high frequency detection loss.

With progressive age, the auditory nerve or related
cochlear nuclei may be at fault which results in loss of
threshold responses to pure tones and, finally, higher level
nuclei or the auditory cortex may be in trouble. The latter
results in speech discrimination loss which is independent
of any loss in hearing tone sensitivity.

Corso (1982) has reviewed the discriminatory tests to
establish hearing loss. Of interest, hearing changes are
not as great in women as in men to pure tone air generated
thresholds.

Hearing is poorer with advancing age to higher frequencies and at higher frequencies pitch discrimination is
altered beyond 55 years of age. What is most critical is
age related inability to discriminate between pure tones
which may involve central processing changes to speech
reception thresholds. These differ in quiet environments as
compared to the adverse effects of controlled noise as a
background during attempts to elicit speech discrimination.
Age related changes, for speech perception, can be quantitated
particularly when measured in the quiet which may be a good
quantitative system for judging functional age.

Harkins (1981) has utilized measurement of brainstem
auditory evoked potentials as an index of age. Response
variables did not change with age in healthy aged women, but

was related to hearing loss. However, it is important to note that there is suggestive evidence that auditory evoked potentials can be used as a technique to identify early Alzheimer patients (Harkins, 1980, Harkins and Lenhardt, 1980).

2.   Vision:

Visual preception alters with age and Sekular (1982) has discussed this in an excellent review at the NIA Biomarkers Conference.

One of the most reliable markers is senile miosis.   In a study at the U.S. Airforce Aerospace Medical Research Laboratory, pupillary diameters decreased significantly in response to a standard assay system.   Seventy per cent of subjects 55 or older had 3 mm pupils while all subjects under 55 had 4 mm pupils.   The exact cause of this change is unknown and may relate to iris muscle tone or pupillary light reflex responses.

Contrast sensitivity varies with age and this technique which can be independent of acuity, is readily applicable to bioquantitation (Sekular and Owsley, 1980).   Dark adaptation also decreases with age (Cinotti et al., 1980) and, in a study that requires facial identification as the goal for contrast modified thresholds, older observers required twice as long to identify faces as younger subjects (Owsley, et al., 1981).

The most widely studied and the earliest visual effect of aging is presbyopia.   This is a valid test of age, but it loses validity above the age of 60 because accomodative amplitude differences stabilize.   However, prior to this event, presbyopic changes represent a good biomarker for each individual subject (Sekular, 1982).

New techniques using laser refraction of the lens can reveal early cataract changes before clinical evidence of opacification by slit lamp technique.   In diabetics, this has been found to indicate lens changes before clinical evidence of visual disturbance (Weiss et al., 1983) and laser technology may provide us with a biomarker for chronologic age.

Stephens et al. (1978) have used the electro-oculogram which measures retinal electrophysiological function to light adaptation.  Apparently, as a biomarker, improvement is seen following response to zinc dietary supplementation. Flicker fusion is also a biomarker for aging as a measure of retinal function (Stephens et al., 1979, 1980).

Most recently, Beck et al., (1980) have reported on long latency of visually evoked potentials of the brain related to specific visual events with evoked potential responses showing an age relationship.

Other methods that are applicable to bioquantitation in opthamalogic practice include distortion of visual preception that provoke nystagmus and vertigo and evaluation of the permeability of iris vascular endothelium to fluoroscein dye injection.

3.  Olfaction and taste:

Murphy (1981) has reported from the Monell Chemical Senses Center, using a Dravnieks dynamic dilution binary scale olfactometer, that menthol odor sensitivity declined with age and Hughes (1968) has shown an increase in taste threshold with progressive age.

Taste sensitivity was measured by Hughes (1969) with weak galvanic stimulation which changed with age, and it would be of interest to see if such assays could be applied in routine clinical settings for age quantitation.

J.  Clinical Neurologic Changes

1.  Presbystasis, "spindle-vertigo", psychomotor performance, cognition, etc.

The extent of neurologic deficits in aging is controversial as a great deal of the clinical data has been obtained from nursing home patients (Greenhouse et al., 1981).  In contrast, matched subjects living independently may show minimal or absent changes.

An area suitable for bioquantitation has recently been reviewed by Ochs et al., (1982) and Sheppard (1978) in regaru to factors responsible for maintenance of balance in the aged.

The loss of equilibrium in the elderly has been termed "presbystasis", but whether it relates to alterations in vestibular function or peripheral nerve afferent loss or the combination of these factors remains to be seen, although it constitutes an excellent biomarker of aging (Overstall et al., 1981).

Presbystasis assay techniques, are varied: Mulch and Petermann (1979) studied caloric induction of nystagmus and found that nystagmus oscillation was 50-57% (51-60 years) above that seen for the youngest age group, but those 61-70 years of age showed a weaker response. This is of interest in view of reports of a decline in motion sickness with progressive age (McCafery and Graham, 1980).

Side to side sway is significantly greater in older persons (Tokumasu and Kawano, 1976). The healthy elderly lift their feet higher than younger subjects (Murray, et al., 1969), and this is associated with a decline in monosynaptic reflex excitability (Sabbahi et al., 1982).

Sabin (1982) has shown that an age related loss of large peripheral nerve fibers can be a significant factor in the senile gait disorder. The longer afferents to the lower limbs decline functionally before proximal afferent muscle innervation fails. This change, which has been termed "spindle-vertigo", can be studied as an office procedure using a simple vibrator. The threshold of stimulation that induces falling is a function of progressive age as the position of the lower limbs is lost to the subject during intense vibratory over stimulation. It is Sabin's contention that this is a major reason as to why falling characterizes our older population.

In another area, Potvin et al., (1980) have found consistent decline with age to a number of simple tasks or tests, i.e., speed of handwriting, removal of shirt and decline in vibration sensitivity. The most sensitive test in Potvin, et al's study was the loss of capability for one legged standing which showed a 100% decline with age.

Salthouse (1982) in the recent NIA conference on bio-markers very ably discusses clinical changes in psychomotor performance. Among the most correlative performance changes, which decline with increasing age, is the Wais Digit Symbol Substitution Test. Salthouse suggests that from the point of view of economy and correlative value, the digit symbol substitution test is the best index of psychomotor age although simple or choice reaction times also provide valid measures that are also easily obtained with minimal equipment outlay. McClaran et al., (1981) reports that Benton's visual retention test was the assay which correlated most with overall physical activity in elderly French managers.

Apart from measuring psychomotor function, Albert and Naeser (1982) have shown that there are quantitative changes in brain volume and density that accompany aging. In support of this, DeLeon et al., (1979), reported cognitive defects that correlate with cortical atrophy on CT scan in senile dementia as have George et al., (1981), who have found increases in ventricular volume in this population. This requires more work as the data is still only preliminary.

The obvious potential of other non-interfering techniques such as positron emission scanning, nuclear magnetic resonance imaging or multiple simultaneous computerized electroenceph-alography have age related biomarker potential as they become available at major centers.

In regard to the above, there is data showing decreased glucose utilization with aging in the brain of rodents (London et al., 1979). This can be clinically evaluated with positron emission via F-18 deoxyglucose (FDG) which is providing diagnostic criteria for senile dementia (Ferris et al., 1980; de Leon et al., 1979, 1980, 1981). The latter group have shown diminished CNS metabolic uptake of 35-45% in senile dementia patients as compared to controls.

An alternative physiologic marker for aging measures changes in sleep patterns which, Dement (1982), in his excellent review, has divided into: time in bed (TIB); total sleep time (TST); wake after sleep onset (WASO). Additional non-EEG parameters that can be measured during sleep include sleep apnea, nocturnal myoclonus and gastroesophageal reflux.

Some of the above changes in sleep parameters can be easily established by obervation and history taking, and may relate to nasopharyngeal obstruction, pulmonary hypertension and myxedema. The most intricate patterns of sleep change require EEG interpretation and the help of a sleep laboratory.

Organic penile erectile function, which correlates with rapid eye movement dreaming, can be quantitated during sleep with the Event Systems Device (Moorestown, New Jersey) that permits, in males, a method to ascertain psychogenic versus organic impotency and which can also be used to quantitate,

REM sleep, as a function of aging (Podolsky, 1980).

Studies of gait and mobility in the elderly can be quantitated using photocell measurements in standard walkways. There is also the Wright (1971) Sway Meter and television tape analysis, using defined criteria for obstacle course traversment (Imms and Edham, 1981), can be routinized for biomarker study.

2.  Motor performance and cognition:

The length, diameter and number of aging skeletal muscle fibers decreases with age in mice (Hooper, 1981). This has been related to loss of joint mobility with aging, and may reflect on motor functional and exercise tolerance capacity of the elderly as measured by performance tests. These areas are reviewed by Sheppard (1978) and Smith and Serfass (1980).

Among the performance tests conveniently applicable is the Crawford Dexterity Test which compares bimanual with unimanual activity (Veray et al., 1980). Of interest, this group reports that differences are seen between elderly obese subjects versus non-obese and those with hyperostosis frontalis.

Reaction time and intelligence: Excellent reviews of this area of age evaluation are found in the Duke Longitudinal Study (Palmore, 1970). More recently, La Rue and Jarvik (1980) have presented data that senile dementia can be diagnosed on the basis of low scores using three tests of cognitive function that may be predictive twenty years before clinical diagnosis. Tests for vocabulary similarities and digit symbol were the most predictive for the development of dementia in later life.

The speed at which mentally retarded subjects can choose among alternatives in a reaction time task is related to their level of intelligence. Individual fluctuations around an average level of performance are correlated with IQ (Vernon, 1982; Vernon and Jensen, 1982) and can be developed as office procedures.

In the above, simple testing systems involving speed of encoding or inspection time; processing (scanning) information of digits; speed of retrieving word information ("same" or "different"), and reaction time response to a positioned light; were compared to Wais and Raven advanced progressive matrices for evaluation as to intelligence. Correlation of intelligence testing with reaction time shows that it measures a key factor in cognitive processing that can be readily applied to the elderly.

Each institution has its own battery of measurements for this purpose which has been used to distinguish dementia from depression or Korsakoff's syndrome (Neville and Folstein, 1979). Psychological testing can also act as a standard stress for study of catechol urinary output changes (Faucheux et al., 1981) with aging.

Good reviews of neural and cognitive function and aging are found in Heron and Chown (1967), Stein (1979), and Craik and Trehub (1982) as well as in the Handbooks on Aging.

        3.   Hippocampal function and adrenocorticoid
            secretion:

Landfield et al. (1978) have found, in rodents, a correlation between hippocampal astrocyte concentration and adrenocorticoid output and hypertrophy which increase with aging. At the upper limits of aging, there may be decreases in levels of aldosterone output. For this reason, we need 24 hour blood sampling systems for determination of ACTh response and adrenocorticosteroid measurement combined with pet scanning or NMR scanning of the hippocampal region. This will help us ascertain correlative changes in CNS and adrenal function that could relate to changes in aging parameters.

As pituitary-adrenocortical response to stress is under hippocampal CNS control and the sensitivity of animals to stress induced ACTh release is modulated via the hippocampus (Landfield et al., 1978; Lanfield, 1981), we need an acceptable clinical neuroendocrine response stress test which can determine the response of the aged to the modulating action of the hippocampus.

An alternative measure to steroid assay in stress are changes in amino acid patterns in blood which can be followed by amino acid analysis (Spackman and Riley, unpublished observation, Pacific N.W. Research Foundation, 1982).

Long term blood measurement of diurinal variations, most important to endocrine evaluation, can now be performed conveniently with the development of subcutaneously implanted venous sideports (i.e., NuTech, Boston, MA) which permits convenient intermittant or continuous blood sampling.

    K.   Endocrine Measurement:

        1.   Steroids, glucoregulation, thyroid, prolactin, parathormone, etc.:

The importance of measures of sexual function with aging is seen in rodents where there is a correlation between the time of reproductive senescence and the absolute length of life (Timiras, 1975, 1979). This area has been reviewed in a number of texts (Greenblatt, 1978) and conferences (Schimore, 1981) and, most recently, in texts edited by Korenman (1982), and by Vernadakis and Timiras (1982).

The decline in estrogen function in the aging female has been well studied (Eisenberg and Walker, 1982) and clinical estrogenic intervention, as an option, is controversial because of the toxic thrombotic and carcinogenic effects of currently available estrogens. As discussed in this text (Purdy and Goldzieher, 1983), we need non-carcinogenic estrogens which are already available or can be readily synthesized and tested.

Of importance to biomarkers, aldosterone levels have been reported to decline as an age factor in women (Cugini et al., 1982) and to have a circadian expression (Halberg, 1982).

In contrast to the obvious changes of the menopause; changes in testosterone function in the aging male are not well defined as changes in testosterone blood levels need not correlate with sexual activity (Tsitoura et al., 1982). In this regard, testosterone decline is felt to be of testicular origin and Ghanadian and Puah (1981) have reported significant differences between age groups 20-39; 40-59; 60-79 in testosterone output. This has been confirmed by Zumoff et al. (1981) who reported a 35% decrease in plasma testosterone content between age 21 to 85 accompanied by a linear increase in FSH. It must be stressed that quantitative assays in males are effected by chronobiological sampling differences. It is hoped that more rapid and reproducible assays reflecting on male hormonal function could be developed by measuring LHRH.

Huemer and Walters (1978), in a retrospective study, have found that 17-keto-steroid production, estrogen and pregnanediol and gonadotrophin levels decrease with age. There is also evidence in the aging rat that serum levels of somatomedins decline with age, but this is not associated with a decline in growth hormone that stimulates the production of these mediators (Florini et al., 1981). In Daughaday's review (1981) he reports on a clinical decline of somatomedins with age. Somatomedin levels, obviously, need clinical evaluation as potential biomarkers.

There are different reports of growth hormone (GH), changes with age and there is a complex relationship between somatomedins and growth hormone production (Tannenbaum et al., 1983): Growth hormone may consist of a family of peptides (Linfoot, 1981) and it may be that clinical immunoassay for GH presence does not identify specific peptide changes which may be specifically altered with age. In view of thyroid releasing hormone (TRH) action in stimulating growth hormone release (Mosier, 1981) as well as arginine and insulin effects on GH levels, it is appropriate to study growth hormone following administration of standard stimuli to its release in clinical assays of GH with aging.

While the level of glucocorticoids is a factor in aging and age related response to stress (Landfield, 1981), the one adrenocortical hormone that clearly declines with age and constitutes a readily evaluable biomarker is dehydroepiandrosterone (DHEA) (Orentreich, 1982; Crilly and Nordin, 1981). This hormone, at age 80, declines to 10-20% of values seen at age 20, as has been discussed by Arthur Schwartz at this meeting. DHEA has anti-obesity and anti-carcinogenesis activity. Most importantly, it aborts diabetes of the adult type and streptozotocin induced diabetes in inbred mice, which may be meaningful to control of adult onset diabetic patterns in man (Coleman, 1982). For a more detailed review of the above, the reader is referred to Cole et al. (1982) and other chapters in the text edited by Verdakis and Timaris (1982).

Many of the age related changes seen with alteration of glucoregulatory hormones may be due to age related obesity which influences plasma glucose, insulin and glucagon (Elahi et al., 1982; Davidson, 1982). For this reason, age quantitation must include anthropometric measures of body fat content. These can be calculated by body weight determinants correlated with skin fold and other anatomic

measurements. Orentreich et al., (1979) have developed an
air displacement method which, in contrast to water displacement specific gravity estimates, could be developed as an
office related technique for bioquantitation of age related
changes in fat distribution.

As mentioned previously, changes in the control of
insulin secretion occur with aging as does glucagon excretion
(Adelman et al., 1981; Adelman, 1982; DeFronzo, 1982).
There is an age related clinical decrease in glucose utiliza-
tion (DeFronzo, 1982), which may relate to insulin resistance.
In rats, glucagon levels rise with age (Klug et al., 1979).
The relationship of the above to changes in glucose tolerance,
in man, requires further evaluation (Adelman, 1982).

Sawin et al. (1979) report an increase in TSH levels in
6% of healthy subjects over age 60. TSH elevation was
associated with a decline in $T_4$ values in 50% of subjects.
Both the total and free levels of serum triiodothyronine
($T_3$) and thyroxine ($T_4$) decrease during age (Adelman et al.,
1981; Muzziol and Mocchegiani, 1982)), and glucocorticoid
levels can effect TSH secretion in man (Otsuki et al.,
1973). This has recently been reviewed in an excellent
paper by Melmed and Hershman (1982), and by Cole et al.
(1982) and is discussed, in this text, in our review of the
pituitary control of aging.

Klug and Adelman (1979) have reported on a decrease in
thyroid hormone with progressive increase of a particular
large molecular form of thyrotropin in the serum of aging
rats (Adelman et al., 1982). For this reason, exploration
of altered hormonal mediators should be explored clinically
and thyroid hormonal relationships are particularly important
to prolactin levels which respond to TRH administration.

Prolactin secretion is under dopaminergic control in
aging male rats (Gudelsky et al., 1981; Neil, 1980) and with
age, prolactin levels, in rats, increase as compared to that
of younger animals (Gudelsky et al., 1981; Meites et al.,
1978).

The clinical importance of prolactin, as an aging
biomarker, is controversial as natural postmenopausal prolactin values are not altered, while, with surgical menopause,
prolactin values may be higher than normal (Notelovitz
et al., 1982). However, prolactin values may reflect on
techniques of sampling as values change as part of circadian

rhythm and season.

Prolactin rises with sleep (Haus et al., 1980; Djursing et al., 1981) and the role of prolactin, in aging, remains to be determined although it is apparently required for normal growth in infant mice (Sinha and Vanderlaan, 1982). In contrast, L-dopa, which blocks prolactin release (Papavasiliou et al., 1981) is associated with maintenance of motor activity and increases in average survival when given throughout life beginning at 8 weeks. In relation to intervention, dopamine agonists have profound effects on pituitary size, growth hormone production (Daughaday, 1982) and prolactin secretion (Thorner et al., 1980) as well as life expectancy.

Prolactin is reduced in manic depression (Mendlewicz et al., 1980) which may be pertinent to the depression of aging. It is of interest that, in aging female rats, copulatory response does not elicit prolactin secretion. This is associated with decreased fertility (Hendricks and Blake, 1981) as an age related event.

Finally, prolactin alters membrane fluidity which may effect receptor availability in similar fashion to what has been seen for lecithin derivatives as reported by Shinitzky at this meeting. This action of prolactin is age related as liver cells, from younger animals, are more sensitive to prolactin membrane fluidizing effects than those derived from older animals (Dave and Knazek, 1983).

The role of dehydroepiandrosterone (DHEA) as a biomarker for aging has been discussed at this meeting by Schwartz. Its decline is age related and DHEA has been shown to possess anti-stress activity in rodents and is marketed in Italy as an anti-stress steroid. DHEA is under prolactin control which may also explain age related changes in DHEA levels (Lobo et al., 1980; Seki and Kato, 1981).

The osteopenia of age is a major clinical problem leading to vertebral collapse, back pain and hip fracture. The mechanisms of bone loss relate to calcium decreased dietary intake, $1,25-(OH)_2D$ levels and parathormone. With enhanced immunoreactive ability to detect parathyroid hormone (PTH) and its fragments, it is apparent that there is a true age related increase in functional PTH levels. Insogna et al. (1981) present good evidence that with aging there is an increase in the level of PTH that could contribute to the bone loss of aging.

2. Vasopressin:

The sensitivity of the aged to dehydration is well
known and Zbuzek and Wu (1982) have reviewed the changes in
hypothalamic and serum levels of vasopressin with age.  In
rat plasma, immunoreactive vasopressin in 30 month old
animals was half of that seen in adult (12 months) and young
(3 months) animals.  However, clinically, with age, physiologic control of antidiuretic vasopressin release becomes more
sensitive to serum osmolarity, but there is a less active
response to hemodynamic or orthostatic changes.

Clinical studies require well defined controlled
stimuli for age comparative studies of vasopressin release
to have significant bioquantitative value (Robertson et al.,
1979).  As is seen in response patterns for prolactin,
vasopressin may alter targeted prostaglandin synthesis and
response (Kinter et al., 1981) which may provide us with
alternative assays related to gerontologic patterns.

L. Gastrointestinal:

This area has been reviewed extensively by Kaye (1981)
and Schmucker and Wang (1981) in the Handbook of Physiology
in Aging.  It is my own personal experience that the simplest
parameter for age changes, in this area, relate to study of
motor control of the esophagous (presbyesophagus) and gastric
emptying rate in the elderly which is significantly prolonged
(Evans et al., 1981).  Unfortunately, roentgen or functional
assays of bowel require great effort, cost and inconvenience
as do most studies of absorption (Fikay et al., 1967) and
further work is necessary to expand the opportunities provided by fiberoptic visualization and biopsy techniques.

The problem of nutritional absorption, or the decrease
in the synthesis of enzymatic cofactors may require dietary
supplementation in the aged.  This has been discussed by
Folkers in regard to the relative pyridoxine deficiency of
aging and the need for tetrahydrobiopterin ($BH_4$) in parkinsonism (see Folkers, 1983 in this text).  Another example is
the obvious need for calcium supplementation as an age related
problem that may reflect on primary gastrointestinal pathology.
The ultimate example of problems of this kind, which may be
more subtle in the aged, is the axonal dystrophy of intestinal
malabsorption syndromes (Cavalier and Gambetti, 1981).

Intervention in aging requires a better understanding of intestinal absorption and changes which could constitute the primary pathology of aging that leads to many of the neurologic and tissue disorders of age. Gastrointestinal absorption and functional assays should be a major priority for biomarker age correlates.

M.   Nuclear Magnetic Resonance (NMR):

An example of recent technology applicable to aging quantitation which is useful for evaluation of the physiologic systems discussed is nuclear magnetic resonance (NMR) which has resulted in clinical imaging devices which have the additional benefit of determining, with a non-interfering method, internal metabolic events.

Surface magnetic coil, or topical magnetic resonance (TMR) permits the focused analysis of NMR signals from internal organs, i.e., liver, heart, kidney, without the need for biopsy (Bore et al., 1982). These techniques have already been applied clinically for analysis of muscle function in peripheral limbs and for the analysis of viability of the human kidney homografts. NMR permits the assay of not only internal pH changes, but the presence of ATP and phosphocreatine which permits us to measure dynamic changes of high energy phosphate levels. Shulman has recently discussed the biomedical applications of NMR in an excellent review (1983).

In the isolated heart, NMR has permitted observations related to pH and internal energy changes (Jacobus et al., 1982; Gadian et al., 1982). The above will become clinically useful with the application of focused NMR which will permit the assay of changes in internal organs; an approach which will be ideally suited to bioquantitation of human aging. This technology will permit, for the first time, the non-interferring assay of mitochondrial function, which is thought to decline with age in specific target organs.

Phosphorous nuclear magnetic resonance ($^{31}$ P-NMR) can be used to measure intracellular pH of intact tissue (Gadian et al., 1982). Changes in pH can reflect on intracellular metabolic events including the metabolic changes of free ammonia, ischemic changes and the integrity of mitochondrial function.

In another area, Moore et al., (1982) have shown that

intracellular pH governs insulin action in control of glycolysis. NMR can be of importance in monitoring diabetic
control and possibly give insight into the progeric action
of the diabetic syndrome.

Lymphocyte proliferative stimulation is governed by
intracellular pH elevations which is correlated with DNA
synthesis (Gerson, 1982) and thus NMR may also become a
rapid monitoring system for lymphocyte age related blasto-
genic response.

NMR will serve as a spur to cytogerontology, where in
tissue culture systems, it could provide age related indicators of senescent changes following biopsy and it will
provide insights as to mechanisms of senescence (Gillies
et al., 1982).

III.  IMMUNOLOGIC PARAMETERS:

It has been shown in a variety of animal and clinical
models that with age immunologic response declines (Friedman
and Globerson, 1978; Dilman, 1978; Leech, 1980; Yunis et al.,
1979; Gozes et al., 1982; Weindruch, 1982; Segre and Smith,
1981; Mark and Weksler, 1982; Weksler, 1982; Staiano-Coico
et al., 1983).  Methodology, in this area, is reviewed by
Adler and Nordin (1981).  Aging and progeric syndromes may
also be associated with decreases in suppressor T cell
levels and the appearance of autoimmune disease (Fudenberg
et al., 1979).

Ninety per cent or more of thymic lymphocytes in humans
less than 20 years of age express the thymic receptor for
sheep erythrocytes while these receptor levels fall with age
so that by 60 years only 60% of lymphocytes within the
thymus have this receptor (Singh and Singh, 1979).

Long term cultures of human T cells show age related
decreases in doubling capacity despite the presence of T
cell growth factors (Walford et al., 1981) which fits within
the criteria for other Hayflick senescence models.

Autorosetting of lymphocytes increases with age (Moody
et al., 1981) which is a reflection of lymphocyte immaturity
and Weksler (1982) has found that the distribution of human
T lymphocytes sub-populations change with age.  In that
regard, Wexler's group has found a significant increase in
the number of helper-induced T lymphocytes which react with

OKT4 monoclonal antibody in elderly humans. There is a significant decrease in the number of suppressor-cytotoxic lymphocytes which react with the OKT5 and OKT8 antibodies (Moody et al., 1981).

With increasing age, there is a progressive decline in the percentage of lymphocytes transformed in cultures exposed to the plant lectin phytohemagglutinin (PHA). T-lymphocytes, in old subjects, contain only one-half as many responsive cells to PHA as do similar preparations from younger individuals (Inkeles et al., 1977). Hollingsworth and Gailotte (1981) have found deficient response to pokeweed mitogen in lymphocyte cultures obtained from aged men.

In measuring *in vitro* vesicular stomatitis virus infection present only in activated T cells, but not in resting T cells, the number of lytic foci generated in cultures from aged donors was only 1/5 the number observed in cultures from younger participants (Inkeles et al., 1977). Cowan et al., (1981) have found results similar to Ikeles that can be modified by thymosin fraction V.

In the presence of colchicine, lymphocyte cultures from old subjects incorporated only 1/2 as much tritiated thymidine as did cultures from young subjects. Not only were there fewer initially responsive T cells in the blood of old donors, but in addition, the replication of these cells in culture was intrinsically defective (Weksler, 1982).

Of interest, colchicine enhances con A induced capping in lymphocytes from aged donors and progeric Downs syndrome subjects suggesting that progressive microtubulin polymerization may be a factor that changes in lymphocytes from aged donors (Naeim et al., 1981).

There is a decline in the number of cells dividing *in vitro* for a second or third time, from older donors, when stimulated by PHA (Hefton et al., 1980). The number of lymphocytes from old donors dividing for a second time were only 1/2 that in cultures from younger individuals.

Weksler (1982) indicates that cultures from old donors have only 1/5 the number of lymphocytes dividing for a third time as did cultures from younger donors. This impairment of old donor replicative potential in cultures is comparable to what has been seen for human fibroblasts and arterial smooth muscle cells from aged populations.

The above decline in reproductive potential of stem cell production of lymphocytes is seen in reconstitution studies of radiated bone marrow of 3 month old mice recepients using old donors (24 months) where lymphocyte decline occurs in contrast to prolonged survival seen in transplants of young marrow (Gozes et al., 1982).

Weksler (1982) Staiano-Coico et al. (1983) suggest that tritiated thymidine, even of low specific activity, inhibits passage of lymphocytes through the cell cycle. Weksler has observed that tritiated thymidine blocks cell proliferation at the G2 or M phase of the cell cycle and preliminary work suggests that lymphocytes from old donors are more lethally sensitive to tritiated thymidine in contrast to those cells obtained from young donors. This is of particular interest to the reports by Lipetz and Stephens and Williams, at this conference, and others (Gensler and Bernstein, 1981) indicating that DNA repair mechanisms may be defective in older cell populations.

The decline in T lymphocyte responses with aging might reside in the availability of interleukin II which is the leukokine peptide driving force for maintenance of T cell proliferation: Lymphocytes from old donors produce less than 1/2 the amount of interleukin II than that produced from young donors (Gillis et al., 1980). Activated lymphocytes from old donors also do not express the receptors for interleukin II normally found in younger subjects.

In contrast to the above, Jamil and Millard (1981) have found no significant changes in T or B lymphocytes or PHA response with age in healthy subjects, although the number of "null" lymphocytes showed a significant decline. This group suggests that clinical differences could reflect on the iron deficiency anemia seen in many elderly subjects. Fernandez and MacSween (1980) have shown a decline in the autologous mixed lymphocyte reaction with age which they feel correlates with age related auto antibody or β cell neoplasia.

In regard to lymphocyte subsets, Fitzgerald and Bennet (1983) have reported that NK cells decline in aging rats. Here is a lymphocyte subpopulation that must be looked for in man as a biomarker of age related change.

In lymphocytes, cyclic GMP increases while cyclic AMP decreases with age (Tam and Walford, 1978) in rodents and

similar results have been reported in man for peripheral
blood leukocytes along with changes in adenylate cyclase and
guanylate cyclase activities (Tam and Walford, 1980).
Although this has not been confirmed by Weksler (1982),
perhaps the decline in lymphocyte response is associated
with an age impairment in glycolysis (Tollesfsbol et al.,
1981).

In another area, Scholar et al., (1980) observed an age
related fall in mouse splenocyte purine nucleoside phosphorylase activity which can lead to T cell functional impairment.
Similarly, two key enzymes, needed for DNA synthesis (deoxynucleotidyl transferase and DNA polymerase alpha) are
reported to fall with age in mouse bone marrow cells enriched
for T cell precursors (Muller et al., 1980).

Purine nucleoside phosphyorylase activity (Scholar
et al., 1980) declines in splenic lymphocytes in correlation
with T cell functional decline in aging mice.  Sun et al.
(1978) have reported increases in 5' nucleotidase in aging
lymphocytes and these enzymatic observations must be confirmed in man.

Reversal of age related lymphocyte abnormalities is
possible:  Rivnay et al. (1979) have reported that membrane
viscosity of old mouse and human lymphocytes was about 20%
higher than that of younger subjects.  Lyte (1982) has shown
that lymphocyte responsiveness, in older mice, can be
restored by egg lecithin phospholipid feeding with return of
lymphocyte membrane fluidity (Shinitzky,  et al., 1982).  Of
interest to this, beta adrenergic lymphocyte receptors have
been reported to decline in human lymphocytes (Shocken and
Roth, 1977) with age and one wonders if this lymphocyte
receptor change correlates similarly with CNS receptor
availability which change as a function of membrane fluidity.
CNS membrane fluidity and receptor availability can be
altered by "active lecithin" feeding as described by Shinitzky
at this meeting.

Lymphocyte surface markers change with age (Nagel et
al., 1981).  Fluorescein-labeled con A effects on lymphocyte
capping decrease with age beginning at 40-60 years (Norohna
et al., 1980), and Rivnay et al., (1980), as discussed
earlier, have found that the lymphocyte membrane viscosity
increase with age correlates with the decline in con A
response.  This is thought to be due to a decrease in phospholipid to cholesterol ratios in the cell membrane.  Changes
in membrane cholesterol/phospholipid ratios are a biomarker

approach which can be developed for automated quantitation
of clinically sampled lymphocytes.

O'Leary et al., (1982) have recently reported changes
in lactic acid dehydrogenase isozyme ratios in lymphocytes
of subjects over 75 years. Cells from older individuals
appear less differentiated in correlation with a decline in
OKT3 leukokine positive cells. As mentioned previously, Sun
et al. (1980) have shown that proliferative capacity in
lymphocyte cell lines was inversely proportional to 5'
nucleotidase which is located at the cell surface.

It will be of interest to examine the above observations
in conjunction with those of DeWeck's group (personal communication, 1983) in Berne, who have shown changes in lymphocyte
populations in the elderly as measured by flow cytofluorometric responses to lectin and leukokine mitogenic stimulation.

Cytofluorometric technique may provide us with a rapid
biomarker system for functional quantitation of lymphocyte
response with aging (Staiano-Coico et al., 1983). This is
supported by evidence that mixed lymphocyte responses decline
(Konen et al., 1973; Merhav and Gershon, 1977) in similar
fashion to what Weksler's group has reported for PHA. Cowan
et al., (1981) have shown that mixed lymphocyte responses
can be corrected by thymosin fraction V. In that regard,
Goldstein's group (Hersh et al., 1983) has now developed a
thymosin fraction V monoclonal antibody which can quantitate
the clinical level of this hormone in blood, and which may
be useful in identifying patients with the acquired immunodeficiency syndrome.

In another area, Goidal et al., (1980) reported that
there is a relative increase in auto-antiidiotypic antibodies
with aging that produces a down regulation of immune response
with age. This effect can be reversed with hapten augmention
in plaquing (Choy and Goidal, 1981) assays.

As immune complex disease is increased with age in both
rodents and man, the assay of such complexes could provide
significant biomarkers: Powell and Fernandez, (1980) have
found an age related increase in immunoglobulin bearing β
cells to pokeweed mitogen in the presence of peripheral
blood mononuclear cells. Nandy et al., (1978) have found
age related increases in autoantibodies to thyroglobulin and
gastric mucosa. Indeed, Nandy (1978; 1981) have reported on

circulating antibodies to central nervous system tissue in senile dementia patients which has been thought by Nandy et al., (1982) to relate to declining thymic regulation. Similar increases have been reported for thyroid and kidney antibodies along with the presence of immune complexes in synovia and glomeruli.

Based on the above, using immunological techniques, one must look for age related immunologically altered thymic hormones or hormonal precursors in serum or lymphocytes. Blaylock (1983), has reported that lymphocytes contain ACTh perhaps derived from interferon. Klug and Adelman (1979) have reported on the presence of large molecular weight forms of thyrotropin (TSH) in the pituitary and serum of male Sprague-Dawley rats. They have found an age dependent accumulation of immunologically cross-reactive large forms of TSH in rat serum associated with a progressive decline in bioassayable levels of normal serum TSH. The large molecular form of TSH inhibits thyroidal response to exogenous TSH and may contribute to the relative hypothyroid state which accompanies aging. (Alternative explanations for the relative hypothyroid state seen with aging is discussed in my chapter on the Pituitary Control of Aging in this volume.)

IV.   NON-REPLICATING TISSUE SAMPLES:

A.   Blood Cells:

Apart from representing a model system for the study of the aging process on cell membranes, a specific study of red cell function from aged donors can reflect on the physical status of age. As an example, an increase in resistance to osmotic fragility of red cells has been reported to reflect chronologic age (Bowdler et al., 1981; Detraglia et al., 1974).

The above changes may reflect on the sphericity index of red cells which measures the volume of the red cell which changes with age. There is also evidence that sodium potassium ATPase falls in red blood cells of older women (Naylor et al., 1980).

Acetylcholine esterase activity increases in aging red blood cells of women, but not males, while plasma choline shows an age related increase (Hartford et al., 1979).

Minimal anemia characterizes those over 60 and in one study this was felt to be corrected by iron supplementation

(Hershko et al., 1979). Independent of iron metabolism, in Swiss mice, there is a change with chronologic age in electrophoretic bands of hemoglobin that deserves clinical exploration (Rodgers and Gass, 1980).

There are distinct changes in red blood cell membrane proteins as determined by electron spin resonance studies depending on the age of the donor (Butterfield and Markesbery, 1981; Butterfield et al., 1982). In addition, red blood cell polyamine levels may change with the age of the donor with a decrease in spermidine and spermine after the fifth and sixth decades (Kremzner and Natta, 1981). This change, which effects beta globulin binding to red cell stroma, may be a factor in membrane deformability and the decreased osmotic resistance seen in aging cells (Natta et al., 1982).

Red blood cells from older mice are more sensitive to perfringolysin O which suggests an expansion of the cholesterol cell membrane compartment with aging (Saito et al., 1982). It has direct bearing on the paper presented by Shinitzky, at this meeting, and red blood cells from old mice are more sensitive to oxidative stress produced by sodium ascorbate (Tyan, 1982).

Hochstein et al. (1982), Hochstein and Jain (1981) and Walls et al. (1976) have described the physiological significance of oxidative changes in red cell membranes. For example, there is an increased hemolytic sensitivity of aging red cells to oxidant action. This is seen as a function of uric acid or the presence of thyroid hormones (Ames et al., 1981; Walls et al., 1976). Importantly, the phosphatidylethanolamine content of red cells does not exchange with plasma phospholipid and the make up of the red cell membrane could thus reflect on the chronologic age of the individual, independent of dietary fluctuation.

An age dependent increase of oxidized glutathione has been reported in the blood of aged rats which Dyundikove et al. (1981) feels might be an effective biomarker of biologic age.

In view of related proteins in the lens and red blood cell (spectrin), one should look at methionine sulfoxide levels as a function of chronologic age in RBC or WBC membranes as it accumulates in the aging lens (Brot and Weissbach, 1982), and might also change in blood cells.

As discussed previously, Bridge (1979) has reported on the presence of distinct increases in monoamine oxidase in platelets derived from subjects beyond the fifth decade.

Cerami et al. (1979) have reported on nonenzymatic glycosylation changes in red cells as a function of glucose levels in diabetes. These changes are now used as measures of diabetic control. It would be of interest to see if such changes occur in white blood cells and platelets and could reflect age related events.

B. Spinal Fluid Assays (CSF Assay):

Although CSF aspiration is a procedure that is not readily accepted by patients, there are significant changes in cerebrospinal fluid neuropeptides with senile dementia (Oram et al., 1981) and in particular patients CSF assay is warranted.

In view of reports of neurotensin, substance P and somatostatin decline in the central nervous system of aging rodents and man (Burks et al., 1981), it would be of interest if these peptides could be measured in the CNS via CSF assay.

In regard to the above, thyrotropin releasing hormone, gonadotropin releasing hormone and somatostatin are lower in patients with dementia in contrast to control patients with cerebral tumors or spinal disc lesions.

Most recently, Yesavage et al. (1982) have reported that CSF lactate is elevated in aging subjects despite normal blood oxygen saturation.

Strain et al. (1981) are studying the quantitative elemental composition of spinal fluid using inductively coupled argon plasma arc spectrometry which, they claim, permits assay of 28 major and minor elements. We look forward to further study by this group to see if they can separate age related differences from that caused by specific disease states in the central nervous system.

C. Hair, Finger Nail and Skin Scrapings:

Tissue for measurement purposes requires concern for the ease of its retrieval. For this reason, base of tongue scrapings have been used for magnesium and trace metal assays (Silver, 1982) as have hair or finger nail studies.

Unfortunately, hair and finger nail trace metal or amino acid profile determinants have never been accepted by clinicians because of their commercial exploitation by chiropractic and naturopathic advocates, but this sampling opportunity requires research validation. Currently, the availability of secondary gamma emission for cation and metallic electron concentration combined with microscopic scanning of single cells might be a useful measure for age correlated studies (Silver, 1980).

The most successful application of this has been the assay of zinc nutritional requirements as seen in values obtained from hair samples (Gentile et al., 1981).

Most recently, Shapiro and Lam (1982) have used atomic absorption techniques to show calcium decline in senescent fibroblasts *in vitro*. These techniques could be applied to non-replicating tissue samples.

D. Sperm:

This source of tissue sampling could conceivably be used as a biomarker for age in functioning males and certainly is a more pleasant clinical alternative to CSF fluid or needle biopsies. In relation to this alternative, there is an age related increase in the percent of spermhead abnormalities in aged mice as compared to young mice (Fabricant and Parkening, 1981), and Lugaro et al. (1982) have found a sperm related factor which stimulates hepatic enzyme induction.

E.  Collagen and Tendon:

Biopsy of tendon or cartilage, while discomforting, can be done without morbidity, and could provide a source for age quantitation. Harrison has discussed mouse tail tendon age related changes at this meeting. In that regard, the solubility of level of collagen in bone, skin and tendon changes with alloxan diabetes in a mouse model (Behera and Patnaik, 1981) and the stability of collagen to heat denaturation increases with age and as early as 1957, Sinex showed that aging had distinct effects on the lability of amide groups in collagen.

Most recently, Williamson (1983) has reviewed changes

in the physical state of cartilage and connective tissue
which shows accelerated age related changes in diabetes.  In
animal models, lysyl oxidase levels, which effects the cross
linking of collagen, are increased in diabetes, an effect
that is blocked by insulin.  It would be appropriate to
examine lysyl oxidase with changes in  the physical state of
collagen on tissue biopsy (Heinegard and Hascall, 1979).

Sorbitol accumulates in diabetic tissue with age
(Williamson, 1983).  Monnier et al. (1981) have found age
related increases in non-enzymatic browning (Maillard
reaction) as a function of heat related protein-sugar
interaction which may be responsible for age pigment that
could be quantitated in biopsiable tissue.  Exploration for
methionine sulfoxide levels should also be made as methionine
sulfoxide increases the lens of the eye with age and cataract
formation.  Changes in cartilage tendon and formed blood
elements (Brot and Weissbach, 1982), should be looked at as
potential biomarkers for the above.

Tendon aging responds to effects of diet and heat and
Everitt et al. (1981) and Miyahara et al. (1982) have found
quantitative differences in solvent solubility and pepsin
digestion of human skin with aging.

What we need are non-interfering techniques that could
evaluate the physical state of collagen.  As collagen is
found with minimal skin covering in the ear, achilles tendon
or nasal septum, perhaps ultrasound, heat, NMR, or electrical
conduction techniques could provide non-interfering measurements to quantitate the clinical aging of collagen.

F.  Skeletal Muscle:

As discussed previously, NMR will probably prove to be
the best technique available for measuring muscle function
and age.

Guanylate cyclase activity was elevated in muscle of
aged (>20 years) as compared to adult (6-11) year old Rhesus
monkeys.  In these biopsies, reducing agents decreased while
dehydroascorbic acid increased along with the level of
guanylate cyclase in old as compared to adult muscle (Beatty
et al., 1981).

Distinct differences were seen in skeletal muscle
lipofuscin content of aged Rhesus monkeys that could be
quantitated (Beatty et al., 1982) with muscle biopsy.

Changes in mucopolysaccharides and glycoproteins have also been described with age (Mohan and Radha, 1981).

V.   BIOCHEMICAL ASSAYS:

A.   Drug Metabolism, HEME Biosynthesis, Delta Amino Levulinic Acid Synthesis:

Paterniti et al. (1978) discusses the role of delta-aminolevulinic acid synthetase, a mitochondrial enzyme, as the first step in HEME biosynthesis.  As HEME pigments are essential to oxidative pathways in mammalian physiology, changes in porphyrin metabolism or HEME biosynthesis are critical to the functional capacity of the aging animal (Marcus et al., 1982).

HEME synthesis is important to drug detoxification (Cytochrome, p. 450); the synthesis of unsaturated fatty acids (cytochrome b$_5$); or to neutralization of peroxides (catalase).  In this regard, delta-aminolevulinic acid synthetase activity decreases in liver, heart, brain and kidney, in an age related fashion.  This enzyme can serve as a salient tissue biomarker for measurement of significant decline in a host of critical enzyme systems.  In support of this, Lugaro et al. (1982) have reported that delta-amino-levulinic acid synthetase is inhibited by ethanol during aging in rats.  This is an observation that could be used for bioquantitation of both *in vivo* or *in vitro* aging systems.

Drug metabolism declines with aging (Schmucker and Wang, 1981) with a rapid decline in middle age with some restoration of function in later life (Rikans and Notley, 1981).  As an example, there is an increase in salicylate metabolites and prolongation of excretion with age in patients on aspirin (Montgomery and Stiar, 1981; Cuny et al., 1979).  These age effects might provide good clinical bio-markers as they do not relate to absorption or to the frequent use of salicylates.

Other compounds that alter endoplasmic reticulum drug hydrolase activity with age related effects on P450, 448 cytochrome activity are coumadin, phenobarbital and ethanol (Ritzmann and Springer, 1980) and numerous papers have been published on the topic of altered drug sensitivities with age.

Of clinical relevance to psychologic or sensory testing, Kaiko (1979) has reported a significant change in the age related response to morphine analgesia in post operative cancer patients. There are striking differences seen in patients in their 70's as contrasted with those in their 20's and 30's. Analgesic response to narcotics could conceivably be developed as an *in vivo* bioquantitation technique for age. In my own clinical experience, there is an increased sensitivity to the euphorant action of narcotics combined with a dramatic increase in dependency associated with senile depression.

B.  Monoamine Oxidase:

There is evidence of an age related progressive elevation of a monoamine degrading enzyme in both the rat and man (Leung et al., 1981; Fowler et al., 1980) and the level of MAO may be higher in Alzheimer's disease (Adolfsson et al., 1980; Smith et al., 1982).

Changes in MAO activity in the central nervous system has an important controlling effect on hypothalamic pituitary and thyroid function in rats (Morley et al., 1981).

Platelet MAO activity increases with aging (Robinson et al., 1971; Bridge et al., 1981). Of interest to this, Sandler's group at Queen Charlotte's Hospital, London, has demonstrated the presence of a small molecular weight monoamine oxidase inhibitor in human urine. Inhibitor output is increased by cold stress in rats (Sandler et al., 1981) and its output is increased by benzodiazepam or alcohol withdrawal. The identity of this agent should be ascertained clinically in an aging population, as it may be important to age related endogenous sensitivity to benzodiazepams, to stress response and alterations in amine function with age.

C.  Volatiles in Expired Air:

Gee and Tappel (1981) have reported on the presence of pentane and ethane in mammalian expired air as an end product reflecting on free radical formation. They feel that changes occur as a function of exercise and that these volatiles are possible predictors of endogenous free radical scavaging activity.

Krotozynski et al. (1977) and Krotozynski and O'Neill (1979) have described methodology developed at the Illinois Institute of Technology measuring expired air volatiles as a quantitative technique for age (Krotozynski, 1979) or diabetic monitoring.

Krotozynski has collected expired air samples and found suggestive differences in the measurement of 115 constituents in comparing aged to younger subjects. This technique measures hydrocarbons, aldehydes and ketones, esters and ethers, nitrogen and sulfur compounds. There were distinct changes in the pattern of respiratory volatiles as a function of age, and the significance of these changes remains to be studied. Unfortunately, Krotozynski's work has not been adequately supported or accepted for publication and should be confirmed and coordinated with that of Robinson's (1976, 1978) studies of amine volatiles in urine, discussed later.

Of particular importance, Krotozynski's group has shown that isoprene/acetone ratios in expired air can identify diabetics and their degree of diabetic control. The work of Krotozynski's group deserves major NIA support and the eventual development of commercial models for routine application to gerontologic intervention and diabetic control studies.

D.  Amino Acid Patterns:

Robinson (1979) discussed the role of deamidation of proteins as a regulator of the aging clock. This group started with studies in Drosophila of different ages, (Robinson et al., 1976), measuring amines, amides and amino acids which correlated with age profiles of the fruit fly. This technique was extended to mice (Robinson et al., 1976a) wherein 174 urine volatile substances were assayed. Sixty of these urine isolates correlated with age and permitted discrimination of young from old mice. This work was then extended to man with identification of 185 urine vapor substances and urinary amines in 235 men 19-94 years of age. Correlates with aging were reported in 60 of these urine isolates (Robinson et al., 1978).

Unfortunately, the above technique utilizing the analysis of urine volatiles has not been developed for routine application to clinical measurement of age or to dietary or clinical intervention in age modulation. These relatively simple observations await validation, computeri- zation and commercial instrument development for clinical exploitation in aging research and disease profiling.

Aspects of this work has been confirmed by the late Vernon Riley and Darrel Spackman (1979) where serum differences in bound to unbound amino acids were found in aging mice. The availability of amino acid analyzer technology makes it convenient for amino acid profiling, particularly as computerization can help us to distinguish differences in patterns between free amino acids and bound to unbound peptides and proteins.

One place where amino acid analysis has shown age related differences is in the composition of human glomerular basement membrane (Smalley, 1980). As renal biopsy is not a simple procedure, Smalley's kidney basement membrane determinations should be applied to skin or collagen biopsies that can be obtained more readily as biomarkers.

E.  Racemization of Proteins:

Masters (1982) has presented data regarding the racemization of structural proteins (conversion of L-enantiomers to the D form) as a biomarker. Unfortunately, these changes are reported for lens and teeth. We need more readily obtained proteins, such as those in skin, serum or red cells for such studies to be of clinical value.

F.  The Peptide/Protein Index:

High resolution two dimensional electrophoretic mapping of human proteins permits us to map the major fractions of 30-50,000 protein gene products (Merril et al., 1979; Anderson, 1979; Anderson et al., 1980). This technology permits the development of a molecular anatomy which can allow us to distinguish between disease states (Anderson, 1979). The improvement in electrophoretic protein/peptide isolation are made possible by advances in gel protein separation and staining of peptides and proteins in the gel (Merril et al., 1979). Combined with a Landsat type of computerized scanning, with this technique we can distinguish between age related or disease caused patterns in serum, urine or tissue specimens.

Under the direction of Norman Anderson of Argonne National Laboratories, The Fund for Integrative Biomedical Research (FIBER) aided in the financing of a protein/peptide task force which proposed the development of an industrial governmental consortium to profile human proteins and peptides to create a library for gene, metabolic, infection and age related disease patterns. This program will allow us to rapidly diagnose metabolic changes and disease states. It will permit us to profile early organ injury, the presence of infectious agents or tissue changes on the basis of peptide/protein leakage into blood and urine long before clinical disease is manifest. A coordinated program for the development of peptide profiling, as a major reference source, will begin in this country, and coordinated work of this kind is underway in Japan and France under governmental financial support and guidance. It is expected that within 7 years, this new technology will allow us to rapidly characterize age changes within 20 minutes of obtaining a urine or blood specimen. Peptide profiling should allow us to rapidly distinguish the presence of infectious organisms on the basis of their protein/peptide products rather than awaiting for growth or immunologic identity.

The application of protein/peptide profiling to diagnosis and aging intervention awaits the development of large scale coordinated studies of clinical disease and study of patterns in subjects of varied age and sex.

G.   Analysis of Individual Altered Proteins:

Scholfield (1980) utilizing circular dichroism spectroscopy has established what could become a rapid screening technique of wide applicability to determine changes in structure with heat denaturation of specific proteins or collagen with age. This was seen in the identification of age related conformational changes in serum albumin for 21 month old C57BL mice as compared to 8 month old mice with heating at 50-80°C. The heat differences are critical and this technique is applicable to study of extractable collagen changes as a function of age (Scholfield, 1980). These observations go back to Sinex (1957) and the hope is that these techniques could be adapted for the limited quantity of protein or collagen available in clinical biopsy specimens.

Gracy's group, at North Texas University (Yuan et al., 1981), have demonstrated that the differences between protein alterations seen in aging animals, as compared to their younger counterparts, may be due to a protein deamidation. Robinson (1979) has discussed this as an age related factor in his assay of urine or tissue isolates in Drosophila and mammals, including man. With age, there is an increase in acidic isoenzymes (Yuan et al., 1981, a,b). These changes occur spontaneously in acidic environments (Westall et al., 1976) and Gracy has suggested that age changes in protein deamidation and isozyme identity may be the result of protease action.

Apart from broad peptide profiling techniques, there
are now simple rapid peptide microsequencing procedures that
can be utilized to quantitate differences in specific proteins
or peptides that correlate with clinical age. This is seen
in the demonstration by Tollefsbol et al. (1982) that there
are increases in triosephosphate isomerase in progeria and
Werner's syndrome fibroblasts.

The above technology provides high sensitivity for
homology structural analysis that allows one to comparatively
identify differences in protein species (Lu et al., 1981).
As discussed previously, while this includes two phase gel
electrophoretic silver staining mapping, once these proteins
are separated and recovered, one can, following peptide
fragmentation, determine peptide alignment based on size,
amino acid composition and amino acid carboxyl terminal
analysis to distinguish qualitative differences in amino
acid sequences. This has been determined for human and
rabbit triosephosphate isomerase.

Tryptic digestion, of the above peptides, has shown
that specific deamidation is a consequence of aging and this
program is distinctly complementary to the protein/peptide
profile discussed by Anderson (1979, 1980).

Another way of studying protein differences with age
would be to examine the action of proteases on accessible
blood proteins, i.e., albumin, ferritin, fibrinogen, etc.,
as a function of age. This has been suggested by the work
of Wiederander et al. (1978) where cytosol protein degredation was more rapid in a variety of proteins obtained from
young versus old animals. There is an excellent review of
protease action on age related proteins in their paper.

The applicability of the above to studies of tissue
culture samples is supported by the work of Houben et al.
(1980) where differences in lysozomal and mitochondrial heat
labile enzymes were found in Werner's syndrome fibroblasts.

H.  Isoenzymes  and Enzymes:

Jacobus and Gershon (1980) reviewed age related changes
in inducible mouse liver enzymes. There are suggestive
differences in the half life of induced ornithine decarboxylase with age. Tyrosine aminotransferase loses specific
activity per unit of enzyme by antigenic determinants with

age, as does heat inactivation change with age for both enzymes.

Kendrick et al. (1979) have shown an age related difference in $Na^+K^+$ ATPase inhibition by oubain in Fisher rat heart, brain and spinal cord. Extending this observation to accessible tissue and formed elements of blood might also provide a good biomarker.

Another area for clinical exploration is based on the observation of Wang and Mays (1978) which showed the loss of specific activity of up to 50% for isozymes of glucose-6-phosphate dehydrogenase (G-6-PD) in livers of aging rats. G-6-PD shows an increase on electrophoresis in hexamer concentration which reacts with 2-deoxyglucose-6-phosphate. This enzyme is easy to obtain from formed blood elements and studies are warranted to see if it could provide a clinical biomarker.

Similar changes in isoenzyme configuration are seen in separation of leukocyte peroxidase isoenzymes by disc electrophoresis. Changes are seen with a rise in isoenzyme D and a decline in isoenzyme B (Struaven et al., 1978), with progressive age.

I.   Methionine Sulfoxide Dismutase:

Reis and Gershon (1978) have described a liver enzyme, methionine sulfoxide dismutase which is altered in the liver of aging animals and which they postulate may have an effect on repairing superoxide dismutase integrity with age. Although this work is controversial, most recently, Brot and Weissbach (1982) of the Hoffmann-La Roche Research Institute, have shown that methionine sulfoxide levels correlate with disease states. Methionine sulfoxide increases in lensatic cataracts (Spector et al., 1982) and the level of methionine sulfoxide is increased in the alpha-1-PI elastase inhibitor in lung which relates to emphysema.

Methionine sulfoxide residues, in accessible blood or tissue protein, should be looked for as a biomarker for aging. Sensitive methods are now available for its quantitation and detection.

J.   Ammonia:

Ammonia levels govern the capacity of cells to survive in tissue culture. $NH_3-N$ levels are toxic to survival of tissue culture lines with increased levels in tissue culture media (McLimans et al., 1981). $NH_3-N$ is more toxic to differentiated cells in contrast to embryonic or tumor lines (McLimans, 1979).

Ammonia levels are increased in the BHE rat (Berdanier and Burrell, 1980; Berdanier and McNamara, 1980) which is a progeric animal that shows deficiencies in mitochondrial function and glucose metabolism with aging.

Ammonia effects a wide range of physiologic events which include: increased glycolysis; effects on respiration through effects on oxidation of NAD; changes in RNA/protein content; chromosomal clumping; inhibition of DNA synthesis; inhibition of urea synthesis as well as effects in orotic acid metabolism. The levels of ammonia should be looked at as a function of age (Visek, 1981).

Ammonia has profound effects on tissue pH and, thus, effects can be indirectly seen on using such NMR techniques which has been discussed in a previous section.

Non-ionic ammonia can be found in the expired air of animals and ammonia is present as a byproduct of gastrointestinal urease bacterial action and it can be present as the end result of infection. Although no significant conclusions were drawn from the study of ammonia levels on controlled protein diets in young versus old sheep (Koenig and Boling, 1980), such studies are warranted in rodents and man.

The arginine-citrulline cycle involved in ammonia metabolism may depend on exogenous arginine needs and protein intake, which varies with age and animal species (Milner and Visek, 1974). It would be appropriate to study the effects of arginine loading on orotate, citrate and urea excretion as a function of age.

K.  Polyamines and Ornithine Decarboxylase:

Campbell (1979) has suggested that the pathology of the uremic syndrome, with its associated high polyamine levels, bears some relationship to the pathogenesis of aging. Polyamines inhibit the immune response and produce neuropathy. Polyamine detoxification can result in free radical formation with tissue injury. Campbell has developed a sensitive radiobiological immunoassay to quantitate the levels of spermine and spermidine in serum which will permit us to follow these growth regulatory amines as factors that may be age related.

Recently, Das and Kanungo (1982) have found that ornithine decarboxylase levels, with the exception of lung, decline in tissue with progressive age. Putrescine levels remain the same while spermidine and spermine concentrations decrease sharply with progressive age. In support of the above, Kremzner and Natta (1981) have found that spermine and spermidine levels decrease with age in red blood cells.

L.  Lipid Metabolism:

Most importantly, Gershfeld (1979) has found that the level of saturated lecithin increases in postcoronary patients. In view of the age related sensitivity to myocardial infarction, differences in saturated to unsaturated phospholipid, in serum, should be looked at as a function of age. It is possible that blood phospholipid differences will reflect on what has been observed in aging neural and lymphocyte membranes. I feel that Gershfeld's observations are of major importance to age related quantitation as they can identify a high risk coronary population.

As mentioned previously, in view of heparin's action in lipid metabolism, it would be of interest to see if heparin administration effects serum lipoproteins in an age related fashion. The work of Pilgeram (1958) showed that there was the suggestion of a chronologic decline in lipoprotein lipase which correlated with coronary disease. Choluverakis (1965) has shown this in rats and these older areas of investigation require renewed interest in view of Gershfeld's data (1979).

M.  Trace Metals:

In a study of major cations assayed by atomic absorption in heart muscle of aging rats, zinc rose uniformly through the aging period with an increase in zinc/copper ratios by 56% between 3 and 24 months of age. Calcium levels rose in heart muscle while magnesium decreased in the atria (Baskin et al., 1979). Studies of these cations should be made of biopsiable tissue.

There is an increase with age in the ratios of copper to ceruloplasmin in human males (Massie et al., 1979). Although not confirmed by Massie et al., Harmon (1965) and Yunice et al. (1974) have reported an increase in serum

copper in older males. Dyundikova et al. (1980) have
shown, in rats, a significant decline in aortic copper
concentration with age which deserves clinical evaluation in
readily obtained tissue. This is important to age related
collagen changes as copper deficiency is associated with
lysyl oxidase decline (Williamson, 1983).

    N.  Selenium:

    Westermarch (1979) has reported that decreasing selenium
tissue levels were age correlated in Finland where selenium
deficiency is endemic. This has been associated with the
presence of neuronal ceroid lipofuscinosis and the high
incidence of myocardinal infarction and multiple sclerosis
in this population. Age related differences correlated with
blood selenium levels and the selenium red blood cell dependent enzyme glutathione peroxidase.

VI.   ASSAY OF WHITE BLOOD CELLS OR CELLS IN TISSUE CULTURE:

    A.  Lysozomal Stability:

    What is needed are lysozomal studies of readily sampled
cells, i.e., leukocytes, or alternatively, utilization of
biopsy capacity to grow cells in culture, (i.e., subcutaneous
fibroblasts) could permit evaluation of age differences in
lysozomal stability.

    In regard to tissue sampling, there are differences in
the temperature response of rat liver lysozomes subjected to
triton or osmotic gradient exposure and these effects, which
are sex dependent, may also involve age related differences
(Ruth and Weglecki, 1979). In rat liver, acid phosphatase
rises during maturation and declines with senescence. There
is also a $\beta$ glucuronidase increase during senescence
(Schmucker and Wang, 1979) which can be stimulated, in the
liver, by previous phenobarbital administration. This is
similar to what has been found in the aging heart where an
increase in aryl sulfatase has also been shown (Trauric and
Papka, 1980). With progressive age, Middleton and Gahan
(1982) have found an acid phosphatase lysozomal rise in
isolated hepatocytes which accompanies an increase in
chromosomal ploidy. There is also an age related sodium
fluoride oubain inhibition of this enzyme. The CRC Handbook
on Aging discusses changed patterns in liver enzyme alteration with age in great detail.

    Glucose aminidase and cathepsin activity is released

from lysozomes and it is of interest that chlorpromazine acts as a lysozomal stabilizer through inhibition of lysozomal lipases (Ruta et al., 1979). Phenothiazine administration to cell populations, *in vitro*, could conceivably act as a modulator that might provide another way to measure lysozomal integrity with age in tissue samples.

B. Membrane Stability and Lipid Metabolism:

The measurable changes in cell membrane fluidity, as a function of phospholipid/cholesterol ratio with aging, have been discussed at this conference by Meir Shinitzky. These membrane changes may also involve the integrity of mitochondrial function as mitochondrial ATP/ADP ratios governing oxidative phosphorylation change in the aging heart (Nohn and Kramer, 1980).

Of interest, changes in cellular lipid composition reflect the age of young and old rats as a function of free radical sensitivity (Hegner, 1980). Using isolated hepatocytes, Stege et al. (1982) have found, in rats given an anti-oxidant free diet, increased lipid peroxidation with age. *In vitro* addition of the proxidant cumene or PADPH to hepatocytes increased lipid peroxidation in older animals (12 and 24 months) as compared to young rats (2 months). Lipid peroxidation products might constitute a measure of age related change using isolated blood or biopsy cells as the target tissue.

Age determines plasma differences in lipid fractionation. This can be seen utilizing ultracentrifugal separation (Malhotra and Kritchevsky, 1978) and the major differences reported for this technique are: high levels of free and esterified cholesterol, triglycerides and free fatty acids in the lipoproteins of rat plasma with age; the increase in sphingomyelin with age; and the predominance of unsaturated fatty acids as compared to saturated, in young versus old animals.

Szymanski et al. (1981) have shown differences in the phospholipid composition of young versus old livers in rats. This work should be translated to assays that could show differences that might exist in accessible blood or tissue culture cells.

VII.  BIOPSY STUDIES OF REPLICATING TISSUE:

A.  Skin and Bone Marrow Culture:  Kinetic, Radiation, DNA, RNA and Enzymatic and Other Changes:

Cristofalo, at this conference, has discussed the role of tissue culture as a technique to study age modulation. Tissue culture studies of aging has been called "cytogerontology" and reviewed in an excellent paper by Hayflick (1981) who has summarized both increases and decreases in age related, *in vitro*, tissue physiologic activity.  Studies of biopsied cells in tissue culture should give us information relative to the age of the donor.  This work has also been discussed in our section on immunologic assay with particular reference to *in vitro* responses of lymphocytes.

There are differences in the sensitivity of *in vitro* cell populations to radiation.  Azarrone et al. (1980), in studies of thoracic skin fibroblasts, distinguished biopsied skin from breast cancer patients as compared to those with benign or non-neoplastic lesions.  Lifespan of cells in tissue culture decrease significantly as a function of donor's age for normal patients in contrast to cancer patients (Azzarone et al., 1980) and the distinction between cells in culture as obtained from cancer prone patient donors has also been described by Kopelovich for Gardner's syndrome (1982).  Distinctions between normal and malignant bowel epithelium, in regard to cancer, have also been made by Allfrey's group (Boffa et al., 1979) with differences reported in the physical state of nucleoprotein.

Our capacity to grow cells in culture and determine growth kinetics, enzyme and DNA repair alterations should make tissue culture techniques useful for quantitation of functional age.  The importance of this is seen in the presentations of Lipetz et al. and Williams, at this conference, where the physical state of DNA and DNA repair capacity ascertained from blood or biopsy samples may relate to chronologic age or to species survival capacity.  This work can be determined on lymphocytes, which are readily obtainable.

Gensler (1981) has looked at this in studies of cells from isolated hamster lung and kidney cells.  Unscheduled DNA repair did not change until the animals had exceeded two thirds of their life span.

Torrelio et al., (1981) have reported that senescent

fibroblast cell lines can be identified by changes in phospho-
ribosylpyrophosphate (P-RIB-PP) levels despite media change
with hypoxanthine. In view of P-RIB-PP role in DNA synthesis
and repair, its measurement in isolated biopsy material
could consititue a potential biomarker for aged cells.

Most recently, Wilson and Jones (1983) have shown that
there is a decline in DNA methylation *in vitro* of human and
rodent fibroblasts on serial passage. These authors discuss
the disparity between the data of Romanov and Vanyushin
(1981) that show similar *in vivo* age related DNA methylation
decline in cattle and salmon versus work that has shown no
such age changes. Immortal cell lines maintain 5-methyl
cytosine residues in their DNA while senescent cells lose
methylated DNA. The changes in DNA methylation may distinguish between embryonic and adult functional differences and
could be critical to the aging process.

In regard to cell sampling techniques, bone marrow cell
culture provides an opportunity (Mets and Verdonk, 1981)
similar to that of skin in estimating age related cloning
efficiency. However, there is less patient acceptability of
bone marrow biopsy in contrast to skin biopsy and it is
obvious that lymphocyte assays from buffy coat may still be
our best source for cell sampling.

Minkowitz et al. (1978) have developed enzyme profiles
from skin biopsies of dermal fibroblasts and found suggestive variation in 5 enzymes which could provide comparative
information with age. This group grows normal fibroblasts
from skin, which can be obtained from 6mm biopsies, and it
is possible to separate fibroblasts from dermal papillary
and reticular layers of skin for separate evaluation.

The observations of Shapiro and Lam (1982) regarding
calcium decline in cultured fibroblasts may provide an age
correlate using skin biopsy fibroblasts.

As discussed previously, Williamson (1983) has found
lysyl oxidase levels to be abnormal in the connective
tissue of diabetic animals. Berenson (1983) discussing the
role of sulfated polysaccharides in atherosclerosis has
found age related differences in blood vessel walls. The
above is pertinent to the age related predicting effect of
hexosamine values in aging rats (Hofecker et al., 1980).

The work of Hochstein's group (Hochstein and Jain,
1981; Walls et al., 1976; Ames et al., 1981) suggest that

the polymerization of red cell membranes is oxidant sensitive
and age related. Aging red cells, under certain circumstances
can be lysed in proxidant environments if free of anti-
oxidants. This work, with red cells, should be extended to
studies of nucleated cells where quantitative information as
to membrane stability to proxidants with age can be obtained
as a function of senescence for all cells.

Okudaira et al. (1980) have found age related increases
in the histamine content of rat mast cells obtained from the
peritoneum. It would be of interest to see if such changes
occur in mast cells that could be obtained in skin biopsy.

In culture, one can measure responses to ultraviolet
induced injury and repair; response to epidermal growth
factor. Changes in monoamine oxidase activity in skin
fibroblasts can be quantitated for donor age. The latter
shows a three to ten fold increase in monoamine oxidase with
senescence of cell lines (Harper and Grove, 1979) and this
is of interest because catecholamines block human keratinocyte mitosis, *in vitro*, (Harper and Flaxman, 1975).

Human diploid fibroblast cells in tissue culture show
increased sensitivity to the ribonucleotide reductase
inhibitor hydroxyurea with increasing passage. This suggests
that ribonucleotide reductase may decline as a function of
aging and changes in this enzyme, necessary for DNA synthesis,
should be looked at as a function of donor age.

Once tissue culture survival patterns are established,
response to peptide growth factors by *in vitro* aging cells
can be ascertained (Van Wyk and Clemmons, 1979). These must
be determined in similar fashion to what is seen for lymphocyte response to lectins and leukokines. Peptide growth
factors have been identified with somatomedins and are under
growth hormone control. The production of somatomedins by
fibroblasts in tissue culture has related to the age of the
donor (Pledger and Clemmons, 1979).

5' nucleotidase could be an important *in vitro* biomarker
as 5' nucleotidase levels increase in human fibroblasts
(Wl38) by 300% from the 20th to 50th population doubling
(Sun et al., 1975). Where population doublings were finite
in tissue culture lines, 5' nucleotidase increased with
accumulated doubling, but where malignant viral transformation occurred, the enzyme levels did not rise (Sun and
Reinach, 1978; Sun et al., 1979). 5' nucleotidase activity
increased up to 20 fold with senescence in tissue culture

(Sun et al., 1979) and was inversely related to proliferation in lymphoid cell lines (Sun et al., 1982).

Most recently, Lee et al. (1983) have identified a peptide in rapidly dividing cells that inhibits 5' nucleotidase and may be a regulator of mitotic activity.

Chen et al. (1980) have found a decrease in fibroblast RNA and protein synthesis in donor cells obtained from subjects 11 years or older. Indeed, Goldstein et al. (1969) and Martin et al. (1970), in similar fashion to what has been found in lymphocytes, have found an inverse correlation between *in vitro* replicative capacity and age of the donor. Martin has discussed this at length in many papers, as has Cristofalo at this conference. Others (Schneider and Mitsui, 1976) have shown this to relate to explant outgrowth, onset of cell culture senescence, life span, doubling time, percent of replicating cells and number of cells at confluence.

Automated systems for monitoring these differences are needed. These were developed by Don Glaser at the University of California program at Berkeley. Glaser's group developed an elaborate computerized TV monitored tissue culture system called "cyclops" and "dumbwaiter" that provided continuous three dimensional monitoring of tissue culture growth patterns from biopsy or single cell clonal lines (Couch et al., 1979). Unfortunately, this program lost federal grant support just as it was ready to be applied. The instrumentation and engineering, at Berkeley, could be reconstituted and made available, if funds could be provided.

The free radical concept of aging has been related to studies of bacterial sensitivity to hyperbaric oxygen. In tissue culture, one should look for amino acid, pantothenate and nicotinamide related deficiencies which may reflect changes in mammalian response similar to that involving key amino acids such as valine which is seen in bacteria (Boehme et al., 1971).

In regard to free radical toxicity, paraquat exposure results in damage similar to that seen for hyperbaric oxygen (Fee et al., 1980). Brown et al. (1981) have shown that niacin can reduce paraquat toxicity in mice. This observation may have significance to clinical biomarkers of aging in that paraquat poisons systems requiring nicotinamide adenine dinucleotide. The de novo synthesis of quinolate depends on NAD and is the same in E-coli, rat and man (Brown et al., 1981). Brown has proposed that one look at

quinolate phosphoribosyltransferase, niacin and pyrimidine
nucleotide coenzymes as key factors in aging which could be
examined in biopsy or tissue culture.

In another area, *in vitro* tissue culture patterns of
glycosaminoglycans appear to change with an associated
progressive decline in population doubling. With senescence,
there is a rise in heparin sulfate synthesis when cell
division ceases (Sluke et al., 1981; Matuoka and Mitsui,
1981). Methodology is needed that could rapidly quantitate
glycosaminoglycan levels in cell culture which might serve
as a rapid measure of population doubling capacity and
senescence. Similar value might be seen in the measure of
fibronectin matrix which appears to decline in late passage
cells (Vogel et al., 1981).

If cutaneously biopsiable tissue explants could be
functionally maintained for *in vitro* assay examination of
biomarker responses, we might also be able to explore subcutaneous adipocyte response to glucagon, catecholamines or
insulin (Masoro, 1982). These responses decline with age as
does the ability of dexamethasone to inhibit glucose oxidation (Roth and Livingston, 1976).

Other measures such as assay of 2 DNA-polymerase, which
declines with cell senescence, may become of value if tissue
culture methods become routine. Similarly, there are changes
in cell morphology, protein content, nucleolar and nuclear
cytoplasmic or RNA ratios with aging.

B.  Histochemical Changes:

Deamer and Pigford (1978) have described lipofuscin
accumulation *in vitro* as a function of aging in tissue
culture. Deamer and Gonzales, (1974) using chick embryonic
fibroblasts subjected to:  serum starvation, $NO_2$ toxicity
and UV light exposure showed increases in the presence of
fluorescent pigment in non-mitotic cells. One wonders if
the donor age of cells could, under *in vitro* standardized
stress conditions, accumulate pigment in a manner that could
act as a biomarker of the biologic age of the donor. Thaw
and Bronk (1983) have developed an *in vitro* lipofuscin model
using glial cells which develop lipofuscin in response to
oxygen concentration and antioxidants.

Cerami (1983) has been concerned with the formation of
age related non-enzymatic pigment as the result of the

Maillard reaction which is responsible for the non-enzymatic browning of food seen on cooking.

As discussed previously, cytogerontologic measurements could utilize NMR technology. In retinal pigment cells, the deposition of age related ceroid-lipofuscin has been measured by electron spin resonance technique (ESR) (Nicolaissen et al., 1981). Thus, ESR technique might also serve as a method to quantitate changes in lipofuscin as a biologic measure of age in biopsy obtained material.

Eddy and Harmon (1977) have demonstrated changes in docasahexanoic acid in the rat brain in relation to free radical injury. Other changes in cytogerontologic measurement that could provide tissue culture as a response for clinical biomarker determination are: distinct increases in the size of nucleoli with aging of cells *in vitro* (Bemiller and Lee, 1978). Preliminary data suggests that it is possible, *in vitro*, (Bemiller et al., 1980) to measure chronologic age by estimates of nucleolar size during replication.

The potential for the above as an *in vitro* method is seen in an age related decline of silver staining of the nucleolar organizing regions in metaphase chromosomes of human lymphocytes and fibroblasts (Buys et al., 1979). Also, in support of this, Lee et al. (1978) have found that there are distinct changes in nuclear size in correlation with donor age. Doubling time and nuclear volume of liver cells increases with age.

One area that is readily accessible for biopsy study in man that shows age related enzyme and morphologic alteration in rats is the proximal small intestinal mucosa. Biopsy of this area for measurement purposes can be obtained as part of fiberscopic endoscopy studies, but is probably not warranted as a routine technique because of the expense and discomfort to the patient (Hohn et al., 1978).

In cells obtained from older animals Bemiller et al., (1981) found, in hepatocytes, an increase in binuclear cells and surface folds. On scanning electron microscopy, cell surface projections are decreased with age. If similar changes are seen in readily sampled fibroblasts or lymphocytes in culture, then it could be used as a biomarker (Engelmann et al., 1981; Porta et al., 1981).

C. Mitochondria:

Marcus et al. (1982) have described an age loss of protein synthesizing capacity from the mitochondrial inner membrane age in rat liver mitochondria. In tissue samples, there is a decrease of 25-40% in hepatic mitochondrial inner membrane protein synthesis in 27 month old rats as compared to 2 month old animals (Abramin et al., 1981).

Measurement of mitochondrial function, *in vitro*, would be critical, as there is an age dependent mitochondrial translation inhibitor which shows ribonuclease activity and which inhibits protein synthesis in rabbit reticulocyte polysomes. It apparently is present in advancing age and may be a regulator of mammalian mitochondrial protein synthesis which may effect the functional capacity of mito- chondria with age.

Berdanier and coworkers (1980) have shown mitochondria to be defective in the BHE progeric rat. Fleming et al. (1982) have reviewed changes in the mitochondrial genome with aging and Piko and Masumoto (1977) have reported an increase in circular dimers of mitochondria obtained from tissues of adult and senescent mice.

In aging Drosophila, Massie et al. (1981) have shown that there is a loss in mitochondrial DNA with age and this has recently been confirmed in mouse tissue (Polson and Webster, 1982). The search for such mitochondrial changes in human cells could be of value as a biomarker. Marcus et al. (1982) suggest that delta aminolevulinic acid synthe- tase activity, which declines with age in rat tissue (Paterniti et al., 1978), could be an indicator of an age related decline in mitochondrial function.

Davies et al. (1982) have shown that mitochondria, with exercise, are damaged although stimulated to increase in numbers possibly through free radical generation. On the basis of biopsy tissue, it would be of interest to determine if there is an age related difference in free radical sensi- tivity to *in vitro* mitochondria.

D. Chromosomal Breakage and DNA Repair:

The reader is referred to Kanungo's monograph (1980) for an excellent review of chromatin structure and function as it is altered in the aging process.

Emerit (1980) has reported on the presence of chromosomal breakage factor, a low molecular weight protein, in the
serum of man and animals that is associated with autoimmune
syndromes. In view of the increase in autoimmunity of
aging, this should be looked for in older patients with
rheumatoid arthritis and related collagen diseases; colitis
and other syndromes thought to be caused by autoimmunity.
Chromosomal breakage factor activity is blocked by superoxide
dismutase.

The importance of DNA damage, as the primary cause of
aging, has been reviewed by Gensler and Bernstein (1981).
DNA repair as an area for aging quantitation has been
discussed by Stephens and Lipetz and Williams at this meeting
where changes in DNA superhelicity and DNA repair mechanisms
and nucleosome structure have been reported to correlate
with chronologic age and species survival. This has also
been described by Turner et al. (1981) in human lymphocytes
where the average molecular weight of DNA declines with
chronologic age.

Age related decrease in $H_1$ histone have been reported
in human fibroblast culture (Mitsui et al., 1980) and this
has also been shown to occur in aging Drosophila (Martinez
and McDaniel, 1981). The assay for histone changes can be
applied to tissue culture samples from biopsies along with
assays of DNA superhelicity, methylation of DNA and DNA
repair as a function of donor age.

Using nuclei from mouse liver cells, following hypotonic
lysis and mechanical shearing, Tas et al. (1980) have shown
that more heavy density chromatin was obtained from old mice
as compared to young. Tas and Walford (1982) have found
quantitative age related differences in nuclease susceptability following the effects of disulfide reducing agents
which provides quantitative differences for evaluating
chromatin structure with age.

Fibroblasts obtained from aged rats, following ethyl
nitrosurea exposure, show age differences that have been
associated with increased fragmentation of DNA in younger
animals (Fort and Cerutti, 1981). This may also reflect
on differences in sister chromatid exchange, which declines
in aging animals (Maciera-Coehlo, 1980; Mann et al., 1981).

The role of DNA changes as relates to nuclear template
function has been reviewed by Whatley and Hill (1980) who
describe physical changes in chromatin as being related to

RNA synthesis capacity and nuclear template activity. In another area, Pvion-Dutilleul, (1982) have shown nuclear electron microscopic changes *in vitro* with aging of human fibroblasts.

The sensitivity of the DNA of aged cells to radiation in tissue culture increases with serial passage. There is an increase in single strand breaks and a progressive sensitivity of DNA to endonuclease digestion with age. This has been reviewed in a paper by Icard et al. (1979) and Paffenholz (1978) and has been discussed by Lipetz et al. and Williams at this meeting.

Preumont et al. (1978) have shown that the binding of tritiated adriamycin to *in vitro* PHA stimulated lymphocytes decline with the age of the donor. It would be of interest to see if this occurs with other cell lines as a quantitative index for aging with or without blastic stimulation.

In relation to chromatin changes with aging, Medvedev et al. (1980) have electrophoretic pattern data showing changes in high molecular weight non-histone proteins derived from mouse liver and spleen chromatin. These changes are not found in hepatoma, and it would be hoped that non-histone chromatin patterns could quantify aging in cell culture populations.

E.  Dysdifferentiative Assays:

Cutler (1982), in an excellent review of mechanisms of aging, proposes that we look for age-dependent derepression of genes. This should be looked for in tissues that are normally not identified with unrelated products, i.e., globin in brain, but which are the result of derepression of structural genes.

In that regard, he has identified age-dependent increases in gene products using radioactive DNA probes of specific genes to detect the presence of a complementary RNA sequences. In RNA preparations from tissues of different aged mice, using this technique, he has identified a two fold increase in globin and endogenous virus genes in the brain of aged animals.

Based on the above, he suggests that we look at structural protein for which human DNA probes are available, i.e., alpha and beta hemoglobin, insulin, growth hormones and adeno and retroviruses to see if their matching RNA sequences are increased with age in given tissue. If this could be developed in tissue culture or buffy coat models, it could serve as an age quantitation measure.

Dysdifferentiation could reflect on methylation of DNA (Jones, 1983) and in tissue culture it would be of interest to see if there is an age related sensitivity to 5 AZA cytidine which blocks methylation of DNA with resultant return to embryonic functional status.

F.    Protein and RNA Synthesis:

There is evidence regarding the decline in protein synthesis and RNA metabolism with aging. In the main, this has been studied in isolated hepatocytes and for this to have meaningful clinical expression as a biomarker, one would have to identify the age related loss or change in character of a particular circulating protein by biochemical or monoclonal assay. The work of Penniall et al. (1980) in rat hepatocytes could be a step in that direction.

Changes in ornithine decarboxylase response and polyamine synthesis govern changes in protein synthesis (Das and Kanungo, 1982) which are age related. Montgomery et al. (1982), in isolated hepatocytes, feel this decline could relate to alterations in cyclic AMP dependent protein kinases.

Several investigators have reported on decreases with age in rat liver RNA synthesis. Isolated nuclei can be stimulated to synthesize RNA to hormone receptor complexes or to dexamethasone administration. Decline in stimulation begins at 6-8 months of age from isolated liver cells (Bolla and Miller, 1980). Of interest, Lugaro et al. (1982) have found a gametic factor linked to DNA which stimulates delta-aminolevulinic acid synthetase inducibility in aged rat liver.

Diamond et al. (1981) have found a decline in RNA polymerase I with aging which accompanies ribosomal RNA synthesis in rat liver nuclei. Apparently, this is associated with a transferable factor from young nuclei which is compatible with the presence of a protein kinase.

Tissue culture methods appropriate to assay of the above, for sperm and nuclear factors on biopsy material, could help us in biomarker determinations. In support of

this, in his excellent reviews on insect versus mammalian
aging, Miquel et al. (1982) has suggested that apart from
similarities of lipofuscin deposition in post mitotic cells
ribosomal alteration also characterizes senescence (Miquel
and Johnson, 1978). The cytoplasm of older mice show fewer
aggregates of endoplasmic reticulum (Johnson and Miquel,
1974), and it would be logical to look for ribosomal changes
in biopsiable tissue to determine age quantitative differences.

VIII.  MISCELLANEOUS AREAS FOR EXPLORATION:

A.  Assays:

Horribin (1981) has described a decrease in delta-6-
desaturase in liver and testes of aging animals. This
enzyme converts cis-linoleic acid to gamma linoleic acid
which is necessary for prostaglandin $E_1$ synthesis. Horribin
claims that diabetes, alcohol, radiation injury and virus
infection can all lower delta-6-desaturase which may be a
controlling factor in aging. If so, this certainly should
be looked at as a biomarker. In regard to this, platelet
aggregability to increases in ADP, epinephrine collagen and
arachidonic acid changes in both men and women with age.

Lipoprotein lipase declines in rats as they age
(Chlouverakis, 1965) and increasing age reduces the ability
of rat adipose tissue to biosynthesize saturated and mono-
saturated fatty acids (Masoro, 1982). It would be of interest,
in view of the role of heparin and mast cells in lipid
metabolism, for heparin action or mast cell morphologic or
functional quantitation to be developed as part of age
related assays of lipid mobilization.

Superoxide dismutase (SOD) levels correlate with life
span and specific metabolic rate in primates (Tolmasoff
et al., 1980). These studies have been done on liver, brain
and heart. Sykes et al. (1980) are developing antibody
assay techniques for circulating SOD, and it will be of
interest to see if SOD values correlate with chronologic age
or clinical disease when these immunoassay techniques become
available.

Bhuyan et al. (1981) have reported that malonaldehyde,
which is a breakdown product of lipid peroxides, was significantly elevated in the aging human lens and highest in
cataract victims. This group also claims that tissue

inhibitors of catalase, superoxide dismutase and glutathione peroxidase are present in cataract lens tissue. As discussed earlier, in regard to methionine sulfoxide, if data for lens assays is valid and similar assays could be developed for red or white blood cells, tissue biopsy or from *in vitro* tissue culture material, these observations could be very significant to age quantitation.

The ratio of reduced to oxidized glutathione blood levels decreases with age and there is suggestive evidence that such changes in mouse kidney are age related (Stohs et al., 1980). With newer techniques, age related changes in glutathione and glutathione peroxidase should be looked for in peripheral blood elements which may reflect selenium action. Such studies should include the assay of methionine sulfoxide and methionine sulfoxide reductase (Brot and Weissbach, 1982).

Bliznakov et al. (1978) have shown that the specific activity of mouse succinate dehydrogenase coenzyme Q reduct-ase was deficient in the age involuted thymus. This is important, as they have reported that treatment with Co Q can protect against infection, maintain immune responsiveness and increase average survival in aging mice. As mentioned earlier, currently, ubiquinone is in clinical use in Japan for the treatment of hypertension, migraine and congestive heart failure.

Plasma 1,25 (OH$_2$) D levels of vitamin D fall in rats with senescence (Gray and Gambert, 1982) and similar results, ascribed to decreased sunlight exposure, are found in man (Baker et al., 1980) which might suggest that it has bio-marker value. Alternative reasons for D deficiency, in the elderly, relate to malabsorption or decrease in thickness of skin with aging, with resultant decrease in vitamin D precursors.

In another area, serum ferritin rises with age, and is higher in males than in females. Changes in ferritin are felt to relate to increases in reticuloendothelial function and increases in iron storage with age (Casale et al., 1981). Ferritin might be a good assay, along with albumin, for measurement of the nutritional state of elderly (Asplund et al., 1981). In contrast, *in vitro* transferrin synthesis does not rise with age although there is an increase in *in vitro* albumin synthesis (Bolla, 1981; Chen et al., 1973; Bolla and Greenblatt, 1982).

B.   Studies Under Special Conditions (i.e., Oxygen Concentration):

   The physiologic response with aging varies in relation to stress and environmental factors. McFarland (1963) has shown evidence of a relationship between aging and oxygen want. By varying the $O_2$ saturation of subjects, in relation to clinical laboratory conditions or altitude, he has reviewed age related differences in regard to visual acuity, dark adaptation, auditory sensitivity, memory and performance status. As is to be expected, decreased oxygen saturation results in greater loss of sensory responses with progressive age. This may provide us with a clinical system to magnify and thus quantify age related sensory differences during middle years when age differences are not apparent at sea level oxygen saturation.

IX.   CONCLUSION:

   This review describes technology in place or readily available for age quantification. In some cases, what is required is validation in human subjects. In addition, for some assays, cost must be controlled for biomarker programs to be applied to gerontologic intervention. Other studies, as described in this chapter, require more extensive preclinical or clinical application before they can be useful.

   Functional bioquantitation of human age is necessary for effective intervention studies that will improve both the quality and length of human survival. Clinical success in aging intervention requires a concerted effort to quantitate chronologic age. At the very least, these studies will revolutionize actuarial data, but it is not enough to passively predict the pattern of our aging or our demise! What is important is that biomarker studies will lead to an understanding of aging as a defined syndrome that will be subject to rational measures that will improve the quality and length of our survival through direct responsible intervention.

ACKNOWLEDGMENTS:

   To Eva Gross and Joyce Fordham for editorial assistance and Marott Sinex and Charles O'Neal for editing.

# X. REFERENCES

Adelman RC, Obenrader MF, Klug TL, Sartin JL (1981). Hormone Interactions During Aging. In Schimke RT (ed): "Biological Mechanisms in Aging Metabolism," Bethesda: NIH 81-2194, p 686.

Adelman RC (1981). Expression of endocrinological change. In Reff ME, Schneider EL (ed): "Biological Markers of Aging," Bethesda: NIH 82-2221, p 27.

Adler WH, Nordin AA (ed)(1981): "Immunological Techniques Applied To Aging Research," Boca Raton: CRC Press.

Adolfsson R, Gottfries GC, Oreland L, Wilberg A, Windblad B (1980). Increased activity of brain and platelet monoamine oxidase in dementia of the Alzheimer type. Life Sci 27:1029.

Agnisola C, Foti L, Genoino IT (1980). Influence of age on 5' nucleotidase in plasma membranes isolated from rat liver. Mech of Ageing & Dev 13:227.

Albert MS, Naeser MA (1982). CT scan measurements as biological markers of aging. In Reff ME, Schneider EC (eds): "Biological Markers Of Aging," Bethesda: NIH 82-2221, p 188.

Ames BN, Cathcart R, Schwiers E, Hochstein P (1981). Uric acid provides an antioxidant defense in humans against oxidant and radical caused aging and cancer: a hypothesis. Proc Natl Acad Sci 78:6858.

Anderson NG, Anderson NL (1981). The human protein index: A proposal for the organization of molecular anatomy. A Report of the Human Protein Task Force. Molecular anatomy program. Argonne Natl Labs, Argonne, IL:60439.

Anderson NG, Anderson NL (1979). Molecular Anatomy: Behring Institute: MITT 63:169.

Anderson F (1976). Old age-normal and abnormal aging. In Practical Management of the Elderly: Blackwell Scientific Publications, Oxford, p 15.

Anderson NL, Edwards JJ, Giometti CS, Willard KE, Tollaksen SL, Nance SL, Hickman BJ, Taylor J, Coulter B, Scandora A, Anderson NG (1980). High resolution two-dimensional electrophoretic mapping of human proteins: Molecular Anatomy Program, Div of Biological and Medical Research, Argonne Natl Lab, Argonne IL: 60439.

Andrew W, Behuke R, Sato T (1964). Changes with advancing age in the cell population of human dermis. Gerontologia 10:1.

Asplund K, Normark M, Pettersson V (1981). Nutritional Assessment of Psychogeriatric Patients. Age & Ageing 10:87.

Avertano B, Noronha C, Antel JP, Roos RP, Arnason GW
(1980). Changes in concanavalin A capping of human
lymphocytes with age. Mech of Ageing & Dev 21:331.
Azzarone B, Diatloff-Zito C, Billard C, Macieira-Coelho
(1980). Effect of low dose irradiation on the division
potential of cells IN VITRO: VII human fibroblasts from
young and adult donors IN VITRO. Mech of Ageing & Dev
16:634.
Baker MR, Peacock M, Nordin BEC (1980). The decline in
vitamin D status with age. Age & Ageing 9:249.
Baskin SI, Uricchio FJ, Kendrick ZV (1979). The effect of
age on the regional distribution of four cations in the rat
heart. AGE 2:64.
Beatty CH, Bocek RM, Herrington PT, Lamy C, Hoskins MK
(1982). Aged rhesus skeletal muscle: histochemistry and
lipofuscin content. AGE 5:1.
Beatty CH, Herrington PT, Hoskin MK, Bocer RM (1981).
Guanylate cyclase activity in the skeletal muscle of adult
(6-11 year) and aged (over 20 year) male rhesus monkeys.
AGE 4:138.
Beck EC, Swanson C, Dustman RE (1980). Long latency components of the visually evoked potential in man: Effects of
aging. Exp. Aging Res 5:523.
Behera HN, Patnaik BK (1981). Recovery from alloxan
diabetes as revealed by collagen characteristics of bone,
skin and tendon of swiss mice. Gerontol 27:32.
Bemiller PM, Lee SC, BeMiller JN, Pappelis AJ (1981).
Determination of the nuclear RNA content of cells from
donors of three different ages during IN VITRO senescence.
Mech of Ageing & Dev 15:349.
Bemiller PM, Lee LH (1978). Nucleolar changes in senescing
Wl-38 cells. Mech of Ageing & Dev 8:417.
Bemiller PM, Lee SC, BeMiller JN, Pappelis AJ (1980).
Relating nuclear RNA content in senescing human fibroblast
cells. AGE 3:108.
Berdanier CD, Burrell BR (1980). Effect of adrenalectomy
on the responses of the BHE rats to either sucrose or
starch diet. J. Nutr 110:298.
Berdanier CD, McNamara S (1980). Aging and mitochondrial
activity in BHE and Wistar strains of rats. Exp. Gerontol
15:519.
Berenson GS (1983). The extracellular matrix of atherosclerosis. In Migaki G, Scarpelli DG (eds). "Comparative
Pathobiology of Major Age-Related Diseases: Current status
and research frontiers," New York: Alan Liss, in press.

Bertolini AM (1969). "Gerontologic Metabolism," Springfield: C.C. Thomas.

Bhuyan KC, Bhuyan DK, Podos SM (1981). Lipid peroxidation in the human as an age linked factor, enhanced in cataract. AGE 4:141.

Billingham RE, Russel PS (1956). Studies on wound healing, with special reference to the phenomenon of contracture in experimental wounds in rabbit skin. Ann Surg 144:961.

Bliznakov EG, Watanabe T, Saji S, Folkers K (1978). Co-enzyme Q deficiency in aged mice. J Med 9:337.

Boehme DE, Vincent K, Brown OR (1970). Oxygen & Toxicity. Nature 262:418.

Boffa LC, Diwan BA, Gruss R, Allfrey VG (1979). Differences in colonic nuclear proteins of two mouse strains with different susceptabilities to 1,2. dimethyl-hydrazine-induced carcinogenesis. Cancer Res 40:1774.

Bolla R (1981). Age associated changes in rat liver synthesis of transferrin. AGE 4:149.

Bolla RI, Miller JK (1980). Effect of hormone receptor complex binding on RNA synthesis in liver nuclei from aged rats. AGE 3:107.

Bolla RI, Greenblatt C (1982). Age related changes in rat liver total protein and transferrin synthesis. AGE 5:72.

Bolton WK, Sturgill BC (1979). Ultrastructural studies of glomerular sclerosis in the aging rat kidney. AGE 2:135.

Bore PJ, Chan L, Gadian DG, Radda GK, Ross BD, Styles P, Taylor DJ (1982). Noninasive pH, measurements of human tissue using 31P-NMR. In Nuccitelli R, Deamer DW (eds): "Intracellular pH Its Measurement, Regulation and Utilization in Cellular Functions". New York, Alan R. Liss, p 527.

Bourliere F (1978). Ecology of human senescence. In Brocklehurst JC (ed), : "Textbook of Geriatric Medicine & Gerontology". New York, Churchill Livingston, p 71.

Bowdler AJ, Dougherty RM, Bowdler NC (1981). Age as a factor affecting erythrocytes osmotic fragility in males. Gerontology 27:224.

Bradfonbrener M, Landowne M, Shock NW (1955). Changes in cardiac output with age. Circulation 12:557.

Bridge TP (1979). Monamine oxidase: age related changes in platelets. "Biomarkers in Aging" Proc. First Fund for Integrative Biomedical Conf. April 11-2, Washington, D.C.

Bridge TP, Jeste DV, Wise CD, Potkin SG, Phelps BH, Wyatt RJ (1981). Platelet monoamine oxidase in an aged general population and elderly schizophrenics. Psychopharmacol Bull 17:103.

Brunk U, Thaw H (1983). Work in Progress
Brot N, Weissbach H (1982). The biochemistry of methionine sulfoxide residues in proteins. Trends in Biochemical Sciences 7:137.
Brown OR, Heitkamp M, Song ES (1981). Niacin reduces paraquat toxicity in rats. Science 212:1510.
Burks TF, Buck SH, Yamamura HI, Deshmukh PP (1981). Levels of substance P, somatostatin and neurotensin in rodent and human CNS in aging. AGE 4:143.
Butterfield DA, Markesberry WR (1981). Spin label studies of human erthyrocyte membranes and aging. AGE 4:151.
Butterfield DA, Ordaz FE, Markesberry WR (1982). Spin label studies of human erythrocyte membranes in aging. J Gerontol 27:535.
Buys CHM, Osinga J, Anders GJPA (1979). Age-dependent variability of ribosomal RNA-gene activity in man as determined from frequencies of silver staining nucleolous organizing regions on metaphase chromosomes of lymphocytes and fibroblasts. Mech of Ageing & Dev 11:55.
Cape R (1979). Physical aspects of aging. In "Aging Its Complex Management", New York: Harper & Row, p 13.
Campbell R (1979). The role of polyamines in aging. "Biomarkers in Aging". Proc First Fund for Integrative Biomedical Conf. April 11-12: Washington, D.C.
Carrel A, Ebeling AH (1923). Antagonistic growth principles of serum and their relation to old age. J Exp Med 38:419.
Casale G, Bonora C, Zurith IE, deNicola P (1981). Serum ferritin and ageing. Age & Ageing 10:119.
Cavalier SJ, Gambetti P (1981). Dystrophic axons and spinal cord demyelination in cystic fibrosis. Neurology 31:714.
Cerami A, Stevens VJ, Monnier VM (1979). Role of nonenzymatic glycosylation in the development of the sequence of diabetes mellitus. Metabolism Suppl 1:431.
Chang MP, Makinodan T, Peterson WJ, Strehler SC (1982). Role of T-cell and adherent cells in age related decline in murine interleukin 2 production. J Immunol 129:2426.
Chen JC, Ove P, Lansing AI (1973). IN VITRO synthesis of microsomal protein and albumin in young and old rats. Biochem Biophys Acta 312:598.
Choluverakis C (1965). Lipoprotein lipase activity in adipose, muscle and aortic tissue from rats of different age and in human subcutaneous adipose tissue. Proc Soc Exper Biol Med 119:775.

Chon SH, Vartsky D, Yasumura S, Aloia JF, Vaswani A, Ellis KJ (1980). Effects of aging on skeletal mass, body cell mass and protein content. AGE 3:118.
Choy JW, Goidl EA (1981). Regulation of the immune response of aged mice by auto-anti-idiotypic antibody. AGE 4:147.
Cinotti AC, Stephens G, Stephens SE, White HJ, Louis H (1980). Dark adaptation photopic phase in the aged. AGE 3:111.
Coburn AF, Grey RM, Rivera SM (1971). Observations on the relation of heart rate, life span, weight and mineralization in the digoxin-treated A/J mouse. Johns Hopkins Med J 128:169.
Cohn SE (1981)(ed). "Non-Invasive Measurement of Bone Mass". Boca Raton, CRC Press.
Cole GM, Segall PE, Timiras PS (1982). Hormones during aging. In Vernadakis A, Timiras PS (eds). "Hormones in Development and Aging." New York, Spectrum Publications: p. 477.
Coleman DL, Leiter EH, Schwizer RW (1982). Therapeutic effects of dehydroepiandrosterone (DHEA) in diabetic mice. Diabetes 31:830.
Collins KJ, Exton-Smith AN, James MH, Oliver DJ (1980). Functional changes in autonomic nervous responses with ageing. Age & Ageing 9:17.
Comfort A (1969). Test battery to measure ageing rate in man. Lancet I:1411.
Comfort A (1979). "The Biology of Senesence". New York, Elsevier.
Corso JF (1982). Auditory clinical markers of Aging. In Reff ME, Schneider EL (eds). "Biological Markers of Aging," Bethesda: NIH Publ #82-2221, April, 1982.
Couch JL, Konrao MW, Glaser DA (1979). Analysis of images of colonies of tissue culture cells and microorganisms in "Pattern Reckognition and Image Processing". New York: Institute of Electrical & Electronic Engineers, p 473.
Cowan, MJ, Fujiwara P, Wara DW, Ammann AJ (1981). Effect of thymosin on cellular immunity of old age. Mech of Ageing & Dev 15:29.
Craik FIM, Trehub S (1982) (eds). "Cognitive Processes". New York, Plenum.
Crilly RG, Nordin BEC (1981). Steroid Hormones and Ageing. Brit Soc For Res. on Ageing. Symposium on Hormones and Ageing: Age & Ageing 10:202.
Cugini P, Scavo P, Halberg F, Schramm A, Pusch HJ, Franke H (1982). Methodologically critical interactions of

circadian rhythm, sex and aging characterize serum aldosterone and the female adrenopause. J Gerontol 37:403.

Cullen MR, Tonna EA (1979). Distribution and density of mast cells in the oral tissues of aging BNL mice. AGE 2:133.

Cunningham DA, Rechnitzer PA, Pearce ME, Donner AP (1982). Determinants of self-selected walking pace across ages 19 to 66. J Gerontol 37:560.

Cuny G, Royer RJ, Mur JM, Serot JM, Faure G, Netter P, Maillard A, Penin F (1979). Pharmacokinetics of salicylate in elderly. Gerontol 25:49.

Cutler RG (1982). The dysdifferentiative hypothesis of mammalian aging and longevity. In Giacobini E, Giacobini G, Filogamo G, Vernadakis A (eds). "The Aging Brain, Cellular and Molecular Mechanisms of Aging in the Nervous System," New York: Raven Press, p 1.

Dave JR, Knazek RA (1983). Changes in the prolactin binding capacity of mouse hepatic membranes with development and aging. In Press.

Davidson MB (1982). The effect of aging on carbohydrate metabolism. A comprehensive review and a practical approach to the clinical problem. In Korenman SG (ed). "Endocrine Aspects of Aging," New York: Elsevier Biomedical, p 231.

Davies KJA, Quintanilha AT, Brooks GA, Packer L (1982). Free radicals and tissue damage produced by exercise. Biochem Biophys Res Commun 107:1198.

Daughaday WH (1981). Growth hormone and the somatomedins. In Daughaday WH (ed). "Endocrine Control of Growth," New York: Elsevier Biomedical, p 15.

Das R, Kanungo MS (1982). Activity and modulation of ornithine decarboxylase and concentrations of polyamines in various tissues of rats as a function of age. Exp Gerontol 17:95.

Deamer DW, Rigford J (1978). Accumulation of fluorescent damage in aging and stressed cells in culture. AGE 1:164.

Deamer DW, Gonzales J, (1974). Autofluorescent structures in cultures WI-38 cells. Arch Biochem Biophys 165:421.

Debes P, Samorajski T (1980). Effects of voluntary wheel exercise on longevity, body weight, liver function and metabolic rate of old male mice. AGE 3:118.

DeFronzo RA (1982). Glucose intolerance and aging. In Reff ME, Schneider EL (eds). "Biological Markers of Aging," Bethesda: NIH Pub #82-2221, p 98.

Dehn MM, Bruce RA (1972). Longitudinal variations in maximal oxygen intake with age and activity. J Appl Physiol 33:805.

deLeon MJ, Ferris SH, George AE, Blau F, Reisberg B (1979). CT correlates of cognitive deficit in senile dementia. AGE 2:130.

deLeon MJ, Ferris SH, George AE, Rosenbloom B, Christman DR, Fowler J, Gentes C, Emmerich M, Wolf A (1981). Positron emission tomography and computed tomography evaluations in regional brain metabolism in senile dementia. AGE 4:146.

deLeon MJ, Ferris SH, George AE, Rosenbloom S, Reisberg B, Christman DR, Fowler J, Gentes C, Emmerich M, Wolf A (1980). Reginal brain metabolism in aging and senile dementia determined by position emission tomography. AGE 3:113.

Delespesse G, Gausset PhD, Sarfati M (1980). Circulating immune complexes in old people and in diabetes. Correlation with autoantibodies. Clin Exp Immunol 40:96.

DeLuca HF, Frost HM, Jee WSS, Johnston CC, Parfitt AM (1981) (eds). "Osteoporosis." Baltimore University, Park Press.

Dement JWC (1982). Physiological markers of aging. Human sleep pattern changes. In Reff ME, Schneider EL (eds). "Biological Markers of Aging," Bethesda: NIH Publ #82-2221, p 177.

Derman U (1972). Changes in the mitral valve echogram with aging and the influence of atherosclerotic risk factors. Atherosclerosis 15:349.

Detraglia M, Cook FG, Stasiw DM, Cerny CC (1974). Erythro-cyte fragility in aging. Biochem Biophys Acta 345:213.

DeWeck A, Kristensen F (1982). Personal communications.

Dick JE, Wright JA (1982). Involvement of ribonucleotide reductase activity in the senescence of normal human diploid fibroblasts. Mech of Ageing & Dev 20:103.

Dietz AA, Marcum VS (eds) (1979). "Aging - Its Chemistry", Washington, D.C.: Am Assoc for Clin Chemistry.

Dill DB, Yousef MK, Vitez TS, Goldman A, Patzer R (1982). Metabolic observations on caucasian men and women aged 17 to 88 years. J Gerontol 37:565.

Dilman VM (1978). Ageing, metabolic immunodepression and carcinogenesis. Mech of Ageing & Dev 8:153.

Dilman VM (1976). In Everitt AF, Burgess JA (eds). "Hypothalamus, Pituitary and Aging," Springfield: C.C. Thomas, p 634.

Dimond PF, Elridi SS, Todhunter JA (1981). Age related control of RNA polymerase I activity by phosphorylatin. AGE 4:148.

Djursing H, Hagen C, Moller J, Christiansen C (1981). Short and long term fluctutions in plasma prolactin concentration in normal subjects. ACTA Endocrinologica 97:1.

DuNouy PL (1916). Cicatrization of wounds. III. The relation between the age of the patient, the area of the wound and the index of cicatrization. J Exp Med 24:461.

Dyundikova VA, Silvon ZK, Dubina TL (1981). Biological age and its estimation I: Studies of some physiological parameters in albino rats and their validity as biological age tests. Exp Gerontol 16:13.

Eddy DE, Harmon D (1977). Free radical theory of aging: Effect of age, sex and dietary precursors on rat brain docosahexanoic acid. J Am Geriatri Soc 25:220.

Eisenberg E, Walker RF (1982). Physiologicalaspects of the menopause. In Vernadakis A, Timiras PS (eds). "Hormones in Development and Aging." New York, Spectrum Publications. p. 587.

Elahi D, Muller D, Tzankoff SP, Andres R, Tobin JD (1982). Effect of age and obesity on fasting levels of glucose, insulin, glucagon and growth hormone in man. J Gerontology 37:385.

Engelmann GL, Richardson A, Katz A, Ficrer JA (1981). Age related changes in isolated rat hepatocytes. Comparison of size, morphology, binucleation and protein content. Mech of Ageing & Dev 16:385.

Emerit I, Michelson AM (1979). Chromosome instability and murine autoimmune disease. Anticlastogenic effect of superoxide dismutase "Free radicals in medicine and biology". ACTA Physiol Scandinav Suppl 492:59.

Epstein S, Wiske PS, Bell NH, Edmondson J, Johnston JC (1979). Serum immunoreactive parathyroid hormone increases with age. In Korenman SG (ed). "Endocrine Aspects of Aging". Proc of Joint NIA, Endocrin Soc and Veterans Adm Conf, Oct 18–20.

Ethier MF, Hickler RB, Saunders RH (1981). Cholesterol concentration in subpopulations of senescent human fibroblasts. AGE 4:134.

Evans MA, Triggs EJ, Cheung M, Broe GA, Creasey H (1981). Gastric emptying rate in the elderly: implications for drug therapy. J Am Geriat Soc 29:201.

Everitt AV, Porter BD, Steele M (1981). Dietary, caging and temperature factors in the ageing of collagen fibres in rat tail tendon. Gerontol 37:37.

Everitt AV (1981). Pituitary function and aging. In Danon D, Shock NW, Marois M (eds). "Aging: A Challenge to Science and Society," IV Biology: Oxford University Press, p 249.

Everitt AV (1976). The Nature and measurement of aging. In Everitt AV, Burgess JA (eds). "Hypothlamus Pituitary and Aging,": Springfield: C.C. Thomas, p 5.

Fabricant JD, Parkening TA (1981). Increased aberrations in spermhead morphology with age in C57Bl/6 mice: AGE 4:150.

Fabris N, Muzzioli M, Mocchegiani E (1982). Recovery of age dependent immunological deterioration in Balb/C mice by short term treatment with L-thyroxine. Mech of Ageing & Dev 18:237.

Faucheux BA, Bourliere F, Baulon , Dupuis C (1981). The effects of psychosocial stress on urinary excretion of adrenaline and noradrenaline in 51 to 55 and 71 to 74 year old men. Gerontol 27:313.

Fee JA, Lees AC, Bloch PL, Gilliland PL, Brown OR (1981). Oxygen stasis of bacterial growth. Analogy between the stasis of E. coli by hyperbaric oxygen and by aerobic paraquat. Biochem Internat 1:304.

Fernandez LA, MacSween JH (1980). Decreased autologous mixed lymphocyte reaction with aging. Mech of Ageing & Dev 12:245.

Fikay ME, Aboul-Wafa MH (1967). Intestinal Absorption in the old. Gerontol Clin 7:171.

Finch CE, Potter PE, Kenney AD (ed) (1978). "Parkinson's Disease II": Adv in Exp. Med. Biol 113: New York: Plenum Press.

Finch CE, Hayflick L (eds) (1977). "Handbook of the Biology of Aging", New York: Von Nostrand Reinhold.

Fitzergerald PA, Bennet M (1983). Aging of natural and acquired immunity of Mice I: Decreased natural killer cell function and hybrid resistance. Cancer Investigation 1:15.

Fleming JE, Miquel J, Cottrell SF, Yengoyan LS, Economos AC (1982). Is cell aging caused by respiration–dependent injury to the mitochondrial genome? Gerontology 28:44.

Florini JR (1981). Growth hormone & the somtomedins. In Schimke RT (ed). "Biological Mechanisms in Aging", Bethesda: NIH Pub 81-2194, p 650.

Florini JR, Harned JA, Richman RA, Weiss JP (1981). Effect of rat age on serum levels in growth hormone and somatomedins. Mech of Ageing & Dev 15:165.

Florini JR, Adelman RC, Roth GS (1981). "Handbook of Biochemistry of Aging", Boca Raton: CRC Press.

Folkers K, Zewoski J, Richardson PC, Ellis J, Shizukuishi S, Baker L (1981). Bioenergetics in clinical medicine XVI. Reduction of hypertension in patients by therapy with coenzyme Q10. Res Comm in Chem Pathol & Pharmac 31:129.

Folkers K, Yamamura Y (eds) (1981). "Biomedical & Clinical Aspects of Coenzyme Q." New York, Elselvier.

Fort FL, Cerutti PA (1981). Altered DNA repair in fibroblasts from aged rats. Gerontology 27:306.

Fowler CJ, Wimberg A, Oreland L, Wiberg A, Winblad B (1980). The effect of age on the activity and molecular properties of human brain monoamine oxidase. J Neural Transmis 49:1

Friedman D, Globerson A (1978). Immune reactivity during aging I. T-helper dependent and independent antibody responses to different antigens IN VIVO and IN VITRO. Mech of Ageing & Dev 7:289.

Frolkis VV, Frolkis R, Pugach BU, Gunina LM, Rushkevich YE (1980). Kallikrein-kinin system and adenosine metabolism system of blood and heart and their changes at hypothalamic-hypophyserl stimulation in rabbits of different age. Gerontol 26:254.

Frolkis V (1979). Physical Aspects of Aging. In Von Hahn HP (ed): "Practical Geriatrics", Karger Basel, p 1.

Fudenberg HH, Goust JM, Vesole DH, Salinas CF (1979). Active and suppressor T cells. Diminution in a patient with dyskeratosis congenita and in first degree relatives. Gerontol 25:231.

Gadian DG, Radda GK, Dawson MJ, Wilkie DR (1982). pH measurements of cardiac and skeletal muscle using 31P-NMR. In Nuccitelli R, Deamer DW (eds). "Intracellular pH Its Measurement, Regulation and Utilization in Cellular Functions", New York: Alan R. Liss, p 61.

Galbo H, Holst JJ, Christensen NJ (1975). Glucagon and Plasma catecholamine response to exercise in man. J Appl Physiol 38:70

Gardin JM, Henry WL, Savage DD, Epstein SE (1977). Echocardiographic evaluation of an older population without clinically apparent heart disease. Am J Cardiol 39:277.

Gee DL, Tappel AL (1981). The effect of exhaustive exercise on expired pentane as a measure of IN VIVO lipid peroxidation in the rat. Life Sciences 28:2425.

George AE, deLeon MJ, Rosenbloom S, Ferris SH, Gentes C, Emmerich M, Kricheff II (1981). CT ventricular volume and its relationship to cognitive impairment in dementia. AGE 4:146.
Gensler HL, Bernstein H (1981). DNA damage as the primary cause of aging. Quart Rev Biol 56:279.
Gensler HL (1981). The effect of hamster age on UV-induced unscheduled DNA synthesis of freshly isolated lung and kidney cells. Exp Gerontol 16:59.
Gentile PS, Trentalange MJ, Coleman M (19810. The relationship of hair zinc concentrations to height, weight, age, and sex in the normal population. Pediatr Res 15:123.
Gershfeld NL (1979) Selective Phospholipid absorption and atherosclerosis. Science 204:506.
Gershon D, Reznick , Reiss U (1979). Characterization and possible effects of age associated alterations. In Cherkin A (ed). "Enzymes and Proteins in Physiology and Cell Biology. New York: Raven Press, p 21.
Gerson PF (1982). The relation between intracellular pH and DNA synthesis rate in proliferative lymphocytes. In Nuccitelli R, Deamer DW (eds). "Intracellular pH Its Measurement, Regulation and Utilization in Cellular Functions", New York: Alan R. Liss, p 375.
Gerstenblith G (1982). Cardiovascular aging. In Reff ME, Schneider EL (eds): "Biological Markers of Aging," Bethesda: NIH Pub #82-2221, p 138.
Gerstenblith G, Fredrikson J, Yin CP, Fortuin NJ, Lakatta EG, Weisfeldt ML (1977). Echocardiographic assessment of a normal adult aging population. Circulation 50:273.
Ghanadian R, Pauh CM (1981). Changes of androgens with age in normal men. Ageing Symposium on Hormones and Ageing. Age & Ageing 10:204.
Gillies RJ, Alger JR, denHollander JA, Shulman RG (1982). In Nuccitelli R, Deamer DW (eds). "Intracellular pH measured by NMR: Methods and results: Proc. Kroc Foundation Conf on Intracellular pH: Its measurement, regulation, and utilization in cellular functions," New York: Alan R. Liss, p 79.
Gillis S. Kozak R, Durante M, Weksler ME (1980). Immunological studies of aging: decreased production of and response to T-cell growth factor by lymphocytes from aged human. J Clin Invest 67:937.
Goidl EA, Thorbecke GJ, Weksler ME, Siskind GW (1980). Production of auto-anti-idiotypic antibody during the normal immune-response. Changes in the auto-anti-idiotypic

antibody response and the idiotype repertoire associated with aging. Proc Natl Acad Sci, USA 77:6788.
Goldman R (1979). Decline in organ function with aging. In Rossman I (ed). "Clinical Geriatrics," Philadelphia: J.B. Lippincott, p 23.
Goldstein S (1969). Life span of cultured cells in progeria. Lancet II:424.
Goldstein S, Littlefield JW, Soeldner JS (1969). Diabetes mellitus and aging. Dimninished plating efficiency of cultured human fibroblasts. Proc Natl Acad Sci, USA 64:155.
Gozes Y, Umiel T, Trainin (1982). Selective decline in differentiating capacity of immunohemopoetic stem cells with aging. Mech of Ageing & Dev 18:251.
Gracy RW, Yuan PM (1980). Molecular basis of accumulation of abnormal triose-phosphate isomerase during aging. AGE 3:110 ABS 19.
Gray RW, Gambert SR (1982). Effect of age on plasma 1,25 (OH)2 Vitamin D in the rat. AGE 5:54.
Greenblatt RB (1978). Geriatric Endocrinology. Aging V:5: Raven Press
Greenhouse AH, Vitu HSM, Yates CS, Golden C, MacInnes W (1981). Do changes occur in the neurological examination of normal elderly persons. AGE 4:146.
Gregerman RI, Gaffney GW, Shock NW, Rowder SE (1962). Thyroxine turnover in euthyroid man with special reference to changes with age. J Clin Invest 41:2065.
Grove GI (1979). Age changes in the cytodynamics of the human epidermis. AGE 2:133.
Gudelsky GA, Nansel DD, Porter JC (1981). Dopaminergic control of prolactin secretion in the aging male rat. Brain Res 204:446.
Gundberg CM, Gallop PM (1981). Osteoporosis and vitamin K dependent bone proteins. AGE 4:140.
Halberg F (1982). Biological rhythms, hormones and aging. In Vernadakis A, Timiras PS (eds). "Hormones in Development and Aging." New York, Spectrum Publications, p 451.
Hall DA, Blackett AD, Zajac AR, Switala S, Airey CM (19810. Changes in skinfold thickness with increasing age. Age & Ageing 10:19.
Halter JB, Pfeifer MA (1982). Aging and autonomic nervous system function in man. In Reff ME, Schneider EL (ed). "Biological Markers of Aging," Bethesda: NIH #82-2221, p 168.

Hardin JC, Patterson JL Jr (1979). Monitoring the state of
the human air-ways by analysis of respiratory sound. ACTA
Astronautica 6:1137.
Harkins SW (1980). Brainstem evoked potentials in aging
and dementia. In Delman RC, Roberts J, Baker GT (eds).
"Neural Regulatory Mechanisms During Aging," New York: Alan
R. Liss, p. 211.
Harkins SW, Lenhardt ML (1980). Age effects on farfield
evoked potentials. In Poon LW (ed). "Contemporary Issue &
New Directions in the Psychology of Aging," Washington,
D.C.: American Psychological Association Press, p 101.
Harkins SW (1981). Effects of age and interstimulus
interval on the brainstem auditory evoked potential.
Intern J Neuroscience 15:107.
Harmon D (1965). The free radical theory of aging. Effect
of age on serum copper level. J Gerontol 20:151.
Harper RA, Grove G (1979). Human skin fibroblsts derived
from papillary and reticular dermis. Differences in growth
potential IN VITRO. Science 204:526.
Harper RA, Flaxman B (1975). Effect of pharmacological
agents on human keratinocyte mitosis IN VITRO. II
Inhibition by catecholamines. J Cell Physiol 86:293.
Harrison DE (1982). Experience with developing assays on
physiological age. In Reff ME, Schneider EL (eds).
"Biological Markers of Aging," Bethesda: NIH #82-2221, p 2.
Hartford JT, Hsu C, Smorajski T (1979). Choline and
cholinergic enzymes in the blood across the life span. AGE
2:131.
Haus E, Kalatua DJ, Halberg F, Halberg E, Cornelissen G,
Sackett LL, Berg HG, Kawsaki T, Veno M, Vezono K, Matsuoka
M, Omae T (1980). Chronobiological studies of plasma pro-
lactin in women in Kyushu, Japan and Minnesota USA . J
Clin Endocrin & Metabol 51:632.
Hayflick L (1965). The limited IN VITRO lifetime of human
diploid cell strains. Exp Cell Res 37:614.
Hayflick L (1980). Recent advances in the cell biology of
aging. Mech of Ageing & Dev 14:59.
Heaney RP (1982). Age related bone loss. In Reff ME,
Schneider EL (eds). "Biological Markers of Aging,"
Bethesda: NIH #82-2221, p 161.
Hefton JM, Darlington GJ, Casazza BA, Weksler ME (1980).
Immunologic studies of aging V impaired proliferation of
PHA responsive human lymphocytes in culture. J Immunol
125:1007.

Hegner D (1980). Age dependence of molecular and functional changes in biological membrane properties. Mech of Ageing & Dev 14:101.
Heinegard D, Hascall VC (1974). Characterization of chondroitin sulfate isolated from trypsin-chymotrypsin/- digests of cartilage proteoglycans. Arch Biochem Biophys 165:427.
Hendricks S, Black CA (1981). Plasma prolactin and progesterone responses to mating are altered in aged rats. J Endocr 90:179.
Hensley JC, McWilliams PC, Oakley GE (1964). Physiological capacitance: A study in Physiological Age Determination. J. Gerontol 19:317.
Hersh E, Reuben J, Rios A, Mansell P, Newell G, McClure J, Goldstein A (1983). Elevated serum thymosin levels associated with evidence of immune dysregulation in male homosexuals with a history of infectious diseases or kaposi's sarcoma. N Eng J Med 308:45.
Hershko C, Levy S, Matzner Y, Grossowicz N, Izak G (1979). Prevalance and causes of anemia in the elderly in Kiryat Shemoneh, Israel. Gerontol 25:42.
Heron A, Chown S (1967). "Age & Function". Little Brown & Company, Boston.
Hochstein P, Jain SK (1981). Association of lipid peroxidation and polymerization of membrane proteins with erythrocyte aging. Fed Proc 40:183.
Hochstein P, Jain SK, Rice-Evans C (1981). The physiological significance of oxidative pertubations in erythrocyte membrane lipids and proteins. Progr Clin Biol Res 55:449.
Hochstein P (1979). Oxidant mechanics in accelerated erythrocyte aging. In "Biomarkers in Aging" Proc Fund for Integrative Biomedical Res Conf, Apr 11-12, Wash, D.C.
Hofecker G, Skalicky M, Kment A, Nieder Muller H (1980). Models of the biological age of the rat I A factor model of age parameters. Mech of Ageing & Dev 14:345.
Hohn P, Gabbert H, Wagner R (1978). Differentiation and aging of the rat intestinal mucosa II Morphological, enzyme histochemical and disc electrophoretic aspects of the aging of the small intestinal mucosa. Mech of Aging & Dev 7:217.
Holick MF, MacLaughlin J (1981). Aging decreases the ability of human skin to produce Vitamin D3. AGE 4:140.
Hollingsworth JW, Gailotte R (1981). B. Lymphocyte maturation in cultures from blood of elderly men. A comparison of plaque forming cells, cells containing

intracytoplasmic immunogloblin and cell proliferation. Mech of Ageing & Dev 15:9.

Hollingsworth MA, Barrowclough J, Evans DL (1981). Age related increases in mitogenic responses and natural immunity to a syngeneic fibrosarcom in rats. Mech of Aging & Dev 17:95.

Hooper ACB (1981). Length, diameter and number of ageing skeletal muscle fibers. Gerontol 27:121.

Horrobin DF (1981). Loss of delta-6-desaturase (D6D) activity as a key factor in aging. AGE 4:139.

Howes EL, Harvey SC (1932). The age factor in the velocity of the growth of fibroblasts in the healing wound. J Exper Med 55:577.

Houben A, Houbion A, Remacle J (1980). Lysozomal and mitochondrial heat labile enzymes in Werner's syndrome fibroblasts. Exp Gerontol 15:629.

Howell TH (1981). Skin treatment of bedsore areas in the aged. Exp Gerontol 16:137.

Howell TH (1982). Skin temperature gradient in the lower limbs of old women. Exp Gerontol 17:65.

Huemer RP, Walters JD (1978). Age related changes in hormone excretion. AGE 1:26.

Hughes G (1968). Changes in taste sensitivity with advancing age. Gerontol Clin 11:224

Icard C, Beaupain R, Diatloff C, Maciero-Coehlo (1979). Effect of low dose rate irradiation on the division potential of cells IN VITRO VI changes in DNA and in radiosensitivity during aging of human fibroblasts. Mech of Ageing & Dev 11:269.

Imms FJ, Edholm OG (1981). Studies of gait and mobility in the elderly. Age & Ageing 10:147.

Inkeles B, Innes JB, Kuntz MM, Kadish S, Weksler ME (19177). Immunologic studies of aging II. Cytokinetic basis for the impaired response of lymphocytes from aged humans to plant lectins. J Exp Med 145:1176.

Insogna KL, Lewis AM, Lipinski Ba, Bryant C, Baron DT (1981). Effect of age on serum immunoreactive parathyroid hormone and its biological effects. J Clin Endocrinol Metab 53:1072.

Jacobus S, Geashon D (1980). Age related changes in inducible mouse liver enzymes: ornithine decarboxylase and tyrosine amino transferase. Mech of Ageing and Dev 12:311.

Jacobs R (1981). Physical changes in the aged: In eldercare. In O'Hara Devereaux M, Andrus LH, Scott CD, Gray MI (eds). "A Practical Guide to Clinical Geriatrics," New York: Grune & Stratton.

Jacobus WE, Pores IH, Lucas SK, Kallman CH, Weisfeldt ML, Flaherty JT (1982). The role of intracellular pH in the control of normal and ischemic myocardial contractivity: A31P nuclear magnetic resonance and mass spectrometry study. In Nuccitelli R, Deamer DW (eds). "Intracellular pH Its Measurement, Regulation and Utilization in Cellular Function", New York: Alan R. Liss, p 537.

Jamil NAK, Millard RE (1981). Studies of T,B, and "Null" Blood lymphocytes in normal persons of different age groups. Gerontol 27:79.

Johnson JE Jr (1979). Electron microscopic comparison of the effects of hypophysectomy on changes in the rat kidney and pineal gland. AGE 2:135.

Johnson JJE, Cutler RG (1980). Effects of hypophysectomy on age related changes in rat kidney glomerulus: Observations by scanning and transmission electron microscopy. Mech of Ageing & Dev 13:63.

Jones PA (1983). The role of DNA methylation in cell differentiation. Cancer Res. In Press

Kaiko RF (1979). Age and pain relief in postoperative cancer patients. AGE 2:132.

Kannel W, Hubert H (1982). In Reff ME, Schneider EL (eds). "Biological Markers of Aging," Bethesda: NIH Pub #82-2221, p 145.

Kanungo MS (1980). "Biochemistry of Aging," New York. Academic Press.

Kay MMB, Makinodian T (1981). "Handbook of Immunology in Aging," Boca Raton. CRC Press.

Kaye MD (1981) Gastrointestinal Physiology. In Masoro EJ (ed). "Handbook of Physiology in Aging," Boca Raton. CRC Press.

Kendrick ZV, Ray JE, Urrichio FJ, Baskin SI (1979). The effect of age on the activity and ouabain inhibition of Na+, K+ ATPase purified from the brain, spinal cord and heart of the Fischer 344 rat. AGE 2:128.

Kenney RA (1982). "Physiology of Aging: A Synopsis," Chicago: Year Book Medical Pubishers, Inc.

Kinter LB, Dunn MJ, Beck TR, Beevwkes R, Hassid A (1981). The interactions of prostaglandins and vasopressin in the kidney. Ann Ny Acad Sci 372:163.

Klevay LM (1970). Hair as a biopsy material I. Assessment of zinc nutriture. Am J Clin Nutr 23:284.

Klug TL, Adelman RC (1979). Altered hypothalamic-pituitary regulation of thyrotrophin in male rats during aging. Endocrinology 104:1136.

Klug TL, Freeman C, Karoly K, Adelman RC (1979). Altered regulation of pancreatic glucagon in male rats during aging. Biochem & Biophys Res Commun 89:907.

Koenig JM, Boling JA (1980). Effect of age and dietary protein level on ovine nitrogen metabolism I evidence for comparable metabolizable nitrogen availability. Exp Gerontol 15:177.

Kohner EM (1977). Diabetic retinopathy. Clin Endocrinol Metab 6:345.

Konen TG, Smith GS, Walford RL (1973). Decline in the mixed lymphocyte reactivity of spleen cells from aged mice of a long lived strain. J Immunol 110:1216.

Kopelovich L (1982). Hereditary adenomatosis of the colon and rectum: Relevance to cancer promotion and cancer control in humans. Cancer Genetics and Cytogenetics 5:333.

Korenman SG (ed) (1982). "Endocrine Aspects of Aging". New York: Elsevier.

Kremzner LT, Naita CL (1981). Red Blood Cell (RBC). Polyamines and Aging 4:151.

Krotoszynski BK (1979) Investigation into correlation between pulmonary effluents and disease processes. IIT project: C118-2 (final report).

Krotoszynski BK, Gabrid G, O'Neill HJ, Claudio MPA (1977). Characterization of human expired air: A promising investigation and diagnostic technique. J Chromatog Sc 15:239.

Krotoszynski BK (1979). Human expired air: A Promising source of biochemical markers for aging (submitted to: J Gerontol).

Krotoszynski BK, O'Neill HJ (1979). Techniques for collecting, processing and analysis of human expired air. (Submitted to: J Gerontol).

Kubicek WG, Kottke FJ, Ramos MU, Patterson RP, Witsoe DA, Labree JW, Remole W, Laman TE, Schoening H, Grameus JT (1974). Non-invasive blood flow monitoring, the Minnesota impedance cardiography-theory and applications. Biomedical Engineering 9:410.

Lakatta EG (1982). Age related changes in rat cardiac muscle. In Reff ME, Schneider EL (eds). "Biological Markers of Aging," Bethesda: NIH Pub #82-2221, p 57.

Lakatta EG (1981). Heart. In Masoro EJ (ed). "Handbook of Physiology in Aging", Boca Raton: CRC Press, p 69.

Landfield PW (1981). Adrenocortical hypothesis of the brain and somatic aging. In Schimke RT (ed). "Biological Mechanisms in Aging," Bethesda. Conf Proc June 1980, NIH Pub #81-2194, p 658.

Landfield PW, Waymire JC, Lynch G (1978). Hippocampal aging and adrenocorticods: Quantitative correlations. Science 202:1098.
LaRue A, Jarvik LF (1980). Reflections of biological changes in the psychological performance of the aged. AGE 3:29.
Lee SC, BeMiller PM, BeMiller JN, Dappelis AJ (1978). Nuclear area changes in senescing human diploid fibroblasts. Mech of Ageing & Dev 7:417.
Lee BY, Thoden WR, Trainor FS, Kavner D (1980). Noninvasive evaluation of peripheral arterial disease in the geriatric patient. J Am Geriat Soc 28:352.
Lee Y-M, Sun AS, Holland JF (1983). 5'nucleotidase and its inhibitor Ehrlich ascites cancer cells. Proc Am Assoc Cancer Res 24:40.
Leech SH (1980). Cellular Immunosenescence. Gerontol 26:330.
Leung TKC, Lai JCK, Lim L (1981). The regional distribution of monoamine activities towards different substrates: effects in rat brain of chronic administration of manganese chloride and of aging. J Neurochem 36:2037.
Lewis RR, Bers Ley MG, Gosling RG (1979). Disease at the Carotid bifurcation. Diagnosis by Doppler Ultrasound Imaging. Gerontol 25:291.
Light M (1983). Doctoral thesis, Weizmann Inst, Rehoveth, Israel.
Linfoot JA (1981). Acromegaly and gigantism. In Daughaday WH (ed). "Endocrine Control of Growth," New York: Elsevier, p 226.
Lobo RA, Kletzky OA, Kaptein EM, Goebelsmann U (1980). Prolactin modulation of dehydroepiandrosterone sulfate secretion. Am J Obstet & Gynecol 138:632.
London ED, Nespor S, Moore L, Mahone P, Rapoport SI (1979). Age Dependent changes in local cerebral glucose utilization. AGE 2:131.
Lu HS, Yuan PM, Talent JM, Gracy RW (1981). A simple manual peptide microsequencing procedure. J Biol Chem 256:785.
Lu HS, Gracy RW (1981). Specific cleavage of glucose-phosphate isomerases at cysteinyl residues using 2-nitro-5-thiocyanobenzoic acid: analysis of peptides eluted from polyacrylamide gels and localization of active site histidyl and lysyl residues. Arch Biochem Biophys 212:347.
Lugaro G, Manera E, Casellato MM, Riboni L (1982). A non steroidal ganetic factor linked to DNA modulates delta-aminolevulinic acid synthase inducibility acting on liver

transcriptional and translational processes. Exp Gerontol 17:365.

Macek K, Deyl Z, Adams M (1980). The effect of age upon the content of gamma carboxyglutamic acid in rat mineralized tissue. Exp Gerontol 15:1.

Macieira-Coehlo A (1980). Implications of the reorganization of the cell genome for aging or immortalization of dividing cells IN VITRO. Gerontol 26:276.

Malhotra S, Kritchevsky D (1978). The distribution and lipid composition of ultra-centrifugally separated lipoprotein of young and old rat plasma. Mech of Ageing & Dev 8:445.

Marcus DL, Ibrahim NG, Freedman ML (1982). Age-related decline in the biosynthesis of mitochondrial inner membrane proteins. Exp Gerontol 17:333.

Mann PL, Kern DE, Kram D, Schneider EL (1981). Relationship between IN VIVO mitomycin C exposure, sister chromatid exchange induction and IN VITRO mitogenic proliferation. II. Effect of aging on spleen cell mitogenesis and sister chromatid exchange induction. Mech of Ageing & Dev 17:203.

Mark DH, Weksler ME (1982). Immunologic studies of aging VIII. No change in cyclic nucleotide concentration in T lymphocytes from old humans despite their depressed proliferative response. Immunol 129:2323.

Martin GM, Sprague CA, Espstein CJ (1970). Replictive life span of cultivated human cells. Effects of donor's age, tissue and genotype. Lab Invest 23:86.

Martinez AO, McDaniel RG (1981). Heterosis for Hl histone content in aging drosophila. Mech of Ageing & Dev 17:141.

Masoro EJ (19820. Adipocyte Function. In Reff ME, Schneider EL (eds). "Biological Markers of Aging," Bethesda: NIH #82-2221, p 13.

Masoro EJ, Delman RC, Roth GS (eds) (1981). "Handbook of Physiology of Aging," Boca Raton: CRC Press.

Massie HR, Colacicco JR, Aiello VR (1979). Changes with age in copper and ceruloplasmin in serum from human and C57Bl/6J Mice. AGE 2:97.

Massie HR, Colacicco JR, Williams TR (1981). Loss of mitochondrial DNA with aging in the Swedish C strain of drosophila melanogaster. AGE 4:42.

Master MA, Oppenheimer ET (1979). A simple exercise tolerance test for circulatory efficiency with standing tables for normal individuals. Am J Med Sc 177:223.

Masters PM (1982). Amino acid racemization in structural protein. In Reff ME, Schneider EL (eds). "Biological Markers of Aging," Bethesda: NIH Publ #82-2221, p 120.

Matvoka K, Mitsui Y (1981). Changes in cell surface glyosaminoglycans in human diploid fibroblasts during IN VITRO aging. Mech of Ageing & Dev 15:153.

McCaffrey RJ, Graham G (1980). Age related differences for motion sickness in the rat. Exp Aging Res 6:555.

McClaran J, Pointrenaud J, Vallery-Masson J (1981). Risk factors for loss of cognitive function in young as well as elderly. AGE 4:145.

McFarland RA (1963). Experimental evidence of the relationship between aging and oxygen want: in search of a theory of ageing. Ergonomics 6:339.

McLimans WF (1979). The role of ammonia in survival of differentiated human cells. "Biomarkers in Aging" Fund for Integrative Biomedical Research Conf, April 11-12, Wash, D.C.

McLimans WF, Blumenson LE, Repasky E, Ito M (1981). Ammonia loading in cell culture systems. Cell Biol Int Rep 5:653.

McLimans WF (1979). "Ammonia and the Cultured Cell in the IN VITRO Expression of Aging". Research proposal to the Fund for Integrative Biomedical Research

Medvedev ZA, Medvedev MN, Robson L (1980). Age associated changes in the electrophoretic pattern of the high molecular weight non-histone proteins from mouse liver. AGE 3:74.

Meites J, Huang HH, Simpkins JW (1978). Recent studies on neuroendocrine control of reproductive senescence in rats. In Schneider EL (ed). "The Aging Reproductive System," New York: Raven Press, p 213.

Melin JA, Piret LJ, Van Butsele RJM, Roussaeu MF, Cosyns J, Brasseur JA, Beckers C, Detay JMR (1981). Diagnostic value of exercise electro- cardiography and thallium myocardial scintigraphy in patients without previous myocardial infarction. Circulation 63:1019.

Melmed S, Hershman JM (1982). The Thyroid and Aging. In Korenman S (ed). "Endocrine Aspects of Aging," New York: Elsevier, p 33.

Mendlewicz J, Van Cauter E, Linkowski P, L'Hermite M, Robyn C (1980). I. The 24-hour profile of prolactin in depression. Life Sciences 27:2015.

Merhan S, Gershon H (1977). The mixed lymphocyte response of senescent mice. Sensitivity to allolantigen and cell replication time. Cell Immunol 34:354.

Merril CR, Switzer RC, Van Keuren ML (1979). Trace polypeptides in cellular extracts and human body fluids
detected by two-dimensional electrophoresis and a highly
sensitive silver stain. Proc Natl Acad Sci, USA 76:4335.
Mets T, Verdonk G (1981). Variations in the stromal cell
population of human bone marrow during aging. Mech Ageing &
Dev 10:81.
Middleton J, Gahan PB (1982). A quantitative cytochemical
study of acid phosphatase in hepatocytes of different
ploidy classes from aging rats. Exp Gerontol 17:267.
Minkowitz S, Minkowitz F, Conklin D (1978). Quantitative
assay of enzyme activity in skin: A new approach to the
correlation of cell biology and physiology. AGE 1:74.
Miquel J, Economus AC, Bensch KG, Atlavo H, Johnson JE Jr
(1973). Review of cell aging in drosophila and mouse. AGE
2:78.
Miquel J, Economus AC, Bensch KG (1981). Insect vs.
mammalian aging. In Johnson JE (ed). "Aging and Fine
Structure,": Plenum Press.
Miquel J, Johnson JE Jr (1979). Senescent changes in the
ribosomes of animal cells IN VIVO and IN VITRO. Mech of
Ageing & Dev 9: 247.
Mitsui Y, Sakagami H, Murota SI, Yamada MA (1980). Age
related decline in histone Hl fraction in human diploid
fibroblast cultures. Exp Cell Res 126:289.
Mittman C, Edelman NH, Norris AH, Shock NW (1965).
Relationship between chest wall and pulmonary compliance
and age. J Applied Physiol 20:1211.
Miyahara T, Murai A, Tanaka T, Shiozawa S, Kameymma M
(1982). Age related differences in human skin collagen:
Solubility in solvent, susceptability to pepsin digestion
and the spectrum of the solubilized polymeric collagen
molecules. J Gerontol 37:651.
Mohan S, Radha E (1981). Age related changes in muscle
connective tissue: Acid mucopolysalccharides and structural
glycoprotein. Exp Gerontol 16:385.
Monnier VM, Stevens VJ, Cermi A (1981). Maillard reactions
involving proteins and carbohydrates in vivo: relevance
to diabetes mellitus and aging. Progr Food Nutr Sci 5:315.
Montgomery D, Bauman TR, Manen CA, Clark JA (1982).
Altered activation of rat hepatic cyclic amp-dependent
protein kinases with increasing age. Exp Gerontol 17:159.
Montgomery PR, Sitar DS (1981). Increased serum salicylate
metabolites with age in patients receiving chrome acetyl-
salicylic acid therapy. Gerontol 27:329.

Moody CE, Innes JB, Stainao-Coico L, Incefy GS, Thaler HT, Weksler ME (1981). Lymphocyte transformation induced by autologous cells XI. The effect of age on the autologous mixed lymphocyte reaction. Immunol 44:431.

Moore RD, Fidelman ML, Hansen JC, Oti JN (1982). The role of intracellular pH in insulin action. In Nuccitelli R, Deamer DW. "Intracellular pH Its Measurement, Regulation and Utilization in Cellular Functions", New York: Alan R. Liss, p 385.

Morgan RF (1981). "Measurement of Human Aging in Applied Gerontology". Dubuque: Kendall/Hunt.

Morley JE, Brammer GL, Sharp B, Yamada T, yuwiler A, Hershman JM (1981). Neurotransmitter control of hypothalamic-pituitary-thyroid function in rats. EuropeanJ Pharmacol 70: 263.

Mosier HD (1981). Thyroid hormone. In Daughaday WH (ed). "Endocrine Control of Growth," New York: Elsevier.

Mulch G, Petermann W (1979). Influence of age on results of vestibular function tests. Ann Otol Rhinol Laryngol 58 (Suppl 56):1

Muller WEG, Zahn RK, Gevrsten W (1980). Age dependent alterations of DNA synthesis. Terminal deoxynucleotidyl transferase and DNA polymerase activities in bone marrow subpopulations from mice. Mech of Aging & Dev 13:119.

Murphy C (1981). Effects of aging on the human threshold and psychophysical function for a chemosensory stimulus. AGE 4:145.

Murray MP, Kory RC, Clarkson BH (1969). Walking patterns in healthy old men. J Gerontol 24:169.

Naeim F, Bergmann K, Walford RL (1981). Capping of conconavalin A receptors on lymphocytes of aged individuals and patients with Down's syndrome. Enhancing effect of colchicine. Possible relation to microtubular system. AGE 4:5.

Nagel JE, Chrest FJ, Adler WH (19810. Enumeration of T-lymphocyte subsets by monoclonal antibodies in young and aged humans. J Immunol 127:2086.

Nandy K, Reisberg B, Ferris SH, deLeon MJ (1981). Brain reactive antibodies and progressive cognitive decline in the aged. AGE 4:145.

Nandy K (1981). Effects of caloric restriction on brain reactive antibodies in SCRR of old mice. AGE 4:117.

Nandy K (1978). Brain reactive antibodies in aging and senile dementia. AGE 1:74.

Nandy K, Aldrich W, Bennett M (1982). Brain-reactive anti-
bodies in young thymectomized mice. 12th Ann Natl Meeting.
Amer Aging Assoc ABS 60:16.
Natta CL, Motyczka AA, Kremzner LT (1982). Polyamines and
globin binding in sickle cell disease. Am J Pediatr
Hematol Oncol 4:73.
Naylor GJ, Dick EG, Smith AHW, Dick DAT, McHarg AM,
Chambers CA (1980). Changes in erythrocyte membrane cation
carrier with age in women. Gerontol 26:327.
Neil JD (1980). Neuroendocrine control of prolactin
secretion. In Martini L, Ganong WF (eds). "Frontiers in
Neuroendocrinology 6," New York: Raven Press, p 129.
Neville HJ, Folstein MF (1979). Performance on three
cognitive tasks by patients with dementia, depression or
Korsakov's syndrome. Gerontol 25:285.
Nicolaissen B, Armstrong P, Vistnes A, Henriksen T, Koppang
N (1981). Lipopigment accumulation in tissue culture. AGE
4:133.
Nohl H, Kramer R (1980). Molecular basis of age-dependent
changes in the activity of adenine nucleotide translocase.
Mech of Ageing & Dev 14:137.
Norohna AB, Antel JP, Roos RP, Arnason BG (1980). Changes
in conconavalin A capping of human lymphocytes with age.
Mech Ageing & Dev 12:331.
Notelovitz M, Ware MD, Buhl WC, Dougherty MC (1982).
Prolactin: Effects of age, menopausal status and exogenous
hormones. Am J Obstet Gyncel 143:225.
Nutrition Rev (1980). Carnitine metabolism in man.
Nutrition Rev 38:338.
O'Brien TJ, Sykes JA, Morrow CP (1979). A sensitive radio-
immunoassay for bovine superoxide dismutase. "Biomarkers in
Aging," Fund for Integrative Biomedical Research Conf,
April 11-12: Wash, D.C.
Ochs AL, Newberry J, Lenhardt ML, Harkins SW (1982).
Balance, imbalance and falls in the elderly: In Birren JE,
Schzie KW (eds). "Handbook of the Psychology of Aging,"
New York: Van Nostrand, Reinhold (In Press).
Okudaira H, Suzuki T, Morita Y, Miyamoto T, Horiuchi Y
(1980). Age dependent increase of histamine content in rat
mast cells. Exp Gerontol 15:195.
O'Leary JJ, Jackola DR, Hallgren HM, Abbasnezhad J,
Yasmineh WG (1982). Evidence of a less differentiated
subpopulation of lymphocytes in people of advanced age. In
Press.
Olsho LW, Harkins SW, Lenhardt ML (1982). Aging and the
Auditory System. In Birren JE, Schzie KW (eds). "Handbook

of the Psychology of Aging," New York: Van Nostrand,
Reinhold (In Press).
Orentreich, N (1982). Ohrentreich Foundation for the
Advancement of Science, 1982 Report.
Orentreich N, Markofsky J, Vogelman, JH (1979). The Effect
of aging on the rate of linear nail growth. J Invest
Dermatology 73:126.
Orentreich N, Vogelman JH, Reizer RL, Markofsky J (1979).
Dehydroepiandrosterone sulfate levels and aging rate of
nail growth changes with age. "Biomarkers in Aging", Fund
for Integrative Biomedical Research Conf, April 11-12,
Wash, D.C.
Otsuki M, Dakoda M, Baba S (1973). Influence of gluco-
corticoids on TRF-induced TSH response in man. J Clin
Endocrinol Metab 36:95.
Overstall PW, Hazell JWP, Johnson L (1981). Vertigo in the
elderly. Age & Ageing 10:105.
Owsley CJ, Sekular R, Boldt HC (1981). Face perception and
human aging. Investigative Opthamology & Visual Science
21:362.
Paffenholz V (1978). Correlation between DNA repair of
embryonic fibroblasts and different life span of 3 inbred
mouse strains. Mech of Ageing & Dev 7:131.
Palgi A, Vanihook S, Lewin A, Cummins J, Blackburn GL
(1981). Serial nutritional assessments of chronically ill
hospitalized elderly. AGE 4:137.
Palmore E (ed) (1970). "Normal Aging: Report from the Duke
Longitudinal Study, 1955-1969". Durham, Duke University
Press.
Palmore E, Jeffers FC (1971) (eds). "Prediction of Life
Span: Recent Findings," Lexington: Heath Lexington Books.
Pandy JP, Ainsworth SK, Fudenberg HH, Loadholt CB (1978).
Aging & Autoimmunity. AGE 1:77.
Papavasiliou PF, Miller FT, Thal LJ, Nerder LJ, Houlihan G,
Rao FN, Stevens JM (1981). Age related motor and
catecholamine alterations in mice on levo-dopa supplemented
diet. Life Sciences 28:2945.
Paterniti JR, Lin CIP, Beattle DS (1978). Delta amino-
levulinic acid synthetase. Regulation of activity in
various tissue of the aging rat. Arch Biochem Biophys
191:792.
Penniall R, Baker M, Holbrook JP, Viskup RW (1981).
Age-associated changes in rat hepatocytes. Studies of the
character of a polypeptide subject to diminished synthesis
at an early age. AGE 4:9

Permutt S, Martin HB (1960). Static pressure - volume characteristics of lungs in normal males. J Appl Physiol 15:819.

Petrofsky JS, Lind AR (1975). Isometric strength, endurance and the blood pressure and heart rate responses during isometric exercise in healthy men and women, with special reference to age and body fat content. Pluegers Arch 360:49.

Pfeiffer MA, Cook D, Brodsky J (1982). Quantitative Emulation of sympathetic and parasympathetic control of iris function. Diabetes Care (In Press).

Pfeiffer MA, Halter JB, Luickie F (1980). Autonomic nervous system. Function and age-related increases of blood pressure and heart rate in man. Clin Res 28:335.

Pieri C, Giuli C, Del Moro M, Pintanelli L (1980). Electron-microscopic morphometric analysis of mouse liver: II effect of ageing and thymus transplantation in old animals. Mech of Ageing & Dev 13:275.

Piko L, Matsumoto L (1977). Complex forms and replicative intermediates of mitochondrial DNA: In tissues from adult & senescent mice. Nucl Acids Res. 4:1301.

Pilgeram LO (1958). Deficiencies in the lipoprotein lipase system in atherosclerosis. J Gerontol 13:32.

Pisciotta AV, Westring DW, Petrey C, Walsh B (1967). Mitogenic effect of phytohaemagglutinin at different ages. NATURE 215:193.

Pledger WJ, Clemmons D (1979). Role of peptic growth factors in modulating the cell cycle of BALB/C 3T3 cell. In Korenman SG (ed). "Endocrine Aspects of Aging," Proc on the Endocrine Aspects of Aging of the Endocrine Soc and the NIA. Oct 18-20, 1979.

Podolsky S (1980). Differentiation between organic and psychogenic erective impotence in aging males. AGE 3:112.

Polson CD, Webster JC (1982). Loss of mitochondrial DNA in mouse tissues with age. Proc 12th Ann Mtg Amer Aging Assoc (ABS 19): p 8.

Port S, Cobb FR, Coleman RE, Jones RH (1980). Effect of age on the response of the left ventricular heart to exercise. N Eng J Med 303:1135

Porta EA, Keopuhiwa L, Joun NS, Nitta RT (1981). Effects of the type of dietary fat at two levels of vitamin E in Wistar male rats during development and aging. III biochemical and morphometric parameters of the liver. Mech Ageing & Dev 15:297.

Potvin AR, Syndulko K, Tourtellotte WW, Lemmon JA, Potvin JH (1980). Human neurologic function and the aging process. Amer Geriatrics Soc 28:1
Powell R, Fernandez LA (1980). Proliferative Responses of peripheral blood lymphocytes to polyclonal activation. A comparison of young and elderly individuals. Mech of Ageing & Dev 13:241.
Preumont AM, Van Gansen P, Bracchet J (1978). Cytochemicl Study of human lymphocytes stimulated by PHA in function of donor age. Mech of Ageing & Dev 7:25.
Purdy RH, Goldzieher JW (1982). Toward a safer estrogen in aging. "Intervention in the Aging Process: Basic Research, Pre-clinical Screening and Clinical Programs". FIBER/Boston University, Nov 5,6,: Boston, Mass.
Pvion-Dutilleul F, Azzarone B, Macieria-Coelho D (1982). Comparison between proliferative changes in nuclear events during ageing of human fibroblasts IN VITRO. Mech of Ageing and Dev 20:75.
Rai GS (1981). Viscosity, vascular disease and the elderly. Age and Ageing 10:221.
Rama Sastry BV, Owens LK (1980). Responsiveness of the dia-phram of the rat as a function of age. AGE 3:115 ABS 40.
Ramwell PW, Uzunova A, Johnson M, Ramsey E (1978). Effect of age on human platelet aggregation and arterial thrombi formation in rats. AGE 1:36.
Reddan WG (1980). Exercise and Aging: The Scientific Basis. In Smith EL, Serfass RC (eds). "Respiratory System and Aging," New Jersey: Enslow Pub, p 89.
Reff ME, Schneider EL (ed) (1982). "Biological Markers of Aging". Bethesda: NIH Pub #82-2221.
Reiss U, Gershon D (1978). Methionine sulfoxide reductase. A novel protective enzyme in liver and its potentially significant role in aging. In Kitani K (ed). "Liver & Aging,": Elsevier, North Holland Biomedical Press, p 55.
Richardson A, Birchenall-Sparks MC, Staekcr JL, Hardwick JP, Liu DSH (1982). The transcription of various types of ribonucleic acid by heptocytes isolated from rats of various ages. J Gerontology 37:666.
Riegle GD (1976). In Everitt AF, Burgess JA (eds). "Hypothalamus, Pituitary and Aging," Illinois: C.C. Thomas, p 547.
Ries W (1974). Problems associated with biological age. Gerontol 9:145.
Rikans LE, Notley BA (1981). Decline in hepatic microsomal monooxygenase components in middle aged Fischer 344 rats. Exp Gerontol 16:253.

Riley V, Spackman D (1982). Pacific NW Research Foundation. Report to the Murdoch Foundation.

Rivnay B, Bergman S, Shinitzky M, Globerson A (1980). Correlations between membrane viscosity, serum cholesterol, lymphocyte activation and aging in man. Mech of Ageing & Dev 12:119.

Rivnay B, Globerson A, Schinitzky M (1979). Viscosity of lymphocyte plasma membrane in aging mice and its possible relation to serum cholesterol. Mech Aging & Dev 10:71.

Ritzmann RF, Springer A (1980). Age differences in brain sensitivity and tolerance of ethanol in mice. AGE 3:15.

Robertson GL, Rowe J, Helderman H, Andres R (1979). The effect of aging on the regulation of vasopressin secretion. In Korenman SG (ed). "Endocrine Aspects of Aging," Bethesda: Proc NIA, Endocrine Soc, Veterans Adm Confer.

Robinson AB, Irving K, McCrea M (1973). Acceleration of the rate of deamidation of Glyarg, Asn, Arg, Gly and of human tranferrin by the addition of l-ascorbic acid. Proc Nat Acad Sci USA 70:21.

Robinson DS, Davis JM, Nies A, Ravaris CL, Sylvester D (1971). Relation of sex and aging to monoamine oxidase activity of human brain, plasma and platelets. Arch Gen Psychiat 24:536.

Robinson S (1938). Experimental studies of physical fitness in relation to age. Arbeitphysiologie 10:251.

Robinson AB, Willoughby R, Robinson LR (1976). Age dependent amines, amides and amino acid residues in drosophila melanogaster. Exp. Gerontol 11:113.

Robinson AB, Dirren H, Sheets A, Miquel J, Lungren R (1976). Quantitative aging pattern in mouse urine vapor as measured by gas-liquid chromatography. Exp Gerontol 11:11.

Robinson AB, Dirren H, Sheets A, Tsao C, Cherkin A (1978). Quantitative urine profiling of human age. Work in Progress.

Robinson AB (1979). Molecular clocks, molecular profiles, and optimum diets: Three approaches to the problem of aging. Mech of Ageing & Dev 9:275.

Rockstein M, Sussman ML, Chesky J (ed)(1974). "Theoretical Aspects of Aging,". Academic Press.

Rodgers JD, Gass GH (1980). Changes in the electrophoretic pattern of hemoglobin in aging Swiss mice. Exp Gerontol 15:73.

Rolsten C, Hicks P, Brizzee DL, Samorajski T (1980). Age related changes in hippocampal capillaries. AGE 3:115.

Roof BS, Fudenberg HH (1978). Changing profiles of serum calcium (SCa) immunoactive parathyroid hormone (iPTH) and albumin (alb) in white, black or oriental males and females correlating with thymic size and age. AGE 1:34.

Romanov GA, VanYushin BF (1981). Methylation of reiterted sequences in mammalian DNAs. Effects of the tissue type, age, malignancy and hormonal induction. Biochim Biophys ACTA 653:204.

Rosenthal M (1978). Age and immunity. III Circulating immune complexes in different age groups. Blut 37:21.

Rosenthal SM (1981). Microcirculation and lymphatics. In Masoro EJ (ed). "CRC Handbook of Physiology in Aging," Boca Raton: CRC Press, p 155.

Rossman I (1979). The anatomy of aging. In Rossman I (ed). "Clinical Geriatrics," Philadelphia: J.B. Lippincott, p 3.

Roth GS, Livingston JN (1976). Reductions in glucocorticoid receptor content in rat adipocytes during aging. Endocrinology 99:831.

Rowell LB (1974). Human cardiovascular adjustments to exercise and thermal stress. Physiol Rev 54:75.

Rowe JW (1982). Renal function and aging. In Reff ME, Schneider EL (eds). "Biological Markers of Aging," Bethesda: NIH #82-2221, p 228.

Rowe JW, Troen BR (1980). Sympathetic nervous system and aging in man. End Rev 1:167.

Ruth RC, Owens K, Weglicki WB (1979). Inhibition of lyso-zomal lipases by chlorpromazine: A possible mechanisms of stabilization. J Pharm Exp Ther 212:361.

Ruth RC, Weglicki WB (1979). The temperature-dependence of the loss of latency of lysozomal enzymes. Biochem J 172:163.

Sabbahi MA, Sedgwick EM (1982). Age related changes in monosynapatic reflex excitability. J Gerontol 37:24.

Sabin TC (1982). Biological aspects of falls and mobility limitations in the elderly. J Am Geriatr Soc 30:51.

Saito M, Ando S, Tanaka Y, Nagai Y, Mitsui K, Hase J (1982). Age development in susceptability of erythrocytes to perfringolysin O. Mech of Ageing & Dev 20:53.

Salthouse T (1982). Psychomotor indices of physiological age. In Reff ME, Schneider EL (eds). "Biological Markers of Aging," Bethesda: NIH Pub #82-2221.

Sandler M, Glover V, Bhattachaaya SK, Armando I, File SE, Petersson H, Reveley MA (1981). Endogenous urinary monoamine oxidase inhibitor and stress: Proc of Intern'l Symp on Monoamine Oxidase: Basic & Clinical Frontiers: Hakone July 25-27, 1981. Amsterdam Excerpta Medica Amsterdam.

Sawin CT, Chopra D, Azizi F, Mannix JE, Bacharach P (1979).
The aging thyroid. JAMA 242:247.
Scheving LE, Roig C, Halbert F, Pauly JE, Hand EA (1977).
Circadian variations in residents of a "Senior Citizens"
home. In Scheving LE, Halbert F, Pauley JE (eds). "Chrono-
biology," Tokyo: Igaku Shoin Ltd, p 353.
Schmucker DL, Wang RK (1981). Effects of aging and pheno-
barbital on the rat liver microsomal drug metabolizing
system. Mech of Ageing & Dev 15:189.
Schmucker DL, Wang RK (1979). Rat liver lysosomal enzymes:
Effects of animal age and phenobarbital. AGE 2:93.
Schmucker DL, Wang RK (1981). Effects of aging and pheno-
barbital on the rat liver microsomal drug metabolizing
system. Mech of Ageing & Dev 15:189.
Schmucker DL, Wang RKJ (1981). Gastrointestinal
physiology. In Masoro EJ (ed). "Handbook of Physiology in
Aging," Boca Raton: CRC Press, p 35.
Schneider EL, Mitsui Y (1976). The relationship between IN
VITRO cellular aging and IN VIVO human age. Proc Natl Acad
Sci USA 73:3584.
Schocken DD, Roth GS (1977). Reduced B-adrenergic receptor
concentration in ageing man. NATURE 267:856.
Scholar EM, Rashidian M, Heidrick ML (1980). Adenosine
deaminase and purine nucleoside phosphorylase activity in
spleen cells of aged mice. Mech Aging and Dev 12:323.
Scholfield JD (1980). Connective tissue aging: differences
between mouse tissues in age-related changes in collagen
extractability. Exp Gerontol 15:113.
Scholfield JD (1980). Altered proteins of ageing organisms
application of circular dichroism spectroscopy to study the
thermal denaturation of purified serum albumin from adult
and ageing C57BL mice. Exp Gerontol 15:533.
Segre D, Smith L (eds) (1981). "Immunological Aspects of
Aging," New York: Marcel Dekker.
Silver B (1979). Electron microscopy and emission scanning
for magnesium and other metals in aging. "Biomarkers in
Aging": Fund for Integrative Biomedical Research Conf,
April 11-12: Washington, D.C.
Schow RL, Goldbaum DE (1980). Collapsed ear canals in the
elderly nursing home population. J Sp Hag Dis 45:259.
Seki K, Kato K (1981). Elevated serum DHEA-S levels in
association with hyperprolactinemia. Endocrinol Japon
28:79.
Sekular R (1982). Vision as a source of simple and
reliable biomarkers for aging. In Reff ME, Schneider EL

(eds). "Biological Markers of Aging," Bethesda: NIH Publ #82-2221, p 220.
Sekular R, Owsley CJ (1980). The spatial vision of older humans. In Sekular R, Kline D, Dismukes K (eds). "Aging and Human Visual Function," New York: Alan Liss, p 185.
Sheppard RJ (ed)(1978). "Physical Activity and Aging," Chicago: Year Book Medical Publishing, p 134.
Sheppard RJ (1981). Cardiovascular limitations in the aged. In Smith EL, Serfass RC (eds). "Exercise and Aging," New Jersey: Enslow Pub, p 19.
Sigel B, Machi J, Beitler JC, Justin Jr, Coelho JCU (1982). Variable ultra sound echogenicity in flowing blood. Science 218:1321.
Shock NW (1960). Discussion on mortality and measurement. In Strehler BL, Ebert JD, Glass HB (eds). "The Biology of Aging," (symposium) Washington, D.C.: Am Inst of Biological Sciences.
Shug AL (1979). Control of carnitine related metabolism during myocardial ischemia. Texas Rpt Biol & med 39:409.
Shulman RG (1983). NMR spectoscopy of living cells. Scientific American 248:86.
Sinha YN, Vanderlaan WP (1982). Effect on growth of pro-lactin deficiency induced in infant mice. Endocrinology 110:1871.
Singh J, Singh AK (1979). Age related changes in the human thymus. Clin Exp Immunol 37:507.
Sinex FM (1957). Aging and the lability of irreplaceable molecules - II the amide groups of collagen. J Gerontol 12:15.
Slavin S (1981). Programming spinning optics technology. Proc IEEE Technical Committee on Computing and the Handicapped. IEEE #TH0092-7, p 210.
Sluke G, Schachtschabel DO, Wever J (1981). Age related changes in the distribution pattern of glycosaminoglycans synthesized by cultured human diploid fibroblasts (WI-38). Mech of Ageing & Dev 16:19.
Smalley JW (1980). Age related changes in the amino acid composition of human glomerular basement membrane. Exp Gerontol 15:43.
Smith RC, Ho BT, Krlik P, Vroulis G, Gordon J, Wolff J (1982). Platelet monoamine oxidase in Alzheimer's disease. J Gerontol 37:572.
Smith EL, Sempos CT, Purvis RW (1981). Bone mass and strength decline with age. In Smith EL, Seafass RC (eds). "Exercise and Aging," New Jersey: Enslow Pub, p 59.

Smith EL, Serfass RC (eds) (1980). "Exercise and Aging: The Scientific Basis," New Jersey: Enslow Pub.
Spector A, Scotto R, Weissbach H, Brot N (1982). Lens methionine sulfoxide reductase. Biochemical and Biophysical Research Communications 108:429.
Staiano-Coico L, Darzynkiewicz Z, Hefton JM, Dutkowski R, Darlington GJ, Weksler ME (1983). Increased sensitivity of lymphocytes from people over 65 to cell cycle arrest and chromosomal damage. Science 219:1335.
Stege TE, Mischke BS, Zipperer (1982). Levels of lipid peroxidation in hepatocytes isolated from aging rats fed an antioxidant free diet. Exp Gerontol 17:273.
Stein DG (ed) (1979). "The Psychobiology of Aging Problems and Perspectives," New York: Elsevier/North Holland.
Steinhagen-Theissen E, Reznik A, Hilz H (1980). Negative adaptation to physical training in senile mice. Mech of Ageing & Dev 12:231.
Steinhagen-Theissen E, Reznick Z, Hilz H (1981). Positive and negative adaptation of muscle enzymes in aging mice subjected to physical exercise. Mech of Ageing and Dev 16:363.
Stell PM (1979). Effect of age on the retraction of skin. Gerontol 25:145.
Stephens G, Cinotti A, Duyk G, Caputo P, Desai R (1978). Zinc and the Electro-oculogram (EOG) in the aged: AGE 1:160.
Stephens G, Cinotti A, Chavis P, Stephens E, Fiorc R (1980). An objective non-invasive test for degree of aging in the retina. AGE 3:111.
Stephens G, Cinotti , Stephens E, Fiorc R (1979). Comparison of electroretinographic response between old (above 60) and young (18-35) people. AGE 2:132.
Stohs SJ, Hazzing JM, Al-Turk WA, Masoud AN (1980). Glutathione levels in hepatic and extrahepatic tissues of mice as a function of age. AGE 3:11.
Strain WH, Lavin P, Hershey LA, Varnes AW, Hershey CO (1981). Influence of age and sex on elemental composition of cerebrospinal fluid as determined by ICAP spectrometry. AGE 4:144.
Strashun A, Horowitz SF, Goldsmith SJ, Teichholz LE, Dicker A, Miceli K, Gorlin R (1981). Noninvasive detection of left ventricular dysfunction with a portable electrocardiographic gated scintillation probe device. Am J Cardiology 47:610.

Strauven TA, Armstrong D, James GT, Austin JH (1978).
Separation of leukocyte peroxidse isoenzymes by
agarose-acrylamide disc electrophoresis. AGE 1:111.
Strozzi C, Cocco G, Destro , Padovavo G, Abbasciaivo V,
Tosatti S (1979). Disorders in peripheral arterial system
in asymptomatic elderly: Plethysmographic semiology at
rest, during posture, effort and pharmacological tests.
Gerontol 25:24.
Sun S, Holland JF, Ohnum T, Slankard-Chahinian M (1982).
5'-nucleotidase activity in permanent human lymphoid cell
lines: implication for cell proliferation and aging IN
VITRO. Biochem Biophys ACTA 714:530.
Sun AS, Alvarez LJ, Reinach PS, Rubin E (1979). 5' nucleotidase levels in normal and virus transformed cells:
implication for cellular aging IN VITRO. Lab Invest 41:1.
Sun S, Reinach P (1978). Increase of 5' nucleotidase
activity with increasing accumulated population doubling in
normal cell lines and its absence in transformed cell
lines. AGE 1:70 ABS 3.
Sun AS, Aggarwal BB, Packer L (1975). Enzyme levels of
normal human cells: Aging in culture. Arch Biochem Biophys
170:1.
Susskind H, Zanzi I, Atkins HL, Harold WH, Cohn SH (1978).
Lung function in primary osteoporosis. AGE 1:72.
Sykes JA (1980). Personal communication re: work in progress.
Szymanski ES, Little NA, Kritchevsky D (1981).
Phospholipid metabolism in livers of young and old Fischer
344 and Sprague-Dawley rats. Exp Gerontol 16:163.
Tam CF, Walford RL (1978). Cyclic nucleotide levels in
resting and nitrogen-stimulated spleen cell suspensions
from young and old mice. Mech of Aging & Dev 7:309.
Tam CF, Walford RL (1980). Alterations in cyclic nucleo-
tides and cyclase specific activities in T-lymphocytes of
aging normal humans and patients with Down's syndrome. J
Immunol 125:1665.
Tannenbaum GS, Guyda HJ, Posner BI (1983). Insulin like
growth factors: a role of growth hormone negative feedback
and body weight regulation via brain. Science 220:77.
Tas S, Tam CF, Walford RL (1980). Disulfide bonds and the
structure of the chromatin complex in relation to aging.
Mech of Ageing & Dev 12:65.
Tas S, Walford RL (1982). Influence of disulfide reducing
agents on fractionation of the chromatin complex by endo-
genous nucleosis and deoxyribonuclease I in aging mice. J
Gerontol 37:673.

Thomsen JH, Shug AL, Yap VU, Patel AK, Karras TJ, DeFelice SL (1979). Improved stress tolerance of the ischemic human myocardium after carnintine administration. Am J Cardiol 43:300.
Thorner MO, Martin WH, Rogol AD, Morris LJ, Pearyman RL, Conway BP, Howards SS, Wolfman MG, MacLeod RM (1980). Rapid regression of pituitary prolactinomas during bromcriptine treatment. J Clin Endocrin & Metabol 51:438.
Timiras PS (1979). Conference on Endocrine Aspects of Aging; Korenman SC (ed) NIA, Endocrine Soc and Veterans Adm. Oct 18-20.
Timiras PS (1972). Differential Aging in Man: In "Developmental Physiology and Aging", New York. MacMillan Co, p 415.
Timiras PS (1972). "Developmental Physiology and Aging": New York, MacMillan Co.
Tokumasu K, Kawano R (1976). Head sway during stepping in old and young adults. Agressologie 17:1
Tollesfsbol TO, Chapman ML, Zaun MR, Gracy RW (1981). Impaired glycolysis of human lymphocyte during aging. Mech of Ageing & Dev 17:369.
Tollesfsbol TO, Zaun MR,, Gracy RW (1982). Increased ability of triosephosphate isomerase in progeria and Werner's syndrome fibroblasts. Mech of Ageing and Dev 20:93.
Torrelio BM, Paz MA, Gallop PM (1981). Modulation of purine synthesis and phosphorbosyl pyrophosphate content in aging human fibroblasts. AGE 4:134.
Tolmasoff JM, Ono T, Cutler RG (1980). Superoxide dismutase: correlation with lifespan and specific metabolic rate in primate species. Proc Natl Acad Sci USA 77:2777.
Trauric HH, Papka RE (1980). Lysozomal acid hydrolase activity in the aging heart. Exp Gerontol 15:291.
Tsitoura PD, Martin CE, Harman SM (1982). Relationship of serum testosterone to sexual activity in healthy elderly men. J Gerontol 37:288.
Turner DR, Morley AA, Seshadri RS, Sorrell JR (1981). Age related variations in human lymphocyte DNA. Mech of Ageing & Dev 17:305.
Tyan ML (1982). Age related increase in erythrocyte oxidant sensitivity. Mech of Aging & Dev 20:25.
Uricchio FJ, Baskin SI (1978). The effect of age on its residual distribution of five metals in Fischer 344 rats. AGE 1:77.
Van Wyk JJ, Clemmons DR (1979). Growth control by peptide growth factors: Approaches to a functional classification

in endocrine aspects of aging. Korenman SG (ed). NIA Conf Oct 18-20.

Verdy M, Levesque HP, Boghen D, Aube M, Guimond J (1980). Manual dexterity test in relation to obesity and hyperostosis frontalis interna in elderly women. Gerontol 26:50.

Vernadakis A, Timiras (1982). "Hormones in Development and Aging." New York, Spectrum Publications.

Vernon PA (1982). Speed of information processing and general intelligence. Intelligence, In Press.

Vernon PA, Jensen AR (1982). Individual and group differences in intelligence and speed of information process. Submitted: J of Educational Psychology.

Visek WJ (1981). The influence of urea hydrolysis and ammonia on animals. Adv in Veter Med 33:64. Supp J Vet Med.

Vogel K, Kelley RO, Stewart C (1981). Loss of organized fibronectin matrix from the surface of aging diploid fibroblasts (IMR-90). Mech of Ageing & Dev 16:295.

Walford RL, Jawaid SQ, Naeim F (1981). Evidence for IN VITRO senescence of T-lymphocytes cultured from normal human peripheral blood. AGE 4:67.

Walford RL, Gottesman SR, Weindruch RH, Tam CF (1981). Immunopathology of aging in Ann Rev of Gerontology and Geriatrics 2:3. Springer, New York.

Walls R, Kumr KS, Hochstein P (1976). Aging of human erythrocytes: differential sensitivity of young and old erthyrocytes to hemolysis induced by peroxide in the presence of thyroxine. Arch Biochem Biophys 174:463.

Wang RKJ, Mays LL (1978). Isozymes of glucose-6-phosphate dehydrogenase in livers of aging rats. AGE 1:2.

Weksler ME (1982). A search for immunological markers of aging in man. In Reff ME, Schneider EL (eds). "Biological Markers of Aging," Bethesda: NIH Publ #82-2221.

Weindruch RH, Kristie JA, Naeim F, Mullen BG, Walford RL (1982). Influence of weaning – initiated dietary restriction on responses to T cell mitogens and on splenic T cell levels in a long lived Fl-hybrid mouse strain. Exp Gerontol 17:49.

Weiss JN, Rand LI, Gleason RE, Soeldner JS (1983). Laser light segttering spectroscopy of in vivo human lenses. Submitted Archives of Ophthalmology.

Westall FC, Thompson M, Robinson AB (1976). Degredation of encephalitogenic protein in ascorbic acid solution. Experentia 32:848.

Whatley SA, Hill ZT (1980). IN VITRO 'Ageing' and Nuclear Template Function. Gerontol 26:138.

White NK, Edwards JE, Dry TJ (1950). The relationship of the degree of coronary atherosclerosis with age, in man. Circulation 1:645.

Wiederanders B, Ansorge S, Bohley P, Kirschke H, Langner J, Hanson H (1978). The age dependence of intracellular proteolysis. Changes of the substrate proteins. Mech of Ageing & Dev 8:355.

Williams BO, Caird FI (1980). Impedance cardiography and cardiac output in the elderly. Age & Ageing 9:47.

Williamson JR (1983). In Migaki G, Scarpelli DG (eds). "Comparative Pathobiology of Major Age-Related Diseases: Current Status and Research Frontiers," New York: Alan Liss, In Press.

Wilson MM, Greer SE, Greer MA, Roserts L (1980). Hippocampal inhibition of pituitary-adrenocortical function in female rats. Brain Res 197:433.

Wilson VL, Jones PA (1983). DNA methylation decreases in aging but not in immortal cells. Science 220:1055.

Wright BM (1971). A simple mechanical ataxia meter. J Physiol 218:27P

Yamaura H, Matsuzawa T (1980). Decrease in capillary growth during aging. Exp Gerontol 15:145.

Yesavage JA, Holman CA, Sarnquist FH, Berger PA (1982). Elevation of cerebrospinal fluid lactate with aging in subjects with normal blood oxygen saturations. J Gerontol 37:313.

Yin FCP, Spurgeon HA, Raizes CS, Greene L, Weisfeldt ML, Shock NW (1970). Age associated decrease in chronotropic response to insoporterenol Circulation 54:11.

Yuan PM, Talent JM, Gracy RW (1981). Molecular basis for the accumulation of acidic isozymes of triosephosphate isomerase on aging. Mech of Ageing & Dev 17:151.

Yuan PM, Talent JM, Gracy RW (1981b). A tentative elucidation of the sequence of human triosephosphate isomerase by homology peptide mapping. Biochem Biophys ACTA 671:211.

Yunice AA, Lindiman RD, Czcawinski AW, Clark M (1974). Influence of age and sex on scrum copper and ceruloplasmin levels. J Gerontol 29:277.

Yunis EJ, Handwerger BS, Hallgren HM, Good RA, Fernandez G (1979). Aging and Immunity. In Cohen S, Ward PA, McClusky RJ (eds). "Mechanisms of Immunopathology," New York: Wiley, p 91.

Ziegler MG, Lake CR, Kopin IJ (1976). Plasma Noradrenaline increases with age. NATURE 261:333.

Zumoff, Strain GW, Kream J, O'Connor J, Rosenfeld RS, Levin
J, Fukushima DK (1981). Age variation of the 24-hour mean
plasma concentration of adrogens, estrogens and gonado-
tropins on normal adult men. AGE 4:140.
Zbuzek VK, Wu W-H (1982). Age related vasopressin changes
in rat plasma and the hypothalamo-hypophyseal system. Exp
Gerontol 17:133.

Intervention in the Aging Process, Part A: Quantitation, Epidemiology, and
Clinical Research, pages 99–111
© 1983 Alan R. Liss, Inc., 150 Fifth Avenue, New York, NY 10011

FACTORS IN CLINICAL AGING: VARIATION IN RATES OF AGING

Gary A. Borkan, Ph.D.

Normative Aging Study, Veterans Administration

Outpatient Clinic, Boston, Massachusetts

As gerontological research progresses, agents will be
found which may potentially alter the rate of aging. It
will be necessary to test these drugs or aspects of behavior
(diet, exercise, etc.), to determine if they actually have
an effect on the progress of aging in humans. Many of the
papers in this volume represent attempts to identify "marker
traits" of aging, which can be used to monitor the progress
of senescence. The purpose of this paper is to discuss one
possible way in which gerontological data may be analyzed to
evaluate the relative impact of different behaviors on the
aging process.

One of the main reasons for the lack of research in
comparative aging is the difficulty of measuring rate of
aging longitudinally or aging status cross-sectionally.
Longitudinal data (follow-up measures on the same individuals) provide the ideal means of comparing aging between
individuals. Large scale longitudinal studies are already
underway, but over 20 years of follow-up are required to
determine accurate individual slopes in many variables
(Schlesselman, 1973). For this reason previous research in
comparative aging has relied on cross-sectional data,
adapting a model similar to that used for child development
assessment. This approach assumes that every individual can
be characterized by a biological age (developmental or
functional age) which may be older or younger than his
chronological age, and presumably reflects his own rate of
change. The assessment of biological age in children is
facilitated by the discernable stages of their skeletal,
dental, or sexual maturation. Unfortunately for gerontol-

ogists, aging is not characterized by stepwise changes, but involves continuous change in many physical parameters.

A number of researchers have attempted to measure biological age in adulthood. The most prevalent method has been to combine a large number of age-related parameters in a multiple regression equation to predict chronological age, with the predicted value viewed as the biological age of the individual (Hollingsworth et al. 1965; Dirken, 1972; Bell, 1972; Heikkinen et al. 1974; Furukawa et al. 1974; Webster and Logie, 1976). Another approach is factor analysis of a large number of aging parameters, with subsequent use of the factor scores as biological age measures (Clark, 1960; Jalavisto and Makkonen, 1963). Only a few researchers have attempted to utilize their biological age scores in further analysis. Costa and McCrae (1980) used biological age to predict longitudinal change in other parameters with little success. Hansen (1973) demonstrated that biological age was a better correlate of periodontal disease than chronological age. Brown and Forbes (1976) suggested that biological age should be predictive of the likelihood of mortality, though no previous investigation has measured this. Two studies (Furukawa et al. 1975; Webster and Logie, 1976) have compared healthy and unhealthy individuals, and found the unhealthy groups to be biologically older.

With the goal of examining the association of lifestyle with aging variability, we have developed a new approach to biological age in adulthood (Borkan, 1978; Borkan and Norris, 1980). This method uses a profile of 24 biological age scores reflecting various aspects of physical function. The profile approach allows the possibility that different body systems may age at different rates within the same individual. We compared the biological age of survivors with now deceased participants in the Baltimore Longitudinal Study, and found statistically significant differences at the time of measurement for 9 of 24 profile variables. Another comparison indicated that men who were subjectively judged as looking older than their actual age were biologically older in many of the profile parameters as well (Borkan and Norris, 1979).

The purpose of this paper is to describe the use of the biological age profile, and demonstrate differences in biological age in men of different marital status, education and self-reported health.

METHODS

The investigation was based on the data collected by the Baltimore Longitudinal Study of Human Aging of the Gerontology Research Center, National Institute on Aging. This longitudinal study was begun in 1958 and since that time the male participants have returned at 18 month intervals for a comprehensive series of physical evaluations, personal questionnaires, and interviews. Participants are from the Baltimore-Washington area and most are white, college educated, and middle income. At entry they ranged in age from 17 to 98 years with an average age of 50. Participants were self-recruited into the study, and no applicant was excluded for health reasons. Further demographic description of this population may be found in Stone and Norris (1966).

For the present study, cross-sectional data for 1086 individuals were analyzed. Data used were the first data points available for each variable for each subject, which generally corresponded to the first study visit.

The rationale behind the biological age profile and the calculation of biological age scores has been described by Borkan (1978) and Borkan and Norris (1980). An overview of the technique follows:

A total of 24 physiological parameters were selected as a representative subset of the very large number of characteristic changes of aging. The criteria for selection were that the variables have a positive or negative linear trend with age in cross-sectional and longitudinal data. Selected parameters had been used in other studies of biological age, had good replicability, and reflected a wide range of physical functions.

The biological age concept implies that for an age-related parameter (with a positive slope, for example), individuals whose scores are above the mean for their chronological age peers are biologically older than those below the mean. That is, their scores are more similar to those of individuals chronologically older than themselves. This suggests that a biological age score should simply be a statistic which describes a man's status relative to his chronological age group for each variable, expressed in standardized units. In statistical terms, the raw data should be corrected for the effects of chronological age, and converted to z-score (standard deviation) units.

The steps in transforming the raw data into biological age scores were:

1. Simple piecewise linear regression (Neter and Wasserman, 1974) of each variable on age.
2. Subtraction of the predicted score from the actual score of each individual (i.e. calculate residuals).
3. Standardization of residual scores using the z-transformation, accounting for increased variance of data with age.
4. Conversion of data so positive scores referred to greater biological age. Positive sloped variables already were in this form; negative sloped variables were multiplied by -1 to facilitate interpretation.

As a result of these procedures, the raw data for 24 age-related variables were transformed into 24 biological age scores reflecting a man's physical status relative to his chronological age peers. Because the biological age scores are in standardized units, all 24 variables can be compared simply. A further advantage is that men of different chronological ages can have the same biological scores (e.g. +1 SD) for a given variable, indicating that their status relative to their own chronological age peers is identical. Because of this correction, men of different chronological ages can be included in the same analysis without confounding the results.

Biological age scores can be plotted on a profile chart using the technique of Garn (1977). The 24 scores of an individual may be graphed, or subgroups may be plotted by their mean scores on the 24 variables and the pairs of means may be analyzed by t-test. Breakdowns of the population based on education, marital status and self-reported health are examined for differences in biological age status in the present report.

RESULTS AND DISCUSSION

The 24 variables selected for inclusion in the biological age profile are listed in Table 1 with their sample size and correlation with age. The quantity of missing data

TABLE 1
Sample size and correlation coefficients with age for
variables selected for biological age test battery

| Variable | N | r |
|---|---|---|
| Forced expiratory volume (1 sec) | 969 | -.698** |
| Vital capacity | 971 | -.606** |
| Maximum breathing capacity | 1029 | -.547** |
| Systolic blood pressure | 1077 | .538** |
| Diastolic blood pressure | 1077 | .368** |
| Hemoglobin | 1071 | -.223** |
| Serum albumin | 777 | -.356** |
| Serum globulin | 777 | .092* |
| Creatinine clearance | 1051 | -.602** |
| Plasma glucose (OGT test) | 739 | .279** |
| Auditory threshold (4000 cps) | 862 | .549** |
| Visual acuity | 940 | -.306** |
| Visual depth perception | 935 | -.232** |
| Basal metabolic rate | 1035 | -.337** |
| Cortical bone percent | 983 | -.435** |
| Creatinine excretion | 1080 | -.538** |
| Hand grip stength | 943 | -.501** |
| Maximum work rate | 892 | -.511** |
| Benton visual memory test (errors) | 905 | .502** |
| Tapping time (medium targets) | 992 | .468** |
| Tapping time (close targets) | 991 | .366** |
| Reaction time (simple) | 687 | .287** |
| Reaction time (choice) | 701 | .220** |
| Foot reaction time | 734 | .222** |

*p<.05, **<.01

differs among the variables because each participant visit
to the Baltimore Longitudinal Study included only a fraction
of the total examination. Certain tests were begun a number
of years into the study, and much of the missing data
resulted from individuals who did not continue after the
initial visit, and therefore did not have all the tests.
All the correlation coefficients are statistically significant. Further screening analyses of these parameters
(Borkan, 1978) indicated that longitudinal slopes paralleled
cross-sectional trends for these variables, demonstrating

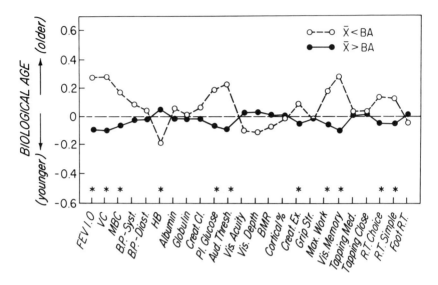

Fig. 1 Biological age profile comparison based on
educational status. Mean scores for subpopulations compared by Student's t-test,
* signifies p<.05.

that secular or cohort trends did not account for the
apparent age-relatedness of these variables.

The subject population was divided into two groups for
comparison based on education (Fig. 1): those who had a
junior college diploma or less (264 individuals) and those
with at least a bachelors degree (787 individuals). We
hypothesized that the less educated group would be biologically older than the more educated group, because more
educated people have better health care, longer life
expectancy, and safer work conditions. However, it is
possible that less educated individuals could be at an
advantage if they have more active occupations. The results
of this analysis show that the less educated group was
biologically older in 17 of 24 variables, and 10 of these
are statistically significant. Significant differences
occur for the three lung measures, plasma glucose, auditory
function, creatinine excretion, maximum work rate, visual
memory, and reaction times. These comparisons indicate that
the less educated group was biologically older in variables
that reflect physiological function and health (the left

side of the profile), were capable of less work, and slower on psychomotor tests. Their poorer visual memory may reflect the influence of education on scores on this test.

Reversals of expectation are notable in hemoglobin and less so in vision, in which the less educated group was biologically younger. Thus, their visual capability was more youthful (i.e. better) but their auditory function was worse than the more educated group. This may reflect hazards of their work environment.

In summary, the biological age profile of less educated individuals indicates generally greater biological age on physiological variables and on psychomotor tasks. Their body composition was very slightly more youthful, meaning that they were somewhat larger in body size than the more educated group.

In stratifying the sample by marital status (Fig. 2) the results are again not reflective of the average U.S. population, as the present group showed greater marital stability. 85 percent were presently married, 5 percent were never married, and 10 percent were widowed, separated, or divorced. The two subpopulations for comparison were the group of men who were presently married and the group which had never married, or were widowed, separated, or divorced. These two groups contain all the individuals for whom marital information was available.

We hypothesized that non-married individuals would have generally greater biological age because married men tend to have greater personal stability and longer life expectancy than non-married men. This hypothesis was supported by the finding that on 19 of 24 test variables, non-married men had greater biological age than married men (Figure 2). Cortical bone percentage was the only significant difference, although moderate differences were observed for lung function, blood pressure, and psychomotor tests. Of the five variables which reversed expectation none were near statistical significance.

From this analysis it is evident that non-married men were biologically older than married men on many aging parameters, but not substantially so. While this may be attributable to the beneficial influence of married life, it is also possible that individuals who never marry or who do

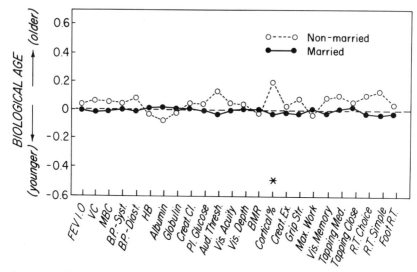

Fig. 2   Biological age profile comparison based on marital
status.  Mean scores for subpopulations are compared
by t-test, * signifies p<.05.

not remain married are a subset of the total population with
less favorable health physical characteristics.

One of the questionnaires filled out by subjects in the
Baltimore Longitudinal Study is "Your Activities and Attitudes" by Burgess, Cavan and Havighurst (Fig. 3).   As
directed in the scoring manual, the scores on four of the
questions were combined to yield a rating of general health
and vitality.  The subpopulations for comparison were the 15
percent of the sample with the poorest health scores (3.5
points or less) and the 15 percent with the best health
scores (9.5 points or more).

We hypothesized that individuals whose health was poor
might be biologically older than those in good health,
because it is a frequent observation that illness accelerates the aging process, at least on the basis of visual
estimation.  This hypothesis was vigorously supported by the
profile comparisons (Figure 3) in which all 24 variables
were in the expected direction.   Significant differences
were found in the three lung variables, two serum proteins,
hearing, vision, and maximum work rate.

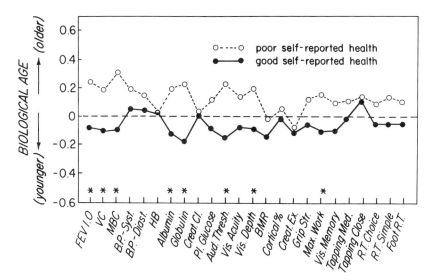

Fig. 3  Biological age profile comparison based on
self-reported health.  Mean scores for subpopulations are compared by Student's t-test,
* signifies p<.05.

The results of this comparison demonstrate that the mean
profile of individuals in poor health was biologically older
than for those who were healthy.  Since illness and aging
are positively correlated, the close relationship between
biological age and health is not surprising.  Whether illness actually accelerates the processes of aging or merely
simulates their appearance is not demonstrated in the
pattern profile analysis.  What is shown is that unhealthy
people have the physical, sensory, and psychomotor traits of
persons chronologically older than themselves.

The foregoing analyses demonstrate the association of
biological age with personal background and lifestyle.  We
also examined the heritability of biological age using the
biological age profile technique.  To study this problem, 96
father-son and 51 brother-brother pairs in the population
were identified.  This large number of related individuals
may be traced to the mode of subject recruitment which
allowed participants to recommend the study to friends and
relatives.

TABLE 2
Correlation of biological age scores
between related individuals

| Variable | Father-Son N | R | Sig. | Brother-Brother N | R | Sig. |
|---|---|---|---|---|---|---|
| Forced expiratory volume | 91 | .144 | | 48 | .006 | |
| Vital capacity | 91 | .248 | * | 48 | .151 | |
| Max. breathing capacity | 94 | .061 | | 50 | .196 | |
| Systolic blood pressure | 95 | .126 | | 50 | .277 | |
| Diastolic blood pressure | 95 | .079 | | 50 | .209 | |
| Hemoglobin | 94 | .129 | | 50 | .365 | ** |
| Albumin | 62 | .305 | ** | 37 | .443 | ** |
| Globulin | 62 | .300 | * | 37 | .271 | |
| Creatinine clearance | 93 | .100 | | 51 | .037 | |
| Plasma glucose | 63 | .120 | | 34 | .134 | |
| Auditory threshold | 79 | .311 | ** | 45 | .069 | |
| Visual acuity | 91 | .163 | | 47 | -.096 | |
| Depth perception | 91 | .031 | | 47 | .092 | |
| Basal metabolic rate | 92 | .039 | | 48 | .306 | * |
| Cortical bone percent | 92 | .319 | ** | 43 | .445 | ** |
| Creatinine excretion | 95 | .308 | ** | 51 | .211 | |
| Grip strength | 81 | .071 | | 37 | .088 | |
| Maximum work rate | 78 | .005 | | 36 | .158 | |
| Visual memory | 85 | .115 | | 40 | .237 | |
| Tapping rate (MN) | 91 | .430 | ** | 49 | .490 | ** |
| Tapping rate (SN) | 91 | .363 | ** | 49 | .456 | ** |
| Reaction time (choice) | 56 | .337 | * | 35 | .182 | |
| Reaction time (simple) | 56 | .095 | | 36 | .185 | |
| Foot reaction time | 63 | .318 | * | 40 | .131 | |

* p<.05, ** p<.01

We correlated the scores of fathers and sons for each of the 24 profile variables (cross-sectional data) and the same for brother-brother pairs. The correlations and their significance levels are given in Table 2. We expected that the correlations between pairs of unrelated individuals should be zero, and that significant positive correlations would suggest a familial and possibly genetic aspect to biological age status.

All but one of the correlations in Table 2 were positive and a substantial number reached statistical significance. High correlations were found for some of the blood biochemistry measures, for some body composition measures, and for tapping and reaction time tests. The differences in correlation levels between variables suggest that the familial component of some aspects of aging is greater than for others. It should be remembered that these results may reflect the influence either of genes or common home environment and shared lifestyle. Therefore, such correlations do not prove that genetic inheritance is a factor in biological age status, though it is clearly a strong possibility.

The foregoing comparisons demonstrate statistically significant differences in biological age status between individuals. However, it is important to bear in mind the assumptions and limitations of the approach. The technique is based on the view that an individual's scores on age related variables, when compared to his chronological age peers, are an indication of his biological age. This is very similar to when a physician tells a patient he has the lung capacity of someone 20 years younger. In this case the physician is making the suggestion that the patient has changed (aged) less than others of his same age group. Of course the patient may have always had a high score on this parameter, due to genetic endowment, large body size, athletic training, or pure chance. The extent to which the man's lung function reflects his actual rate of pulmonary change is the extent to which such an observation is a good measure of aging.

Another problem, true of all aging research, is the differentiation of aging from disease. It is well accepted that advancing age is associated with increased incidence of many diseases. There are few parameters in the biological age profile which could not be viewed as aspects of health as well as aging, and none on which truly poor scores would not be of medical concern. Considerable debate could be undertaken to prove whether this or any aging profile measures aging or disease. But from a practical standpoint such an argument is moot, because these are all measures of functional status in late adulthood, and are indications of relative viability of the individual. And ultimately, the purpose of aging research is to improve the health and well being of the last part of the life cycle. Whether these variables are measures of aging or disease becomes less important.

The approaches reported here are one way in which it is possible to examine factors which may possibly influence the course of aging. The biological age test battery proposed is not immutable, but can be composed of any measures that are indicative of aging. Indeed, there could be an entire profile devoted to visual function or exercise performance, rather than the broad one described. The important aspect is that the parameters in the profile comprise significant aspects of the aging process. Particularly important would be inclusion of parameters which represent the basic biochemical "causes" of aging. When these underlying processes of aging are identified, they can be incorporated into a profile technique such as the one describe here to learn which pharmacological agents or behavioral traits may influence the course of the aging process.

LITERATURE CITED

Bell B (1972). Significance of functional age for interdisciplinary and longitudinal research in aging. Aging Hum Devel 3:145.
Borkan GA (1978). The assessment of biological age during adulthood. (Doctoral Dissertation, University of Michigan), Dissertation Abstracts International, 39/06-A:3682. (University Microfilms No. 78-2286).
Borkan GA, Norris AH (1980). Assessment of biological age using a profile of physical parameters. J Gerontol 35:177.
Brown KS, Forbes WF (1976). Concerning the estimation of biological age. Gerontology 22:428.
Clark JW (1960). Aging dimension: a factorial analysis of individual differences with age of psychological and physiological measurements. J Gerontol 15:183.
Costa PT Jr, McCrae RR (1980). Functional age: a conceptual and empirical critique. In Haynes GS, Feinleib M (eds): Epidemiology of Aging. NIH Pub. No. 80-969.
Dirken JM (1972). Functional age of industrial workers. Groningen, Netherlands: Wolters-Noordhoff.
Furukawa T, Inoue TM, Kajiya F, Takeda H, Abe H (1975). Assessment of biological age by multiple regression analysis. J Gerontol 30:422.
Garn SM (1977). Patterning in ontogeny, taxonomy, phylogeny, and dysmorphogenesis. In Wetherington RK (ed):

Colloquia on Anthropology, The Fort Burgwin Research Center 1:83.
Hansen GC (1973). An epidemiologic investigation of the effect of biologic age on the breakdown of periodontal tissues. J Peridontol 44:269.
Heikkinen E, Kiskinen A, Kayhty B, Rimpela M, Vouri I (1974). Assessment of biological age: methodological study of two Finish populations. Gerontologia 20:33.
Hollingsworth JW, Hashizuma A, Jablon S (1965). Correlations between tests of aging in Hiroshima subjects: an attempt to define "physiologic age". Yale J Biol Med 38:11.
Jalavisto E, Makkonen T (1963). On the assessment of biological age. I. A factor analysis of physiological measurements in old and young women. Ann Acad Sci Fenn Med 100:1.
Schlesselman JJ (1973). Planning a longitudinal study: I. Sample size determination. II. Frequency of measurement and study duration. J Chron Dis 26:553.
Stone JL, Norris AH (1966). Activities and attitudes of participants in the Baltimore Longitudinal Study. J Gerontol 21:575.
Webster IW, Logie AR (1976). A relationship between age and health status in female subjects. J Gerontol 31:546.

Intervention in the Aging Process, Part A: Quantitation, Epidemiology, and
Clinical Research, pages 113–125
© 1983 Alan R. Liss, Inc., 150 Fifth Avenue, New York, NY 10011

THE H-SCAN  - AN INSTRUMENT FOR THE AUTOMATIC
MEASUREMENT OF PHYSIOLOGICAL MARKERS OF AGING

Richard Hochschild
Hoch Company
2915 Pebble Drive
Corona del Mar, California 92625

Test batteries to assess biological,
physiological or functional age have been utilized
in the past by Hollingsworth et al. (1965), Conard
et al. (1966), Dirken (1972), Furokawa et al.
(1975), and others.  In the H-SCAN, fourteen
age-sensitive tests are brought together for the
first time in a single instrument which is
computer-driven and does not need an operator.

Looking a bit like an unusual video game set,
with a screen, six push-buttons, earphones, a
breathing tube, an optical viewer, vibrometers,
printer, and so on, the unit fits on a desk top.


SUMMARY OF OPERATION

After name, height and age are entered, the
keyboard is covered with a metal cover.  The H-SCAN
then goes to work automatically, giving the
participant step-by-step instructions on the screen
for performing each test.  Aside from the initial
information that is keyed in, the tests are
self-administered by the participant without need
for a test operator.

If the participant makes an error in technique
(or tries to cheat), the computer responds -
sometimes with humor - giving individualized
instructions about what was done wrong and how to

correct the procedure.

At the end of testing, the H-SCAN prints out
the results in duplicate (one copy for the
participant), giving scores obtained on each test
and the age of which each score is typical. The
computed test ages depend on sex (and for lung
function, on height as well) and are based on
results obtained for a heterogeneous reference
population which currently consists of about 1,400
subjects. As the final item on the printout, the
participant's net "H-SCAN age" is given, a
combination of the individual test ages.


ADVANTAGES OF H-SCAN FORMAT

We know of few if any medical tests that are
routinely enjoyed by participants. An H-SCAN
session is an exception. Participants regularly
comment that they found the tests fun to perform,
and there is no lack of volunteers when the tests
are offered. Most persons are interested in
learning their H-SCAN test age.

A typical test takes four minutes, the entire
H-SCAN session about 45 minutes. This compares with
half-day sessions previously required to administer
the same tests using operators and separate
instruments for each test. When 6 H-SCANS are used
together, 50 or more subjects can be tested in an
8-hour day.

Besides participant acceptability and speed,
another advantage of the H-SCAN format is
standardization. In earlier test batteries, the
operator was a source of variabilty. Not only do
different test operators instruct and motivate
subjects differently, but the same operator may
interact differently with subjects at different
times of the day. By executing its program in a
reproducible manner, the H-SCAN offers uniformity of
instruction and motivation. Results obtained at
different locations may be compared and combined.

Data collection occurs automatically onto the

same diskette which carries the program. Each diskette can hold some 23 items of test data for each of 150 participants. From these diskettes, the data for a given study is copied and combined onto special data-only diskettes, reformatted and transferred to the analysis computer, avoiding potential errors due to manual data entery steps.

But the most obvious and pleasant advantage of the H-SCAN is the ability to test large numbers of participants with almost no manpower investment and no training of operators - or worry if they are doing their job right.


CRITERIA FOR TEST SELECTION

In designing the H-SCAN, we surveyed over 250 clinical tests reported in the literature as candidate physiological and psychological - i.e. functional - markers of aging. A number of those which appeared most promising were first used by us on subject populations in non-computer-driven form to further evaluate their potential for inclusion in a fully automated battery.

The final selection was based on statistical parameters (especially correlation coefficients vs. chronological age), mimimum redundancy of body systems tested, adaptability to the computer-driven format, length of time required by the test, and relevance of the test to mental and physical faculties that are important in handling every-day tasks and challenges. I.e., besides the quantitative considerations, we wanted the H-SCAN to be testing functions whose decline with age is recognizably associated with the quality of life.


HARDWARE AND SOFTWARE DEVELOPMENT

Since some of the needed computer circuits and test apparatus did not exist, we developed them. With the exception of lung function, none of the selected tests had been previously automated, and this produced some hardware design challenges.

Especially time consuming, but ultimately highly successful, was the design of a computer driven lens system for the measurement of visual accommodation.

Most of the development time went into writing the software and revising it as experience with the tests showed how they could be made to run more smoothly.

AGE-EQUIVALENTS OF OBTAINED SCORES

Data accumulated on the 1,400 participants tested to date shows that the regression curves relating test scores to chronological age by sex are nonlinear for each test. Coefficients for cubic equations relating score to age for each test, by sex, have been computed from the available data. These coefficients are entered into the computer program for the printout to provide the age-equivalent shown for each obtained test score.

INDIVIDUAL TESTS IN THE H-SCAN PROTOCOL

The following is a list of the fourteen tests which currently make up the H-SCAN battery, a brief description of how each test is performed and examples of scores obtained by subjects near opposite ends of the age range.

HIGHEST AUDIBLE PITCH

The participant puts on earphones (capable of reproducing up to 21,000 Hz) and listens to a tone which randomly starts and stops while it rises or falls in pitch. As long as the tone is heard, the participant presses a button. When the tone is not heard, he releases the button. Tone volume remains a constant 80 DB over the entire available range of pitch from 2,600 Hz to 21,000 Hz.

The computer senses when the tone (which starts in mid-range) is too high to be heard, responds by reducing the pitch in small steps until it is once more heard and then raises the pitch again. After several passes through the upper boundary zone of audibility, the computer records the highest pitch heard. Because the tone turns on and off for periods of random length, the test is cheat-proof. (Participants with a hearing deficit are given the opportunity to skip this test).

On average, the highest pitch that an 18-year-old male can hear is 18,100 Hz. For the average 70-year-old male, it is 6,000 Hz.

AUDITORY REACTION TIME

The participant presses a button as quickly as possible after hearing a tone (easily heard at all ages) on the earphones. Reaction time, in thousandths of a second, is displayed on the screen after each trial to challenge the participant to beat it. After a practice session of four trials, the test is repeated ten times, the five fastest times of response being averaged for the score. Premature depressions are caught and rejected.

Average reaction times for males are 0.114 sec at age 18, 0.168 sec at age 70. This loss with age may have several contributing CNS factors, especially an increase in synapse transmission time.

VISUAL REACTION TIME

This test is similar to the preceding test, but in place of the audible tone, the stimulus is a visual signal on the screen. In response, the participant quickly releases a button he was holding down. Waiting time before the signal is randomized in this and the other timing tests. The recorded score is the average of the best 5 of 10 trials after a practice session. Male response speed averages 0.175 sec at age 18, 0.280 sec at age 70.

MOVEMENT TIME

Measured simultaneously with visual reaction time, this is the time it takes for the finger to jump the 7 inch distance to a predetermined new button from the instant of release of the starting button, a measure of muscle movement speed.

Technique errors (premature response, use of two fingers, wrong target button, etc.) result in appropriate reprimands and instructions for doing it right. After the practice trials, the best 5 of 10 scored trials are averaged. Typical times for males: 0.122 sec at age 18, 0.281 sec at age 70.

REACTION TIME WITH DECISION

The target signal now jumps randomly from button to button and the object is to follow it rapidly with one finger. Timing is unpredictable. This test is similar to the first half of the preceding two-test combination, but the destination button is unknown until the visual signal appears above it. After each jump, the destination button becomes the start button for the next jump. If a wrong button is hit, that score is discarded and a jump is added. After the practice run, the 5 best of 10 good jumps are averaged.

The added decision step slows typical male scores to 0.180 sec at age 18, 0.315 sec at age 70.

MOVEMENT TIME WITH DECISION

Second half of the preceding procedure, this test measures the time required for the finger to travel to the new button (whose position cannot be anticipated) after the release of the start button, a measure of muscle movement speed when a decision step is added. Averages of the best 5 of 10 for males are: 0.120 sec at age 18, 0.240 at age 70.

LUNG FUNCTION #1: VITAL CAPACITY

The three lung function tests reflect the integrity of the overall respiratory system, including structural parameters, muscle strength and tissue elasticity. Participants with lung disease (or loose dentures) may elect to skip these tests.

Forced vital capacity (FVC) is measured by having the participant take the deepest breath possible and then blow it out forcefully and exhaustively through a 1" diameter, 6.5" long plastic tube. The best effort of 3 trials is recorded. According to the Framingham study, FVC is one of the best predictors of longevity.

The sensor is a heated thermistor centered in the breathing tube. A computer circuit calibrated for air at body temperature senses the cooling effect on the thermistor as air flows over it. The resulting change in thermistor resistance is converted to liters of air. A diaphragm allows only exhaled air to pass through the breathing tube.

At the same time as breath is exhaled through the tube, the curve of exhaled volume (vertically) vs. time (horizontally) is traced on the computer screen to help motivate the participant to maximum effort. Any prior curves stay on the screen for comparison during this maneuver. Incorrect technique is recognized by the computer and generates an "invalid trial" response followed by an explanation and a repeat of the trial.

Both sex and height (entered at the start of testing) are used in the subsequent computation of the age typical of the obtained vital capacity score. Lung function values tend to peak at age 25. At this age, on average, males 178 cm in height have a FVC of 6.03 liters. For 65-year-old males of the same height, the value is 4.87 liters.

LUNG FUNCTION #2: FEV-1

Forced Expiratory Volume-1 (FEV-1) is the air exhaled during the first second of a forced maximum exhalation. This data is extracted from the flow data generated for vital capacity - i.e. no new breathing effort is necessary. The breath computer integrates the volume exhaled during the first second of each of the three valid trials, recording the best FEV-1 (which may come from a different effort than best FVC.)

Males aged 25 and 178 cm in height have an average FEV-1 of 4.90 liters. This drops to 3.82

liters for 65-year-old males of the same height.

LUNG FUNCTION #3:  PEAK FLOW

Measured along with FVC and FEV-1 in the same
three breathing efforts, peak flow (PF) is the flow
rate at the steepest portion of the volume vs. time
curve, in liters per minute. Again, the best of the
three scores is recorded. At age 25, 178 cm high
males reach 590 l/min on average. At age 70,
average PF is 465 l/min.

TOUCH SENSITIVITY

Sensitivity of touch is measured at the finger
tip by means of a 120 Hz mechanical vibration. The
participant holds a small round magnet, about the
size of a dime but 1/4" thick, between thumb and
index finger. He must identify which of three
target areas is the source of the vibration in the
magnet (produced by solenoids energized with 120 Hz
current under the target areas).

Following each correct identification, the
vibration drops one step in amplitude. After each
erroneous response, vibration amplitude rises one
step. Target location may change randomly or remain
the same for the next trial. The procedure is
repeated until the amplitude boundary between a
perceptable vibration and an imperceptable one has
been crossed several times and carefully defined by
the computer.

Males aged 18 score 23 (arbitrary units) on
average. The average score for 70-year-old males is
12. This reflects an age-associated decrement in
the function and number of touch receptors.

RECOGNITION OF INCOMPLETE PICTURES

After two practice pictures, a series of 21
pictures flashes on the screen. The pictures are
rough line drawings of common objects (tree, house,
cup, woman, etc.) but they are incomplete, random
parts having been omitted to make the identification
difficult. The participant is asked to identify the

object shown by depressing the button (one of six) under the letter with which the name of the object begins. If there is no response in 8 seconds, the next picture appears.

Scores recorded are number of pictures right, number not answered and average time (sec) taken to identify a picture. The picture recognition test measures perceptual organization and the ability to concentrate, and is quite age sensitive. Males aged 18 identify 16 pictures correctly on average. By age 70 the average number correctly identified is 10.

MEMORY

The H-SCAN memory test is designed to be uninfluenced by differences in verbal, numerical or tonal memory or memory for shapes. It is abstract in nature, involving a target spot that moves on the screen above the six push buttons. As the target jumps in an irregular sequence from button to button, the participant is asked to watch and memorize the sequence. Upon completion of the sequence, he is asked to repeat it by depressing the buttons in the same order.

The first sequence is 2 positions long. With each correct repetition by the participant, the previous sequence is repeated and one new position is added. If the participant makes an error, no position is added and the sequence is shown again. The test terminates after two errors in succession or when the sequence reaches a length of 16 positions. Length of the longest sequence correctly memorized and location of error are recorded.

On average, males aged 18 can remember an 11 position sequence while males aged 70 can remember a 7 position sequence.

ALTERNATE BUTTON TAPPING

This is a test of muscle speed, control and coordination. The object is to move one finger as rapidly as possible back and forth between two

buttons spaced 7 inches apart.  The score is the
time required to make 30 round trips.  Number of
misses is also recorded.

Males aged 18 require 16.2 sec on average to
make the 30 round trips while 70-year-old males
require an average time of 28.3 sec for the same
task.

VISUAL ACCOMMODATION

The usual way that this test is performed in an
opthalmologist's office is unadaptable to computer
operation.  The opthalmologist places one end of a
special kind of ruler on the participant's nose.  A
card with very small printed sentences on it is
positioned successively at various points along the
ruler.  The participant tries to read the card as it
is moved from far away to close up.  The ruler is
calibrated in diopters (and sometimes in age).  The
score is the diopter difference between the near and
far limits of readability.

The same test is performed in the H-SCAN by a
novel computer-driven lens system.  The participant
looks into a hand-held viewer (overall dimensions
3.5" x 5" x 5.5").  Visible in the viewer is a small
luminous red symbol, either a number or letter,
which changes after each look into the viewer.  The
object is to identify the symbol by pressing the
button (one of five) above which the symbol appears
on the screen.

Reading glasses may not be worn during the test
but glasses which provide distance vision may be
worn if desired.  (Such corrective lenses do not
invalidate the results as long as they are kept on
throughout the test.)  To assure that the eye
remains in the correct position with respect to the
viewer, a button on the viewer must be depressed
with the forehead before the symbol will light up.

To begin, the computer adjusts the viewer
optics to place the symbol near infinity, where it
is easily read by most participants.  After a
correct identification of the symbol, the computer

adjusts the position of the lens system to move the symbol still slightly farther away. These stepwise changes begin small but increase after each correct identification to shorten testing time (typically, the symbol is read about 24 times during this 4 minute test).

An error causes a reversal of direction by a small step. Direction is reversed again after the next correct identification. In this way, the far limit of focus is probed by moving the symbol through it two or three times. The computer then takes the symbol to the starting point and moves from there to probe the near limit of focus in the same way. The diopter difference between the near and far focal limits is computed and recorded as the score.

There is a dramatic decrease in visual accommodation with increasing age as the eye lens and lens capsule become less elastic, less easily deformable by the associated muscles. This explains why most persons begin to need reading glasses during their fourties. Visual accommodation differences can even be recognized between groups of 10- and 15-year-olds (suggesting that aging begins well before development ends).

The average 10-year-old has a focal range of 13.4 diopters. By age 15, this has dropped to 12.3 diopters. At age 30 it is 8.7, at age 40, 5.7. Then comes the precipitous change to 2.1 diopters by age 50, occasioning the need for reading glasses. At age 60, the average range is only 1.2 diopters, about 10% of the focal range which the average person had early in life.

H-SCAN APPLICATIONS

The H-SCAN was designed for group comparisons. In a clinical setting, it detects differences in certain markers of aging between a group receiving an active agent and a group receiving a placebo. Before-and-after comparisons may be made for individual members of each group to detect changes brought about during the period of administration.

In an epidemiological setting, the H-SCAN can be used to detect effects in groups exposed to different environmental, dietary or life style conditions.

For example, some 600 participants were recently H-SCAN tested at San Diego State University to determine if an exercise-oriented life style either retards or accelerates age changes. Both sexes were included and participants ranged in age from about 25 to 80, and in physical activity level from the completely sedentary to marathon runners. (It is hoped to follow up this study with an exercise-intervention study.)

Another application area is the study of effects of dietary habits on physiological markers of aging. Whole populations exist that follow unusual diets. Seventh Day Adventists, for example, are largely vegetarians and live 7 years longer, on average, than a comparable non-Adventist population. It would be interesting to know if, age-by-age, they score relatively younger on the H-SCAN as well.

A stimulus for studying environmental influences on aging is the observation by Sauer (1980) that some of the 3,055 counties of the United States are consistently long-lived while others are consistently short-lived.

In 82 long-lived counties, Sauer found that the natural causes, age-adjusted death rate for white males aged 35 to 74 is under 9.6 per thousand per year. In 21 short-lived counties, the death rate is over 20 per thousand per year. Such two-to-one differences translate into life span differences of about 7 years. This is not an effect due to differences in the average age of county populations since the rates are age-adjusted. Nor can it be explained by differences in the quality of medical care.

For reasons that are largely unknown, longevity depends on where one happens to live in the U.S.

(and of course elsewhere in the world). The impact
of identifying some of the responsible geographical
factors and of their subsequent modification is hard
to assess, but it goes without saying that it is
large. Involved is the health, functional capacity,
length of life and productivity in later life of
most of the population which does not live in the
longest-lived areas.

Since human longevity studies are too time
consuming and population-specific mortality data is
too coarse, biomarkers of aging now offer the best
approach to the identification of environmental,
dietary and life style influences on aging and the
clinical testing of intervention strategies.

REFERENCES

Conard A, Lowrey A, Eicher M, et al. (1966). Ageing
studies in a Marshallese population exposed to
radioactive fall-out in 1954. In Lindop & Sacher
(eds): "Radiation and Ageing," London: Taylor &
Francis, Ltd.
Dirken JM (1972). Functional age of industrial
workers. Gronigen, The Netherlands: Wolters-
Noordhoff.
Furukawa T, Inoue M, et al. (1975). Assessment of
biological age by multiple regression analysis. J.
Gerontology 30 (4):422-434.
Hollingsworth JW, Hashizume A, et al. (1965). Corre-
lation between tests of aging in Hiroshima
subjects: an attempt to define "physiologic age".
Yale J Biol & Med 38: 11-36.
Sauer H (1980). Geographic patterns in the risk of
dying and associated factors, ages 35-74 years,
U.S. Department of Health and Human Services
Publication No. 80-1402  Hyattsville, MD.

# CLINICAL RESEARCH AND
# EPIDEMIOLOGY

Intervention in the Aging Process, Part A: Quantitation, Epidemiology, and
Clinical Research, pages 129–139
© 1983 Alan R. Liss, Inc., 150 Fifth Avenue, New York, NY 10011

AN OVERVIEW: THEORETICAL CONSIDERATIONS AS TO INTERVENTION
IN THE AGING PROCESS: ALZHEIMER'S DISEASE AND AGING

F. Marott Sinex, Ph.D.

Section on Bio-Medical Gerontology
Boston University School of Medicine
80 East Concord Street, Boston, MA   02118

Our conference deals with how one might intervene in
the aging process, and thereby ensure better health and
longer life.  This theme was suggested by Dr. Jerry Williams,
a member of our scientific advisory committee.  The papers
speak to the complex nature of aging and the fact that
intervention in the aging process, given our present state
of knowledge, may involve a number of different therapies.
This is not to say that aging does not have one or more
primary causes in molecular terms, but they may affect a
number of enzymes, regulatory processes and body systems.
A rigorous system analysis of the failure of aging humans
is not possible at this time, but may some day be part of
the technology transfer to which the Fund for Integrative
Biomedical Research is dedicated.

A major part of this program deals with biomarkers for
aging.  To study aging we must be able to measure it.  If
we are to determine that a particular intervention procedure
helps, we will need to evaluate the benefit with minimal
risk and at reasonable cost.

The main themes of gerontology of the last forty years
run through our program.  We certainly owe a debt to E.V.
Cowdry (1939), Nathan Shock (1961) and H.S. Simms (1946).
Bernard Strehler advocated invertebrates for the study of
aging in his book, Time, Cells, and Aging, in 1962.  When
Meir Shinitsky talks of changes in the microviscosity of
cell membranes with age in this volume, one may hear faint
echoes of the crosslinkage of collagen, an earlier fashion
in physical structure.

While the aging of plants is in many instances hormone directed (Woolhouse, 1974), it has not been so clear that this is the case in human subjects. We now have a new array of neuropeptide hormones including releasing factors and releasing factor inhibitors to evaluate. New information will be reported on two hormone of particular interest to gerontologists, dehydroepiandosterone, and a new pituitary factor which may increase with age and inhibit the thyroid hormone.

Immunology is one of the success stories of gerontology. The immune system becomes less responsive with age. We don't know why, but this has enormous implications. We are fortunate to have Roy Walford, M.D. and Allen Goldstein, Ph.D. with us to talk of T cells, B cells and natural killer cells and interleukin, thymosin and HLA.

There is a good deal about nutrition, exercise and life style. I doubt that we will be able to modify aging with a single nutrient; however, it should become apparent during our discussion that some nutrients may be particularly important for the optimal support of the aging human. Dr. Lovenberg will tell us about how tetrahydrobiopterin, a nonvitamin cousin of folic acid may be an important support for the aging brain.

There is growing evidence that people will indeed live longer and healthier if they eat reasonable diets, exercise and avoid toxic things such as cigarettes. While we have a beginning design and evaluation of mutifactor support systems is going to be difficult with many methodological problems.

The mutation theory of aging (Sinex-1977; Williams, this volume) had fallen on bad times when it was rediscovered via repair. For repair to be significant, there must be injury. This does not necessarily mean that point mutation is important in mammalian aging, but recombinations and deletions may be. I regret that we do not have more on the organization of genes in the mammalian chromosome on the program. For the moment our molecular biological friends are concerned with problems such as cancer and embryogenesis. Aging is the other half of development and when we can make the link between aging, embryonic development and cancer, I believe, that important insights will follow.

I am among those who believe that the physical properties of chromatin in many cells change with age. Investigators tend to see in this change what they want to see: The search for changes in spacer regions (Berkowitz, 1983), in supercoiling, in methylation of DNA (Wilson and Jones, 1983), in gene activation, in protein composition, or in the rearrangement of chromosomal sequences.

I hope each of you can relate our program to your own experience. My colleagues and I at Boston University School of Medicine are searching for a group of genes whose regulation may be affected by aging, and which may be responsible for Alzheimer's disease, of particular concern to the elderly. To study regulation one must first find that which is regulated.

## ALZHEIMER'S DISEASE

The chances of developing Alzheimer's disease become more likely as we get older. This is true of all three forms which may be identified; the familial form, the senile dementia of the Alzheimer type and the dementia of the Down's adult. We have discussed the relationship between age of onset and inheritance in a previous paper (Sinex and Myers, 1982).

We really know little about why the elderly victims of senile dementia of Alzheimer type (SDAT) develop the disease even though they are a major component of our nursing home population. The victim is more likely to be a woman because women live longer. Inheritance in SDAT is difficult to establish, and the disease could originate for reasons having little to do with inheritance.

The separation of the form inherited as in autosomal dominant from senile dementia of the Alzheimer's type (SDAT) cannot be done with any great precision because the later Alzheimer's occurs in a family, the more likely death is from other causes (Larrson, 1963).

Alzheimer's disease's classical division into two forms with a separation at age 65 is too soon. The two or more forms of Alzheimer's must overlap to a considerable extent between the ages of 70 and 75 (Sinex and Myers, 1982). The figure shows the data that first suggested to us the bimodal distribution of Alzheimer's, and it also shows the appearance of new cases as a function of age.

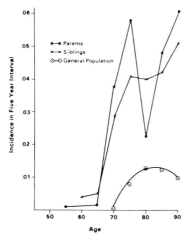

FIGURE 1. The incidence of Alzheimer's disease, from the data of Heston, at intervals of 5 years for the general population compared with that for first-degree relatives plotted against age. Assuming autosomal dominant inheritance, the incidence of the gene in the general population can be calculated.

In one of the most extensive families to be studied, originally described by Feldman and Froisant, age at diagnosis seems to vary from 35 to 70, with a median age of 50. This family has an unusually early age of onset, but in most familial, pedigrees the age of onset is later, perhaps 15 years, so that the number of cases appear to increase with age. This represents the left side of the distribution curve. Substantial numbers of those at risk, based on the principles of autosomal inheritance, never express the curve merges with the mortality curve. The majority of victims with the familial form of the disease contact the disease when they are healthy and vigorous (Seltzer and Shermin, 1983).

The third group of Alzheimer victims is particularly interesting. In their forties and fifties almost all Down's adults show the characteristic plaques and tangles, but while such pathology is quite evident, only a portion of these adults become demented (Ball and Nuttall, 1980; Lott 1982; Whalley, 1982; Wisniewski, 1982). The distribution of plaques and tangles in Alzheimer and Down's-Alzheimer brains is very similar but not identical. There seems to be more involvement of basal ganglia in Down's-Alzheimer's (Wisniewski, 1982), and some differences in the distribution of hippocampal lesions (Ball and Nuttall 1980).

The study of Alzheimer's disease is therefore not limited to a single group of victims. A number of different populations must be considered.

|  | | AGE-MATCHED |
| AT RISK | VICTIM | NORMAL CONTROLS |
| Down's victims<br>without dementia | Adult Down's<br>with dementia | Adults |
| First degree re-<br>lative victims | Familial Alz-<br>heimer's | Adults |
| Elderly | SDAT | Elderly |

The question of whether or not Alzheimer's is a focal disease that begins in a particular area of the brain, and then spreads to other areas is of critical importance in finding ways of preventing the disease, or retarding its progression. We have very little sequential pathological information because autopsies usually done on advanced patients.

If the disease is focal, are particular noncholinergic transmitters important at different stages of the disease such as norepinepherin. (Perry et al., 1981), dopamine, enkephalin or GABA (Roberts, 1982). We do know that there is some significant variation in the behavioral profile of early patients, and that the different stages of the disease show very different requirements for medication (Bartus, 1981). Depression is common in the early stages, while later on patients may become agitated and difficult to manage. The variable degrees of depression may reflect the loss in structures such as the locus coeruleus. In the final stages there may be convulsions and other symptons which seem autononic.

The cholinergic neurones of the association cortex play a central role in Alzheimer's disease, first because of the anatomical distribution of plaques and tangles, and second because of the rather substantial loss of choline acetyl-transferase (Davis, 1979). Neurofibrillary tangles and senile plaques are found in areas of the brain where the cells are primarily of a pyramidal type. Both types of lesion, qualitatively identical to those in Alzheimer's are found in the aging brain but are much less prominent. In Alzheimer's the lesions are centered in areas receiving cholinergic innervation, particularly the hippocampus temporal lobe and the amygdala while the motor and sensory cortex is usually spared (Kemper, 1983a, Kemper 1983b). Neuronal loss is a more wide spread phemomina as is decreased blood flow and glucose utilization (Frachowiski, 1981; Invar 1981).

Coyle, Price and Delong (1983), believe that the first cells involved in Alzheimer's disease are those in the septal region which contains such structure as the nucleus basalis of Meynert, and the substantia inominata. From the septal region cholinergic afferents go to the association cortex and the hippocampus. There is still the question of what might drive the septal area prior to these cholinergic tracts, and what other structures might be affected in turn.

In early onset conventional Alzheimer's there is considerable cell loss in the locus coeruleus (Bondareff, 1981). While there is a marked decline in the number of cells in the locus coeruleus after 70 in normal populations, the victims of late onset do not seem to show much additional loss (Perry et al 1981). The loss of cells in the locus coeruleus with age has attracted considerable attention among gerontologists (Brody, 1979), and is considered one of the most obvious changes in the aging brain.

The noradrenergic innervation of the hippocampus which seems to be involved in memory loss originates in the locus coeruleus. The fibers reach the hippocampus by ascending via the forebrain bundle through the caudate into the septal region. Other locus coeruleus axones enter the hippocampus from the corpus callosum (Carpentier, 1982). It is reasonable to assume the fibers from the locus ceoruleus also enter the septal region directly from the forebrain bundle and innervate the substantia innomenata and nucleus basalis of Meynert. Thus, in some individuals Alzheimer's may begin in the locus coeruleus and end in the amygdala taking out large regions of association cortex in between.

How much of the Alzheimer effort should be devoted to cholinergic systems, and how much to other transmitters is an important issue to investigators of Alzheimer's disease and the pharmaceutical industry. Contemporary studies with choline acetyl agonists or physostigmine can be considered either encouraging or discouraging depending on one's point of view. Some individuals seem helped.

The possibility that significant initial aging changes, which were once though of as rather global, may be restricted to some discrete sections of the brain has important implications for preventing neurological illness. For example, locus coeruleus neurones require tyrosine hydroxylase for the synthesis of norepinepherine. The cofactor for tyrosine hydroxylase is tetrahydrobiopterin which is becoming available for clinical trail and which will be discussed by Drs. Lovenberg, Levine and Folkers (this volume).

Lymphocytes are available throughout the course of the disease, and may provide new clinical and metabolic clues. My colleague, Dr. Linda Kraus of the Department of Neurology, (Kraus, 1982) has observed a decrease in natural killer cell function in Alzheimer's. This is most clearly seen in the lysis of target cells when lysis is plotted against effector/target cells ratio. Under these circumstances the Alzheimer subjects show a flatter response and seem less responsive to interferon. It would seem that the maturation and recruitment of natural killer cells is retarded in Alzheimer's disease, and might be related to the changes in the brain or in gene expression. Lymphocytes have a rather full complement of receptors for neurotransmitters, (Katz, et al., 1981) and in a sense express a memory.

In our studies at Boston University, we have sought a human gene segment that seemed to change with age, so that we could study its regulatory function (Sinex and Meyers 1982; Sinex, 1983). The presence of a segment of Alzheimer gene on the long arm of chromosome 21 seemed a possibility. An individual who has three copies of this chromosome, has Down's syndrome, and as discussed previously, Down's adults develop Alzheimer's disease. There are five known loci on this chromosome: glycinamide ribonucleotide synthetase (Bartley and Epstein, 1980), aminoimidazole ribonucleotide synthetase (Irvin and Patterson, 1979), liver phosphofructokinase (Vora and Francke, 1981), the receptor for alpha interferon (Epstein, et al. 1982), and superoxide dismutase (Phillip et al., 1978).

We have searched for elevated levels of the products

of the five loci in Alzheimer patients, using lymphocytes as a test system. We are still studying liver phosphofructokinase and interferon receptor. Such studies are complicated by the general depression of lymphocyte metabolism which seems to occur in Alzheimers. It would seem important to study Down's adults with and without Alzheimer's disease.

Perhaps the most important variable in Alzheimer's is age of onset. If it occurs early it is a catastrophe, and if significantly late it may never be expressed. Age of onset may be most easily studied in families in which the disease is inherited, where at least part of the genetic casuality of the disease can be assumed to be the same. Studying the disease in the elderly may be more difficult, with more physiological variables to consider.

Whether extending life span would increase or decrease the incidence of senile dementia is a matter of speculation. I believe life extension will make a bimodal distribution of the disease more obvious. Survival might make it more probable that first degree relatives of the familial group would not escape the disease, so there might be an increase in early onset of 50-70 percent. However, there is the other group of late onset elderly. Whether extended life span would increase or decrease the number of demented persons in nursing homes may depend on the means we use to increase longevity that would affect the brain as opposed to other organ systems, such as the heart.

Dementia is not an acceptable price to pay for the long life we are beginning to enjoy and, therefore, is a problem that must be solved.

## REFERENCES

Ball, M.J. and Nuttall, K. (1980) Neurofibrillary tangles, granulovacular degeneration and neuron loss in Down's syndrome. Neurology 30, 639-44.

Bartus, R.T. and Dean, R.L., (1981) Age related memory loss and drug therapy: possible directions based on animal models. In Brain Neurotransmitters and Receptors in Aging and Age-Related Disorders, Enna, S.J. Samorajski, T. and Bee, B. Eds. Raven, New York, 209-223.

Berkowitz, E.M. Sanborn, A.C. and Vaughn, D.W. (1983) (this volume) Chromatin structure in neuronal and neuroglical cell nuclei as a function of age. Jour. Neurochem. in press.

Bondareff, W. (1981). Selective loss of neurones of origin of adrenergic projection to cerebral cortex (neucleus locus coeruleus in senile dementia). Lancet 1, 783-4.

Carpenter, M.B. and Sutbin, J. (1983). Human Neuroanatomy, 8th ed. Williams and Wilkins, Baltimore, pages 403-406.

Coyle, J.T. Price, D.L. and Delong, M.R. (1983). Alzheimer's disease: A disease of critical cholinergic innervation. Science 219, 1184-90.

Cowdry E.V., (1939). Problem of Aging, Biological and Medical Aspects. Baltimore.

Davis, P. (1979). Neurotransmitter related enzymes in senile dementia of the Alzheimer type. Brain Research 171, 319-27.

Frachowisk, R.S.J., Poyzill, C., Legg, N.J., Du Boulay, G.H., Marshall, J., Lenzi, G.L. and Jones, T. (1981). Regional cerebral oxygen supply and utilization in dementia. A clinical and physiological study with oxygen-15 and position tomography. Brain 104, 753-78.

Herzog, A.G. and Kemper, T.L. Amydaloid changes in aging and dementia. Arch. Neurol. 37, 625-29 (1980).

Katz P., Zaytoum, M. and Farci, A.S. (1983). Modulation of natural killer cell activity by cyclic nucleotides. Jour. Immunol. 129, 287-76.

Kemper, T.L. (1983a). Neurochemical and neuropathological changes in aging, In: The Clinical Neurology of Aging. Albert, M.L. (Ed). Oxford Univ. Press, In Press

Kemper, T.L. (1983b). Organization and neuropathology of the amygdala in Alzheimer's disease. Cold Springs Harbor Symposium, Oct. 24, 1982, Cold Springs Harbor (in press)

Kraus, L. (1982). Human natural killer cell activity and association with neurologic disease, Ph.D. Thesis University Microfilms, Ann Arbor, Mich.

Larrson, T., Sjogren, T. and Jacobson, S. (1963). Senile
dementia. A clinical, sociomedical and genetic study
Acta Pschiat. Scand., Suppl., 167, 1-259.

Lott, I. Down's syndrome, aging and Alzheimer's disease
A clinical review. Alzheimer's Disease, Down's Syndrome
and Aging, by Sinex, F.M. and Merril, C., ed. Annals New
York Acad. Science, 396, 151-19.

Lovenberg, W., Levine, R.A. and Folkers, C. Regulation of
biogenics amine synthestase by the hydroxylase cofactor and
its relation to aging and Parkinsonism, (this volume).

Perry, E.K., Tomilinson, B.E., Blessed, G., Perry, R.H.,
Cross, A.J. and Crow, T.J. Neuropathological and biochemical
observations on the noradrenergic system in Alzheimer's
disease. Jour. Neurol. Sciences 51, 279-87, (1981).

Roberts, E. Potential therapies in aging and senile
dementia: In Sinex, F.M. and Merril, C.R. ed. Alzheimer's
Disease, Down's Syndrome and Aging, Annals New York Acad.
396, 165-178.

Rossor, M.N. (1981). Parkinson's disease and Alzheimer's
disease as disorders of the isodendritic core. British
Medical Jour. 283, 1588-90 (1981).

Seltzer, B. and Sherwin, 1. A comparison of clinical
features in early and late-onset primary degenerative dementia.
Achieves of Neurology 40, 143-46, (1983).

Shock, N.W., (1961). Physiological aspects of aging in man.
Ann Rev. Physiol. 23, 97-122.

Sims, H.S. (1946). Logarithmic increase in mortality as a
manifestation of age. J. Gerontl. 1, 13-26.

Sinex, F.M. (1977). The molecular genetics of aging; in
Handbook of the Biology of Aging, Finch, C.E. and Hayflick,
L. eds., Van Nostrand, New York, pages 39-62.

Sinex, F.M. and Myers, R.H. (1982). Alzheimer's disease,
Down's syndrome and Aging in: Alzheimer's Disease, Down's
Syndrome and Aging, by Sinex, F.M. and Merril, C., ed.
Annals New York Acad. Science, 396, 3-12.

Strehler, B.H. (1962). Times Cells and Aging, New York, Academic Press.

Whalley, A.J. (1982). The dementia of Down's syndrome and its relevance to aetiological studies of Alzheimer disease: In Sinex, F.M., and Merril, C. ed., Alzheimer's Disease, Down's Syndrome and Aging, Annals New York Acad. of Science, 396, 39-54.

Williams, J. (this volume, Part B).

Wilson V.L. and Jones, P.A. (1983). DNA methylation decreases in aging but not in immortal cells. Science 220, 1055-57.

Wisniewski, K.E., French, J.H., Rosen, J.F., Kozlowski, P. B., Tenner, M. and Wisniewski, H.M. (1982). Basal ganglia calification (BGC) in Down's syndrome (DS)-Another manisfestation of premature aging: In Sinex, F.M. and Merril; C.R. ed. Alzheimer's Disease, Down's Syndrome and Aging, Annals New York Acad. Science, New York, pages, 179-91.

Woolhouse, H.W. (1974). Longevity and senescence in plants, Science Progress, (Oxford) 61, 123-47.

Intervention in the Aging Process, Part A: Quantitation, Epidemiology, and
Clinical Research, pages 141–149
© 1983 Alan R. Liss, Inc., 150 Fifth Avenue, New York, NY 10011

EPIDEMIOLOGY OF AGING:  SEVENTH-DAY ADVENTISTS - A
BELLWETHER FOR FUTURE PROGRESS

David A. Snowdon, Ph.D., M.P.H.

Schools of Health and Medicine,
Loma Linda University
Loma Linda, CA 92350

AGING AND HUMAN FUNCTIONS

Aging is characterized by changes in biological and
psychological functions.  As a child ages there are
improvements in physical and mental functions.  As the
adolescent matures and enters adult life there are declines in
some physical functions (e.g. coordination) and improvements
in other functions (e.g. mental and emotional).  As the adult
ages several functions may change.  There may be a gradual
loss of hearing, a change of some healthy tissues into
diseased tissues, and sometimes an improvement in a person's
outlook on life.  So aging is not just the occurrence of
dysfunction in older individuals.  Aging is the sum of
positive and negative changes in human function that are
associated with the passage of time.

Aging is a necessary and inevitable component of human
life.  Various aspects of aging, however, can be eliminated or
deferred.  Death can be postponed until a later age, and
biological and psychological dysfunction associated with aging
can be eliminated or at least delayed.

LENGTH AND QUALITY OF LIFE

Unquestionably the average American lifespan could be
greatly extended by reducing the rate of occurrence of the top
four causes of death - heart disease, cancer, stroke, and
accidents (Table 1).  Luckily there is substantial overlap in
the etiology of the top three killers.  For example, cigarette

TABLE 1

THE TEN LEADING CAUSES OF DEATH IN THE
UNITED STATES, 1980

| RANK | CAUSE OF DEATH | NUMBER OF DEATHS IN 1980 [a] IN THE U.S. |
|---|---|---|
| 1 | Heart Disease | 751,000 |
| 2 | Cancer | 411,000 |
| 3 | Stroke | 168,000 |
| 4 | Accidents | 104,000 |
| 5 | Chronic obstructive pulmonary diseases and allied diseases | 54,000 |
| 6 | Pneumonia and influenza | 50,000 |
| 7 | Diabetes mellitus | 34,000 |
| 8 | Chronic liver disease and cirrhosis | 30,000 |
| 9 | Atheroslerosis | 29,000 |
| 10 | Suicide | 26,000 |

[a] Source of information is National Center for Health
Statistics, 1982.

smoking is a major cause of both heart disease and cancer,
while diabetes and high blood pressure are major causes of
heart disease and stroke. The fourth leading cause of death,
accidents, is a major killer of the very young (by motor
vehicle accidents) and the very old (by falls). The majority
of accidents could be prevented by a lifestyle change (e.g.
reduction of excessive alcohol use) and by engineering a safer
environment (e.g. safer cars or padded linoleum that,
respectively absorb the initial impact of vehicular crash
or a human fall).

Engineering a safer environment, reducing cigarette
smoking, and controlling diabetes and high blood pressure
could extend the average American lifespan and improve the
quality of life. Other tentatively identified or yet to be
identified factors may also have a major impact on the length
and quality of life. A rich source of new information on the
causes of disease are populations that have an unusually low
risk of disease, such as the Seventh-day Adventists.

SEVENTH-DAY ADVENTISTS

Members of the Seventh-day Adventist Church have a low
risk for each of the ten leading causes of death in the U.S.
(Phillips, et al 1980; Phillips, 1975).   This reduction in
risk is probably due, in part, to their unique lifestyle.
Adventists generally avoid the use of alcohol, tobacco,
spices, and pork.  Adventists are also encouraged to
avoid the use of meat and fish, as well as
caffeine-containing beverages.  Approximately 50% of all
Adventists adhere to a lacto-ovo-vegetarian diet--a
vegetarian diet that includes egg and milk products.


ELIMINATE OR POSTPONE DISEASE

Some aspects of the Adventist lifestyle may result
in the elimination or postponement of some causes of
death.  For example, the virtual absence of cigarette
smoking among Adventists has resulted in the almost total
elimination of lung cancer. While lung cancer is the most
common cancer in American men, it is a rare cancer among
Adventist men.  The absence of cigarette smoking also may
explain, in part, the Adventists low risk of heart
disease.  Heart disease, however, accounts for the same
percentage of deaths among Adventists as in the U.S.
general population.  This means that non-smoking probably
postpones, rather than eliminates, the development
of fatal heart disease.  Therefore, in general,
lifestyle and environmental factors may influence aging
by either eliminating or postponing the appearance of
disease.


TEN MODIFIABLE FACTORS

Other factors, besides non-smoking, also influence
the production and prevention of disease in Adventists.
Table 2 presents ten modifiable lifestyle factors that
conceivably could explain the low risk of major diseases
in Adventists.  The first factor, cigarette smoking, is
clearly related to a major proportion of disease,
disability, and death in the American public.  The
Adventist church proscribes the use of tobacco.  The lack
of smoking in Adventists is one of the major reasons for
their low risk for a multitude of diseases including

heart disease and cancer.

TABLE 2

TEN MODIFIABLE LIFESTYLE FACTORS THAT EITHER ARE
RELATED, OR MAY BE RELATED TO DISEASE PRODUCTION

| MODIFIABLE FACTOR | RELATIONSHIP TO DISEASE |
|---|---|
| 1. Tobacco | Definite |
| 2. Alcohol | Definite |
| 3. Sexual and reproductive | Definite |
| 4. Social Support | Probable |
| 5. Animal products | Probable |
| 6. Fruits and vegetables | Probable |
| 7. Obesity | Probable |
| 8. Exercise | Probable |
| 9. Seat belts | Definite |
| 10. Early detection and treatment of disease | Definite |

Alcohol consumption is also strongly discouraged by
the Church. The Adventist's very low consumption of
alcohol probably explains, in part, their low risk for
accidents, liver cirrhosis, and suicide. There is,
however, some evidence that alcohol consumption may offer
some protection against coronary heart disease (Snowdon,
1981; Stason et al, 1976; Yano et al, 1977). What, if
any, impact alcohol consumption has on heart disease
among Adventists is unknown at this time.

Premarital and extramarital sex is also proscribed
by the Church. Conservative sexual habits may explain
the Adventists low risk of cervical cancer (Phillips,
1975). This may occur because Adventist women probably
have few sexual partners, and other studies clearly show
that the smaller the number of sexual partners, the lower
the risk of cervical cancer (Doll and Peto, 1981).

The reproductive habits of Adventists, however, may
actually cause the development of some disease. Children
raised in Adventist homes are strongly encouraged to
pursue university training. As a result many Adventist
women postpone their first pregnancy until later in their
life. While early age at first birth may reduce a women's

risk of breast cancer, a full term pregnancy after age 30
increases her risk (MacMahon et al, 1973; Kelsey, 1979).
Therefore, the reproduction habits of Adventists may
actually result in the production of some breast cancer.
Sexual and reproductive factors may also be related to
other diseases (e.g. prostate cancer).

The Adventist lifestyle also may be characterized by
a high degree of social support. This social support
comes from spouses, friends, and church members. The
actual level of social support has not yet been compared
to the U.S. general population. Adventists, however,
probably enjoy more social support because of their
participation in the Church's religious and social
functions. Results from recent studies of nonAdventists
suggest that lack of social support is a risk factor for
premature death (Berkeman and Syme, 1979, House et al,
1982, Blazer, 1982). Preliminary results from our
studies of Adventists, suggest that the loss of social
support (associated with the death of a spouse) is
strongly related to fatal heart disease in men, and fatal
stroke in women. The social support from a spouse, or
friends may therefore be a major determinant of longevity
(because of it's apparent effect on two major causes of
death).

Another unique characteristic of Adventists is their
low consumption of meat and other animal products.
Preliminary research suggests that current and past meat
consumption is positively associated with fatal coronary
heart disease (Snowdon and Phillips, 1982). The positive
association between meat consumption and fatal coronary
heart disease is stronger in men than in women, and
overall strongest in young men. In men, meat consumed
during the early and middle years of life has a stronger
relationship to risk than meat consumed later in life.
In women, however, only the meat consumed after menopause
has a measurable effect on risk. Preliminary results
also suggest that other diseases (e.g. prostate cancer)
are related to meat consumption. However, more research
is needed before we can definitely state that meat
consumption causes disease.

By nature of their low animal product consumption,
Adventists probably consume large amounts of fruits and
vegetables. We have not yet investigated the possible

effect of fruit and vegetable consumption in Adventists. However, studies of nonAdventists suggest that fruit and vegetable consumption may offer some protection against cancer of the mouth, larynx, lung, esophagus, stomach, colon, rectum, and bladder (Bjelke, 1973; Doll and Peto, 1981; National Research Council, 1982).

Vitamin A and C in fruits and vegetables may be the protective factor responsible for the apparent low cancer risk. The work of Wattenberg at the University of Minnesota also suggests that indoleamines in some vegetables (e.g. brussel sprouts, cauliflower, and cabbage) may favorably alter the liver's metabolism of carcinogens. While we can't definitely say whether Vitamin A or C, or the indoleamines are responsible, we can safely suggest that cancer risk might decrease by adding more fruit and vegetables to the diet.

Preliminary results from our studies of Adventists also suggest that obesity is related to risk of death from several diseases. Studies of nonAdventists suggest that obesity is related to risk of death from heart disease, stroke, colon and breast cancer, other cancers and other diseases (Lew and Garfinkel, 1979). While more research is needed, it appears that obesity, by way of it's deleterious effect on several diseases, is another major determinant of longevity.

Excessive weight can be shed by increasing the level of exercise. Several studies of nonAdventists have suggested that exercise may offer protection against coronary heart disease (Paffenbarger et al, 1978; Morris et al, 1973; Salonen et al, 1982). Anecdotal evidence also suggests that exercise may help relieve stress, and improve a person's outlook on life. The effect of exercise in Adventists is currently being investigated.

Unfortunately no studies have been implemented to investigate the protective effect of seat belts and other safety devices in the Adventist population. However, other studies clearly show a life-saving, and injury-reducing effect of seat belts and shoulder harnesses. Wearing a seat belt may reduce your chances of dying in your car by as much as 50% (U.S. Department of Transportation, 1980). Wearing seat belts is a

simple, yet vastly under used "vaccine" against the epidemic of trauma, disability, and death associated with
motor vehicle travel.

The last modifiable lifestyle factor to be addressed
is the phenomena of "early detection and treatment of
disease". In general, the earlier a disease is detected
and treated, the better the prognosis. As already mentioned, the early detection and treatment of diabetes
and high blood pressure may lower a person's risk of
heart disease and stroke. The early detection in
Adventists of diabetes, high blood pressure, heart disease, and cancer may, in part, explain the Adventists
low risk of fatal cancer and cardiovascular disease.

SYNOPOSIS

Aging is the sum of positive and negative changes
in human function that are associated with the passage
of time. Some of the disease-producing changes in biological functions can be eliminated or postponed. Engineering a safer environment, reducing cigarette smoking, and controlling diabetes and high blood pressure
could extend the average American lifespan and improve
the quality of life. Studies of Seventh-day Adventists
and nonAdventists also suggest that meat, fruit, and
vegetable consumption, obesity, exercise, social support, certain sexual and reproductive habits, use of
seatbelts, and the early detection and treatment of
disease are related to longevity and the quality of
life. Luckily, most of the major factors that cause
disease and shorten life are modifiable by simple
changes in lifestyle.

REFERENCES
Berkman LF, Syme SL (1979). Social networks, host resistance, and mortality: a nine-year follow-up study
of Alameda County residents. Am J Epidemiol 109:186-
204.
Bjelke E (1973). "Epidemiologic Studies of Cancer of
the Stomach, Colon, and Rectum; with Special Emphasis
on the Role of Diet. Case-Control Study of Digestive
Tract Cancers in Minnesota." Michigan: University
Microfilms.
Blazer DG (1982). Social support and mortality in an
elderly community population. Am J Epidemiol 115:684-94.

Doll R, Peto R (1981). The causes of cancer. J Natl Cancer Inst 66:1191-1308.

House JS, Robbins C, Metzner HL (1982). The association of social relationships and activities with mortality: prospective evidence from the Tecumseh Community health study. Am J Epidemiol 116:123-40.

Kelsey JL (1979). A review of the peidemiology of human breast cancer. Epid Reviews 1:74-109.

Lew EA, Garfinkel L (1979). Variations in mortality by weight among 750,000 men and women. J Chronic Dis 32:563-76.

MacMahon B, Cole P, Brown J (1973). Etiology of human breast cancer: a review. J Natl Cancer Inst 50:21-42.

Morris JN, Chave SPW, Adam C (1973). Vigorous exercise in leisure-time and the incidence of coronary heart disease. Lancet 1:333-9.

National Center for Health Statistics (1982). Births, marriages, divorces, and deaths for1981. Monthly Vital Statistics Report 30(12):1-12.

National Research Council (1982). "Diet, Nutrition, and Cancer." Washington, D.C.: National Academy Press.

Paffenbarger RS, Wing AL, Jr., Hyde RT (1978). Physical activity as an index of heart attack risk in college alumni. Am J Epidemiol 108:161-175.

Phillips RL (1975). Role of life-style and dietary habits in cancer among Seventh-day Adventists. Cancer Research 35:3515-22.

Phillips RL, Kuzma JW, Beeson WL, Lotz T (1980). Influence of selection versus lifestyle on risk of fatal cancer and cardiovascular disease among Seventh-day Adventists. Am J Epidemiol 112:296-314.

Salonen JT, Puska P, Tuomilehto J (1982). Physical activity and risk of myocardial infarction, cerebral stroke and death: a longitudinal study in Eastern Finland. Am J Epidemiol 115:526-37.

Snowdon D (1981). "Alcohol Use and Mortality from Cancer and Heart Disease Among Members of the Lutheran Brotherhood Cohort". Michigan: University Microfilms.

Snowdon D, Phillips R (1982). Risk of fatal ischemic heart disease among vegetarian and nonvegetarian Seventh-day Adventists (abstract). Am J Epidemiol (in press).

Stason WB, Neff RK, Mietinen OS, Jick H (1976). Alcohol consumption and non-fatal myocardial infarction. Am J Epidemiol 104:603-608.

U.S. Department of Transportation (1980). "Automobile Occupant Crash Protection". Washington, D.C.: National

Highway Traffic Safety Administration.
Yano K, Rhoads GG, Kagan A (1977). Coffee, alcohol and risk of coronary heart disease among Japanese men living in Hawaii. N Engl J Med 297:405-9.

Intervention in the Aging Process, Part A: Quantitation, Epidemiology, and Clinical Research, pages 151-166
© 1983 Alan R. Liss, Inc., 150 Fifth Avenue, New York, NY 10011

PROGERIC SYNDROMES

Dorothy B. Villee, M.D.
Assistant Professor of Pediatrics
Harvard Medical School; Children's Hospital
           Medical Center
300 Longwood Avenue
Boston, Massachusetts 02115

Scientists interested in the pathophysiology of aging have long sought models of accelerated aging. One approach has been that of George Martin who selected 21 phenotypes possibly associated with senescence. He then tabulated those human genetic disorders with the most number of these phenotypes (Martin, 1978). Ten syndromes could be recognized as having many aspects of the senescent phenotype (Table 1).

Table 1: Segmental Progeroid Syndromes

Down syndrome
Werner syndrome
Cockayne syndrome
Progeria (Hutchinson-Gilford syndrome)
Ataxia telangiectasia
Seip syndrome (generalized lipodystrophy,
     hereditary type)
Cervical lipodysplasia, familial
Klinefelter syndrome
Turner syndrome
Myotonic dystrophy (Steinert disease)

Martin called these progeroid syndromes. I should like to concentrate this morning on one of these ten: progeria (Hutchinson-Gilford Syndrome). Progeria presents the anthropomorphic features of aging: dry, tight or wrinkled skin with pigmented spots; flexion deformities of the joints; prominent joints; a prominent venous pattern in the skin.

Progerics exhibit certain biochemical characteristics that
are similar to those found with aging; however, some features
of aging are distinctly lacking in this syndrome. There is
no clinical or pathologic evidence of senile dementia or of
the other neurologic stigmata of aging. The degenerative
osteoarthritis, cataracts, and arcus senilis seen with
advancing age are not found in classical progeria.

Nevertheless, progeria and its adult counterpart,
Werner's syndrome, have attracted interest particularly
because of the extensive atherosclerosis and collagen changes
found in these patients. Although there are many progeroid
syndromes, the classical progeria of Hutchinson-Gilford is
readily differentiated from them on the basis of its characteristic features.

An excellent review by DeBusk gives details of the
early findings on progeria (DeBusk, 1972). First reported
in the medical literature in 1866 (Hutchinson, 1866), a
century later DeBusk could find reports of some 60 cases in
the literature. The incidence of progeria in the United
States is estimated to be 1 per 8,000,000 births. Progeria
is found in all races and in all parts of the world. The
reported cases include slightly more male than female
patients. Because of its unique phenotype, it is believed
to be a simple gene defect. There is no increased incidence
of consanguinity; this fact and the increased paternal age
suggest progeria could be due to a sporadic dominant mutation; however, the finding of certain cellular changes in
the parents of progerics argues that it is a recessive gene.


Clinical Features

Patients with classical progeria usually appear normal
at birth. At about 6 months to 1 year of age they begin to
lose their hair and subcutaneous tissue. With time they
become totally bald, lose their eyebrows and often eyelashes,
too, and lose most of the visible subcutaneous fat except
that of the pubic area. Growth slows and finally ceases.
Characteristically they achieve the height of an average
5-year old and the weight of an average 3-year old. The
skin becomes thinner. It is dry and warm, tight over the
face and abdomen but loose and wrinkled over the hands. This
thin skin permits better visualization of the superficial
veins. Thus the veins of the skull, chest, and hands are

usually quite prominent. With age increasing numbers of
brownish pigmented spots appear over the body, particularly
in those areas exposed to sunlight. The nails become
dystrophic and the terminal phalanges may be shortened. As
the child starts to walk, a bilateral coxa valga develops.
In later years the clavicles resorb and are replaced with
fibrous tissue.

The face of the progeric child is unusual. The beaked
nose and underdevelopment of the lower portion of the face
give the progeric a bird-headed look. The mouth is small
and the teeth are crowded together. Primary dentition is
delayed; the secondary teeth may fail to erupt. The anterior
fontanelle remains patent. The ears often have missing lobes.
There may be a circumoral pallor or cyanosis in early life.
The voice is thin and high pitched. The body of the progeric
child is small, thin and frail looking. The joints are
prominent and tend to have flexion deformities. The coxa
valga deformity gives a horse-riding stance to the child.

Sexual development is limited. Death occurs usually
in the teens but even those few patients who reach their
third decade show very little sexual development. A 26-year
old female progeric has been reported to have no breast
development and only some scanty periods. One male progeric
in his twenties was reported to have spermatogenesis but
other progerics in their late teens have had little or no
spermatogenesis. No progerics have reproduced.

Patients with progeria have normal or above average
intelligence.

The terminal event in these children is most often
related to occlusive coronary artery disease. Myocardial
infarction and/or fibrosis has been reported. After 6 years
of age the mean systolic blood pressure of progeric patients
was greater than 1 SD above the mean of normal age-matched
children. The mean diastolic blood pressure was more than
2 SD above the normal mean (Makous et al, 1962). In addition
to hypertension the progeric child often develops cardiac
murmurs. In the year or two before death angina and congestive heart failure may necessitate medical treatment but
almost uniformly such treatment is of only temporary pallia-
tive benefit. The process proceeds inexorably and death
ensues.

A.

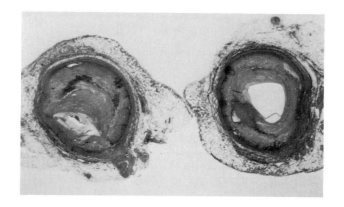

B.

C.

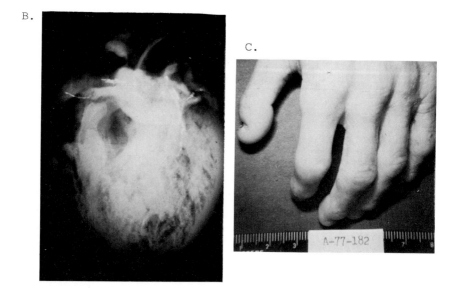

Figure 1.  Post-mortem findings in a patient with progeria
   A. Two sections of the left main coronary showing greater
      than 95% occlusion by calcified ulcerated atherosclerotic
      plaque.  Recent plaque hemorrhage is present.  The
      material filling the lumen consists of concentric rings
      of thickened condensed eosinophilic material.
   B. Roentgenogram of the heart showing calcification of the
      coronary arteries.
   C. Hand showing wrinkling of skin, prominence of joints
      and dystrophic nails.

The most striking findings at autopsy are related to the cardiovascular system. There is usually extensive atherosclerosis of the coronary arteries and/or aorta with calcification of the atherosclerotic plaques (Fig. 1). Often there is occlusion of the coronary arteries, the right coronary being the most commonly involved (Fig. 1). Arteriosclerosis elsewhere is not necessarily extensive or advanced but is usually present. Nephrosclerosis has been reported in some patients but involvement of the cerebral arteries is rare.

The skin of progeric patients is atrophic with hyperkeratotic epithelium and dense dermal collagen. The thickened dermis shows extension of collagen into the submucosa enveloping sweat glands.

The other area of interest is the brain. In reported autopsies of patients with progeria, no neurofibrillar tangles or senile plaques were noted. In one of our patients who came to autopsy there were some changes suggestive of hypertension such as patchy subarachnoid hemorrhages and foci of perivascular groups of hemosiderin-laden macrophages. There was no atherosclerosis of the cerebral vessels; this is a characteristic finding in progeria.

Biochemical Findings in Vivo

Attempts to find the molecular basis for the abnormalities found in progeria have been largely unsuccessful. Most of the chemical substances found in serum or urine in normal individuals are present in normal quantities in progeria (Villee et al, 1969). Some patients have elevated levels of serum cholesterol and lipids; however, these findings are not consistent and the elevations are usually not marked. If repeated samplings of blood are examined for cholesterol concentration, most progeric patients over 4 years of age will show at least one elevated value (Makous, 1962).

Perturbations of homeostatic systems reveal intact regulatory responses in these patients. For example, glucose tolerance tests are normal. In three male progeric patients that we studied, a relative insulin resistance could be demonstrated (Villee et al, 1969). Doses from 0.15 to 0.2 unit insulin per kg body weight (twice the normal) were required to reduce the blood glucose concentration by 50 percent. There was no indication that this insulin resistance altered blood glucose levels; the latter were normal in all patients at all times tested. A relative insulin resistance was also reported in a 3-year old girl with progeria (Rosenbloom, 1970). This child's sleep values for insulin ranged from 21 to 42 μU/ml, distinctly high for the blood glucose concentration and above the range of normal fasting insulin values (5 to 24 μU/ml). Double the usual insulin dose was required to produce a 50 percent decrease in blood glucose. Growth hormone release was studied in this child and shown to be normal in response to arginine, insulin and sleep stimuli. The least impressive growth hormone response was after insulin-induced hypoglycemia; a finding compatible with other reports of impaired growth hormone response to this stimulus (Villee et al, 1969; Kaplan, 1968).

Biochemical Findings in Vitro

One of the earliest in vitro studies with progeric tissues involved the analysis of skin, muscle, and bone (Villee et al, 1969). The most striking abnormality found concerned the properties of skin collagen. The collagen fibers from the skin of progeric patients had a higher shrinkage temperature and were less soluble than those from normal skin. These are characteristics of highly cross-linked collagen; the latter is found in increasing amounts with age.

In several studies the propagation of fibroblasts from progeric skin has been studied to assess the growth potential of these cells. The life span of these cells in vitro was shortened considerably compared to that of normal fibroblasts (Goldstein, 1969; Martin et al, 1970) and resembled more the lifespan of fibroblasts from aged individuals rather than that from normal children. Danes reported markedly decreased mitotic activity, DNA synthesis and cloning efficiency in progeric fibroblasts (Danes, 1971). Cells from the patients' parents showed intermediate values for these parameters, suggesting a heterozygous state of the parents.

Several investigators have looked at the quantity and/or activity of several proteins formed in normal and progeric cells. Goldstein reported an increased fraction of heat-labile enzymes in cultured progeric fibroblasts (Goldstein and Moerman, 1975) as well as in circulating erythrocytes from a progeric patient (Goldstein and Moerman, 1978). They postulated that accumulated errors of protein synthesis might be responsible for the accelerated aging seen in progeria (Goldstein and Moerman, 1976). The finding of decreased proteolysis in aging and progeric fibroblasts may be a reflection of an increased proportion of defective proteins (Goldstein et al, 1976). Brown (1980), however, could find no increased thermolabile enzyme components in the erythrocytes of three unrelated progeric patients. Holliday and Tarrant (1972) reported increased thermolabile enzymes in senescing cultured fibroblasts; however, Pendergrass et al (1976) found no evidence of this.

Goldstein found increased procoagulant activity in cultured fibroblasts from patients with progeria (Goldstein and Niewiarswski, 1976) as well as diminished HLA expression on these cells (Singal and Goldstein, 1973). Using cells from nine patients with progeria, Brown et al (1980) found no abnormality of HLA expression. At least one of these patients had been previously shown to be HLA deficient by Goldstein. Thus the hypothesis of accumulated errors of protein synthesis with age and progeric syndromes is yet to be resolved. The fidelity of protein synthesis appears to be normal in fibroblasts from aged individuals as well as from patients with progeria (Wojtyk and Goldstein, 1980).

Several investigators have studied DNA repair in progeric cells. The original reports of Epstein (Epstein et al, 1974) and Regan and Setlow (1974) differed in their conclusions. Epstein studied four patients, only two of whom showed impaired DNA repair after irradiation. Regan and Setlow studied the same patients and could not find evidence of poor DNA repair in their cultured cells. Weichselbaum et al (1980) found evidence for poor DNA repair in the cells from two progeric patients but normal repair in others. Rainbow and Howes (1977) reported decreased DNA repair in two strains of progeric cells. Brown et al (1976) showed that cocultivation of progeric cells previously shown to have severe deficiency of DNA repair with normal fibroblasts or with cells from another progeric patient with decreased DNA repair can bring about normal repair in the progeric cells. In a more recent study, using a variety of of growth conditions, cells from one patient with progeria had normal DNA repair while cells from another were severely deficient (Brown et al, 1980). The authors conclude that DNA

repair capacity is not a consistent marker for progeria.
Another aspect of nucleic acid alteration, namely, sister
chromatid exchange, has been described as normal in progeric
fibroblasts (Darlington et al, 1981).

Finally, our laboratory has looked at the responsiveness
of progeric tissues and fibroblasts to insulin in vitro
(Villee and Powers, 1978). The results were compared with
those from cells of normal individuals of various ages.
Both glucose-$^{14}$C incorporation into glycogen-$^{14}$C and labeled
amino acid incorporation into labeled protein in response to
insulin were studied. Explants of skin and muscle maintained
in organ culture for 24 hours were tested for incorporation
of $^{14}$C labeled amino acids into protein (Table 2).

Table 2:  Effect of Insulin on Incorporation of Amino Acids
into Protein in Explants of Human Skin and Muscle

| Donor | Percent Increase in Specific Activity of Cell Protein in Cells Exposed to Insulin Relative to Control Cells | |
|---|---|---|
| | Skin | Muscle |
| Fetus, crown-rump length | | |
| 5.5 cm | 45 | |
| 6.5 cm | 45 | 48 |
| 9.7 cm | | 36 |
| 11.5 cm (male) | | 67 |
| 12.4 cm (male) | | 85 |
| 15.3 cm (male) | 137 | 41 |
| Child | | |
| 10 yr (female | 158 | |
| 11 yr (male) | | 137 |
| Progeric | | |
| 7 yr (male) AK | 0 | 0 |

Each value represents the average of three incubations.
Culture medium consisted of 4 ml CMRL-1066 to which was
added 0.1 ml of uniformly $^{14}$C-labeled amino acids (10mCi/mmol
each amino acid) ± insulin 0.1 U/ml. The cultures were
maintained in 95% oxygen and 5% $CO_2$ for 24 hrs. at 37$^{\circ}$C.

One-half the dishes contained insulin at a concentration of
0.1 unit/ml. Control tissues were obtained from aborted
fetuses and two normal children incidental to orthopedic
surgery. Informed consent was obtained in each case. After
24 hours in culture the tissue protein was analyzed for
specific activity (DPM/μg protein). Control tissues showed
appropriate response to insulin in vitro with increased
specific activity of protein in the cells exposed to insulin.
However, explants of skin and muscle from a 7-year old boy
with classical progeria showed no response to insulin
(Table 2).

In other studies fibroblasts from skin of normal children and adults (obtained incidental to surgery) and from
two patients with classical progeria were cultured as monolayers in minimum essential medium +10% fetal calf serum in
room air +5% carbon dioxide. At confluency the cells were
used for experiments or passaged for use in future experiments.

Early and late passage fibroblasts from skin of young
and old donors were studied for their responsiveness to
insulin and the results compared with those obtained using
progeric cells. The increase in the incorporation of labeled
glucose into glycogen in response to insulin was much greater
in the early passaged fibroblasts from young donors (4-day
old male foreskin) than in the later passaged cells from the
same two donors (Table 3). Far less responsive were cells
from a 67-year old male, and progeric cells were the least
responsive. Progeric cells also showed poor response to
insulin when tested for incorporation of labeled amino acids
into total cellular protein (Table 4). In contrast fibroblasts from three normal children responded well to insulin.
The specific activity of the collagen secreted into the
medium was also determined. The response to insulin was a
37.6 percent (mean of three dishes) increase in collagen
specific activity for the cells from the 8-year old male,
a 55.7 percent (mean of three) increase for the cells from a
13-year old male and no increase (three dishes) for the
progeric cells. These experiments show a profound impairment in response to insulin in progeric cells.

Progeric fibroblasts and late-passage normal fibroblasts
also show diminished response to non-suppressible insulin-
like activity (NSILA) compared to that of early passage cells
(Goldstein and Harley, 1979). Using intravenous glucose

Table 3: Effect of Insulin on Glucose Incorporation into Glycogen in Cells Aged In Vivo and In Vitro

| Donor Age (sex) | Population doubling | CPM $^{14}$C-glucose in glycogen per μg cell protein mean (s.e.) | | % increase over control |
|---|---|---|---|---|
| | | Control | Insulin | |
| 4 d (M) | 5 | 6.07(0.37) | 19.1 | 215 |
| 4 d (M) | 7 | 10.80(0.40) | 28.90(2.28) | 168 |
| 12 yr (M)* | 4 | 3.69(0.38) | 4.30(0.61) | 16 |
| 12 yr (M)* | 6 | 10.30(0.09) | 11.49(0.34) | 12 |
| 4 d (M) | 19 | 3.92(0.45) | 6.88(0.87) | 76 |
| 4 d (M) | 21 | 5.64(0.47) | 10.08(0.22) | 79 |
| 67 yr (M) | 16 | 6.92(0.03) | 8.68(0.20) | 25 |
| 5 mo (F)* | 22 | 6.89(0.44) | 7.43(0.32) | 8 |

*Classical progeria (A.K. and S.K.)

Fibroblasts grown to confluency, fed with serum-free medium and then exposed to glucose-D-$^{14}$C (0.25μCi/ml) ± 0.1 u/ml insulin for 24 hours.

Table 4: Effect of Insulin on Amino Acid Incorporation into Total Protein in Fibroblasts

| Donor Age (sex | Population doubling | N | CPM/µg protein mean (s.e.) | | % increase over control |
|---|---|---|---|---|---|
| | | | Control | Insulin | |
| 8 yr (M) | 8 | 4 | 59.2(4.6) | 96.2(8.7) | 62.5 |
| 12 yr (F) | 2 | 6 | 23.5(1.7) | 38.1(2.6) | 62.1 |
| 13 yr (M) | 8 | 4 | 95.3(9.0) | 162.8(5.3) | 70.8 |
| 5 mo (F)* | 8 | 4 | 22.1(1.3) | 22.4(2.5) | 0 |

*Classical progeria (S.K.)
Fibroblasts grown in monolayers to confluency, fed serum-free medium and then exposed for 24 hrs to $^3$H-labeled amino acids (0.2µCi/ml) ± 0.1 u/ml insulin.

and/or insulin, DeFronzo (1979) has shown impaired tissue
sensitivity to insulin in vivo with age.  The mechanism of
this age-related resistance to insulin is unknown; however,
several examples of diminished hormone responsiveness with
age have been cited in a review by Roth (1979).

The accumulated data from studies of progeric and aging
cells suggest certain similarities (Table 5).  However, the
differing results in regard to DNA repair, HLA expression,
and thermolabile enzymes do not make it likely that these
findings are primarily involved in the pathobiology of progeria and/or aging.  No abnormality of lipid metabolism has
been found to explain the increased atherosclerosis and
arteriosclerosis found in progeria and aging.  The connective
tissue changes of accelerated aging could alter the structure
of vessel walls and predispose to the deposition of lipid.
Insulin resistance may shift glucose uptake to those tissues
not so dependent upon insulin.  Increased concentrations of
intracellular glucose in such tissues may exceed the capacity
of the glycolytic and pentose pathways diverting the glucose
into other pathways such as the aldose reductase path or
metabolic reactions involving glycosylation of proteins.
These changes are, of course, reminiscent of the cellular
changes which occur in diabetes mellitus.  The latter is
found with increasing frequency in older individuals.  Many
of the tissue alterations of aging are found in accelerated
form in diabetics and progerics.

Other progeroid syndromes such as Werner's syndrome and
Down's syndrome manifest many of the characteristics of aging.
Senile dementia, shortened lifespan, and osteoporosis are
just a few of the senescent features in Down's syndrome.
Lymphocytes from patients with Down's syndrome show decreased
HLA expression (Boxer and Yokoyama, 1972).  There is some
evidence in mice to suggest a relationship between the major
histocompatibility complex and DNA repair and lifespan (Hall
et al, 1981).  Werner's syndrome has features of shortened
lifespan, osteoporosis, stunted growth, cataracts, hair loss,
increased atherosclerosis, and diabetes mellitus (Epstein,CJ
et al, 1966).  Fibroblasts from skin of these patients have
shortened lifespans.  As in progeria there are differing
reports on the presence of altered proteins.

Thus the progeric syndromes provide examples of human
mutations which mimic to varying degrees the process of aging.
Studies of such patients may provide a better understanding

Table 5:  Comparisons of In Vitro Studies in Progeria and Aging

| | Progeria | Aging |
|---|---|---|
| **Accumulation of Altered Proteins** | | |
| 1) stability of collagen | ↑ (Villee et al, 1969) | ↑ (Viidik, 1979) |
| 2) procoagulant activity | ↑ (Goldstein & Niewiarswski, 1976) | |
| 3) thermolabile enzymes | ↑ (Goldstein & Moerman, 1975, 1978) | ↑ (Holliday & Tarrant, 1972) |
| | normal (Brown & Darlington, 1980) | normal (Pendergrass et al, 1976) |
| **Immune System** | ↓ HLA expression (Singal & Goldstein, 1973) | correlation of MHC with DNA repair and lifespan (Hall et al, 1981) |
| | normal HLA expression (Brown et al, 1980) | |
| **DNA Repair** | ↓ (Epstein et al, 1974; Rainbow & Howes, 1977) | ↓ (Little, 1976; Hart & Setlow, 1976) |
| | normal in some or all (Regan & Setlow, 1974; Bradley et al, 1976; Brown et al, 1980) | normal (Bradley et al, 1976) |
| **Insulin Resistance** | ↑ (Villee & Powers, 1978; Goldstein & Harley, 1979) | ↑ (Villee & Powers, 1978; DeFronzo, 1979; Goldstein & Harley, 1979) |

of the action of genes relevant to longevity.

ACKNOWLEDGEMENT

This research was supported by the Grant Foundation (New York) and the Milton Fund of Harvard Medical School.

REFERENCES

Boxer LA, Yokohama M (1972). Lymphocyte antigens in patients with Down's syndrome. Vox Sanguinis 22:539.
Bradley MO, Erickson LC, Kohn KW (1976). Normal DNA strand rejoining and absence of DNA cross-linking in progerial and aging human cells. Mutation Res 37:279.
Brown WT, Darlington GJ (1980). Thermolabile enzymes in progeria and Werner syndrome: evidence contrary to the protein error hypothesis. Am J Hum Genet 32:614.
Brown WT, Darlington GJ, Arnold A, Fotino M (1980). Detection of HLA antigens on progeria syndrome fibroblasts. Clin Genetics 17:213.
Brown WT, Epstein J, Little JB (1976). Progeria cells are stimulated to repair DNA by co-cultivation with normal cells. Exp Cell Res 97:291.
Brown WT, Ford JP, Gershey EL (1980). Variation of DNA repair capacity in progeria cells unrelated to growth conditions. Biochem Biophys Res Comm 97:347.
Danes BS (1971). Progeria: a cell culture study on aging. J Clin Invest 50:2000.
Darlington GJ, Dutkowski R, Brown WT (1981). Sister chromatid exchange frequencies in progeria and Werner syndrome patients. Am J Hum Genetics 33:762.
De Busk FL (1972). The Hutchinson-Gilford progeria syndrome. J Pediatr 80:697.
De Fronzo RA (1979). Glucose intolerance and aging: evidence for tissue insensitivity to insulin. Diabetes 28:1095.
Epstein CJ, Martin GM, Schultz AL, Motulsky AG (1966). Werner's syndrome: a review of its symptomatology, natural history, pathologic features, genetics and relationship to the natural aging process. Medicine 45:177.
Epstein J, Williams JR, Little JB (1974). Rate of DNA repair in progeric and normal human fibroblasts. Biochem Biophys Res Comm 59:850.
Goldstein S (1969). Lifespan of cultured cells in progeria. Lancet 1:424.
Goldstein S, Harley CB (1979). In vitro studies of age-associated diseases. Fed Proc 38:1862.

Goldstein S, Moerman E (1975). Heat-labile enzymes in skin fibroblasts from subjects with progeria. N Engl J Med 292:1305.

Goldstein S, Moerman EJ (1976). Defective proteins in normal and abnormal human fibroblasts during aging in vitro. Interdiscip Top Gerontol 10:24.

Goldstein S, Moerman EJ (1978). Heat-labile enzymes in circulating erythrocytes of a progeria family. Am J Hum Genetics 30:167.

Goldstein S, Niewiarswski S (1976). Increased procoagulant activity in cultured fibroblasts from progeria and Werner's syndromes of premature aging. Nature 260:711.

Goldstein S, Stotland D, Cordeiro RAJ (1976). Decreased proteolysis and increased amino acid efflux in aging human fibroblasts. Mech Ageing & Develop 5:221.

Hall KY, Bergmann K, Walford RL (1981). DNA repair, H-2, and aging in NZB and CBA mice. Tissue Antigens 16:104.

Hart RW, Setlow RB (1976). DNA repair in late-passage human cells. Mech Ageing & Develop 5:67.

Holliday R, Tarrant GM (1972). Altered enzymes in ageing human fibroblasts. Nature 238:26.

Hutchinson J (1886). Congenital absence of hair and mammary glands. Medico-Chirurgical Trans 69:473.

Kaplan SL, et al (1968). Growth and growth hormone. Pediatr Res 2:43.

Little JB (1976). Relationship between DNA repair capacity and cellular aging. Gerontologia 22:28.

Makous N, et al (1962). Cardiovascular manifestations in progeria. Report of clinical and pathological findings in a patient with severe arteriosclerotic heart disease and aortic stenosis. Am Heart J 64:334.

Martin GM (1978). Genetic syndromes in man with potential relevance to the pathobiology of aging. In Bergsma D, Harrison DE (eds): "Birth Defects," Vol XIV, No 1, p 5.

Martin GM, Sprague CA, Epstein CJ (1970). Replicative life-span of cultivated human cells: effects of donor's age, tissue, and genotype. Lab Invest 23:86.

Pendergrass WR, Martin GM, Bornstein P (1976). Evidence contrary to the protein error hypothesis for in vitro senescence. J Cell Physiol 87:3.

Rainbow AJ, Howes M (1977). Decreased repair of gamma ray damaged DNA in progeria. Biochem Biophys Res Comm 74:714.

Regan JD, Setlow RB (1974). DNA repair in human progeroid cells. Biochem Biophys Res Comm 59:858.

Rosenbloom AL, Karacau IJ, DeBusk FL (1970). Sleep character-istics and endocrine response in progeria. J Pediatr 77:692.

Roth GS (1979). Hormone action during aging: alterations and mechanisms. Mech Ageing & Develop 9:497.

Singal DP, Goldstein S (1973). Absence of detectable HLA antigens on cultured fibroblasts in progeria. J Clin Invest 52:2259.

Viidik A (1979). Connective tissues - possible implications of the temporal changes for the aging process. Mech Ageing & Develop 9:267.

Villee DB, Nichols G,Jr, Talbot NB (1969). Metabolic studies in two boys with classical progeria. Pediatrics 43:207.

Villee DB, Powers ML (1978). Progeria: a model for the study of aging. In Nandy K (ed): "Senile Dementia: A Biomedical Approach," New York: Elsevier/North Holland Biomedical Press, p 259.

Weichselbaum RR, Nove J, Little JB (1980). X-ray sensitivity in fifty-three human diploid fibroblast cell strains from patients with characterized genetic disorders. Cancer Res 40:920.

Wojtyk RI, Goldstein S (1980). Fidelity of protein synthesis does not decline during aging of cultured human fibroblasts. J Cell Physiol 103:299.

# CLINICAL INTERVENTION IN THE AGING PROCESS

**Intervention in the Aging Process, Part A: Quantitation, Epidemiology, and
Clinical Research, pages 169–197**
© **1983 Alan R. Liss, Inc., 150 Fifth Avenue, New York, NY 10011**

THYMOSIN:  CAN IT RETARD AGING BY BOOSTING IMMUNE CAPACITY ?

A.L. Goldstein, T.L.K. Low, N. Hall, P.H. Naylor
and M.M. Zatz
Department of Biochemistry, The George Washington
University School of Medicine
2300 Eye St., N.W. Washington, D.C.   20037

SUMMARY

     The thymus gland controls the development and mainte-
nance of immune balance by secreting a family of polypeptide
hormones termed thymosin.  These hormones, and possibly
others, act on thymic-dependent lymphocytes (T cells) at
several points in the maturation sequence to ensure the
cells' development and function.  Ongoing studies suggest
that the lack of adequate production and utilization of
these thymic factors causes an immune imbalance and may contribute to the etiology of many of the diseases of aging.
Using a partially purified preparation, thymosin fraction 5,
we have established that thymosin can correct some of the
immunologic deficiencies resulting from the lack of thymic
function in several animal models, as well as in humans with
primary and secondary immunodeficiency diseases.  Several
biologically active peptides present in thymosin fraction 5
contribute to its biologic activity.  Several of these peptides have now been purified, and two, thymosin $\alpha_1$ and
thymosin $\beta_4$, have been sequenced and synthesized.  It appears
that these peptides act individually, sequentially or in
concert to influence the development of T cell subpopulations.
Thymosin $\alpha_1$ is a highly acidic (pI 4.1), heat stable protein
with a molecular weight (MW) of 3,108.  Biologically,
thymosin $\alpha_1$ is from 10 to 1,000 times as active as fraction
5 in inducing maturational and functional changes in T cell
subpopulations in specific <u>in vitro</u> and <u>in vivo</u> assays.

     Currently, a number of Phase I and II randomized
clinical trials with thymosin fraction 5 and/or $\alpha_1$ are

ongoing to establish dose, regimen, safety and efficacy in
cancer patients and patients with autoimmune and infectious
diseases.  An RIA for $\alpha_1$ has been developed which has en-
abled us to initiate pharmacokinetic studies and to quantitate absolute blood levels of $\alpha_1$ in patients during their
course of therapy.  The RIA is proving to be a valuable
diagnostic tool in monitoring dose regimens.  Recently, we
have found that some of the thymosin peptides act directly
in the CNS and influence neuroendocrine function.  Both
in vitro (using a superfusion system) and in vivo (admin-
instering thymosin directly into the lateral ventricle) experiments have revealed that thymosin $\beta_4$ stimulates the
release LRF and LH.  We have observed in the rat that
thymosin $\alpha_1$ is present in high concentrations in the anterior
pituitary and that plasma levels in the human are negatively
correlated with cortisol levels in the blood.  These thymus-
CNS interactions point to an important homeostatic role for
the endocrine thymus in the modulation of the neuroendocrine
axis.


INTRODUCTION


Aging of the Immune System

    A marked increase in the average life span of humans
has occurred in the last century as a result of the reduction of early deaths due to infectious diseases (Makinodan,
T. & Yunis, E. (eds.), 1977).  This has led us to become
more cognizant of the so-called "diseases of aging", which
include infectious diseases, autoimmune diseases, and cancer
(Walford, 1969).  One of the various theories of aging that
has been proposed (Walford, 1969; Orgel, L.E., 1963; Comfort,
1964; Medvedev, 1964; Krohn, P.L. (ed.), 1966; Strehler, B.
L., 1967; Burch, P.R., 1969; Burnet, F.M. 1974; Walford,
R.L., 1974) is the hypothesis that the diseases of aging are
a direct result of the senescence of immunity.  As the immune
system ages, it loses its capacity to maintain the balance
necessary to react vigorously against foreign invaders
(bacteria, viruses, malignant cells, etc.) and loses its
capacity to remain totally nonreactive against self-antigens.
Thus, as the immune system declines, it becomes more difficult for the individual to maintain adequate responses
against infections or malignancy, while at the same time,
it becomes more reactive toward normal "self" antigens, re-

sulting in an increase in autoimmune disorders.

Age related changes in normal immunological function may be due to changes in the cellular microenvironment, maturational rates, or immunological recognition and reactivity. Using cell transfer experiments, investigators have determined that the decline in responsiveness of lymphocytes from aged animals is due largely to intrinsic changes within the cells themselves (Price, G.B. & Makinodan, T., 1972a; Price and Makinodan, 1972b;Hammer, J.A., 1906). However, evidence of microenvironmental changes is also evident since spleen cells from young animals in diffusion chambers elicit lower humoral antibody responses in older animals than they do in young animals (Price, G.B. & Makinodan,T., 1972b).This suggests the decline in the aged mice of essential factor or factors related to immunological responsivity. An obvious source for these factors could be the thymus gland as it is the first gland to atrophy with age (Hammer, J.A., 1906). Thus, changes in lymphocyte functions in aged animals may be secondary to changes in the hormonal influence of the thymus.

Studies of mouse bone marrow stem cells have indicated that although there is a decrease in concentration of stem cells in the bone marrow with age, the overall increase in the total cell population results in the maintenance of a relatively constant number of stem cells throughout life (Price, G.B. & Makinodan, T., 1972b;Albright, J.F. & Makinodan, T., 1966; Coggle, J.E. & Proukakais, C., 1970; Davis, M.L., et al., 1971). One possible cause for the decline in peripheral lymphocyte numbers with aging may be a reduction in the rate of stem cell maturation and differentiation. This reduction could result from the atrophy of the thymus gland if one postulates a feedback mechanism whereby the thymus gland induces proliferation of lymphoid stem cells through circulating thymus factors such as thymosin (Goldstein, A. L., et al., 1981).

Since the related decline of immunity has been shown to be partly a result of decreased cellular function, any one of the various cell types involved in immune responses could be responsible for decreased reactivity. The macrophage is essential for most immune responses, but its function in old mice has been characterized as equal to or superior to that seen in young mice (Perkins, E.H. and Makinodan, T., 1971; Heidrick, M.L. and Makinodan, T., 1973). B-lymphocytes could also be responsible for the decline in immunity with

aging, however, there is little evidence to support this.
It has been shown that the number of B cells in the spleens
and lymph nodes of mice does not change appreciably with age
(Makinodan, T. & Adler, W.H., 1975), although their responsivity to certain antigens may decline (Makinodan, T. &
Peterson, W.J., 1962). This decline may be related to a
loss in helper T cell activity or to an increase in T cell
suppressor activity.


Senescence of Thymus-dependent Immunity with Age

The thymus gland is vital to the normal development and
function of the immune system. It has been known since the
time of Galen (Duckworth, W.L., 1962) that the thymus is the
first gland in the body to involute (Fig. 1).

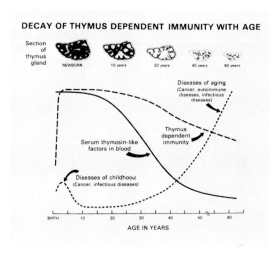

FIGURE 1

Fig. 1. Involution of the thymus with the increasing age of
the individual. Thymic factors in the blood and cellular immune mechanisms are shown to decline in similar fashion.
The incidence of age-related diseases increases in inverse
proportion to the involution of the thymus and to the decrease of thymic-dependent immunity. From Goldstein et. al
1977.

The two most critical periods of life with regard to susceptibility to disease occur shortly after birth and after
the sixth decade of life.  After puberty, both cellular
(Albright, J.F. & Makinodan, T., 1966) and humoral
(Makinodan, T., 1966; Makinodan, T. & Peterson, W.J., 1964)
immunity gradually deteriorate with age.  There is increasing support for the concept that the deterioration of thymic-
dependent, cell-mediated immunity is causally related to the
observations that the incidence of malignancies (Teller,
M.N., et al., 1964) and autoimmune disorders (MacKay, I.R.
et al., 1964) increases with age.

We also know, as illustrated in Figure 1, that thymosin
or thymosin-like serum activities are very high in young
people and that between the ages of 25 and 45 years of ages,
the levels decrease significantly in the blood and continue
to fall with age (Goldstein, A.L., et al., 1974; Goldstein,
A.L., 1975).

The involution of the thymus gland begins in man and
most other mammals just prior to puberty and primarily involves a slow depletion of the lymphoid elements of the
cortex and medulla (Hammer, J.A., 1906).  As involution progresses, thymic lymphoid cells are gradually replaced by
adipose tissue; however, the medullary epithelial cells (the
hormone-secreting cells) remain.  This explains why serum
thymosin and thymosin-like activity remain demonstrable by
both bioassay (Goldstein, A.L., et al., 1974; Goldstein, A.L.
et al., 1975; Bach, J.F., et al., 1973) and radioimmunoassay
(Schulof, R.S., Ph.D. Thesis, 1973; McClure, J.E., et al.,
1981) with advancing age, albeit at markedly lower levels.
It had not, however, been established whether thymic involution is in itself a consequence of aging or is an etiologic
factor in the process.

It has been demonstrated that adult thymectomy accelerates
the age related decline of the immune system (Metcalf, D.,
1965; Taylor, R., 1965) and that the success of a thymic
transplant in reconstituting T-cell-deprived mice is inversely
proportional to the age of the adult thymus gland donor
(Hirokawa, K. & Makinodan, T., 1975).  Specifically, the
thymus gland loses its capacity with age to confer the following functions in T-cell-deprived mice:
   -Repopulation of thymus-dependent areas of lymphoid
    tissue.

- Responsivity of lymphocytes to PHA and Con A of spleen cells.
- Ability of lymphocytes to serve as helper cells to T-dependent antigens.
- Ability of lymphocytes to respond to allogeneic lymphocytes.

It thus appears that the primary immunological consequence of aging is on the T-cell populations (and is due to
alterations in the differentiation and/or maturational pathways). Deficiencies that develop during aging in the thymic
hormones or factors that induce differentiation of the
various subpopulations of T-cells may be responsible for the
immunological decline seen during the aging process.

Recent progress in thymosin research, including a
successful Phase I (Wara, D.W., et al., 1975; Goldstein, A.
L., et al., 1976; Shafer, L.A., et al., 1977; Costanzi, J.J.,
et al., 1977; Rossio, J.L. & Goldstein, A.L., 1977; Costanzi,
J.J., et al., 1977) and Phase II (Cohen, M.H., et al. 1979;
Lipson, D.S., et al., 1979; Chretien, P.B., et al., 1978)
clinical trials, make it possible to explore the role of the
endocrine thymus gland and its constituent polypeptides in
the aging process. It is known that thymosin or thymosin-
like activity decreases in the blood with age, and that we
can artifically elevate serum thymosin levels by injection
of thymosin preparations. It is therefore possible to investigate what effects the maintenance of increased levels
of circulating thymosin (regardless of the state of atrophy
of the thymus gland) will have on the decline of the immune
system with age.

Endocrine Role of the Thymus Gland

Although the exact mechanism by which the thymus exerts
its influence on host resistance is still being defined,
present evidence supports the concept that the thymus functions as both a donor of cells to the peripheral lymphoid
system and as an endocrine gland (Goldstein, A.L. et al.,
1981). Our focus in this paper is with the latter
function, i.e., the endocrine role of the thymus and the
potential use of thymosin as a means of achieving immune reconstitution in aged individuals and in individuals afflicted
with diseases of aging.

A prerequisite for establishing endocrine function for any organ is the demonstration that cell-free extracts of the tissue will replace, in whole or in part, the specific biological functions which have been assigned to that organ. This has now been adequately demonstrated for the thymus. Reconstitution studies with crude and partially purified thymic extracts from various animal sources - mouse, calf, pig, rat, sheep, guinea pig, and man - have established that cell-free preparations can act in lieu of an intact thymus and restore deficiencies due to removal or dysfunction of the gland (Goldstein, A.L., et al., 1981). Ongoing studies point to a major role for thymosin and other thymic factors in maintaining immune balance (Figure 2). There is now a considerable body of evidence indicating that genetic, viral,

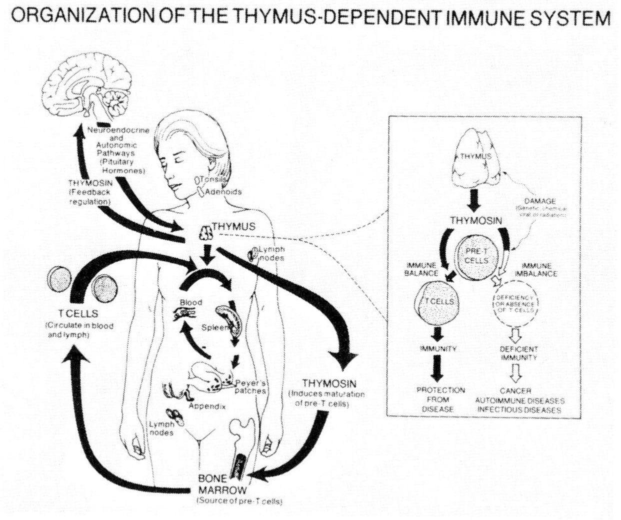

ORGANIZATION OF THE THYMUS-DEPENDENT IMMUNE SYSTEM

FIGURE 2

Fig. 2. Thymus contribution to immunity. Impairment of lymphoid elements, including the thymus and immunocompetent cells, by various deleterious agents causes deficiencies in immunity which may lead to a variety of disease manifestations. These conditions may in part be the result of a malfunctioning thymus and inadequate levels of thymic secretions. From Goldstein et al. (Goldstein, A.L., 1982).

radiation, or chemical insults to the thymus may result in severe immune imbalances involving both T-and B-cells and may contribute to a number of serious diseases (c.f. Goldstein, A.L., et al., 1981).

Activity similar to that of thymosin (the most extensively studied of the thymic factors) has been demonstrated in the blood of normal adult mice by means of a rosette bioassay (Bach, J.F. & Dardenne, M., 1971) and appears in the blood of immunodeficient patients shortly after administration of thymosin (A. Astaldi, 1978). The development of rabbit antibodies to bovine thymosin has provided confirmatory evidence using RIA techniques that circulating thymosin is detectable in the blood of all mammals tested (McClure, J.E., 1981). We have also found that levels of circulating thymosin decrease with age in man and other mammals, and ongoing studies indicate that thymosin levels are altered in patients with specific immunodeficiency diseases and malignancies (c.f. Goldstein, A.L., et al., 1981). Such observations fulfill a second requirement for designating an organ as endocrine in function - i.e., its secretory products can be demonstrated in the circulation. These results suggest that the thymus, in addition to influencing endogenous lymphoid stem cells and cells traversing the gland in situ, may affect the behavior of certain populations of immature lymphoid cells outside the thymus.

Numerous cell-free thymic fractions (such as thymic humoral factor, serum thymic factor and thymopoietin) have been reported to have biological activities in vivo and in vitro. Several comprehensive reviews of these factors have been written (Goldstein, A.L. & White, A., 1970; Goldstein, A.L. & White, A., 1973; Trainin, N., 1974) and a discussion of each of these would be beyond the scope of this proposal. Suffice it to say, there is evidence that the thymus secretes several factors, some of which play a role in the expression of immunity.

Review of Biochemical and Biological Studies with Thymosin.

Our own efforts have contributed to the elucidation of the endocrine function of the thymus gland in the development and maintenance of the immune system. The principal investigator (ALG) was the co-discoverer of thymosin in 1966 (Goldstein, A.L., et al., 1966) with the late Dr. Abraham

White and has had a continuing major role in a program which has resulted in the purification, chemical characterization, and definition of some of the biological properties of thymosin. Our group, in collaboration with our clinical colleagues, has also been responsible for the successful iniation of the first clinical trials with thymosin in patients with primary immunodeficiency diseases (Wara, D.W, et al., 1975; Rossio, J.L. & Goldstein, A.L., 1977) and advanced malignancies (Shafer, L.A., et al., 1977; Costanzi, J.J., et al., 1977; Cohen, M.H., et al., 1979; Chretien, P.B., et al., 1978).

Our initial studies, in 1966 described the isolation from thymus tissue of fractions that stimulated in vivo (Klein, J.J., et al., 1965) lymphoid cell proliferation and metabolism. Subsequent studies demonstrated that the activity of the stimulatory fraction resided with a protein fraction which was given the name "thymosin" (Goldstein, A.L., et al., 1966). Subsequent studies indicated that the action of the inhibitory thymic factor in vitro was of a nonspecific nature and that the stimulatory protein fraction, thymosin, con- sisted of a family of thymic-specific heat-stable acidic polypeptides (Goldstein, A.L., et al., 1975).

A standardized procedure has been developed for the large-scale production of a partially purified thymosin pre- paration for calf thymus which is termed thymosin fraction 5 (Hooper, J.A., et al., 1975). The yield of thymosin frac- tion 5 is approximately 1 gm/kg thymus tissue. Most of the clinical trials and animal studies to date have been con- ducted with this partially purified preparation. Thymosin fraction 5 is used as the starting material for the further isolation and characterization of its component biologically active peptides.

Review of Chemistry of Thymosin Peptides.

Thymosin fraction 5 contains a family of acidic poly- peptides with molecular weights ranging from 1,000 to 15,000 (Figure 3). Ongoing studies indicate that some of the pep- tides in thymosin fraction 5 are produced specifically by thymic epithelial cells and should properly be termed thymic hormones; other peptide components of thymosin fraction 5 are thought to be products of thymocytes (possibly lymphokines), and still other molecules in the fraction 5 preparation are

thus far biologically inactive and are thought to be contam-
inating peptides (Goldstein, A.L., et al., 1981).

In order to facilitate the identification and comparison
of thymic polypeptides from one laboratory to another, we have
proposed a nomenclature for the identification of each of
the polypeptides based upon the isoelectric focusing patterns
of thymosin fraction 5 in the pH range 3.5 - 9.5 (Goldstein,
A.L. et al., 1977).        Thymosin polypeptides are divided
into three major regions based upon their isoelectric points.
These regions are identified by the Greek letter alpha ($\alpha$),

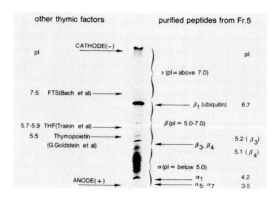

FIGURE 3

Figure 3.  Isoelectrically focused sample of thymosin fraction 5 showing the distribution of mostly acidic peptide
components.  The $\alpha$, $\beta$, and $\gamma$ regions indicate segmentation
of the gel based upon pI ranges suggested for peptide nomenclature.  Peptides that have been isolated are indicated by
the nomenclature $\alpha_1$ through $\alpha_8$ and $\beta_1$ through $\beta_4$.  After
Goldstein et al. (Goldstein, A.L., et al., 1977)

beta ($\beta$), and gamma ($\gamma$).  The alpha region consists of the
polypeptides with isoelectric points (pI) below 5.0 (acidic);
the $\beta$ region 5.0-7.0; the $\gamma$ region above 7.0 (basic). Sequential
numbering is used to identify polypeptides purified to homo-
geneity (Figure 3).  Eight of the purified polypeptides are
from the alpha region and four are from the beta region.
To date, no polypeptides from the gamma region have been
purified.  Two of the polypeptides have been sequenced and
the primary structure of several others are currently being
studied.

Thymosin $\alpha_1$

    Thymosin $\alpha_1$, the first of the biologically active poly-
peptides to be sequenced (Figure 4), contains 28 amino acid
residues and has a molecular weight of 3,108. (Goldstein,
A.L., et al., 1977; Low, T.L.K. and Goldstein, A.L., 1979;
Low, T.L.K., et al., 1979).     As summarized in
Table 1, it is from 10 to 1,000 times as active as thymosin
fraction 5 in some functional in vivo and in vitro assays
while inactive in others. The observation that a purified
isolated from thymosin fraction 5 not active in all of the

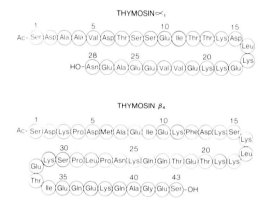

FIGURE 4

Figure 4.  Amino acid sequence of thymosin $\alpha_1$ and thymosin
        $\beta_4$.

fraction 5 bioassays gave us the first conclusive data that
there were several distinct biologically active components
in fraction 5. Thymosin $\alpha_1$ induces the expression of certain T-cell markers Thy 1.2, Lyt 1,2,3 and functional activity associated with lymphocyte maturation (helper T-cell
activity, specific antibody production, production of macrophages inhibitory factor, etc.) At high concentrations of
$\alpha_1$, it increases TdT positive cells in the bone marrow
and spleen. It also suppresses TdT activity in murine
thymocytes in vitro at low concentration ( Goldstein, A.L.,
1982). Furthermore, incubation of thymocytes in vitro with
thymosin f5 or $\alpha_1$ results in an increase in the percentage
of glucocorticoid-resistant cells (Osheroff, P.L., 1981) and
in vivo enhances survival in tumor-bearing mice (Zatz, M.M.

et al., 1981) and immunosuppressed mice with lethal candida infection (Bistoni, F., et al., 1982). Huang et al have demonstrated that $\alpha_1$ is a potent inducer of $\alpha$-interferon production (Huang, K-Y., et al., 1981). More recently, we have found also that intercerebral injection of $\alpha_1$ in mice stimulates corticosterone production (Hall, N.R., 1981; Hall, N.R. and Goldstein, A.L., 1981).

Thymosin $\beta_4$.

Thymosin $\beta_4$ is the first of the biologically active polypeptides from the $\beta$ region of thymosin f5 to be completely characterized (Low, T.L.K. and Goldstein, A.L., 1982). Thymosin $\beta_4$ is composed of 43 amino acid residues with an acetyl group at the N-terminal end. It has a molecular weight of 4,963 and an isoelectric point of 5.1. The complete amino acid sequence of thymosin $\beta_4$ is shown in Figure 4.

A computer search for possible sequence homology between the sequence of thymosin and other published protein sequences has been conducted at the National Biomedical Research Foundation, Washington, D.C. The results do not indicate a statistically significant relationship of thymosin to any other sequenced protein currently stored in the data bank. However, there is an interesting internal duplication between residues 18 to 30 and 31 to 43, as illustrated in Figure 5.

REGIONS OF INTERNAL DUPLICATION IN THYMOSIN $\beta_4$

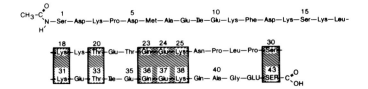

FIGURE 5

Fig. 5. Regions of internal duplication in thymosin $\beta_4$.

Using data for prediction of protein conformation, described by Chou and Fasman (Chou, P.Y. and Fasman, G.D., 1974)
two regions were identified to contain high helical potential.

Thymosin $\beta_4$ has been found to induce TdT expression in
TdT-negative murine bone marrow cells in vivo and in vitro
(Pazmino, N.H., et al., 1978). It also increases TdT
activity in thymocytes from hydrocortisone immunosuppressed
mice in vivo (Goldstein, A.L., 1982). Thus, it appears that
thymosin is acting on lymphoid stem cells and may influence
the early stages of maturation process of thymus-dependent
lymphocytes.

Furthermore, thymosin $\beta_4$ has been found to inhibit
macrophage migrations (Thurman, G.B. et al., 1981).
Preliminary studies indicate that this molecule acts directly
on the macrophages to inhibit their migrations. However, the
possibility that they act on lymphocytes and induce them to
produce a macrophage migration inhibitory factor (MIF) has not
been completely ruled out.

Most recently, thymosin $\beta_4$ has been shown to stimulate
secretion of luteinizing hormone-releasing factor (LRF) from
superfused medial basal hypothalami of female rats (Rebar, R.,
et al., 1981). In addition, luteinizing hormone (LH) is
released from pituitary glands superfused in sequence with
hypothalami (Rebar, R.W., et al., 1981) and when injected
directly into the ventricles of male mice (Hall, N.R., et al.,
1982). These data provide the first evidence of a direct
effect of the endocrine thymus on the central nervous system
hypothalamus and pituitary and suggest as illustrated in
Figure 2, a potentially important role for thymic peptides in
feedback regulation parts of the neuroendocrine system.


Thymosin $\alpha_5$ and thymosin $\alpha_7$

Both thymosin $\alpha_5$ and thymosin $\alpha_7$ are highly acidic polypeptides with isoelectric points around 3.5 (Rovensky, J.,
1977; unpublished observations). They still contain some
impurities. Their molecular weights are approximately 3,000
(Goldstein, A.L., et al., 1981) and 2,000 (Goldstein, A.L.,
et al., 1981) respectively.

Biologically, thymosin $\alpha_7$ has been shown to be a potent
inducer of suppressor cells in humans (S. Horowitz, personal

communication) and in mice (Ahmed, A., et al, 1978; Ahmed, A., et al., 1978) and is also active in inducing T-cell markers ( Ahmed, A., et al., 1978). Most recently, we have found that thymosin $\alpha_7$ can inhibit the production of interferon in vivo (Huang, K-Y., et al., 1981; unpublished observations). Our preliminary results indicate that there is a family of thymic polypeptides that may act on the maturation of different T-cell subpopulations. As shown in Figure 6, the thymosin peptides act on precursor T-cells

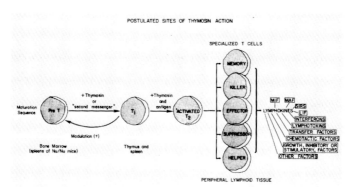

FIGURE 6

Fig. 6. Postulated sites of thymosin action.


(prothymocytes) to form specialized T-cells. The mechanism by which these T-cells appear to act to influence immunity is by releasing lymphokines, the soluble mediators of immunity.


REVIEW OF BIOLOGICAL STUDIES WITH THYMOSIN

Studies in Animals.

    Partially purified thymosin preparations have been found to be effective in partially or fully inducing and maintaining many aspects of immune function in a variety of normal and immunodeficient animal models (cf. Goldstein, et al., 1981). Thymosin treatment has been shown to increase the survival of neonatally thymectomized mice and restore or accelerate the development of immune functions in newborn mice. Thymosin affects the responsivity of lymphocytes from nude, normal and tumor-bearing mice and causes immature mouse lymphoid cells to acquire distinctive T-cell surface antigens (cf. Goldstein, et al., 1981). Experimental approaches utilizing thymosin have shown its effectiveness in modulating immune parameters and inducing specific types of lymphocytes (killer, helper and suppressor cells), and have shown that specific purified thymosin peptides isolated from thymosin fraction 5 can induce certain marker (TdT, Thy-1, and Ly) and functional expressions of lymphocyte maturation. The mechanism of inducing functional responses seen with thymosin fraction 5 and $\alpha_1$ appears to be associated with the capability of these peptides to stimulate the production of the lymphokines, MIF, $\alpha$ and $\gamma$ interferons and lymphotoxin (c.f. Goldstein, A.L., 1981).

Most recently it has been demonstrated that thymosin fraction 5 and thymosin $\alpha_1$ are effective in reducing tumor growth and prolonging survival in mice bearing MOPC-315 plasmocytomas (Zatz, M.M., et al., 1981) and L1210 leukemias (Asanuma, Y., et al., 1970).

Aging and Autoimmune Diseases.

The studies that have been completed in animal models of autoimmune diseases and aging have shown that:

- Thymosin treatment of NZB/W mice can reconstitute suppressor cell and other T-cell functions and temporarily cause remission of some of the symptoms of autoimmune disease commonly seen in these mice, including induction of suppressor T-cells and restoration of antigen-induced depression of DNA synthesis (Talal, N., et al., 1975).

- Administration of thymosin significantly increases the hemagglutinin response of aged mice (Strausser, H.R., et al., 1971).

- In vitro administration of thymosin to aging thymectomized rats shortens the median S + $G_2$ phase of the cell cycle to levels seen in young rats (Dabrowski, M.P. & Goldstein, A.L., 1976).

- Thymosin $\alpha_1$ significantly increases antibody production in aged mice (G. Doria, personal communication).

Studies in Humans.

In vitro.
Incubation with thymosin in vitro increases the percent of total E-rosette levels of some patients with primary immunodeficiencies (Wara, D.W., et al., 1975; Goldstein, A.L., et al., 1976), cancer (Rossio, J.L. and Goldstein, A.L., 1977; Costanzi, J.L., et al., 1978; Lipson, D.S., 1979; Kenady, D.E., 1977) and allergies (J. Hobbs, personal communication), severe burns (Sakai, H., 1975), leprosy (unpublished observations), viral infections (Strausser, H.R., 1971), SLE, rheumatoid arthritis (Moutsopoulos, H., 1976; Scheinberg, M.A., 1975), and in aged normal individuals (Rovensky, J., 1977; and S. Ishizawa, personal communication).

In a study of 388 patients with head and neck, medastinal and pelvic malignancies during radiation therapy, and of 277 normal adults, the in vitro positive to response to thymosin correlated with radiation portal for the cancer patients, and with initial T-cell levels for both groups (Kenady, D.E., et al., 1977).

Incubation with thymosin in vitro induces the appearance of suppressor T-cells in the peripheral lymphocytes of patients with active SLE (Horowitz, S., et al., 1977).

Incubation with thymosin of a subpopulation of null cells isolated by bovine serum albumin density gradient from normal adult controls results in the induction of T-cell rosettes (Kaplan, J. & Peterson, W.D., Jr., 1978). These same cells have enhanced responsiveness to phytohemagglutinin and have increased MLC capacities. Within the null cell compartment following incubation with thymosin fraction 5, no changes in B cells, monocytes, Fc positive or C3 receptor bearing cells could be documented. Therefore, in normal adult controls, putative stem cells can be induced to form T-cell rosettes following incubation with thymosin fraction 5. Cells contained within the null cell HTLA+ compartment enriched by sequestial nylon column filtration and E-rosette depletion could be induced by thymosin fraction 5 incubation in vitro to form T-cell rosettes; HBLA+ cells were not altered by thymosin incubation. Thus, a subpopulation of null cells, isolated from normal human peripheral blood lymphocytes, can be induced to form T-cell rosettes by incubation with thymosin fraction 5.

CLINICAL TRIALS WITH THYMOSIN

The thymic hormones have entered into clinical trials
on a sound theoretical basis. Their therapeutic usefulness
has been demonstrated in immunodeficient animals and in
animal models of human disease. They have exhibited immune
potentiating properties in vitro using PBL obtained from
children with primary immunodeficiency disorders and adults
with autoimmune, infectious and neoplastic disorders. The
rationale for administering thymic hormones to children
with primary immunodeficiencies is to replace the activity
of the endocrine thymus in an attempt to induce non-functional
precursor cells to become immunologically competent T lymphocytes. The rationale for employing thymic hormones therapeutically in adults is somewhat different. It is based on
the observations that circulating thymic hormone levels
decrease dramatically after puberty as the thymus undergoes
its physiologic age dependent involution. This age
associated diminution of thymus function precedes the well
documented deterioration of immune function with age and it
has been suggested that the increased incidence of autoimmune and neoplastic diseases in the elderly population may
reflect the loss of homeostatis control on the part of the
endocrine thymus (Goldstein, A.L., et al., 1981). Thus,
it is hoped that the administration of thymic hormones to
patients with autoimmune disorders can help to normalize the
aberrant immunoregulatory cell activity which are characteristic of the diseases. In cancer patients it is hoped that
the thymic hormones can be employed as adjuncts to conventional chemotheraphy or radiation therapy, in an attempt to
ameliorate the immunosuppressive side effects associated with
their use. By maintaining and/or restoring T-cell dependent
immunity, the cancer patient should be more capable of mount-
ing a host response to the tumor, as well as to the various
viral, bacterial and fungal pathogens that he would otherwise be susceptible to.

To the present time, most clinical studies of thymic
preparations have been reported with four products; namely,
bovine thymosin fraction 5 (Wara, D.W., et al., 1975),
thymosin fraction 5-like preparations such as TP-1 (Falchetti,
R., et al., 1977), THF (Shohat,B., et al., 1978), TFX
(Aleksandrowicz, J., et al., 1975) and thymopoietin (Di Perri,
T., et al., 1980). Currently, it is estimated that over
500 patients have been treated with thymosin and there are
several studies in progress.

To the present time, most of the reported thymic hormone trials in patients with a variety of immunodeficiency
or infectious disorders cannot be critically evaluated since
either the number of treated patients with a clinical syndrome was too small to permit proper statistical analysis
of the findings or subjects receiving placebo were not included.  Nonetheless, the overwhelming evidence would
suggest that thymic hormones exert a therapeutic role in
selected patients with primary immunodeficiencies.  In addition, several randomized trials in cancer patients have indicated that thymosin fraction 5 may be efficacious when
administered as an adjunct to conventional chemotherapy
(Cohen, M.H., et al., 1979; Lipson, D.S., et al., 1979) or
radiation therapy (Wara, W.M., et al., 1978; Wara, W.M., et
al., 1981).  In the following sections, the reported and
ongoing clinical trials with the thymic hormones will be
reviewed.


Primary Immunodeficiency.

Over 100 children have now received thymosin fraction
or other thymic factors for a variety of primary immunodeficiency diseases in non-randomized studies.  The greatest experience has been with thymosin fraction 5.  Most
patients have received 60 mg/m$^2$ (1 mg/kg) of thymosin by
subcutaneous injection for periods of up to five years.
In general, patients have been administered a loading dose
regimen in which daily injections of fraction 5 are given.
(Wara, W.M., et al., 1978; Barrett, D.J., et al., 1980).
Bovine fraction 5 has been well tolerated and there has
been no evidence of liver, renal or hematologic toxicity.
Approximately 60% of treated patients did not experience
any side effects.  About 20% of patients have experienced
mild local skin reactions, and about 10% have experienced
moderate skin reactions or systemic allergic manifestations
requiring discontinuation of injections.  A summary of
clinical results reproted by Wara (Wara, D.W., 1981) in
children with primary immunodeficiency diseases is given
in Table 1.  Thymosin $\alpha_1$ has not yet   been employed in
such patients.

TABLE 1

THERAPEUTIC RESPONSE TO THYMOSIN FRACTION 5
BY PATIENTS WITH PRIMARY IMMUNODEFICIENCY DISEASES

| Finding | Clinical Improvement | Increased T Cell Nos. | Increased T Cell Function |
|---|---|---|---|
| Severe combined immunodeficiency | 0/1 | 0/1 | 0/1 |
| DiGeorge syndrome | N.A.* | 4/6 | 4/6 |
| Ataxia telangiectasia | 2/4 | 3/4 | 2/4 |
| Wiskott-Aldrich syndrome | 1/3 | 2/3 | 2/3 |
| Chronic mucocutaneous candidiasis | 1/4 | 1/4 | 1/4 |
| Nezelof's syndrome | 2/2 | 2/2 | 1/2 |

N.A.* = not applicable

From Wara, D.W., Adv. Pediatr. 28, 229 (1981).

Autoimmune Diseases.

There are very few published studies concerning the
therapeutic efficacy of thymic hormones in patients with
autoimmune disorders, probably because the clinical trials
are currently in progress or are just being initiated.
There are preliminary reports of thymosin fraction 5
(Lavastida, M.A., et al., 1981) administration in patients
with rheumatoid arthritis or SLE. Lavastida et al.
(Lavastida, M.A., et al., 1981) presented results of a
small phase I thymosin fraction 5 trial in 4 patients with
SLE and one with rheumatoid arthritis and Sjogren's syndrome. Patients were treated intramuscularly with either
20 mg or 60 mg a day for either 5 or 14 days followed by
various maintenance schedules. Two patients were off
steroids, and the other 3 were on 10 mg or less of predni-
sone daily. Treatment duration varied from 2-35 months.
All patients receiving thymosin showed a reduction to
zero of serum cytotoxic antibodies against murine thymocytes. There were no changes observed in PBL proliferative
responses to mitogens and antigens, and there was no
influence of thymosin administration on anti-nuclear antibody (FANA) titers. It was reported that the dominant
clinical features of disease activity (eg. arthritis/
arthralgias, thromboytopenia, dermatidis) either improved
or did not recur, but no details were given. No side
effects were encountered.

One randomized Phase II clinical trial with thymosin
fraction 5 in rheumatoid arthritis has recently been
initiated here at The George Washington Medical Center by
Dr. Robert Jacobs. Because of limited patient numbers and
the non-randomized nature of reported studies, little hard
data is available regarding the clinical efficacy of
thymic factors in the autoimmune diseases. It is anticipated that Dr. Jacobs controlled randomized trial will help
to provide an answer.


Phase I, II and III Cancer Trials.

Most of the clinical trials designed to evaluate the
efficacy of thymic hormones in cancer patients have been
performed with thymosin fraction 5 and thymosin $\alpha_1$. Approximately 300 patients have been treated to date. In

phase I studies with fraction 5, there have been no biochemical or hematological toxicity observed with SQ doses
as high as 400 mg/m$^2$ (Schafer, L.A., et al., 1977; Rossio,
J.L. and Goldstein, A.L., 1977; Costanzi, J.J., et al.,
1977). As with pediatric patients, local erythmatus reactions were observed in approximately 30% of patients and
severe allergic manifestations requiring discontinuation
in 10%. The early phase I studies confirmed that in vivo
administration could augment T cell numbers in advanced
cancer patients but only in patients who exhibited low pre-
treatment T cell numbers. A correlation was observed between in vitro and in vivo responsiveness. Recently phase
I studies with thymosin $\alpha_1$ have been performed (Chretien,
P., 1982; Schulof, R.S., et al., 1982) and no significant
side effects have been observed at SQ doses up to 900 µg/m$^2$.

Following the early phase I thymosin fraction 5 trials,
a small, non-randomized study of patients with stage III
melanoma was performed in 28 patients (Patt, Y.Z., et al.,
1979). This study was difficult to interpret because
various groups of patients received concurrent chemotherapy
or other immunotherapy along with fraction 5, administered
subcutaneously either at 4 mg/m$^2$ or 40 mg/m$^2$. Immune
competence was assessed by DTHS skin testing and enumeration of E-RFC and PBL proliferative responses to mitogens.
It was observed that whereas high dose thymosin improved
survival in immunoincompetent patients, it was detrimental
to patients that were immunologically normal prior to
treatment. Thus, these results suggested that the therapeutic benefits of thymosin are restricted to immuno-
compromised patients.

The first randomized phase II trials of thymosin
fraction 5 were designed by Chretien and colleagues
(Chretien, P.B., et al., 1978; Cohen, M.H., et al., 1979;
Lipson, D.S., et al., 1979) in patients with small cell
lung cancer and by Wara and colleagues (Wara, W.M. et al.,
1978; Wara, W.M., et al., 1981) in patients with squamous
cell carcinoma of the head and neck. The first trial was
a three armed study of 55 patients in which thymosin
(either 20 mg/m$^2$ or 60 mg/m$^2$) or placebo was administered
by SQ injection twice weekly during 6 weeks of intensive
combination chemotherapy. Surviving patients received one
of several different forms of maintenance therapy. Although
overall tumor response rates did not differ significantly

among the three treatment groups, it was found that thymosin (60 mg/m$^2$), as shown in Figure 7, significantly prolonged survival in patients who had eradication of all
detectable disease by chemotherapy. Prolonged survival was

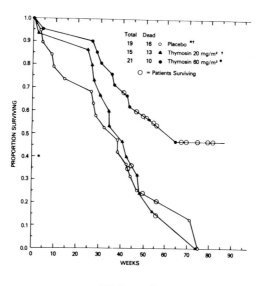

FIGURE 7

Figure 7. Thymosin in conjunction with chemotherapy in
patients with small cell bronchogenic carcinoma. Thymosin,
in chemotherapy of cancer patients (after Cohen et al.,
1979 and P. Chretien, personal communication). Survival
kinetics of oat-cell carcinoma patients given 60 mg/M$^2$
thymosin (●), 20 mg/M$^2$ thymosin fraction 5 (▲), or a placebo
(0) twice weekly subcutaneously during the first    weeks
of intensive chemotherapy. Thymosin increased median survival from 240 days to over 450 days.

found to correlate directly with initial low levels of T
cells and depressed serum $\alpha_2$HS glycoprotein levels. The
patients who benefited most from thymosin were those with
relatively low immune reactivity. Thus, this study was
interpreted to indicate that whereas thymosin had no detectable direct antitumor effects, it may have ameliorated the
immune defects due to the tumor or induced by the chemo-

therapy.  Although this trial can be criticized for employing small patient numbers, and for lack of stratification
based on those patients who received radiation therapy
(which is immunosuppressive) and those who did not, it was
the first positive controlled trial involving a thymic
hormone in patients.

The study of Wara et al. (Wara, W.M. et al., 1978;
Wara,W.M., et al., 1981) is a randomized trial of SQ thymosin fraction 5 (60 mg/m$^2$ SQ) or placebo administered as an
adjunct to conventional radiotherapy for treatment of head
and neck cancer.  Thymosin/placebo administration began
concurrently with radiation therapy and continued for one
year or until relapse.  A loading dose schedule of administration was utilized in which patients received 10 days
of daily injections followed by twice weekly maintenance.
Seventy-five patients with stage II-IV squamous cell cancer
have been entered into this trial.  With a median follow-up
time of 2 years, the thymosin-treated groups exhibited an
improved relapse-free survival which was of borderline significance (p<.08).  The thymosin-treated group of patients
exhibited an accelerated reconstitution of MLC reactivity of
PBL (by 6 months) compared to patients who had received
placebo.  Patient entry for this study can be criticized for
having an inequality of patient numbers between the 2 groups,
and for not stratifying patients on the basis of surgical
reduction of disease, it is the first randomized trial reported with a thymic hormone in which serial immune analyses
were performed.

In September, 1980, under the auspices of the newly
created Biological Response Modifiers Program of the National
Cancer Institute, sponsored phase I/II trials of thymosin
fraction 5 and $\alpha_1$ were initiated at 5 medical centers in the
United States.  These studies have as goals the establish-
ment of the maximal tolerated dose, and maximal immuno-
modulatory dose and schedule of each of the thymosin preparations.  All of the participating institutions are performing
a battery of serial immune analyses, including an evaluation
of T cell subsets by monoclonal antibodies.  It is hoped that
these studies can generate the guidelines upon which future
phase II and phase III trials with thymic hormones will be
based.  Preliminary results of these studies have recently
been published (Schulof, R.S., et al., 1982; Wara, W.M., et.
al. 1982; Fabrega, R., et al., 1982, Dilman, R.O.,.et al.,

1982).


FUTURE PROSPECTIVES FOR THYMIC HORMONES IN CLINICAL MEDICINE
& TREATMENT OF DISEASES OF AGING

The ultimate clinical application of the thymosins
should be in providing a means of safely augmenting specific
T lymphocyte functions in patients with diminished thymic-
dependent immunity due either to disease processes or aging.
In anergic cancer patients, the thymic hormones may be of
importance as an adjunct to conventional treatments by increasing T-cell function in response not only to tumor
cells, but also to pathogens, thus reducing the high incidence of infection that often accompanies cancer treatment. The positive preliminary clinical trials to date
with thymosin fraction 5 and most recently with thymosin
$\alpha_1$ offer a strong rationale for rapidly confirming the
clinical studies and expanding the basic research programs
with the goal of further purifying, characterizing and
increasing the availability of the thymosins. Confirmatory
clinical trials in cancer patients are already in progress
in several centers.
Further clinical assessment of the synthetic thymosins
and thymosin-like polypeptides is needed. The availability
of active agents that can be synthesized in the laboratory
will circumvent the technical problems associated with
the isolation of thymic hormones from bulk quantities of
thymus tissue or serum.

It will also be important to develop experimental
animal models which can be used to explore the efficacy of
administering thymic hormones by various routes (locally,
systemically) and in combination with other biological
response modifiers, such as lymphokines, adjuvants, inter-
ferons or with tumor cell antigens. It is to be anticipated
that over the next decade, well planned clinical trials
will help to determine the optimal conditions for employing
thymic hormones as a therapeutic modality in the treatment
of a wide variety of diseases associated with immune
deficiency and aging. It is also anticipated that unravel-
ing the endocrine thymus interrelationships with other
systems will provide new approaches for treatments of many
endocrine disorders associated with thymic malfunction.

## ACKNOWLEDGEMENTS

The studies reported were supported in part by grants from the National Cancer Institute (CA 24974), the National Institute of Aging (AG 02848,AI 17710) and Hoffmann La Roche, Inc.

## REFERENCES

Ahmed A, Smith AH, Sell KW (1978). In Chirigos MA (ed): "Immune Modulation and Control Neoplasia by Adjuvant Therapy," New York: Raven Press.
Ahmed A, Smith AH, Wong DM, Thurman GB, Goldstein AL, Sell KW (1978). Cancer Treat. Rep. 62:1739.
Albright JF, Makinodan T (1966). Cell. Physiol. 67 (Suppl. 10):185.
Asanuma Y, Goldstein AL, White A (1970). Endocrinol. 86: 600.
Astaldi A, Astaldi GCB, Wijermans P, Groenewoud P, Schellekens TA, Eijsvoogel VP (1978). J. Immunol. 119.
Bach JF, Dardenne M (1971). Transpl. Proc. 4:345.
Bach JF, Dardenne M, Solomon JC (1973). Clin. Exp. Immunol. 14:247.
Barrett DJ, Wara DW, Ammann AJ et al. (1980). J. Pediat. 97:66.
Bistoni F, Marconi P, Frati L, Bonmassar E, Garaci E (1982). Infection and Immunity 36:609.
Burch PRJ (1969). In "Growth, Disease and Aging," Toronto: University of Toronto Press.
Burnet FM (1974). Prog. Immunol. II 5:27.
Hammer JA (1906). In "Die Normal--Morphologische Thymus Forschung In Leitzten Viertei Jahrlundert Leipzig: Barton.
Hardy MA, Quint J, Goldstein AL, State D, White A (1968). Proc. Natl. Acad. Sci. 61:875.
Chou PY, Fasman GD (1974). Biochemistry 13:211
Chretien PB, Lipson SD, Makuch R, et al. (1978). Cancer Treatment Reports. 62:1787
Chretien P (1982) Proc. Internatl. Symp. on Current Contents in Humman Immunology and Cancer Immunomodulation (In Press).
Coggle JE, Proukakais C, (1970). Gerontologia 16:25.
Cohen MH, Chretien PB, Ihle DC, et al. (1979). J.A.M.A. 241:813.
Comfort A (1964). In "Aging, the Biology of Senescence," London: Routledge and Kegan Paul.

Costanzi JJ, Gagliano RG, Loukas D, Delaney F, Sakai H, Harris NS, Thurman GB, Goldstein AL (1977). Cancer 40:14.
Costanzi JJ, Harris N, Goldstein AL (1978). Proc 3rd Conference on Modulation of Host Resistance In Prevention and Treatment of Neoplasias. In Chirigos MA (ed): "Immune Modulation and Control of Neoplasia by Admuvant Therapy," New York: Raven Press.
Dabrowski MP, Goldstein AL (1976). Immunol Commun. 5:695.
Davis ML, Upton AC, Satterfield LC (1971). Proc Soc Exp Biol Med 137:1452.
Dillman RO, Beauregard JC, Zavanelli MI, et al. (1982) Proc Amer Soc Clin Oncol 1:42
Di Perri T, Laghi PF, Auteri A (1980). J Immunopharmacol 2:567
Duckworth WL (1962). In Lyans MC and Towers B (eds.): "Galen on Anatomical Procedures," London and New York: Cambridge University Press, p. 160.
Fabrega R, Pinsley C, Braun D, et al. (1982). Proc Amer Assoc Canc Res 3:39
Goldstein AL, Slater FD, White A (1966). Proc Natl Acad Sci USA 56:100.
Goldstein AL, White A (1970). In Litwack G (ed) "Biochemical Actions of Hormones," New York: Academic Press, pp 462-502.
Goldstein AL, White A (1973). In Davies AJS and Corti RC (eds.) "Contemporary Topics in Immunobiology," vol. 2 New York: Plenum Publishing Co., pp 339-350.
Goldstein AL, Hooper JA, Schulof RS, Cohen GH, Thurman GB, McDaniel MC, White A and Dardenne M (1974). Fed Proc 33(9): 2053.
Goldstein AL, Thurman GB, Cohen GH and Hooper JA (1975). In Van Bekkum DW (ed.), "The Biological Activity of Thymic Hormones, " Rotterdam:Kooyker Scient Publ 145.
Goldstein AL, Cohen GH, Rossio JL, Thurman GB, Brown CN, Ulrich JT (1976). Medical Clinics of North America 60(30): 591.
Goldstein AL, Low TLK, McAdoo M, McClure J, Thurman GB, Rossio JL, Lai C-Y., Chang D, Wang S-S., Harvey C, Ramel AH, Meienhofer JL (1977). Proc Natl Acad Sci 74: 725.
Goldstein AL, Low TLK, Thurman GB, Zatz MM, Hall NR, Chen CP, Hu S-K, Naylor PB and McClure JE (1981). Recent Prog Horm Res 37:369.
Goldstein AL (1982). Executive Health XVIII.
HallNR, Goldstein AL (1981). In Ader R (ed.) "Psychoneuro-immunology," New York: Academic Press.

Hall NR (1981). In Nemeroff CB and Dunn AJ (eds.) "Molecular and Behavioral Neuroendocrinology," New York:Spectrum.
Hall NR, McGillis JP, Spangelo B, Palazynski E, Moody T and Goldstein AL (1982). In Serrou B (ed.) "Current Concepts in Human Immunology and Cancer Immunomudulation," New York: Elsevier Press.
Hammer JA (1906). In Die Normal -- Morphologische Thymus Forschung in Leitzten Viertei Jahrlundert. Leipzig:Barton
Heidrick ML, Makinodan T (1973). J Immunol 111:1502.
Hirokawa K, Makinodan T (1975) J Immunol 114:1659.
Hooper JA, McDaniel MC, Thurman GB, Cohen GH, Schulof RS, Goldstein AL (1975). Annals NY Acad Sci 249:125.
Horowitz S, Borcherding CO, Moorthy AV, Chesney R, Schulte-Wisserman H, Hong R (1977) Science 197:4307.
Huang K-Y, Kind PD, Jagoda EM, Goldstein AL (1981). J. Interferon Res. 1:411.
Kaplan J and Peterson WD, Jr. (1978). Clin Immunol Immunopathol 9:436.
Kenady DE, Chretien PB, Potvin C, Simon RM, Alexander JC, Goldstein AL (1977). Cancer 39:642.
Klein JJ, Goldstein AL, White A (1965). Proc Natl Acad Sci 53:812.
Krohn PL (ed.) (1966). In "Topics in the Biology of Aging", New York:Interscience.
Lavastida MA, Goldstein, AL, Daniels JC (1981). Thymus 2: 287.
Lipson DS, Chretien PB, Makuch R, et al. (1979). Cancer 43: 863.
Low TLK, Goldstein AL (1979). J Biol Chem 254:987.
Low TLK, Thurman GB, McAdoo M, McClure JE, Rossio JL, Naylor PH, Goldstein AL, (1979) J Biol Chem 254:981.
Low TLK, Goldstein AL (1982). J. Biol. Chem. 257:1000.
MacKay IR, Masel M, Burnett FM (1964). Anst. Ann. Med 13:5.
Makinodan T (1966). Dev. Biol. 14:96.
Makinodan T, Peterson WJ, (1962). Proc Natl Acad Sci USA 48:234.
Makinodan T, Peterson WJ (1964). J Immunol 93:886.
Makinodan T, Adler WH (1975). Fed Proc 34:153.
Makinodan T, Yunis E (eds.) (1977) "Immunology and Aging," New York:Plenum Publishing Co.
McClure JE, Lamaris H, Wara DW, Goldstein AL (1981). J. Immunol 128:368.
Medvedev ZA, (1964) Adv Gerontol Res 1:181.
Metcalf D (1965). Nature (London) 208:1336.
Orgel LE (1963) Proc Natl Acad Sci 49:517.
Osheroff PL (1981). Cell Immunol 60:376.

Patt YZ, Hersh EM, Schafer LA, et al. (1979). Cancer
Immunol. Immunotherap. 7:131.
Pazmino NH, Ihle JN and Goldstein AL (1978). J. Exp. Med.
147:708.
Perkins EH, Makinodan T (1971) In "Proceedings from the
First Rocky Mountain Symposium on Aging," Ft. Collins,
Colorado:Colorado State University, pp. 80-103.
Price GB, Makinodan T (1972a) J Immunol 108:403.
Price GB, Makinodan T (1972b) J Immunol 108:413.
Rebar RW, Miyake A, Low TLK, Goldstein AL (1981) Science
214:669.
Rossio JL, Goldstein (1977). World J. Surgery 1:605.
Schafer LA, Gutterman JU, Hersh EM, Mavligit GM, Goldstein
AL (1977). In Chirigos MA (ed.) "Progress in Cancer
Research and Therapy," vol. 2, New York: Raven Press
pp 329-346.
Shohat B, Spitzer S, Topilsky M, et al. (1978). Biomedicine
Exper. 29:91.
Schulof RS, Ph.D. Thesis: Radioimmunological Studies of
Thymosin, (unpublished observations).
Schulof RS, Lloyd M, Cos J, et al. (1982). In Serrou B,
(ed.) "Current Concepts of Cancer Immunology and Immuno-
modulation," Amsterdam:Elsevier-North Holland Press
(In Press).
Strausser HR, Bober LA, Busci RA, Schillcock JA, Goldstein
AL (1971). Exptl. Gerontol. 6:373.
Strehler BL (1967) Ann. N.Y. Acad. Sci. 138:661.
Talal N., Dauphinee M, Philarisetty R, Goldblum R (1975).
Ann. N.Y. Acad. Sci. 249:438.
Taylor R (1965). Nature (London) 208:1334.
Teller MN, Stohr G, Cartlett W, Kubisek ML and Burtis D
(1964). J. Natl. Cancer Inst. 33:649.
Trainin N, (1974). Physiol. Rev. 54:272.
Walford RL (1969). "The Immunologic Theory of Aging."
Copenhagen:Munksgaard.
Walford RL (1974). Fed Proc 33:2020
Wara DW, Goldstein AL, Doyle N, Ammann AJ (1975) New Eng
J Med 292:70.
Wara DW (1981). Adv Pediatr 28:229
Wara WM, Ammann AJ, Wara DW (1978). Cancer Treat Rep 62:
1775.
Wara WM, Neely MH, Amman AJ, Wara DW (1981). In Chirigos
MA and Goldstein AL (eds.) "Lymphokines and Thymic Hormones:
Their Potential Utilization in Cancer Therapeutics, "
New York: Raven Press, p. 257.

Wara WM, Wara DW, Neely MH and Carter SK (1982).   In
Serrou B  (ed.) "Current Concepts of Cancer" Amsterdam:
Elsevier/North Holland Biomedical Press (In Press).
Zatz MM, Glaser M, Seals CM, Goldstein AL (1981).   In
Goldstein AL and Chirigos MA (eds.) "Lymphokines and
Thymic Hormones: Their Potential Utilization in Cancer
Therapeutics. New York: Raven Press.

Intervention in the Aging Process, Part A: Quantitation, Epidemiology, and Clinical Research, pages 199–214
© 1983 Alan R. Liss, Inc., 150 Fifth Avenue, New York, NY 10011

ENZYME COFACTORS AND AGING

Karl Folkers

Institute for Biomedical Research, The University of Texas at Austin, Austin, Texas   78712

My presentation on enzyme cofactors and aging is concerned with pyridoxal 5'-phosphate (vitamin $B_6$), coenzyme $Q_{10}$ ($CoQ_{10}$) and 5,6,7,8-tetrahydrobiopterin ($BH_4$). In biochemistry, $CoQ_{10}$ and $BH_4$ are also established as coenzymes or cofactors.  The present status of biomedical and clinical research on these coenzymes includes not only positive evidence for new therapy of aging processes, but shows great promise for new medical milestones for control of aging.

PYRIDOXAL 5'-PHOSPHATE AND A CONCEPT ON THE CLINICAL EFFECTIVENESS OF A COENZYME

Vitamin $B_6$ consists of a group of biochemically related compounds.  Pyridoxine is one member of this group, and it is commonly referred to as vitamin $B_6$.  Although it is pyridoxine hydrochloride which is orally administered to subjects or patients, it is pyridoxal 5'-phosphate which is the prime coenzyme.  The oral intake of pyridoxine hydrochloride, in tablet or capsule form, results in conversion to the coenzyme, pyridoxal 5'-phosphate.

In a series of over 20 publications in the period of 1975–1982, my associates and I have reported that patients with the carpal tunnel syndrome (CTS) invariably have a very significant deficiency of vitamin $B_6$.  When pyridoxine hydrochloride was administered to such patients, not only was the deficiency of vitamin $B_6$ corrected, but the signs and symptoms of the carpal tunnel syndrome were very significantly alleviated.  Then, this study of vitamin $B_6$ and CTS was conducted on a double blind basis.

In this controlled study, the specific activities and percent deficiencies of the glutamic oxaloacetic transaminase of the erythrocytes (EGOT) were determined for patients with CTS who had been diagnosed by clinical examination and electrical conduction data. The EGOT data revealed a severe deficiency of vitamin $B_6$ for all of the subjects of this trial. After double blind treatment with pyridoxine hydrochloride and placebo for 10-12 weeks, two physicians identified those individuals receiving pyridoxine (clinically improved) and those receiving placebo (did not improve) without error; $P<0.0078$.

This double blind trial and the results were published in December, 1982 (Proc. Natl. Acad. Sci. USA, Vol. 79, pp. 7494-7498, Medical Sciences). As this 7-year study evolved, and was described in 24 publications, a relatively new concept also evolved, which is as follows. Correcting a deficiency of the coenzyme (pyridoxal 5'-phosphate) at the receptors of existing molecules of the apoenzyme (the apoenzyme of EGOT) appears to take place within days. Correction of the deficiency in the number of molecules of the transaminase (EGOT) appears to take place over a period of 10-12 weeks. The clinical response of the carpal tunnel syndrome as appraised by diminution of the signs and symptoms of the neurological disease, was correlated only with the restored levels of the transaminase (EGOT) and which presumably results from a translational long-term increase in the number of molecules of the transaminase (EGOT) by a mechanism which is activated by correcting a deficiency of the coenzyme (pyridoxal 5'-phosphate).

This concept is in great contrast to the common thinking of many scientists and physicians that pyridoxine (vitamin B ) may be considered just like a drug or a synthetic medicinal. Drugs and synthetic medicinals reveal their activities by pharmacodynamic mechanisms within minutes, hours, or a day or so. It became surprisingly clear in this 7-year study that the clinical efficacy of pyridoxine to treat patients with the carpal tunnel syndrome does not result from a pharmacodynamic mechanism like that of a drug, but rather from mechanisms of molecular biology which are long-term changes.

The specific activity of EGOT was always more diagnostic than was the percentage deficiency of the activity of EGOT, although both values have significance. An increase in specific activity from <0.20 → 0.25 to <u>ca.</u> 0.7 over <u>ca.</u> 10-12 weeks was unambiguously associated with clinical improvement.

It has apparently not been customary to relate vitamin $B_6$ to aging, but the demonstration of the efficacy of pyridoxine to treat the carpal tunnel syndrome and recognition of the incidence of the carpal tunnel syndrome in the advancing decades of life may now bring new attention and emphasis to the potential importance of correcting deficiencies of vitamin $B_6$ in many age brackets. The carpal tunnel symdrome has been commonly recognized not only in the elderly, but recently in university students in their 20's.

This relatively new concept about the molecular mechanisms of pyridoxal 5'-phosphate as a coenzyme to explain the clinical efficacy for the treatment of a disease is believed to have some general applicability to the clinical use of other coenzymes to treat diseases. In particular, this concept appears to be presently contributing to the succesful guidance of the clinical use of coenzyme $Q_{10}$ to treat cardiovascular disease. Surely, this concept should also be tested in future clinical trials on tetrahydrobiopterin to treat appropriate disease states.

COENZYME $Q_{10}$

Coenzyme $Q_{10}$ has structure I (Chart 1). It is a benzoquinone with two adjacent methoxy groups, one methyl group and a decaprenyl side chain attached to the nucleus. One isoprenoid unit has structure II, and since there are ten of these units in the isoprenoid side chain, the quinone was designated coenzyme $Q_{10}$. The coenzyme functionality of the molecule is based upon its reversible oxidation and reduction, as for structures III and IV. $CoQ_{10}$ is like a vitamin.

Coenzyme $Q_{10}$ has a biochemical role in electron and proton transport. The location of $CoQ_{10}$ in the respiratory chain is depicted in Chart 2 (Ernster and Nelson, 1981). Semiquinone intermediates are also presumably involved in some processes. For a decade, $CoQ_{10}$ has been scientifically accepted as an indispensable member of respiration in human tissue.

CHART 1

STRUCTURE OF COENZYME $Q_{10}$

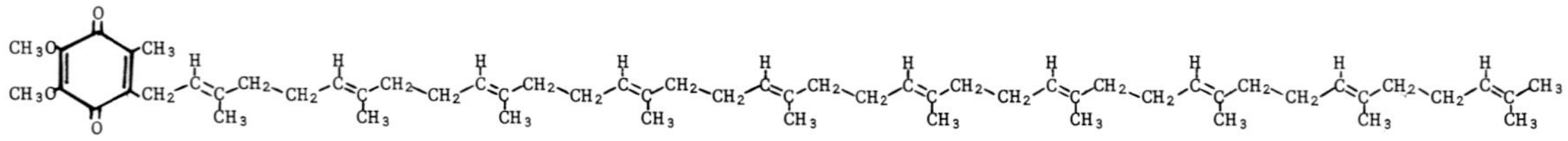

ONE ISOPRENOID UNIT IS:

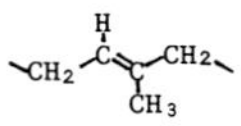

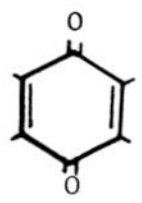

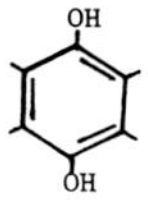

COENZYME $Q_{10}$ IS LIKE A VITAMIN.

CHART 2

FUNCTIONS OF COENZYME Q

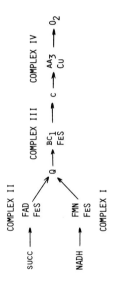

LOCATION OF Q IN THE RESPIRATORY CHAIN

L. ERNSTER AND B.D. NELSON (1981) IN BIOMEDICAL AND CLINICAL ASPECTS OF COENZYME Q, VOL. 3, K. FOLKERS AND Y. YAMAMURA (EDS.) ELSEVIER/NORTH HOLLAND BIOMEDICAL PRESS, AMSTERDAM.

The biochemical and animal studies over many years clearly indicate that $CoQ_{10}$ is necessary for human life to exist. There are some basic concepts for consideration concerning therapy with $CoQ_{10}$. Since $CoQ_{10}$ is apparently necessary for human life to exist, then deficiencies of $CoQ_{10}$ in human tissues may be expected to cause one or more disease states. A patient with a zero deficiency may be expected to show no clinical response to oral $CoQ_{10}$. Therefore, it is important to determine and know about the possible existence and degree of $CoQ_{10}$-deficiency in patients before therapy with $CoQ_{10}$.

Table 1 shows a summary of the levels of the specific activities of the succinate dehydrogenase $CoQ_{10}$-reductase of biopsies of heart tissues and increases in activities which show deficiencies of $CoQ_{10}$. There are 13 categories of cardiopathies which are represented in the study. The conclusion of such biochemical diagnosis was that 75% of the 132 patients showed varying deficiencies of $CoQ_{10}$ in their heart tissue.

$CoQ_{10}$-enzyme analyses on blood samples of cardiac patients have also been performed. In 1978, we had analyzed 406 patients and by 1979, we had extended the analyses to 1002 cardiac patients. The mean specific activity (S.A.) was $3.05 \pm 1.07/1002$ patients, and the mean S.A. was $4.20 \pm 2.73$ for a control group ($p < 0.001$). The conclusion from the analyses of blood samples from cardiac patients was that the incidence of $CoQ_{10}$ deficiency in cardiac patients was very high (Folkers et al., 1978-1980).

Table 2 shows data from the monitoring of the cardiac function by impedance cardiography during treatment of cardiac patients with $CoQ_{10}$. Eight exemplary patients constituted this group. Their age ranged from 38 to 78 years. The period of treatment ranged from 4 to 9 months. Since impedance cardiography is non-invasive, it was feasible to make a very large number of measurements of cardiac function during the control period and the treatment period. The P values for significance show that cardiac output and stroke volume were significantly improved. It was concluded that therapy with $CoQ_{10}$ significantly improved cardiac function, but the positive clinical response was slow to become evident.

TABLE I. SUMMARY OF LEVELS OF SPECIFIC ACTIVITIES OF THE SUCCINATE DEHYDROGENASE-COENZYME $Q_{10}$ REDUCTASE OF BIOPSY HEART TISSUES AND INCREASES WHICH SHOW DEFICIENCIES OF COENZYME $Q_{10}$

| TABLE | NUMBER OF PATIENTS | CARDIOPATHIES | SPECIFIC ACTIVITIES | SPECIFIC ACTIVITIES WITH $CoQ_3$ | % INCREASES WITH $CoQ_3$ |
|---|---|---|---|---|---|
| I | 13 | CONTROLS | 58 (16-137)* | 64 (16-152)* | 9 (0-28)* |
| II | 9 | THORACIC AORTIC ANEURYSM | 64 (16-137) | 71 (16-152) | 11 (0-28) |
| III | 8 | INTERVENTRICULAR SEPTAL DEFECT | 52 (24-91) | 71 (24-183) | 30 (0-100) |
| IV | 12 | INTERATRIAL SEPTAL DEFECT | 48 (22-73) | 76 (29-186) | 62 (0-87) |
| V | 10 | TETRALOGY OF FALLOT | 40 (9-75) | 57 (18-128) | 42 (0-106) |
| VI | 4 | ANOMALOUS VENOUS RETURN | 64 (34-117) | 78 (50-117) | 29 (0-50) |
| VII | 5 | RARE CONGENITAL HEART DEFECTS | 74 (69-94) | 105 (80-140) | 41 (23-50) |
| VIII | 3 | VENTRICULAR ANEURYSM ATRIUM SPECIMENS | 51 (26-84) | 82 (42-126) | 64 (50-78) |
| IX | 3 | VENTRICLE SPECIMENS FROM PAPILLARY MUSCLE (MITRAL VALVE) | 123 (79-146) | 139 (133-150) | 27 (0-70) |
| X | 31 | AORTIC VALVULAR DEFECTS | 45 (9-111) | 63 (13-154) | 40 (0-100) |
| XI | 16 | MITRAL VALVULAR DEFECTS | 57 (18-108) | 88 (24-149) | 52 (0-122) |
| XII | 19 | MITRAL AND AORTIC DEFECTS | 63 (9-130) | 85 (13-148) | 39 (0-95) |
| XIII | 4 | CARDIOPATHIES ASSOCIATED WITH DIABETES | 39 (33-44) | 68 (49-83) | 73 (48-100) |
| XIV | 10 | TRICUSPIDAL DEFECTS | 57 (22-78) | 103 (33-154) | 82 (49-132) |

*RANGE

CONCLUSION - 75% OF THE 132 PATIENTS SHOWED VARYING DEFICIENCIES OF $CoQ_{10}$ IN THEIR HEART TISSUE.

K. FOLKERS, G. LITTARRU, L. HO, T.M. RUNGE, S. HAVANONDA AND D. COOLEY (1970) INT. J. VIT. RES. 40, 374.

G. LITTARRU, L. HO AND K. FOLKERS (1972) INT. J. VIT. RES. 42, 413.

TABLE II. DATA FROM MONITORING OF CARDIAC FUNCTION BY IMPEDANCE CARDIOGRAPHY DURING TREATMENT OF CARDIAC PATIENTS WITH COENZYME $Q_{10}$

| PAT. | SEX | AGE | PERIOD (MONTHS) | N | CARDIAC OUTPUT | p | STROKE VOLUME | p | HEATHER INDEX | p |
|---|---|---|---|---|---|---|---|---|---|---|
| GA | M | 75 | 9 | 6 | 3.59±0.46 | | 45.00±4.30 | | 10.10±1.10 | |
| | | | | 6 | 4.83±0.29 | <0.001 | 59.65±3.60 | <0.001 | 10.56±1.23 | N.S. |
| FB | M | 66 | 4 | 6 | 2.42±0.20 | | 24.70±2.96 | | 7.70±1.10 | |
| | | | | 6 | 3.23±0.32 | <0.001 | 43.53±6.96 | <0.001 | 9.24±1.81 | N.S. |
| RG | M | 51 | 8 | 13 | 2.43±0.95 | | 26.40±11.2 | | 4.70±1.10 | |
| | | | | 6 | 3.64±0.27 | <0.001 | 38.82±1.96 | <0.001 | 5.80±0.40 | <0.05 |
| WH | M | 58 | 6 | 6 | 3.06±0.15 | | 43.55±2.40 | | 6.68±0.53 | |
| | | | | 6 | 3.65±0.35 | <0.01 | 55.05±2.60 | <0.001 | 5.87±0.32 | <0.01 |
| WL | F | 59 | 5 | 4 | 2.57±0.10 | | 28.80±0.50 | | 12.90±0.90 | |
| | | | | 6 | 3.03±0.19 | <0.01 | 36.37±1.86 | <0.001 | 12.32±2.59 | N.S. |
| HM | M | 71 | 5 | 6 | 2.05±0.10 | | 20.95±0.78 | | 4.99±0.19 | |
| | | | | 6 | 2.89±0.35 | <0.001 | 32.05±3.45 | <0.001 | 7.76±0.96 | <0.001 |
| RS | M | 38 | 6 | 6 | 3.65±0.38 | | 45.30±5.00 | | 7.30±1.10 | |
| | | | | 2 | 3.25±0.19 | N.S. | 51.80±0.70 | <0.05 | 7.39±0.06 | N.S. |
| DR | M | 78 | 6 | 6 | 1.99±0.24 | | 28.20±3.10 | | 6.18±0.75 | |
| | | | | 6 | 2.56±0.39 | <0.01 | 30.65±3.62 | N.S. | 6.45±1.04 | N.S. |

IN GENERAL, THE DAILY DOSE OF $CoQ_{10}$ WAS 60-100 MG.

CONCLUSION

THERAPY WITH $CoQ_{10}$ SIGNIFICANTLY IMPROVED CARDIAC FUNCTION, BUT THE POSITIVE CLINICAL RESPONSE WAS SLOW TO BECOME EVIDENT.

K. FOLKERS, L. BAKER, P.C. RICHARDSON, S. SHIZUKUISHI, K. TAKEMURA, J. DRZEWOSKI, J. LEWANDOWSKI, AND J.M. ELLIS (1981) IN BIOMEDICAL AND CLINICAL ASPECTS OF COENZYME Q, VOL. 3, K. FOLKERS AND Y. YAMAMURA (EDS.) ELSEVIER/NORTH HOLLAND BIOMEDICAL PRESS, AMSTERDAM, PP. 399-412.

Chino et al., 1980, reported on the administration of $CoQ_{10}$ to patients having had myocardial infarction. Their objective was to determine the effects of $CoQ_{10}$ after acute myocardial infarction. The prognosis of myocardial infarction was followed for 52 patients who had lived longer than one and one-half years after their first attack. Group A consisted of 26 such patients who were treated with 30 mg of $CoQ_{10}$. Group B consisted of 26 patients as controls. It was concluded that the death rate because of heart disease for Group B without $CoQ_{10}$ was about three times as high as that for Group A with $CoQ_{10}$. It was inferred that reduction of sudden death was due to a decrease in ventricular arrhythmia. There are obviously many variables in such a study with patients who have had an infarction, but the basis for this study appears to be sound, and the results justify extension toward probable confirmation.

There has been a study by Tanaka et al., 1982, on the administration of $CoQ_{10}$ for a prophylactic effect on the low cardiac output which is known to follow cardiac valve replacement. It is known that a low post-operative cardiac output is a major cause of early death following a cardiac operation. The objective of this study was to test the possible effectiveness of pre-operative $CoQ_{10}$ on a post-operative low cardiac output. The protocol involved 50 patients who had valvular diseases. Twenty-five of these patients were in a control group and 25 others received 30-60 mg of $CoQ_{10}$ daily for six days before operation. Tanaka et al. concluded that the $CoQ_{10}$-treated group showed a lower incidence ($p<0.05$) of low cardiac output during recovery than that of the control group.

There have been a number of studies over several years on the inhibition of $CoQ_{10}$-enzymes by beta-receptor antagonists. A summary of the status of all these studies is as follows.

To reduce the elevated blood pressure of a patient, it is known that a beta-blocker has a prompt pharmacodynamic activity, but there can be an important side effect which can be inhibition of $CoQ_{10}$-enzymes. Extensive clinical studies have shwon that $CoQ_{10}$ may reduce blood pressure of hypertensive individuals and presumably in deficiency states. However, the anti-hypertensive activity of $CoQ_{10}$ is a slow response by improved bioenergetics (Folkers et al., 1982). It became evident that combined therapy with a beta-blocker

and $CoQ_{10}$ may have clinical advantages. Such therapy combines
the anti-hypertensive activity of a beta-blocker and that of
$CoQ_{10}$. Such therapy protects against the inhibition of $CoQ_{10}$
by a beta-blocker, and provides the prompt anti-hypertensive
activity of $CoQ_{10}$. This combined therapy offers a protocol
to withdraw the beta-blocker after reduction of hypertension
and maintain a normal blood pressure on $CoQ_{10}$, at least for
some patients (Folkers et al., 1982).

There has been a clinical evaluation of the effects of
$CoQ_{10}$ combined with a beta-blocker on ischemic heart disease.
Beta-blockers are widely used to treat angina pectoris, and
it is commonly believed that the negative inotropic effect
should be tolerated. Nagoshi et al., 1977, questioned whether
$CoQ_{10}$ could prevent the negative inotropic effect. They
studied 21 patients with ischemic heart disease, 13 of whom
had angina pectoris. Group A was treated with pindrol and
$CoQ_{10}$ (30 mg), and Group B was treated with $CoQ_{10}$ and no
beta-blocker. The results were as follows. The angina
pectoris on exertion disappeared after eight weeks on $CoQ_{10}$.
The angina pectoris persisted in 50% of the patients on a
beta-blocker. The ejection fraction increased in 19 of 21
patients on $CoQ_{10}$, and the ejection fraction increased in
patients on the beta-blocker and $CoQ_{10}$. Nagoshi et al.,
1977, concluded that $CoQ_{10}$ increased the ejection fraction
and stroke volume with and without a beta-blocker, and that
$CoQ_{10}$ plus a beta-blocker eliminated the thoracic pain of a
beta-blocker and dyspnea on exertion.

Observations have been reported on significant reductions
of arrhythmias by treatment with $CoQ_{10}$ in patients having
cardiovascular disease (Folkers et al., 1982). A summary of
these observations is as follows. Six patients were treated,
two of whom were on no conventional medication and four of
whom were on conventional medication. All six patients had
primarily either coronary heart disease or essential hypertension, and one clearly had both coronary heart disease and
essential hypertension. Holter recordings were made for two
of the patients. It was concluded that $CoQ_{10}$ caused a
substantial reduction of arrhythmias, and that this reduction
of arrhythmias is likely based on improved bioenergetics. A
variety of the commonly used drugs for such patients had not
interfered with the reduction of arrhythmia by $CoQ_{10}$.

From all this diversified biomedical and clinical research on $CoQ_{10}$, in conjunction with other data which could not be included in this presentation because of time, it is concluded that cardiovascular disease is significantly due to a deficiency of $CoQ_{10}$.

TETRAHYDROBIOPTERIN

Tetrahydrobiopterin is biochemically established as a coenzyme or cofactor. Its systematic name is [6-(L-erythro-1',2'-dihydroxypropyl)-2-amino-4-hydroxy-5,6,7,8-tetrahydro-pteridine. It has Structure I. It is common-y known as tetrahydrobiopterin, and this simplified name is often abbreviated as $BH_4$.

STRUCTURE I

The elucidation of the chemistry of $BH_4$ may be said to have been initiated in 1955 by the first isolation and identification of biopterin from human urine by Patterson, Broquist, Albrecht, von Saltza and Stockstad. Biopterin is 6-(2,3-dihydroxypropyl)pterin.

In 1958, Kaufman found that $BH_4$ functions as the natural coenzyme in the hydroxylation of phenylalanine to tyrosine. In 1966, Hosoda and Glick reported the similar conversion of tryptophan to 5-hydroxytryptophan. In 1972, Nagatsu, Mizutami, Nagatsu, Matsuura and Sugimoto reported on the role of $BH_4$ for the conversion of tyrosine to dopa.

These hydroxylations of aromatic amino acids are physiologically important for the biosynthesis of neurotransmitters, and have been widely investigated by many biochemists. The role of enzymatic diagnosis of biopterin derivatives in disease has also been widely investigated.

The role of tetrahydrobiopterin in neurological disease has been reviewed by Leeming et al., 1981, who concluded that tetrahydrobiopterin appears to have a key role in normal neurological and intellectual function.

Inherited defects in the metabolism of $BH_4$ have been reported to lead to "malignant hyperphenylalaninaemia". Classical phenylketonuria has been recognized for patients on a normal diet, but who have high serum levels of phenylalanine and reduced levels of neurotransmitters. Such patients may become severely handicapped and often have seizures and behavioural problems. Disturbed metabolism of biopterin has been reported for active coeliac disease. Reduced serum levels of dihydrobiopterin have been reported in senile dementia. Reduced levels of $BH_4$ have been reported in cerebrospinal fluid for patients having a variety of neurological diseases, including Parkinson's disease, Alzheimer's disease, Steel Richardson syndrome, Huntington's chorea and dystonia. Levels of $BH_4$ of cerebrospinal fluid may be a direct measure of $BH_4$ levels in the brain.

It has been known that in Parkinsonism, there is a great reduction in the level of dopamine in the brain. It appeared that this reduction may be caused by a decrease in biosynthesis.

In autopsy brain tissue from patients with Parkinson's disease, it was found by Nagatsu et al., 1981, that there was a reduction of the activity of tyrosine hydroxylase for 12 patients to about 5% of that of controls. This hydroxylation requires $BH_4$.

It was also found that biopterin levels in the caudate nucleus from autopsy were reduced for patients with Parkinsonism, according to a new radioimmunoassay. However, the levels of biopterin in the urine of Parkinsonian patients was not different from that of controls.

Data on the levels of biopterin in the caudate nucleus of controls and Parkinsonian patients are:

|  | Biopterin (nmol/g.w.w.) | |
|---|---|---|
| Controls | $1.25\pm0.25$ | $(0.59 - 2.45)$ |
| Parkinsonism | $0.30\pm0.06$ | $(0.12 - 0.62)$ |

There has been and still is substantial ambiguity on the degree that peripherally administered $BH_4$ can actually enter the brain. Kapatos and Kaufman in 1980 described data showing that the content of $BH_4$ in the rat brain was doubled by the intraperitoneal administration of $BH_4$. Rats were injected with the compounds dissolved in 1% ascorbic acid at pH 7. The control animals received only ascorbic acid. The levels of biopterin are expressed as means and represent accumulations above the control level, which was $0.486\pm0.031$ nmole/g. These data showing that $BH_4$ does lead to elevated levels of pterin in the brain indicate that administration of pterins might become an effective therapy for the related diseases. These data are:

| TREATMENT | DOSE (µmole/g) | N | BIOPTERIN ACCUMULATED (nmole/g) | |
|---|---|---|---|---|
| DL-tetrahydrobiopterin | 0.10 | 12 | 0.466 | 0.028 |
| L-tetrahydrobiopterin | 0.08 | 6 | 0.412 | 0.064 |
| D-tetrahydrobiopterin | 0.08 | 66 | 0.258 | 0.043 |

Levine, Miller and Lovenberg, 1981, studied levels of
$BH_4$ in the striatum and found that the hydroxylase cofactor,
$BH_4$, and its biosynthetic system are localized in dopaminergic nerve terminals in the striatum.  Their findings appear
to have implications for the treatment of Parkinson's disease
and other disorders which appear to have a deficiency of
biogenic amines.  Since $BH_4$ and its biosynthetic systems in
the nigrostriatal system appear to be localized in the dopaminergic neurons, it appeared of importance that the major,
if not exclusive physiological role of $BH_4$ in this area, is
to serve as the coenzyme for tyrosine and tryptophan hydroxylases.  They projected that the therapeutic administration
of $BH_4$ should increase neurotransmitter synthesis, specifically within aminergic neurons.

Narabayashi of Juntendo University and his colleagues
have conducted diversified studies on biotperin and BH  over
many years.  The BH  which he has clinically used was
synthesized from L-erythro-biopterin by Sugimoto and Matsuura.
The erduction of biopterin to BH  was by the method of Bailey
and Ailing.  The natural isomer has the 6R absolute configuration.  This synthesis yielded mixtures of the 6R and 6S
isomers, which were used clinically.  It had been known that
both of the 6R and 6S isomers have cofactor activity for
tyrosine hydroxylase.

It is informally known that Narabayashi and his co-
workers have made oral clinical reports at conferences on
the administration of BH  to patients having Parkinsonism.
It is understood that he had reported that single dosage of
BH  has shown a definite but mild benefit to symptoms of
Parkinsonism, including akinesia, rigidity and tremor.
Apparently, the patients were relatively "fresh" and had
moderate symptoms.

Professor Narabayashi has informed me that his manu-
script on these studies will be published, probably before
the end of '82.

SUMMARY

   Tetrahydrobiopterin is a coenzyme which is biosynthesized
de novo.  Blood levels and other tissue levels of $BH_4$ have
been found to be significantly reduced for certain diseases
states and plausible biochemical explanations for the
existence of a deficiency of $BH_4$ have been proposed.

   Although the organic synthesis of $BH_4$ has been achieved,
substantial improvements in the synthesis are needed.
However, $BH_4$ is becoming available on an ever-increasing
scale and more systematic clinical studies are now possible.

   Even the present exploratory and very limited clinical
data on the administration of $BH_4$ to human subjects, particularly those with Parkinsonism, support the prediction that
$BH_4$ will become of very great clinical importance for therapy,
particularly for neurological and behavioural conditions.

REFERENCES

Chino M, Takahashi T, Fujii I, Nara M, Ono K, Soma Y, Ito T
(1980).  Clinical experience with coenzyme $Q_{10}$ on patients
with myocardial infarction. The Diagnosis and Treatment 68:3.
Ernster L, Nelson DB (1981) Functions of coenzyme Q. In
Folkers K, Yamamura Y (eds): "Biomedical and Clinical Aspects
of Coenzyme," Vol 3, Amsterdam: Elsevier North Holland
Biomedical Press, p. 159.
Folkers K, Watanabe T (1978).  Bioenergetics in Clinical
Medicine XIV. Studies on an apparent deficiency of coenzyme
$Q_{10}$ in patients with cardiovascular and related diseases.
J Med 9:67.
Folkers K, Baker L, Richardson P, Shizukuishi S, Kaji M,
Combs A, Choe J, Kwen YZ, Nishii S, Lowell J, Lewandowski J,
Liu R, Hurst G (1980) Biomedical and clinical research on
coenzyme Q.  In Yamamura Y, Folkers K, Ito Y (eds):
"Biomedical and Clinical Aspects of Coenzyme Q," Vol 2,
Amsterdam: Elsevier North Holland Biomedical Press, p 447.
Folkers K, Takemura K, Sartori M (1982) Inhibition of
coenzyme $Q_{10}$-enzymes by beta-receptor antagonists.  In
Kuemmerle HP (ed): "The Effects of Beta-Receptor Antagonists
on the Myocardium," Munich-Deisenhofen: Dustri-Verlag Dr.
Karl Feistle, p 127.

Folkers K, Sartori M, Baker L, Richardson P (1982). Observations of significant reductions of arrhythmias in treatment with coenzyme $Q_{10}$ of patients having cardiovascular disease. IRCS Med Sci 10:348.

Kapatos G, Kaufman S (1981). Peripherally administered reduced pterins do enter the brain. Science 212:955.

Leeming RJ, Pheasant AE, Blair JA (1981). The role of tetrahydrobiopterin in neurological disease: A review. J Ment Defic Res 25:231.

Levine RA, Miller LP, Lovenberg W (1981). Tetrahydrobiopterin in striatum. Science 214:919.

Nagatsu T, Yamaguchi T, Kato T, Sugimoto T, Matsuura S, Akino M, Nagatsu I, Iizuka R, Narabayashi H (1981). Biopterin in human brain and urine from controls and Parkinsonian patients: Application of a new radioimmunoassay. Clin Chim Acta 109:305.

Hagoshi H, Hattori S, Kawamura Y (1977). Effects of coenzyme $Q_{10}$ combined with beta-blocker on ischemic heart disease. The Clinical Report 11:11.

Tanaka J, Tominaga M, Yoshitoshi M, Matsui K, Komori M, Sese A, Yasui Y, Tokunaga K (1982). Coenzyme $Q_{10}$: The prophylactic effect on low cardiac output following cardiac valve replacement. Annals of Thoracic Surgery 33:2.

Intervention in the Aging Process, Part A: Quantitation, Epidemiology, and Clinical Research, pages 215–224
© 1983 Alan R. Liss, Inc., 150 Fifth Avenue, New York, NY 10011

REGULATION OF BIOGENIC AMINE SYNTHESIS BY THE HYDROXYLASE COFACTOR AND ITS RELATION TO AGING AND PARKINSONISM

Walter Lovenberg, Robert A. Levine, Michael A. Aiken, Leonard Miller and Peter LeWitt*
Section on Biochemical Pharmacology, National Heart, Lung, and Blood Institute, Building 10, Room 7N262, Bethesda, Md. 20205. *Experimental Therapeutic Branch, NINCDS, Bethesda, Md 20205

INTRODUCTION

The discovery and characterization of biogenic amine neurotransmitters in the central nervous system has been a major step in man's attempt to understand psychiatric, neurologic, and functional disorders. The fact that these neurotransmitters have been the predominant ones under investigation undoubtedly relates to the fact that sensitive analytical systems have been available for these compounds. Biogenic amine neurotransmitter systems have been directly implicated in Parkinson's disease, and indirectly related to the aging process since partial loss of these neurons seems to be involved in both parkinsonism and aging. A further understanding of the aging process could be gained by studying biosynthetic pathways for the biogenic amines.

Catecholamines and serotonin are respectively derived from the amino acids tyrosine and tryptophan. Our laboratory has studied the biosynthetic pathways of these enzymes and we have focused on the initial and rate-limiting enzyme, tyrosine and tryptophan hydroxylase. These two enzymes which are mixed function oxidases are similar in many respects including the fact that tetrahydrobiopterin ($BH_4$) is a cosubstrate for their catalytic activity. Recent studies from our laboratory (Levine et al., 1981) have demonstrated a special relationship between the amount of tyrosine hydroxylase and one of its cosubstrates, $BH_4$, in dopaminergic neurons. These data suggest that $BH_4$ may have a significant regulatory role in catecholamine biosynthesis. This chapter will focus primarily on $BH_4$ metabolism as it relates to central dopaminergic systems.

REGULATION OF TYROSINE HYDROXYLASE

Tyrosine hydroxylase was first described as a mixed function oxygenase by Nagatsu et al. (1964). It was clear from these early studies that the biosynthesis of L-DOPA catalyzed by tyrosine hydroxylase required three substrates. L-tyrosine, molecular oxygen and a reduced pterin, presumably $BH_4$. It was quickly appreciated that the catecholamines which were subsequently formed from L-DOPA were powerful end-product inhibitors that appeared to be competitive with $BH_4$ (Ikeda et al., 1966). This work suggested a very simple regulatory system for tyrosine hydroxylase, i.e., as the catecholamine content in active neurons was repleted, further synthesis would be limited by endproduct inhibition. Further, it also suggested that the concentration of $BH_4$ relative to that of free catecholamines was an important factor regulating the activity of tyrosine hydroxylase. This basic premise is still valid, although in succeeding years we have learned that the regulatory system for tyrosine hydroxylase is much more complex.

About a decade ago, results from several lines of experimentation began to raise questions about the validity of this simple end-product control system. Some of the most important experiments were done by Carlsson and his colleagues (1974). These workers were able to identify conditions in the nigrostriatal pathway which led to marked increase in tyrosine hydroxylase activity in vivo in the presence of apparent constant or increased amounts of endproduct. In 1974 Zivkovic et al demonstrated that with dopamine receptor blockade tyrosine hydroxylase extracted from a region of brain rich in dopamine terminals was activated. This activation was manifested by a decrease in the Michaelis constant for $BH_4$. In a practical sense this suggested that at the prevailing $BH_4$ and dopamine concentrations in tissue, tyrosine hydroxylase would be more active.

Based on the above, a number of laboratories, including our own, quickly addressed the molecular basis for the kinetic activation of tyrosine hydroxylase.

Because this regulation appeared to be mediated by dopamine receptors and it was known that these receptors were associated with an adenylate cyclase, we examined the effect of phosphorylation by a cAMP dependent protein kinase. Results in our own (Lovenberg et al., 1975) and several other laboratories (Morganroth et al., 1975; Lloyd and Kaufman, 1975; and Goldstein et al., 1975) quickly revealed that protein phosphorylation could mimic the in vivo activation by reducing the apparent $K_m$ of tyrosine hydroxylase for $BH_4$. In subsequent work (Ames et al., 1978), we found that a very important component of this mechanism is an increase in the $K_i$ for end-product following protein phosphorylation. Thus dopamine neurons had a system in which they could override the end-product inhibitor.

These earlier studies were primarily done in in vitro systems, which were maintained near the pH optimum of tyrosine hydroxylase (pH 5.8-6.0). Examining the system over a wider pH range we found (Pradhan et al., 1981) that when the enzyme was phosphorylated the kinetic properties were essentially independent of pH whereas the nonphosphorylated enzyme had kinetic properties that were pH dependent. The net effect of this study was to verify (Goldstein et al., 1975) that the effect of phosphorylation of tyrosine hydroxylase is much more pronounced at physiological pH.

A kinetic examination at pH 6.8 of enzyme extracted from tissue revealed two distinct kinetic forms (Lovenberg et al., 1982). One had a $K_m$ for $BH_4$ of 20uM and the other a $K_m$ of about 500uM. In both adrenal and striatal tissue it appeared that between 65 and 80% of the enzyme was in the less active, presumably nonphosphorylated form.

A MODEL FOR THE DOPAMINE BIOSYNTHETIC SYSTEM

To be able to fully understand the regulatory system for dopamine synthesis, it seemed essential to know the in vitro concentration of $BH_4$. Work on $BH_4$ has lagged behind that of other components of the biogenic amine systems because of its low gross concentration in tissues and the prior lack of appropriate analytical tools.

Another problem in $BH_4$ analysis relates to its anatomic localization, as the brain consists of many different cell types. Simple analysis of tissue is of little help unless we can determine if $BH_4$ is distributed evenly in all cell types or is localized to specific cells. As CNS biogenic amine containing cells have an uneven distribution across various brain regions, our first experiments (Levine et al., 1979) attempted to correlate $BH_4$ levels with the distribution of hydroxylase enzymes which are markers for biogenic amine neurons.

The results of our $BH_4$ distribution studies demonstrated:

1) that the apparent gross concentration of $BH_4$ was very low in all brain regions and significantly below the $K_m$ value for even the activated form of tyrosine hydroxylase; and

2) that there was a highly significant relation between the amount of hydroxylase and $BH_4$.

This latter observation was circumstantial evidence for the localization of $BH_4$ within biogenic amine containing neurons.

A very important experiment was next devised by Robert Levine (Levine et al., 1981 and Levine, 1982). In these studies unilateral 6-hydroxydopamine lesions in the substantia nigra of rats were produced and confirmation of the anatomic lesion was confirmed pharmacologically. The lesion was relatively specific for the dopaminergic cell bodies in the substantia nigra. This highly specific unilateral loss of dopamine terminals in the corpus striatum demonstrated that over 90% of tyrosine hydroxylase and about 75% of $BH_4$ were lost in the lesioned side. Since these subunits (100 µM) appearing to be greater than the concentration of tyrosine (70 µM), under control conditions only 20% of tyrosine hydroxylase appeared to be active. However, following dopamine receptor blockade a much greater proportion of the enzyme was in the activated state. We asked the question as to whether in the presence of dopamine receptor blockade was dependent upon the synthesis of tyrosine transmitter uptake into receptor terminals? This question may have been answered by independent study of Wurtman and his colleagues (1982) who showed that in control animals, dopamine turnover in striatum was independent of circulating tyrosine whereas in animals treated with dopamine receptor blockers there was a good correlation between plasma-tyrosine concentration and striatal dopamine synthesis. This concept of tyrosine dependency in activated neurons is important not only for our basic understanding, but also for the practical purpose of trying to modulate dopamine synthesis in human diseases.

HYDROXYLASE COFACTOR IN NEUROLOGICAL DISEASES AND AGING

With our background knowledge of dopamine synthesis as described above, we sought to determine if we could apply this information to the treatment of clinical states thought to result from either a reduced or enhanced synthesis of dopamine.

From our early work as described, it was clear that the hydroxylase cofactor ($BH_4$) may be an important factor in the overall regulation of dopamine synthesis. The first question we addressed was whether cerebrospinal fluid (CSF) contained measurable quantities of $BH_4$ and whether this might reflect $BH_4$ concentration and activity of biogenic amine neurons in man. Although the concentration of $BH_4$ hydroxylase cofactor activity in the CSF was very low, we were able to modify the existing radioenzymic assay system to make it sensitive enough for routine analysis.

More recently we have been able to utilize differential oxidation techniques and High Performance Liquid Chromatography (HPLC) to measure specifically the reduced forms of biopterin in tissue and cerebrospinal fluid. We applied these techniques to the measurement of CSF from patients with Parkinson's disease because of the known loss of nigrostriatal dopaminergic neurons that occurs in parkinsonism. Examination of the cofactor content of CSF from patients with this disease indicated that parkinsonian patients exhibited a significant reduction in CSF cofactor levels. The fact that these patients in general were older than our control group, made it necessary to age match our groups.

A more careful study using age-matched groups still revealed that parkinsonian patients have about a 50% reduction of cofactor content in the CSF (Lovenberg et al., 1979). Of interest was the observation that the

CSF-cofactor content showed an inverse correlation with age in both normal subjects and patients with Parkinson's disease. While the slope of the decline was generally similar in both normal and parkinsonians, the level was similarly reduced with age progression. This observation on the loss of CSF cofactor has been more recently further supported by Nagatsu and his colleagues (1981) who found that the striatal $BH_4$ levels were even more severely decreased in parkinsonian patients. At this time we have to conclude that the reduction in $BH_4$ concentration in Parkinson's patients reflects the known loss of dopamine neurons, but we cannot rule out the possibility that loss of ability to synthesize $BH_4$ might be involved in the etiology of this disease.

Returning to the question of age, we have recently re-examined the relation between age and reduced biopterin levels with HPLC techniques. In this study we have reaffirmed the inverse age correlation although the decrease with increasing age was less marked (LeWitt et al., 1983).

In contrast to most experimental animals, tissues and CSF from man contain a significant amount of neopterin. The phosphorylated form of this compound appears to be an intermediate in the biosynthetic pathway for $BH_4$, (Curtius et al., 1983). Thus in man the rate limiting enzyme in $BH_4$ biosynthesis may not be the enzyme known as GTP cyclohydroxylase, but rather an enzyme subsequent to neopterin formation. Because the HPLC technique allows us to simultaneously monitor neopterin and biopterin levels in the CSF we have observed that in contrast to $BH_4$, neopterin levels appear to increase with age and the neopterin/biopterin ratio show a very strong positive correlation with age. Thus the dramatic increase in neopterin/biopterin ratio with age may indicate a progressive decline in the ability of neurons to synthesize $BH_4$. The significance of this observation remains to be determined.

In regard to the above, it is interesting that Neiderweiser et al., (1982) reported that a patient with a form of atypical phenylketonuria resulting from a genetic defect in the biosynthesis of biopterin had an extremely high neopterin/biopterin ratio in the urine. In this extreme case, the patient suffered severe neurological symptoms that could be corrected by administering the hydroxylated precursors of the biogenic amine or $BH_4$ alone. Although the changes with aging do not approach this extreme case, the question of whether the ability to synthesize biogenic amines in the CNS decreases with age as a result of decreased $BH_4$ synthesis, remains to be determined.

We have also examined the CSF from patients with a variety of other neurological diseases that may involve dopamine systems. Of particular interest we have found that certain individuals with familial dystonia have a markedly reduced level of $BH_4$ in the CSF. These findings prompted us to explore the possibility of whether it would be possible to alter tissue levels of $BH_4$ in experimental animals or man and whether such an alteration would have any impact on biogenic amine biosynthesis.

The first reported attempt to do this experiment was by Kettler et al., (1974). These workers found that peripheral administration of $BH_4$ resulted in little penetration of the compound into the brain. When given dirrectly into the brain they noted an increase in the parameters of catecholamine synthesis.

In a recent study (Kapatos and Kaufman, 1981), administered to rats 0.1 umole of $BH_4$ per gram of body weight and found about a 2 fold increase in brain $BH_4$ concentration and it appeared that the natural isomer was more effective in penetrating the CNS. They also noted that 6-methyltetrahydropterin, a compound that will also serve as a cosubstrate for the hydroxylases, is more effective in penetrating the CNS. Levine et al., (1983) has recently completed a similar study once again showing minimal penetration of $BH_4$ in rats and also showing no significant impact on biogenic amine synthesis. Work is continuing in several laboratories with the hope of being able to significantly modify biogenic amine synthesis.

TETRAHYDROBIOPTERIN IN MAN

The above discussion leads to the question of whether the administration of tetrahydrobiopterin to patients with certain neurological disorders would have a beneficial effect. To summarize briefly, we know that the majority of tyrosine hydroxylase is present in a form that is essentially inactive at the normal tissue concentration of

$BH_4$. It is possible that a significant increase in $BH_4$ levels would allow this portion of the enzyme to contribute to the dopamine synthesis within specific neurons. Thus in a situation such as parkinsonism, an increase in the activity of remaining dopamine neurons would result in clinical improvement. Against the above optimistic appraisal are the observations in our own and other laboratories that it is difficult in rats to obtain a major increase in brain levels of $BH_4$ by systemic administration and it appears that the small increases result in minimal changes in biogenic amine synthesis. On the other hand, such an approach is strengthened by the clinical observations that in certain cases of atypical phenylketonuria with a $BH_4$ deficiency, a dramatic correction of the neurological symptoms has been observed. (Neiderweiser et al., 1982). These studies suggest that in man a significant amount of $BH_4$ could reach the brain and have an impact on neurotransmitter synthesis.

Within the past year, clinical studies on the administration of $BH_4$ to patients with Parkinson's disease have been initiated in our own and two other laboratories. While it is too early to evaluate this work, it is apparent that each of the research groups found that certain of their patients had demonstrable improvement of their clinical symptoms. While clinical improvement was only seen in about one-half the patients treated, the fact that some responded suggests that it may be possible to increase the effectiveness of the remaining nigrostriatal dopaminergic neurons with $BH_4$.

In support of these observations, LeWitt et al. (1983) has administered $BH_4$ to several patients with familial dystonia. In two of these individuals who had previously been shown to have decreased $BH_4$ in their CSF (Williams et al., 1979), a significant clinical improvement which lasted several hours was observed following a large single dose of $BH_4$.

The importance of these preliminary experiments in man lie both in their apparent therapeutic potential and as a tool to further understand fundamental aspects of biogenic amine metabolism. The need for a large clinical pharmacological study with $BH_4$ is of obvious importance and the pharmacokinetics of $BH_4$ in man must be explored with the hope of developing analogues of $BH_4$ that more readily penetrate the brain.

REFERENCES
Ames MM, Lerner P, Lovenberg W (1978). Tyrosine hydroxylase: Activation by tyrosine hydroxylase and end-product inhibition. J Biol Chem 253:27.
Carlsson A, Kehr W, Lindqvist M (1974). Short-term control of tyrosine hydroxylase. Adv in biochem Psychopharm 12:135.
Curtius HC, Hausermann M, Heintel D, Niederwieser A, Levine RA (1983). Perspectives on tetrahydrobiopterin biosynthesis in mammals. In the symposium on pterin, in press.
Goldstein M, Ebstein B, Bronaugh RL, Roberge C (1975). Stimulation of tyrosine hydroxylase by cyclic AMP. In Almgren O, Carlsson A, Engel J (eds): "Chemical Tools in Catecholamine Research," North Holland Publishing Co., p. 251.
Ikeda M, Fahien L, Udenfriend S (1966). A kinetic study of bovine adrenal tyrosine hydroxylase. J Biol Chem 241:4452.
Kapatos G, Kaufman S (1980). Periphically administered reduced pterins do enter the brain. Science 212:955.
Kettler R, Bartholini G, Pletscher A (1974). IN VIVO enhancement of tyrosine hydroxylation in rat striatum by tetrahydrobiopterin. Nature 249:476.
Levine RA (1982). Pharmacological and Neuroanatomical Studies on Tetrhaydrobiopterin in the Nigrostriatal System of the Rat: Relation to neurological Disorders. PhD Dissertation, George Washington University.
Levine RA, Kuhn DM, Lovenberg W (1979). Regional distribution of hydroxylase cofactor in rat brain. J Neurochem 32:1575.
Levine RA, Miller LP, Lovenberg W (1981). Tetrahydrobiopterin in striatum: Localization in dopamine nerve terminals and its role in catecholamine biosynthesis. Science 214:919.
Levine RA, Lovenberg W, Niederwieser A, Leembacher W, Redwelk U, Staundenman W, Curtius HC (1983). Penetration of reduced pterins into rat brain: Effect on biogenic amine synthesis. Int Symposium on Pterin, in press.
LeWitt PA, Newman RP, Miller LP, Lovenberg W, Eldridge R (1983). Treatment of dystonia with tetrahydrobiopterin. N Engl J Med, submitted.
LeWitt PA, Miller LP, Newman RP, Beusis RS, Insel T, Levine RA, Lovenberg W, Calne DB, Chase TN (1983). Tyrosine

hydroxylase cofactor (tetrahydrobiopterin) in parkinsonism. Int Symposium on Parkinson's Disease, in press.

Lovenberg W, Bruckwick E, Hanbauer I (1975). ATP, cyclic AMP, and magnesium increase the affinity of rat striatal tyrosine hydroxylase for its cofactor. Proc Natl Acad Sci USA 72:2955.

Lovenberg W, Levine RA, Miller LP (1982). The hydroxylase cofactor and catecholamine synthesis. Usdin E, Weiner M, Youdim M (eds): "Second Conference on Monoamine Enzymes." Macmillan, New York, in press.

Lovenberg W, Levine RA, Robinson DR, Ebert M, Williams AC, Calne DB (1979). Hydroxylase cofactor activity in cerebrospinal fluid of normal subjects and patients with Parkinson's disease. Science 204:624.

Morganroth VH III, Hegstrand LR, Roth RH, Greengard P (1975). Evidence for involvement of protein kinase in the activation of adenosine 3'5'-monophosphate of brain tyrosine 3-monooxygenase. J Biol Chem 250:1940.

Nagatsu T, Levitt M, Udenfriend S (1964). Tyrosine hydroxylase: the initial step in norepinephrine biosynthesis. J Biol Chem 239:2910.

Nagatsu T, Yamaguchi T, Kaio T, Sugimoto T, Matsuura S, Akino M, Nagatsu I, Iisuka R, Naraboyashi H (1981). Biopterin in human brain and urine from control and parkinsonian patients: Application of a new radioimmunoassay. Clin Chim cta 109:305.

Niederwieser A, Curtius HC, Wary M, Leupold (1982). Atypical phenylketonuria with defective biopterin metabolism. Monotherapy with tetrahydrobiopterin as seprapterin, screening and study of biosynthesis in man. Eur J Pedatr 138:110.

Pradhan S, Alphs L, Lovenberg W (1981). Characterization of naloperidol-mediated effects on striatal tyrosine hydroxylase. Neuropharm 20:149.

Williams AC, Eldridge R, Levine RA, Lovenberg W, Paulson G (1979). Low CSF hydroxylase cofactor (tetrahydrobiopterin) levels in inherited dystonia. Lancet 2, 8139:410.

Wurtman RJ, Hefti F, Melamed E (1982). Precursor control of neurotransmitter synthesis. Pharm Res, in press.

Zivkovic B, Guidotti A, Costa E (1974). Effect of neuroleptics on striatal tyrosine hydroxylase: Changes in the affinity for the pteridine cofactor. Mol Pharmac 10:727.

Intervention in the Aging Process, Part A: Quantitation, Epidemiology, and
Clinical Research, pages 225–245

# REMARKABLE POTENTIATION AMONG MEMORY-ENHANCING CHOLINERGIC DRUGS IN MICE

Arthur Cherkin and James F. Flood, Geriatric
Research, Education and Clinical Center (GRECC)
VA Medical Center, Sepulveda, CA 91343
Dept. of Psychiatry and Biobehavioral Sciences
UCLA School of Medicine, Los Angeles, CA 90024

Senile dementia is reaching epidemic proportions;
some 4.0 million Americans over age 65 suffer mild to
severe dementia. The tragic cost in human suffering to
patients and families and the economic cost to society are
immense. In nursing homes in the United States alone, 56%
of the 1.3 million elderly residents are diagnosed as
"chronic mental condition or senility" and 5-6% as "senile
dementia." We estimate the annual nursing home costs for
these 730,000 residents to exceed seven billion dollars.
The problems of senile dementia will be magnified if
interventions in the aging process result in prolonging
life without preserving brain function.

The DSM-III (American Psychiatric Association, 1980)
labels senile dementia as "primary degenerative dementia
(PDD), senile onset" and describes it as "dementia with
insidious onset and gradually progressive course for which
all other specific causes for dementia have been excluded...[It] involves a multifaceted loss of intellectual
abilities...severe enough to interfere with social and/or
occupational functioning - especially memory impairment
plus impairment in abstract thinking, judgment or impulse
control (personality change)." A Task Force sponsored by
the National Institute on Aging (1980) has identified 61
individual "reversible causes of mental impairment."
Careful diagnosis of "irreversible" senile dementia is
therefore critical in order to exclude patients with other
disorders (e.g., drug toxicosis, infection, vitamin
deficiency) or psychiatric problems (e.g., depression)

whose symptoms mimic those of senile dementia but which are reversible.

For several reasons, this chapter will focus upon the memory impairment characteristic of age-related conditions variously referred to as Alzheimer's disease, Alzheimer's syndrome, chronic brain syndrome, chronic organic mental syndrome, idiopathic senile dementia, organic brain disease, organic dementia, senile brain disease, senile dementia of Alzheimer's type (SDAT), or senility. One reason for this focus is that failing memory is the hallmark of dementia - it is the earliest symptom of these disorders and it is observed in 100% of the cases (Mohs, Rosen and Davis, 1982). Another reason is that memory failure is also clearly involved in symptoms which, for clinical convenience, carry different labels, e.g., confusion, disorientation and impairment in mathematical calculations, in thinking and in judgment. Indeed, one might ask what symptoms would appear in an individual with a perfectly healthy central nervous system but with total amnesia for all learning experiences since child-birth. He might be aphasic simply because he remembers no words. He might have locomotor difficulties because he has "forgotten" trained walking skills and incontinent because he has lost his toilet-training. Obviously, this is not to imply that aphasia, gait disorders and incontin-ence result only from causes related to memory loss. But enhancement of memory alone has the potential of alleviating certain symptoms which are not ordinarily considered to result from failing memory.

Finally, another reason for our focus on amnesia is as follows. Hare (1978) evaluated 200 patients in a psychogeriatric assessment unit, using a clinical check list. She concluded that "amnesia alone was an unreliable indicator of dementia" because amnesia occurs in other conditions, including old age itself. The multimodal approach suggested in this chaper is in principle applic-able to rehabilitation of failing memory, whatever the clinical diagnosis may be. Thus, our interest is focused upon the amnesia component of the senile dementias and of other age-related conditions.

Attempts to treat senile amnesias have involved both pharmacotherapy and non-drug interventions. The research strategy in pharmacotherapy of senile amnesia has followed the precedent of L-dopa therapy of Parkinson's disease, i.e., the disorder is assumed to arise from a single cause and to be responsive to a unitary treatment. A unimodal intervention permits relatively clear assessment of its effectiveness in improving memory but no single intervention has yet proved to be reliably effective as a practical clinical treatment of senile amnesia.

An alternative strategy suggested in this chapter is the use of multimodal treatments based on an assumption of multiple etiologies of senile amnesias. A review of past studies in the separate unimodal areas, with emphasis on cholinergic drug treatment, will be followed by examples of recent efforts to apply a limited multimodal approach in the treatment of senile amnesias and by our suggestion of a broader multimodal therapy, to combine combination drug therapy with psychological and other non-drug treatments. Encouragement of this approach is provided by the findings to date of our our pre-clinical screening program in mice,to be presented below, that two-drug combinations of cholinergic memory enhancers can strongly potentiate improvement of memory retention.

If similar potentiation could be demonstrated clinically in senile amnesia, a way would be opened for utilizing combinations of presently available memory-enhancing drugs, while efforts continue to develop more effective single drugs. We consider this to be valid even if drug combination therapy requires individual dose titration and proves to be successful in only a sub-set of responders.

NEUROBIOLOGICAL CHANGES IN THE AGING BRAIN

The correlation of characteristic neuropathological changes with senile dementia is well established (Amaducci, Davis and Antuono, 1980; Katzman, Terry and Bick, 1978) but we have reservations about claims for a causal relationship. The major neuropathological changes in Alzheimer's disease are increased neurofibrillary tangles, senile (neuritic) plaques, and granulovacuolar bodies. But changes in the aging brain include: reduced brain weight; enlarged ventricles; regional loss of neurons, dendrites and dendritic spines; increased lipofuscin; loss of cerebral extracellular space; and altered ratios of gray to white matter. At the molecular level, changes reported in the aged brain include: decreased choline acetyltransferase, acetylcholinesterase and tyrosine hydroxylase; increased butyrylcholinesterase and monoamine oxidase; decreased metabolic rate; and neuroendocrine disturbances. Each of the above changes involves structures and molecules which are associated with normal memory processing. What is lacking to support a unitary etiology of dementia is convincing evidence that any one of the reported anatomical or molecular changes observed in brains of senile amnesia patients is the sole or predominant cause of memory impairment. It is equally plausible that senile amnesia is a multifactorial syndrome, with multiple insults in the CNS contributing to impaired memory. Furthermore, the relative contribution of each factor to the overall impairment may differ from patient to patient, fluctuate over the course of the disease, and vary as a result of environmental changes, including administration of therapeutic drugs for a variety of illnesses.

## MULTIPATHWAY HYPOTHESIS OF MEMORY FORMATION

The multipathway hypothesis (Cherkin, in preparation) holds that: (1) a memory trace (engram) is formed by multiple pathways, each with multiple phases and steps and (2) impairment of a primary pathway, phase or step can be reversed by enhancement of a secondary or a separate pathway, phase or step. The argument for this hypothesis is summarized as follows:

1. Biological processes in general and memory processes in particular are characterized by complexity and redundancy.

2. Complexity in biology is illustrated by the alternative pathways, multiple steps and interactive effects which are evident in metabolic maps and in maps of neurotransmitter function, as well as in a hypothetical schema of memory processing (Matthies, 1974).

3. A specific step in one pathway of the complex network of engram formation can be controlled, modulated or substituted by a step in a different pathway of the network.

4. Impairment of one memory pathway may leave intact a secondary pathway, which compensates for the impairment

spontaneously or upon exogenous stimulation, e.g., through reactive synaptogenesis (Bowen, Davison and Sims, 1981).

5. Multiple neuropathologies can exert a cumulative amnestic effect, even when each pathology alone would have no detectable effect.

It may be added that the concept of parallel processing has been suggested for many mnemonic phenomena, including: a dual structure of permanent memory; parallel hierarchies for different sensory dimensions; formation of short-term, medium-term and long-term memory; simultaneous acquisition of multiple memories; and separate, concurrent learning in the two brain hemispheres.

MULTIMODAL INTERVENTIONS - PHARMACOLOGIC

The state-of-the-art of pharmacologic treatment of memory dysfunctions indicates that current research strategy follows the precedent which led to successful L-dopa pharmacotherapy of Parkinson's disease. Marchbanks (1980) has questioned whether the current effort to improve the central cholinergic system "is going to be a successful re-run of the L-dopa story." He points out that replacement of the total tissue store of dopamine in the human caudate nucleus requires about 1 hour, compared to approximately 10-20 seconds for replacement of acetylcholine stores. Thus, choline acetyltransferase (CAT) may normally be present in such large excess that the reduction of CAT observed in brains of senile dements may not result in a corresponding reduction of acetylcholine. Despite the uncertainties of applying the L-dopa precedent to the central cholinergic system, Marchbanks accepts the pharmacological evidence which suggests cholinergic involvement in senile amnesia and asks: "What strategies might be used to capitalize on this in the interest of therapy?" His reply is a dual attack, namely: (1) increase the acetylcholine available, as by choline therapy and (2) preserve the action of acetylcholine by administering anticholinesterase drugs. As will be noted later, this dual approach has been applied clinically, with occasional improved results as compared to precursor (choline or lecithin) therapy alone.

The foregoing considerations lead to the present

proposal of a plausible alternative to the current unitary drug strategy, namely, a multimodal approach. This suggests that therapy should be directed at rehabilitating as many causes of memory dysfunction as possible and at recruiting all available compensatory mechanisms. For example, neuronal loss is considered to be an "irreversible" cause of memory dysfunction because lost neurons are not replaced. But the concept of multiple pathways of memory processing postulates that compensatory mechanisms could be recruited to reverse the functional loss, even in the face of cellular loss. Compensation for lost neurons may occur, for example, through reactive synaptogenesis, i.e., increased dendritic branching of remaining neurons (Bowen, Davison and Sims, 1981).

If the multimodal approach is valid, a sub-set of responder patients may be discovered who show substantial improvement in memory retention by psychometric tests and by daily performance, at individualized combination drug doses. The responders may represent only a small proportion of amnestic patients, thus careful subject selection is necessary to exclude all cases of "reversible dementia" from a clinical trial population. Further exclusion of subjects will be necessary because the brains of some patients with advanced amnesia are so deteriorated that the potential for rehabilitation of degenerated memory systems, and for recruitment of compensatory systems, is too small to permit any substantial improvement of memory.

Even if the multipathway hypothesis turns out to be incorrect, rational multimodal intervention merits exploration in senile amnesia because of the successful clinical precedents in other conditions. Modern behavioral medicine emphasizes multimodal approaches. Multimodal therapy is increasingly accepted in psychotherapy, including psychotherapy of the elderly (Karpf, 1980). Therapy of stroke patients utilizes multiple modalities to repair the impairments of speech and motor functions resulting from brain damage of abrupt onset; the modalities include family counseling, occupational therapy, physiotherapy, psychotherapy, rehabilitation counseling, speech therapy, and aids to daily living (Peszczynski et al., 1972). Yesavage, Westphal and Rush (1981) have combined two modalities to treat dementia, namely, pharmacotherapy (Hydergine[R]) and psychotherapy (cognitive training). Brinkman et al. (1982), following a suggestion of Boyd et al. (1977), tested a combination of lecithin administration plus memory training; although the overall results were disappointing, the significant effect of memory training was considered to be "suggestive of clinical potential." These clinical precedents justify a broader exploration of multimodal therapy of senile amnesias utilizing pharmacological and non-drug measures.

The pharmacotherapy area of the multimodal approach involves combinations of drugs at low doses, aimed at several neurochemical systems. Polypharmacy is the unfortunate rule in geriatric practice and irrational combinations are properly the subject of criticism (Cooper, 1979). Nevertheless, rational drug combinations have proved their usefulness under certain conditions to increase effectiveness, reduce side effects, or both. For example, to achieve these goals modern cancer chemotherapy employs combinations of 3-5 different drugs, further combined with other modalities, i.e., surgery, radiotherapy and hormonal manipulation (Carter and Slavik, 1974). In antibacterial therapy, a long-accepted fixed combination (Bactrim[R]; Septra[R]) of two antibiotics permits a markedly reduced dose of each drug (Rudoy, Nelson and Haltalin, 1974). A theoretical basis for the empirical observation that drug combinations may potentiate therapeutic effects without potentiating side effects has been developed for drugs that bind to separate but equivalent binding sites (Ehrenstein and Huang, 1981).

The rationale for low dosage combinations of memory-enhancing drugs goes beyond the reduction of side effects. Low doses are generally obligatory because of a rule of thumb for drugs which can improve memory: "Low doses enhance; high doses impair." This important dose-response relationship has been observed in animal experiments with carbachol, diethyl ether, flurothyl, imipramine, pemoline, pentylenetetrazol and physostigmine (all cited in Cherkin and Riege, in press), and recently with eight cholinergic drugs (Flood, Landry and Jarvik, 1981), namely, arecoline, choline, dimethylaminoethanol, 1,1-dimethyl-4-piperazine, edrophonium, muscarine, oxotremorine, and physostigmine. This interesting biphasic dose-response relationship is emphasized here because insufficient attention has been paid to it in the past. For a reliable dose-response curve, the relationship must be determined over a sufficiently wide range of doses; for some drugs, the doses must be closely spaced in order to locate a narrow therapeutic window. When doses are properly selected, an inverted-U dose-response curve is often revealed, with increasing enhancement followed by an amnestic effect as the dose is increased (Flood, Landry and Jarvik, 1981).

A constraint imposed on clinical application of this laboratory finding is the fact that many amnestic patients are receiving medications which may interact with a memory-enhancing drug or combination of drugs to increase the potency and thus shift the response toward an amnestic effect. Such patients would not be suitable for this form of pharmacotherapy, especially if their pre-existing drug regimen already approaches the amnestic range and cannot be reduced. (As a corollary, we suggest that mild memory impairments due to drug toxicosis may be more widespread than is generally recognized at present.)

The effects of combinations of memory enhancing drugs in human studies have attracted little attention in the past but the potentialities for multiple pharmacologic intervention are now becoming recognized. For example, Summers et al. (1981) point out three sites of possible drug intervention in the cholinergic system: (1) presynaptic enhancement by increasing the level of the acetylcholine precursor, choline (e.g., with choline or lecithin); (2) synaptic enhancement by blocking cholinesterase (e.g., with physostigmine); and (3) postsynaptic enhancement by direct stimulation of muscarinic receptors (e.g., with oxotremorine). Until recently, however, the few drug combinations reported to improve human memory have included: imipramine plus tetrabenazine (Il' Yuchenok, 1976); d-amphetamine plus chlorpromazine (McGaugh, 1973); and combinations of d-amphetamine plus atropine or methylatropine or hexamethonium (Izquierdo and Elisabetsky, 1979). A non-enhancing dose of physostigmine (a scopolamine antagonist) improved memory in normal adults when combined with an amnestic dose of scopolamine (Drachman and Sahakian, 1980). Pentylenetetrazole plus niacin gave conflicting results in senile patients (Jarvik, 1974). Very recently, combinations of an acetylcholine precursor with a second drug intended to enhance precursor action have come under limited clinical study (Corkin et al., 1982).

As indicated in the foregoing examples, a growing body of evidence strongly implicates the cholinergic system in memory failure. Bartus et al. (1982) recently reviewed this evidence critically. To quote from their summary:

"Significant cholinergic dysfunctions occur in the aged and demented central nervous system, relationships between these changes and loss of memory exist, similar memory deficits can be artifically produced by blocking cholinergic mechanisms in young subjects, and under certain tightly controlled conditions reliable memory improvements in aged subjects can be achieved after cholinergic stimulation. Conventional attempts to reduce memory impairments in clinical trials have not been therapeutically successful, however. Possible explanations for these disappointments are given and directions for future laboratory and clinical studies are suggested."

Among the directions for the future suggested by Bartus et al. (1981) is the following, with which we are in full accord (Cherkin and Riege, in press):

"The most significant improvement in aged memory may be achieved when multiple, interactive neurochemical dysfunctions in the brain are corrected or when activity in more than one aspect of a deficient metabolic pathway is enhanced. These preliminary data from aged rats suggest that solutions to this problem may not be simple, for different physiological functions may have to be affected; alterations may be necessary at more than one point in the cholinergic or other metabolic pathway, or alternatively, the balance or tone between two or more neurotransmitter systems may need to be improved."

Suggestions for possible combinations offered by Leo Hollister and by Peter Davies, in Crook and Gershon (1981), include: choline plus piracetam (p. 10); choline plus dihydroergotoxine (p. 10); a nicotinic agonist plus a muscarinic agonist, such as arecoline (pp. 9, 10, 25); arecoline plus thyrotropin releasing hormone (p. 15); and choline or lecithin plus thyrotropin releasing hormone (p. 27).

As will be described in the following section, our pre-clinical screening strategy employs a systematic series of experiments to: (1) study the interactive effects of two-drug and three-drug combinations of cholinergic memory enhancers in mice, using drugs whose individual effects on memory retention after intracerebroventricular injection are already well defined (Flood, Landry and Jarvik, 1981); (2) select promising combinations for evaluation by the subcutaneous route; (3) select appropriate combinations for long-term chronic administration by the oral route, which is the most feasible for ultimate clinical applications; and (4) expand the study to drug combinations aimed at modulating other neurochemical systems, in addition to the cholinergic system.

To return to the survey of relevant prior reports, of special interest are the results of two-drug clinical treatments. Five clinical research groups reported results with two-drug combinations, in small groups of demented patients, at the International Study Group on the Pharmacology of Memory Disorders Associated with Aging (Corkin et al., 1982). For example, Peters and Levin (pp. 421-426) examined the separate and combined effects of lecithin and physostigmine. Five demented patients were tested in a preliminary study: three received physostigmine, three received lecithin plus physostigmine, then lecithin plus placebo. (One subject was tested in all conditions.) Each subject was compared with his baseline response. Physostigmine alone and lecithin alone did not produce significant improvement over baseline, and even seemed to depress performance below baseline. However, the combined drugs improved performance above baseline in all three subjects, significantly so in two subjects.

The four other reports are as follows. Bajada (pp. 427-432) administered oral choline (1g every 4 hr) plus oral physostigmine (0.4mg every 4 hr); no beneficial effects were observed, as compared to either compound alone or to placebo. Kaye et al. (pp. 433-42) combined oral lecithin (3x20g) and oral tacrine (3x10 mg tetrahydroaminoacridine); less impaired patients scored higher on serial learning ($p < 0.05$), compared to either compound alone or to placebo, but no patients reached normal functioning. Ferris et al. (pp. 475-481) administered oral choline (9g per day) plus piracetam (4.8g per day) for 7 days. Four responders were found in the study group of 15 patients; these four "showed marked improvement in memory storage and retrieval," not previously observed with either compound alone.

Finally, combinations of drugs acting upon different organ systems merit consideration. As pointed out by Goldfarb (1975): "There are benefits to be derived from the rational use of cerebral, pulmonary and central nervous system stimulants in chronic organic brain syndrome to favor the optimal use of remaining physical and mental assets and to encourage their use by the alerting, motivating and euphorizing effects of the medications."

## EXPERIMENTS WITH CHOLINERGIC DRUG COMBINATIONS

We now report the mouse experiments referred to above. The rationale of these experiments was explained in the preceding sections. The route of drug administration was by subcutaneous injection; prior experiments using the intracerebroventricular route gave similar results (Flood, Smith and Cherkin, in preparation). By both routes, the results indicate that combinations of cholinergic drugs can enhance memory retention at greatly reduced doses (95% in some cases), compared to single drug doses.

The procedure has been described in detail (Flood, Landry and Jarvik, 1981). The subjects, CD-1 male mice, 6 weeks of age and weighing 33-38g, were individually caged starting 24-48 hr prior to training and until retention was tested one week after training on a T-maze active avoidance task. The T-maze start box was separated from the start alley by a door which prevented the mouse from entering the alley until training started. A training trial consisted of placing the mouse in the start box, raising the door and sounding a buzzer (conditioned stimulus). Mice not moving to the correct goal box within 5 sec were foot-shocked (0.30ma) until they did so. At the end of each trial, the mouse was removed to its home cage, then replaced in the start box for the next trial. Mice were given 3 training trials, with 20 sec elapsing between trials. A response latency of 5 sec or less was scored as an avoidance, since the mouse did not receive foot shock.

Mice were injected subcutaneously (0.35 ml) within 1 min after training. The dose of drug per mouse is given in Figs. 1-3. All solutions were blind-coded to eliminate experimenter bias. The drugs were obtained from the following sources: edrophonium chloride (EDR; Tensi-lon[R]; F.W. 201.7) was a gift from Hoffman La-Roche; arecoline hydrobromide (ARE; F.W. 236.1), oxotremorine sesquifumarate (OXO; F.W. 380.4) and tetrahydroamino-acridine (TAC; tacrine; F.W. 198.3) were purchased from Sigma Chemical. All doses are expressed in terms of the salt (e.g., arecoline hydrobromide) but are referred to by the name or acronym of the base (e.g., arecoline or ARE). Drug solutions were prepared immediately prior to use.

The measure of memory retention one week after training corresponds with usual reporting practice. Mice which made one avoidance response in three trials or less were considered to remember the original training. This criterion was adopted because it provided maximal separation between the retention test scores of naive mice (with no T-maze training) and well-trained mice. The percent of each group which met criterion was expressed as the "percent recall score." Each group comprised 20 mice (drug-treated ) or 40 mice (saline controls).

Dose-Response Effects of Individual Cholinergic Drugs on Retention

The purpose of this experiment was to determine the optimal dose of four cholinergic agonists (ARE, EDR, OXO, TAC) to improve retention test performance. The dose injected in each group within 1 min after training is given in Fig. 1. The saline control mice showed poor retention, with only 25-30% classed as remembering. The dose-response curve for each drug was an inverted U. Low doses had little effect compared to saline, higher doses improved retention test performance, and still higher doses impaired performance relative to the optimal dose (Fig. 1).

Dose-Response Effects of Two-Drug Combinations on Retention

The purpose of this experiment, still in progress, was to determine if combinations of drugs would improve memory retention when administered at reduced doses in the six possible pairs of the four drugs shown in Fig. 1. The results to date indicate that the ratio of drugs in each pair and the total dose are important in reaching maximal retention test scores. To simplify presentation here, we summarize the results (Fig. 2) as the maximum percentage reduction in the one-drug dose which has been achieved to date by using two-drug combinations. The percentage reduction is calculated as follows.

In order to compare the potency of a drug combination with the potency of its component single drugs, a common denominator can be established, as a first approximation. We have arbitrarily selected ARE as the common denominator drug. The optimal dose of ARE is 44.0 ug (Fig. 1). The equipotent doses for the other drugs are: EDR, 245.0 ug; OXO, 87.0 ug; and TAC, 52.5 ug. Since 245.0 ug of EDR is equipotent with 44.0 ug of ARE, the factor for converting an EDR dose to its equivalent ARE dose is $44.0/245.0 = 0.180$. The corresponding factor for OXO is 0.506 and for TAC it is 0.838. Thus, a combination of 19.6 ug of EDR plus 7.0 ug of OXO is equivalent to 3.53 ug of ARE plus 3.54 ug of ARE, respectively, or a total of 7.07 ug of ARE.

The transformation to ARE equivalents permits calculation of potentiation factors and finally of the percent of single-drug doses which are equipotent in two-drug combinations (Fig. 2). For comparison, the previous results with intraventricular injection are displayed in the same way (Fig. 3), for ARE+EDR, ARE+OXO, EDR+OXO and also for the three-drug combination, ARE+EDR+OXO. The equipotent percentages for two-drug combinations range from 4.6-32.8 by subcutaneous injection (5.0 by intraventricular injection). The corresponding reductions in dose required for peak retention test scores are 67.2-95.4% (subcutaneous) and 95.0% (intraventricular).

The advantage of potentiated memory enhancement by drug combinations would of course be invalidated if toxicity were equally potentiated. Current animal experiments (Cherkin and Flood, in preparation), however, indicate that additivity but not potentiation of acute toxicity is characteristic of combinations of cholinergic system drugs, namely, arecoline plus physostigmine, physostigmine plus diethylaminoethanol, and arecoline plus diethylaminoethanol plus physostigmine.

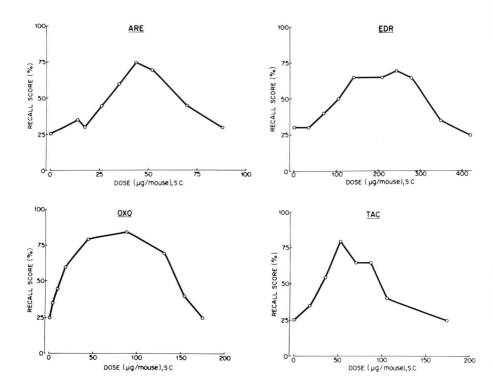

Fig. 1. Dose-response curves of four individual cholinergic drugs. ARE=arecoline hydrobromide; EDR=edrophonium
chloride; OXO=oxotremorine sesquifumarate; TAC=tetrahydro-
aminoacridine. ARE and OXO are muscarinic agonists; EDR
and TAC are cholinesterase inhibitors. Administration was
by subcutaneous injection, within 1 min after training in
a T-maze to avoid foot-shock applied 5 sec after sounding
a warning buzzer. Retention of the trained avoidance was
tested one week later, using a criterion of 1 avoidance
response within 3 test trials. The ordinate represents
the percentage of each group (N=20) which met criterion.

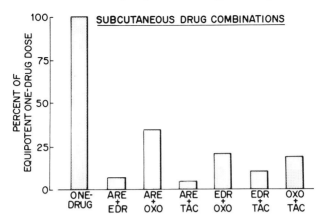

Fig. 2. Reduced subcutaneous doses of two-drug combinations required for peak response (75% or higher recall
score). The doses in each optimal combination were
converted to the equipotent dose of ARE (see text).
The ordinate represents the percent of this one-drug dose,
normalized to 100 percent. The first bar refers to ARE,
EDR, OXO or TAC, each administered by itself.

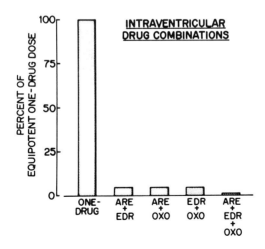

Fig. 3. Reduced intraventricular doses required for peak
response (see legend, Fig. 2). The intraventricular doses
are much smaller than the subcutaneous doses (Fig. 2) but
the potentiating effect of the drug combinations is
similar.

The results of these experiments suggest that carefully selected combinations of drugs may provide the
degree of memory enhancement needed for "meaningful"
clinical improvement in patients with failing memory,
while reducing drug dosage and possibly reducing undesir-
able side effects and development of drug tolerance.

MULTIMODAL INTERVENTIONS - NON-PHARMACOLOGIC

The concept that memory impairments associated
with senile dementia result from the cumulative effects of
numerous insults to the brain suggests that all available
means be mobilized to counteract the effects of those
insults. Pharmacotherapy offers only one such means.
Indeed, in dealing with psychotherapy of the elderly, some
psychologists and psychiatrists regard psychopharmaco-
logic treatment as simply an adjunct to behavioral
modalities (Lazarus, 1976). Non-drug modalities which
have been reported to improve cognitive performance in
elderly subjects include cognitive skills training of
various types (Labouvie-Vief and Gonda, 1976; Plemons,
Willis and Baltas, 1978; Sanders and Sanders, 1978;
Schmitt, Murphy and Sanders, 1981; Zarit, Gallagher
and Kramer, 1981); reality orientation (Eisdorfer, Cohen
and Preston, 1981); sensory stimulation and exercise
therapy (Diesfeldt and Diesfeldt-Groenendijk, 1977;
Dustman, Ruhling, Russell and Shearer, in preparation;
Ernst et al., 1977, 1978; Oster, 1976; Powell, 1974). The
pros and cons of these non-drug modalities have been
discussed in detail by Cherkin and Riege (in press). As
might be expected, the improvement of elderly cognitive
function by non-drug interventions is inconsistent (as it
is by pharmacologic treatments). For example, patients
with moderate to severe mental impairment showed no
benefit from physical and occupational therapy for one
year and those with mild mental impairment showed only
equivocal benefit (Schuman et al., 1981). Nevertheless,
we concur with Ernst et al. (1977), who suggest that "it
seems reasonable to provide sensory stimulation and
isolation-reducing therapies to most clinically-diagnosed
cases of chronic brain syndrome, in addition to any other
medicopharmacological therapies..."

CAVEATS TO MULTIMODAL INTERVENTIONS

There are disadvantages of any multimodal regimen,

even if one can be shown to be effective. Kendall (1979), in a critical analysis of the question: "Will drugs help patients with Alzheimer's disease?", has emphasized the formidable research problems which must be solved in order to generate the meaningful data required to permit a positive answer to his question. Direct extrapolation of data from our normal young mice to demented old patients is of course neither sensible nor intended. We have yet to establish whether the potentiation observed with intraventricular and subcutaneous injections can be achieved with oral administration. The probable necessity of individual titration of drug doses is a constraint which will be complicated by the widespread and variable daily intake of caffeine (in coffee and soft drinks), nicotine (in tobacco) and alcohol (in beverages), because each of these drugs affects memory processing and can interact with memory-enhancing drugs.

A theoretical problem is the near impossibility of determining the individual contribution of each modality to the overall effect and of deciding which modalities are essential for a given patient and which are superfluous. At the present stage of knowledge, however, we consider it premature to be overly concerned with this disadvantage. The short-term goal is to determine whether any "irreversible" amnesias will yield to multimodal therapy under the best of conditions. It is unacceptable to condemn patients and their families to years of sorrow with the sentence of "irreversible" dementia, when some of those dementias are potentially reversible. If multimodal intervention redeems only a small percent of such patients, it merits serious consideration.

CONCLUSION

To assume a single etiology of senile dementias may foster misconceptions about the nature of its characteristic memory dysfunctions and thus about effective therapeutic strategies. The search for a "magic bullet" aimed at some assumed single etiology should continue, but alternative strategies must be considered. One alternative, based on an assumption of multiple interacting etiologies of senile amnesia, is a frankly "shotgun" approach based upon rational multimodal therapy. As applied to senile amnesias, this approach involves synergistic combinations of memory-enhancing drugs at low doses, in conjunction with a variety of non-drug modalities, including cognitive skill training, exercise, sensory stimulation, and socialization. There are significant advantages to the multimodal approach. A practical advantage is the diminished likelihood of unfavorable side effects. More important is the possible potentiation of effects from combined pharmacotherapy and non-drug treatments. Minor successes have attended the pharmacological or psychological treatment modality alone, but the unimodal approaches have not yet provided satisfactory treatment of senile amnesias. Combination drug therapy may set up the prerequisite neural conditions to allow the amnestic patient maximum benefit from non-pharmacological treatment - benefit which would not be realized from either approach alone. The powerful potentiation of cholinergic memory enhancers in mice, achieved in two-drug and three-drug combinations, encourages further exploration of combination drug interventions.

REFERENCES

Amaducci L, Davison AN, Antuono P (1980). "Aging of the Brain and Dementia." New York: Raven Press.

American Psychiatric Association (1980). "Diagnostic and Statistical Manual of Mental Disorder," 3rd ed. DSM III, Washington: APA.

Bartus RT, Dean RL, Beer B, Lippa AS (1982). The cholinergic hypothesis of geriatric memory dysfunction. Science 217:408-417.

Bowen DM, Davison AN, Sims N (1981). Biochemical and pathological correlates of cerebral ageing and dementia. Gerontology 27:100-101.

Boyd WD, Graham-White J, Blackwood G, Glen I, McQueen J. (1977). Clinical effects of choline in Alzheimer senile dementia. Lancet 2:711.

Brinkman SD, Smith RC, Meyer JS, Vroulis G, Shaw T, Gordon JR, Allen RH (1982). Lecithin and memory training in suspected Alzheimer's disease. J Gerontol 37:4-9.

Carter SK, Slavik M (1974). Chemotherapy of cancer. Ann Rev Pharmacol 14:157-183.

Cherkin A, Riege WH. Multimodal approach to pharmacotherapy of senile amnesias. In Cervos-Navarro J, Sarkander HI (eds): "Brain Aging: Neuropathology and Neuropharmacology," New York, Raven Press (in press).

Cooper SJ (1979). Behavioral studies of drug interactions. In Brown K, Cooper SJ (eds): "Chemical Influences on

Behavior," New York: Academic Press, pp 533-597.
Corkin S, Davis KL, Growdon JH, Usdin E, Wurtman RJ (1982). "Alzheimer's Disease: A Report of Progress in Research," New York: Raven Press.
Crook T, Gershon G (1981). "Strategies for the Development of an Effective Treatment for Senile Dementia," New Canaan, Conn.: Mark Powley Associates.
Diesfeldt HFA, Diesfeldt-Groenendijk H (1977). Improving cognitive performance in psycho-geriatric patients: The influence of physical exercise. Age Ageing 58:58-64.
Drachman DA, Sahakian BJ (1980). Memory, aging and pharmacosystems. In Stein DG (ed): "The Psychobiology of Aging," New York: Elsevier/North Holland, pp 347-368.
Ehrenstein G, Huang LM (1981). Side-effect reduction by use of drugs that bind to separate but equivalent binding sites. Science 214:1365-1366.
Eisdorfer C, Cohen D, Preston C (1981). Behavioral and psychological therapies for the older patient with cognitive impairment. In Miller NE, Cohen GD (eds): "Clinical Aspects of Alzheimer's Disease and Senile Dementia," New York: Raven Press, pp 209-226.
Ernst P, Beran B, Badash D, Kosovsky R, Kleinhauz M (1977). Treatment of the aged mentally ill: Further unmasking the effects of a diagnosis of chronic brain syndrome. J Am Geriatr Soc 25:466-469.
Ernst P, Beran B, Safford F, Kleinhauz M (1978). Isolation and the symptoms of chronic brain syndrome. Gerontologist 5:468-474.
Federal Council on the Aging (1981). "The Need for Long Term Care." Washington: U.S. Department of Health and Human Services, DHHS Publication No. (OHDS) 81-20704, p 33.
Flood JF, Landry WD, Jarvik ME (1981). Cholinergic neurotransmitter-receptor interactions and their effects on long-term memory processing. Brain Res 215:177-185.
Goldfarb AI (1975). Memory and aging. In Goldman R, Rockstein M (eds): "The Physiology and Pathology of Human Aging," New York: Raven Press, pp 149-183.
Hare M (1978). Clinical check list for diagnosis of dementia. Brit Med J 2:266-267.
Il'yuchenok RY (1976). "Pharmacology of Behavior and Memory." Washington: Hemisphere Printing.
Izquierdo I, Elisabetsky E (1979). Physiological and pharmacological dissection of the main factors in the acquisition and retention of shuttle behavior. In Brazier MAB (ed): "Brain Mechanisms in Memory and Learning: From

the Single Neuron to Man," New York: Raven Press, pp 227-248.

Jarvik ME (1974). Improving mental function in the aged with drugs. Drug Therapy 4:140-160.

Karpf RJ (1980). Modalities of psychotherapy with the elderly. J Am Geriatr Soc 8:367-371.

Katzman R, Terry RD, Bick KL (1978). "Alzheimer's Disease: Senile Dementia and Related Disorders," New York: Raven Press.

Kendall MJ (1979). Will drugs help patients with Alzheimer's disease? Age Ageing 8:86-92.

Labouvie-Vief GV, Gonda JN (1976). Cognitive strategy training and intellectual performance in the elderly. J Gerontol 31:327-332.

Lazarus AA (1976). "Multimodal Behavior Therapy." New York: Springer.

Marchbanks RM (1980). Choline, acetylcholine and dementia. Psychol Med 10:1-3.

Matthies H (1974). The intracellular regulation of the interneuronal connectivity: The macromolecular foundation of learning. In Knoll J, Knoll B (eds): "Symposium on Pharmacology of Learning and Retention," Budapest: Akademiai Kiado, pp 61-72.

McGaugh JL (1973). Drug facilitation of learning and memory. Ann Rev Pharmacol 13:229-241.

Mohs RC, Rosen WG, Davis KL (1982). Defining treatment efficacy in patients with Alzheimer's disease. In Corkin S et al., ibid., pp 351-360.

Oster C (1976). Sensory deprivation in geriatric patients. J Am Geriatr Soc 10:461:464.

Peters BH, Levin HS (1982). Chronic oral physostigmine and lecithin administration in memory disorders of aging. In Corkin et al., ibid, pp 421-426.

Peszczynski M, Benson DF, Collins JM, Darley FL, Diller L, Greenhouse AH, Katzen FP, Lake LF, Rothberg JS, Waggoner RW (1972): Stroke rehabilitation. Stroke 3:375-407.

Plemons JL, Willis SL, Baltes PB (1978). Modifiability of fluid intelligence in aging: A short term longitudinal training approach. J Gerontol 33:224-231.

Powell RR (1974). Psychological effects of exercise therapy upon institutionalized geriatric mental patients. J Gerontol 2:157-161.

Rudoy RC, Nelson JD, Haltalin KC (1974). In vitro susceptibility of Shigella strains to trimethoprim and sulfamethoxazole. Antimicrob Agents Chemother 5:439-443.

Sanders RE, Sanders JAC (1978). Long-term durability

and transfer of enhanced conceptual performance in the elderly. J Gerontol 33:408-412.

Schmitt FA, Murphy MD, Sanders RE (1981). Training older adults free recall rehearsal strategies. J Gerontol 36:329-337.

Schuman JE, Beattie EJ, Steed DA, Merry GM, Kraus AS (1981). Geriatric patients with and without intellectual dysfunction: Effectiveness of a standard rehabilitation program. Arch Phys Med Rehab 62:612-618.

Summers WK, Viesselman JO, Marsh GM, Candelora K (1981). Use of THA in treatment of Alzheimer-like dementia: Pilot study in twelve patients. Biol Psychiat 16:145-153.

Task Force, National Institute on Aging (1980). Senility reconsidered. J Am Med Assoc 244:259-263.

Yesavage JA, Westphal J, Rush L (1981). Senile dementia: Combined pharmacologic and psychologic treatment. J Am Geriatr Soc 29:164-171.

Zarit SH, Gallagher D, Kramer N (1981). Memory training in the community aged: effects on depression, memory complaint, and memory performance. Educ Gerontol 6:11-27.

Zepelin H, Wolfe CS, Kleinplatz F (1981). Evaluation of a yearlong reality orientation program. J Gerontol 36:70-77.

Portions of the introduction of this chapter are adapted with the permission of Raven Press, from Cherkin A, Riege W H (in press). Multimodal approach to pharmacotherapy of senile amnesias. In Cervos-Navarro J, Sarkander H-I. (eds): "Brain Aging: Neuropathology and Neuropharmacology," New York: Raven Press.

Intervention in the Aging Process, Part A: Quantitation, Epidemiology, and
Clinical Research, pages 247–266
© 1983 Alan R. Liss, Inc., 150 Fifth Avenue, New York, NY 10011

TOWARD A SAFER ESTROGEN IN AGING

Robert H. Purdy[1] and Joseph W. Goldzieher[2]

[1]Southwest Foundation for Research and Education,
 Department of Organic Chemistry, San Antonio, TX   78284
[2]Baylor College of Medicine, Department of Obstetrics
 and Gynecology, 6720 Bertner Avenue, Houston, TX   77030

There are approximately 33 million women over the age
of 50 in the United States at the present time.  This
represents the single largest candidate population for the
occurrence of a major deficiency disease - estrogen deprivation.  For decades the menopausal syndrome has been dealt
with by the medical community in a manner that can only be
described as male chauvinism.  McKinlay and McKinlay (1973)
have analyzed this attitude as originating in two factors:
"menopause, as it is generally perceived in Western cultures, is a stigmatizing event in a woman's life, marking
the end of her social usefulness - procreation...The second
(factor) relates to the power of physicians in most Western
societies...the imputation of competence has served to
shield the knowledge and practices of the medical profes-
sion, including the quality of their research...regardless
of its lack of objectivity and substantiation through adequately controlled studies.  This reliance of physicians on
subjective 'experience' is particularly evident with regard
to the menopause.  Discussions of symptomatology and treatment recommendations, usually with no clear empirical
basis, form the bulk of the medical literature on this
subject."

These comments were made as recently as a decade ago.
Fortunately, a number of important medical observations
have focused serious scientific attention on the consequences of estrogen deprivation, and this in turn has
legitimized inquiries into the overall problem by trained
investigators.  Epidemiological studies have shown that hip
fractures after the age of 65 are eight times more common

in women than in men, and in Scandinavia the frequency of
hip fracture doubles every 5 years after the age of 65.
Using data from Rochester, Minn., North Carolina vital
statistics, and the National Health Survey, we estimate
that between 113,000 and 120,000 hip fractures occur in
elderly white women in the United States each year, at a
cost for medical and nursing care in excess of a billion
dollars a year and resulting in 12,000 to 15,000 deaths.
Thus, this single complication of estrogen deprivation
ranks as the twelfth leading cause of death - a statistic
that can hardly be ignored.

Less lethal complications of estrogen deprivation,
such as increased frequencies of diabetes, cardiovascular
disorders, and neuropsychiatric problems, all to be discussed below, have received more careful evaluation than
heretofore.

On the other hand, two major potential hazards of
estrogen therapy - increased incidences of endometrial and
breast cancer - have been the object of intensive epidemiological and endocrinological investigation. Until the
benefits and risks of estrogen deprivation vs. estrogen
replacement therapy have been adequately evaluated, it is
clearly impossible to make precise public health or even
individual recommendations. We will now attempt to examine
each of these areas of clinical concern in turn.

In 1940 Fuller Albright noted that nearly all of his
42 osteoporotics were postmenopausal white women, and that
estrogen therapy reversed their negative calcium and phosphorus balance. Today we know that there is ethnic poly-
morphism in bone mass which parallels skin pigmentation
(Gordan, 1976). In all races women lose bone mass earlier
and to a greater extent than men, and this is seen most in
white skinned people, less in Asiatics, and least in
blacks, where it is rare in women at any age and is simply
not seen in males except with immobilization or certain
disease states. In recent years accurate methods of bone
density measurement - photon absorption densitometry and
various radiographic techniques, to mention a few - have
been developed. The reproducibility of certain CAT scanning techniques is better than 1% - an accuracy which is
essential for therapeutic evaluation since the rate of
spontaneous bone loss in postmenopausal women is of the
order of 1-2% per year. However, the simplest and one of

the clearest demonstrations of this phenomenon, carried out
in 1959, required no sophisticated instrumentation:
Wallach and Henneman (1959) simply followed the height of
women with and without estrogen treatment as the years went
by. The contrast shown in Figure 1 between height loss
(due to vertebral compression) in the untreated, versus the
stable height in the treated women is dramatic. Eventually,

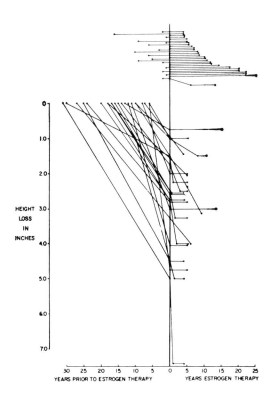

Fig. 1. Height loss in postmenopausal women before and
after estrogen therapy. Upper dots represent 27 women
treated prior to development of osteoporosis, lower dots 22
women with osteoporosis at beginning of treatment. In 16
women with osteoporosis, height loss ceased within 2 years
of initiating therapy. From Wallach and Henneman (1959),
Journal of the American Medical Association 171:1640, copyright 1959, American Medical Association.

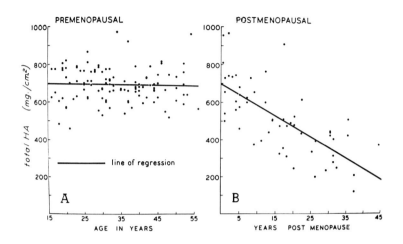

Fig. 2. Bone mineral mass (total hydroxyapatite content) in normal premenopausal women according to age (A), and in normal postmenopausal women in relation to number of post-menopausal years (B). From Meema et al. (1965). Reprinted with permission of the author and The American College of Obstetricians and Gynecologists.

bone densitometry also showed (Figure 2) that loss of bone mass was related not to age but to years after menopause (Meema et al., 1965). Biochemically, the sparing effect of estrogens on urinary calcium loss could be demonstrated and, interestingly, both the 19-norprogestational steroids used in oral contraceptives and certain anabolic steroids also diminished calcium loss. The beneficial effect of estrogen treatment is most apparent from the statistics on the fre-quency of wrist and hip fractures in women with and without estrogen replacement therapy (Weiss et al., 1980). Without going into endocrinological detail, it is thought that the calcium loss is initiated by a relative excess of parathy-roid hormone, which mobilizes bone calcium, and that this hormonal action is counteracted by the effect of estrogen on certain activated metabolites of vitamin D. In addition to estrogen, Table 1 shows that the intake of calcium, of vitamin D, and of fluoride have a substantial effect on bone loss as demonstrated by the unequivocal criterion of fracture incidence (Riggs et al., 1982). The problem of

fluoride treatment is unresolved, as this substance is
toxic in larger doses and treatment regimens which are
effective and have a wide margin of safety have not yet
been perfected.

Table 1
Treatment of Postmenopausal Osteoporosis
(From:   Riggs et al., 1982)

| Treatment Regimen | Fracture Rate, Vertebral, per 1000 Person-years |
|---|---|
| None | 834 |
| Calcium (1.5-2.5 g/day)<br>    + vitamin D. | 419 |
| Fluoride (40-60 mg/day)<br>    + calcium + vit. D. | 304 |
| Estrogen (.6-2.5 mg/day)<br>    + calcium + vit. D. | 181 |
| Fluoride + estrogen + calcium<br>    + vit. D. | 53 |

Fluoride: 38% adverse reactions
Estrogen: 13% menorrhagia
Reprinted by permission of The New England Journal of
Medicine 306:447 (1982).

The psychosomatic benefits of estrogen therapy, which
include relief from vasomotor instability ("hot flashes")
and a variety of other symptoms difficult to quantitate,
have now been demonstrated beyond question by carefully
designed placebo-controlled double-blind studies (Sheffery
et al., 1969; Lebherz and French, 1969).   An equally important and insightful criterion studied by Hammond et al.
(1979) has been the number of new prescriptions written for
the treatment of various disorders such as hypertension,
other cardiac disorders, nervous conditions, etc., in women
given or not given estrogen replacement therapy.   These
differences shown in Table 2 are statistically highly
significant.   Compare them to the "new occurrences" of

diseases shown in Table 3 that were diagnosed in these
hypoestrogenic women.

Clearly, we have come a long way in the decade since
the indictment voiced by McKinlay and McKinlay (1973).

Table 2
Frequency (%) of New Prescriptions in Menopausal Women
With and Without Estrogen Replacement
(From:  Hammond et al., 1979)

| Medication | No Estrogen Therapy | Estrogen Therapy |
|---|---|---|
| None | 26.9 | 47.8* |
| Antidiabetic | 9.7 | 3.7* |
| Antihypertensive | 40.1 | 20.6* |
| Cardiac | 26.5 | 7.0* |
| Sedatives | 13.3 | 4.3* |
| Tranquilizers | 34.6 | 20.3* |

*P < 0.01

Table 3
Percent Occurrence of New Diseases in Menopausal Women
With and Without Estrogen Replacement
(From:  Hammond et al., 1979)

| Disease Category | No Estrogen Therapy | Estrogen Therapy |
|---|---|---|
| Hypertension | 31.7 | 16.3* |
| Diabetes | 11.3 | 3.3* |
| Fractures | 15.9 | 8.6* |
| Osteoporosis | 25.6 | 5.6* |

*P < 0.01

Tables 2 and 3 are reprinted with permission of the author
and publisher, from the American Journal of Obstetrics and
Gynecology 133:525 (1979)

Why, then, are not all nonblack women automatically
placed on estrogen replacement therapy?  It must be admit-
ted, first of all, that not all practicing physicians are

fully aware of the scientific evidence, described so
briefly above, that has accumulated in this past decade.
Some overworked practitioners may still be too busy "saving
lives" to take the time to save hips and wrists.  The
important reasons, however, go deeper.  In women who still
have a uterus, the cyclic administration of estrogen is
very likely at some time, even with individualized dosage
adjustment, to produce endometrial withdrawal bleeding.  It
has been a dictum in gynecology that postmenopausal
bleeding is a sign of endometrial cancer until proven
otherwise.  This dogmatic stricture is of course obsolete,
but the physician who disregards it, does so at his peril.
Thus, estrogen therapy results in many needless curettages
and in any event, frequently results in a phenomenon which
postmenopausal women do not accept kindly.

There have been numerous epidemiological studies of
endometrial cancer and its relation to estrogen therapy,
and there are authoritative oncologists who believe that a
causal relationship exists (Bancroft et al., 1981).  There
are also recent, careful studies which question this conclusion.  Moreover, the nature of "case-control" epidemiological procedures is so subject to subtle biases that
causal inferences must be viewed with the greatest caution.
Finally, all endometrial cancer is not the same:  well over
90% is grade 0 or 1 and the permanent cure rate by hysterectomy is of the order of 95%.  Indeed, some are of the
opinion that much of the grade 0 variety is not true
malignancy at all.  The importance of the distribution of
cancer types is illustrated in the following data from
Studd (1976) shown in Table 4.

Table 4
Histology of Endometrial Pathology
(From Studd, 1976, in cases of Smith et al., 1975)

| Histological Type | | Treatment A | Treatment B |
|---|---|---|---|
| 0 | | 16 | 7 |
| 1 | | 129 | 115 |
| 2 | | 6 | 20 |
| 3 | | 2 | 15 |
| 4 | | 0 | 7 |
| | Total | 153 | 164 |
| Invasive | | 17% | 44% |
| Deeply Invasive | | 1% | 18% |

Reprinted with permission of the author and editor, from
the British Medical Journal 1:1144 (1976)

Considering the increasingly bad prognosis of cancer from grade 0 to grade 5 observed with two types of treatment we shall call "A" and "B", which would you opt for if you were a woman? Now if we "unblind" these data, we find that "A" is the estrogen-treated group and "B" is the nonestrogen group. It is clear that the "cancers" associated with estrogen-treated women in this study were far more likely to be of the low-grade curable variety than those seen in women who had no estrogen treatment.

Equally important, recent epidemiological data have shown that the concurrent use of progestational compounds, as in birth control pills, appears to have decreased the eventual incidence of endometrial cancer by about half, and 5 years or more of use reduced the risk to a third (Hulka et al., 1982). Weiss and Sayvetz (1980) have presented the data in Table 5 showing that the use of progestational drugs along with estrogen therapy in postmenopausal women has a similar prophylactic effect. However, the latter regimens clearly carry with them the nuisance of repeated withdrawal bleeding in these postmenopausal women.

Table 5
Effect of Use of Combined Oral Contraceptives on
the Incidence of Endometrial Cancer, According to Duration
of Use of Menopausal Estrogen
(From:  Weiss and Sayvetz, 1980)

| Use of Menopausal Estrogen | Relative Risk* | 95 Per Cent Confidence Limits ** |
|---|---|---|
| None | 0.4 | 0.1-1.1 |
| 1-2 years | 0.1 | 0.0-1.1 |
| $\geq$ 3 years | 1.3 | 0.3-6.6 |

*Risk of endometrial cancer in women who used combined oral  contraceptives for one or more years relative to that of  nonusers (standardized for age).
Reprinted by permission of The New England Journal of Medicine 302:553 (1980).  **Author's note:  A 95% confidence limit which includes 1 means that the difference between the two groups being compared could easily have occurred by random chance.  This is clearly the case for all three subsets.

Obviously, the woman with a hysterectomy is particularly fortunate in regard to the convenience and acceptability of estrogen therapy.

While the hazard of estrogen-related endometrial malignancy may have been overrated, and may now be substantially prevented, the potential carcinogenic hazard of estrogen therapy cannot be ignored. Moreover, this idea has been so intensively propagated and publicized by the oncological community that it is a fact of life which will not be eradicated from the minds of the public regardless of evidence showing it to be a far less substantial hazard than originally supposed.

The question of the relationship of estrogen to breast cancer is far more complex and far more important from the viewpoint of public health, for while there are about 35,000 new endometrial cancers in the U.S. per year, one out of 11 women will develop breast cancer. It is the preeminent cause of cancer deaths in women. The known sensitivity of a minority of breast cancers to estrogen is well known, hence this potential hazard of estrogen therapy in the menopausal woman is a serious concern. Unfortunately, the data regarding this question are largely epidemiological, and we have already referred to the problems with the interpretation of, and confidence in, such non-experimental information. The early "anecdotal" longterm studies were encouraging but the numbers are far too small to be truly meaningful. Numerous large epidemiological studies have yielded conflicting data, some of which suggest that the hazard of estrogen therapy is related to duration of use (Brinton, 1981). On the other hand, we have information that when estrogen therapy is discontinued after any number of years of use, osteoporosis resumes promptly.

Clearly, we do not have the answer to this problem, nor a good estimate of the magnitude of the risk. Benefit/risk estimates (Weinstein, 1980) are therefore inherently unsatisfactory at the present time. It is not likely that additional epidemiological studies are going to resolve this question. We must therefore take another tack. A task force of the International Union against Cancer has concluded that "breast cancer is hormonally mediated and estrogens are the prime agents in tumor expression" (Miller and Bulbrook, 1980). A similar workshop on the "Hormonal Biology of Endometrial Cancer" suggested as a goal for future research that "First, more detailed information is needed on the natural history of this disease including the role of hormones, particularly the estrogens..." (Richardson and MacLaughlin, 1978). Assuming that estrogens have an oncogenic potential of whatever degree, what is the mechanism or mechanisms of such a potential, and how could it be modified? Obviously an enormous amount of effort has been devoted to a study of existing cancers, as well as to cancer induction in various strains of animals with estrogens. There is no possible way at this time even to give a thumbnail sketch of the multitude of approaches that have been used.

In our laboratory, we have elected to take a tack which is based on the mechanism of action of other chemical carcinogens, in the hope that certain chemical analogies and resemblances might provide a fruitful hypothesis.

The key to an understanding of the mutagenic and carcinogenic potential of polycyclic aromatic hydrocarbons is their biological activation by a class of enzymes, termed cytochrome P-450 mixed function oxidases, that are found in the endoplasmic reticulum (microsomes) of certain mammalian cells that are transformed by these activated metabolites (Tsang and Griffin, 1979). Strong carcinogenic activity is induced by the metabolic activation products of certain compounds of this class which not only have the same carbon skeleton as naturally occurring estrogens, but also contain oxygen functions at positions commonly oxygenated in natural and synthetic estrogens (Coombs et al., 1973, 1976). Figure 3A shows the structure of an epoxide intermediate, proposed by Coombs et al. (1979), that is formed during the metabolism of the parent phenanthrene by liver microsomes and then reacts with DNA. Knowledge of the structure of this type of activated intermediate prompted Soloway and Le Quesne (1980) to propose an epoxide of the type shown in Figure 3B as an intermediate in the formation of catechol estrogens which are principal metabolites of estrogens in women (Ball and Knuppen, 1980). Subsequently, three of these types of intermediates were synthesized in small amounts for our biological investigations (Le Quesne et al., 1980).

At this time we had been testing a number of lines of mammalian cells in culture for their use in the *in vitro* assay of the mutagenic and carcinogenic potential of estrogens because the available Ames bacterial assays were not suitable for estrogens. From the structure of the epoxide

shown in Figure 3B, you would expect that an atom of tritium at carbon 2 of estradiol would be released as tritiated
water in the medium if this intermediate was formed by cells
growing in culture.  The results shown in Figure 4 were

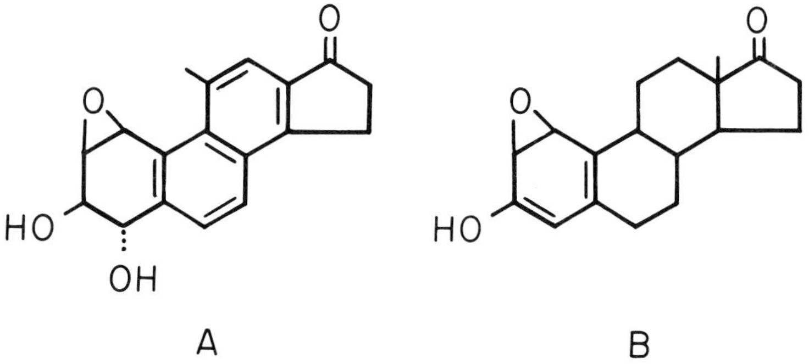

A                              B

Fig. 3.  (A).  Structure proposed by Coombs et al. (1979)
for one of the ultimate forms of the carcinogen 15,16-
dihydro-11-methylcyclopenta[a]phenanthrene-17-one.  (B).
Structure proposed by Soloway and Le Quesne (1980) for one
of the tautomeric forms of an intermediate in the formation
of 2-hydroxyestradiol.

obtained when $[2-^3H]$estradiol was added to a culture of a
cloned line of Balb/c 3T3 mouse fibroblast cells of embryonic origin (Kakunaga, 1973).  This subclone, obtained from
Dr. Kakunaga at the National Cancer Institute, is particularly sensitive to polycyclic aromatic hydrocarbon-induced
neoplastic transformation (Kakunaga et al., 1980) and has
proven to be most useful in our efforts to evaluate the
carcinogenic potential of estrogens.  McLachlan and coworkers (1982) have been using Syrian hamster embryo fibroblasts in similar assays of the neoplastic transformation
of these cells by DES and its analogs.  An *in vivo* model
system for demonstrating liver tumorigenesis by certain
estrogens implanted as pellets in Syrian golden hamsters
has recently been developed by Li et al. (1982).  Thus
there are now at least three mammalian systems that can be
utilized to explore the relationship between estrogen
structure and carcinogenic potential.  *The use of the term
potential is most important here, since these efforts are*

*directed toward understanding the mechanism(s) of estrogen-mediated carcinogenesis as a rare event in biological expression, rather than to any extrapolation of these results to the frequency of human disease.*

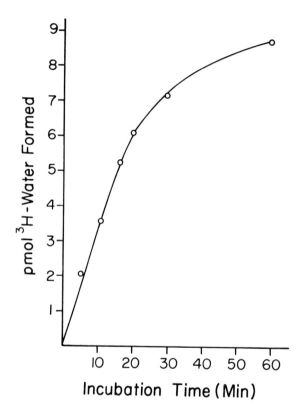

Fig. 4. Release of tritium into the medium as $^3H_2O$ when [2-$^3$H]estradiol was incubated with Balb/c 3T3 cells at 37°.

With this caveat always in mind, we have found that DES, estradiol, ethynylestradiol and certain other estrogens cause the morphologic transformation of Balb/c 3T3 cells from the contact inhibited control cells shown in Figure 5A, to the spindle-shaped cells with a criss-crossed random orientation shown in Figure 5B. These transformed cells grow as multicellular tumor spheroids, and cause

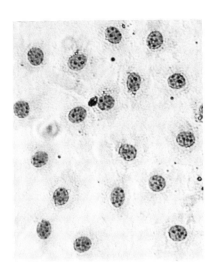 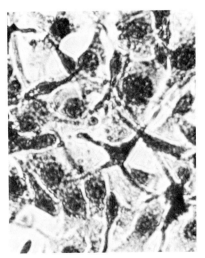

A                                    B

Fig. 5. (A). Morphology of the untreated heteroploid line
of Balb/c 3T3 (A-31-1-13 subclone) used in the transformation assay. (B). Morphology of transformed Balb/c 3T3
cells isolated from Type III foci obtained after 72 hr
treatment with 25 µM estradiol and subsequent expression of
transformation for 28 days in culture in normal media
according to the procedure of Kakunaga (1973).

tumor formation (Figure 6) when injected into NIH nude mice
(Purdy et al., 1983). The mechanism we postulate to be
involved in this process is illustrated in Figure 7.
Estradiol (I) is metabolically activated to an arene oxide
intermediate which stabilizes as the epoxyenone II. II is
then converted to 4-hydroxyestradiol (III) by spontaneous
aromatization or by enzymatic catalysis. We have demonstrated that II is also an effective inducer of the neoplastic transformation of these cells (Le Quesne et al.,
1980; Purdy et al., 1983). Microsomes from these cells can
metabolically activate estradiol to 4-hydroxyestradiol.
Furthermore, 4-hydroxyestradiol (III) can also cause transformation, although a higher concentration is required than
is needed for II in these assays. Thus at present we can't
assign II as the unique ultimate carcinogenic metabolite of
estradiol metabolism. When we incubated [6,7-$^3$H]estradiol
with microsomes from human mammary tumor cells growing in

Fig. 6. Tumor (fibrosarcoma) produced in an NIH nude mouse
5 weeks after 5 x 10⁶ cells transformed by estradiol
(Fig. 5) were inoculated subcutaneously. See Purdy et al.
(1983) for details.

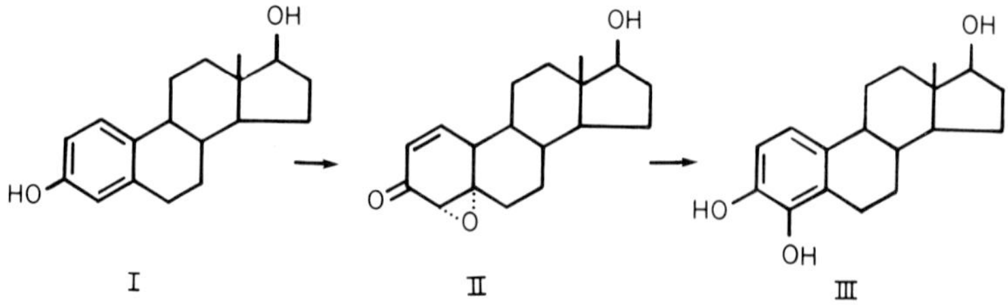

Fig. 7. Postulated metabolic pathway for the formation of
4-hydroxyestradiol (III) from estradiol (I) via the $4\alpha,5\alpha$-
epoxyenone (II).

culture, we were able to trap a portion of the radioactivity
in a form with the properties of an epoxyenone of the type
shown in Figure 3B, rather than compound II which was not
isolated. We now need data on the comparative reactivity
of these epoxides with DNA before we can provide a more
specific mechanism.

We have compared the frequency of neoplastic transformation of Balb/c 3T3 cells by certain estrogens with the
relative rates of catechol estrogen formation by microsomes
from these cells. These data show that the rates of
metabolic activation as catechols roughly parallels the
observed frequency of cellular transformation. The
relative rates of catechol formation are illustrated in
Figure 8 for ethynylestradiol > estradiol. We call your

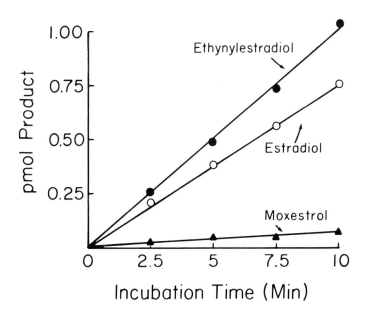

Fig. 8. Radioenzymatic assay of catechol estrogen formation from 50 μM estrogens with microsomes from Balb/c 3T3
cells. The total pmol of the monomethyl ethers obtained in
the heptane extracts according to the procedure of Purdy et
al. (1982) is shown as a function of incubation time (min).

attention to the fact that there was virtually no catechol formation with the 11β-methoxy derivative of ethynylestradiol, termed moxestrol.  On the other hand, moxestrol is by far the most potent estrogen of the three (Raynaud et al., 1973).  Ethynylestradiol is the estrogenic component of oral contraceptives.  The structures of ethynylestradiol and moxestrol are shown in Figure 9.  The remarkable

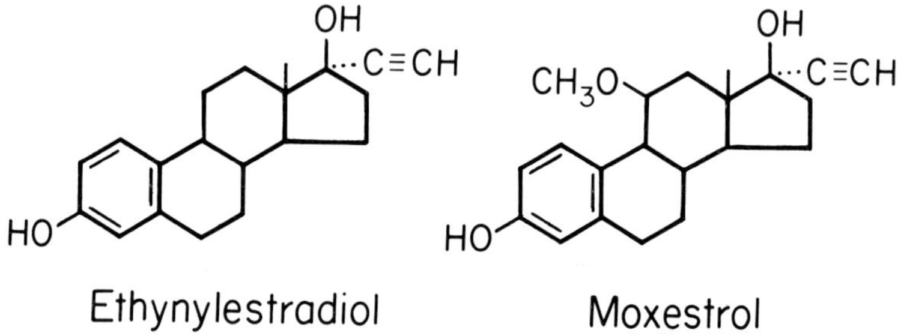

Fig. 9.  Chemical structures of estrogens.

biological potency of moxestrol is due to the combination of effects produced by the 11β-methoxy and 17α-ethynyl groups that are attached to the naturally occurring human hormone, estradiol.

In keeping with our hypothesis, moxestrol, which does not form activated metabolites such as these catechols, did not lead to any detectable morphologic transformation of Balb/c 3T3 cells.  Ethynylestradiol, which does form catechols, not only was clearly always positive in this assay system, but also induced liver tumors *in vivo* in the Syrian hamster model system (Li et al., 1982).

It has been the prevailing opinion of pathologists concerned with estrogens and cancer that "if one estrogen is harmful, they probably all are" (e.g., Silverberg, 1978).  Our data with ethynylestradiol versus moxestrol clearly argues against this attitude.

When moxestrol was administered to postmenopausal women as a single dose of 0.1 mg per week, it compared

favorably to 1.25 mg of conjugated estrogens per day
(De Forteza et al., 1980). In a double-blind study comparing moxestrol (5 μg/day) and ethynylestradiol (25 μg/day)
in postmenopausal women, Robyn et al. (1978) found serum
prolactin levels doubled with ethynylestradiol but were
unchanged with moxestrol. Since prolactin has a role in
accelerating the growth of mammary tumors in experimental
animals (Meites, 1972), this property of moxestrol may
therefore have an advantage in long-term therapy. It has
been available in France since 1974, with no adverse
reports yet brought to our attention. The low amounts of
catechol estrogen formation from moxestrol compared to
ethynylestradiol has recently been documented in pharmacokinetic studies in women by Salmon and coworkers.

Since ethynylestradiol was introduced shortly after
1938, there have been no basically new estrogens that have
become available for women in this country. From the present reports of its clinical effectiveness, and our genotoxicity studies where moxestrol has not been found active
as a transforming agent, moxestrol deserves to be evaluated
further as a safer estrogen in aging. The costs of additional genotoxicity studies are certainly modest compared
to the costs of clinical trials. However, the likelihood
of the acceptance of a French estrogen in the near future
in this country is hardly comparable to the arrival of the
Concorde. We can nevertheless predict with some confidence
that the overall effectiveness obtained by introducing one
or more functional groups at structurally critical positions of natural estrogens will lead to new synthetic
estrogens that will materially and biologically benefit our
future population of 36 million aging but active women.

ACKNOWLEDGEMENTS

This investigation was supported by Grant CA 24629
awarded by the National Cancer Institute, DHHS. We are
indebted to the American Cancer Society for their support
of our initial studies by Grant No. RD-47. We are most
grateful to Perry H. Moore, Jr., for performing the microsomal incubations, to Dr. Jean-Pierre Raynaud of Roussel-
UCLAF for generous gifts of estrogens and other assistance,
and to Drs. Philip W. Le Quesne of Northeastern University
and Johng S. Rhim of the National Cancer Institute for
their invaluable collaborative efforts.

REFERENCES

Albright F, Bloomberg E, Smith PH (1940). Post-menopausal
osteoporosis. Trans Assoc Am Physicians 55:298.
Ball P, Knuppen R (1980). Catecholoestrogens. Acta
Endocrinol Suppl 232:1.
Bancroft J, Burger HG, Devi PK, Mack TM, Nordin BE,
Naylander P, Ryan KJ, Sas M, Sinnathuray TA (1981).
Research on the menopause. WHO Tech Rep Ser 670:1.
Brinton LA, Hoover RN, Szklo M, Fraumeni JF Jr (1981).
Menopausal estrogen use and risk of breast cancer.
Cancer 47:2517.
Coombs MM, Bhatt TS, Croft CJ (1973). Correlation between
carcinogenicity and chemical structure in cyclopenta-
[a]phenanthrenes. Cancer Res 33:832.
Coombs MM, Dixon C, Kissonerghis A-M (1976). Evaluation of
the mutagenicity of compounds of known carcino-
genicity, belonging to the benz[a]anthracene,
chrysene, and cyclopenta[a]phenanthrene series, using
Ames's test. Cancer Res 36:4525.
Coombs MM, Kissonerghis A-M, Allen JA, Vose CW (1979).
Identification of the proximate and ultimate forms of
the carcinogen 15,16-dihydro-11-methylcyclopenta[a]-
phenanthrene-17-one. Cancer Res 39:4160.
De Forteza IE, Tejss CE, Quaglia E, Colillas R (1980).
Accion de un nuevo estregeno de sintesis (moxestrol)
en climatericas recientes y antiguas. Sem Med
156:358.
Gordan GS (1976). Preface to papers presented at the
symposium on postmenopausal osteoporosis. Isr J Med
Sci 12:593.
Hammond CB, Jelovsek FR, Lee KL, Creasman WT, Parker RT
(1979). Effects of long-term estrogen replacement
therapy. I. Metabolic effects. Am J Obstet Gynecol
133:525.
Hulka BS, Chambless LE, Kaufman DG, Fowler WC Jr,
Greenberg, BG (1982). Protection against endometrial
carcinoma by combination-product oral contraceptives.
JAMA 247:475.
Kakunaga T (1973). A quantitative system for assay of
malignant transformation by chemical carcinogens using
a clone derived from Balb/3T3. Int J Cancer 12:463.
Kakunaga T, Lo K-Y, Leavitt J, Ikenaga M (1980). Relationship between transformation and mutation in mammalian
cells. Jerusalem Symp Quantum Chem Biochem 13:527.

Lebherz TB, French L (1969). Nonhormonal treatment of the menopausal syndrome. Obstet Gynecol 33:795.

Le Quesne PW, Durga AV, Subramanyam V, Soloway AH, Hart RW, Purdy RH (1980). Biomimetic synthesis of catechol estrogens: potentially mutagenic arene oxide intermediates in estrogen metabolism. J Med Chem 23:239.

Li JJ, Kempf RA, Li SA (1982). High incidence of malignant hepatomas induced by DES or ethynyl estradiol in Syrian golden hamsters. In 13th International Cancer Congress, Seattle, WA, Sept 8-15, Proceedings p 679(3884).

McKinlay SM, McKinlay JB (1973). Selected studies of the menopause. J Biosoc Sci 5:533.

McLachlan JA, Wong A, Degen GH, Barrett JC (1982). Morphological and neoplastic transformation of Syrian hamster embryo fibroblasts by diethylstilbestrol and its analogs. Cancer Res 42:3040.

Meema HE, Bunker ML, Meema S (1965). Loss of compact bone due to menopause. Obstet Gynecol 26:333.

Meites J (1972). Relation of prolactin to mammary tumorigenesis and growth in rats. In Boyns AR, Griffiths K (eds): "Prolactin and Carcinogenesis." Cardiff: Alpha Omega Alpha Publishing, p 54.

Miller AB, Bulbrook RD (1980). The epidemiology and etiology of breast cancer. N Engl J Med 303:1246.

Purdy, RH, Moore PH Jr, Williams MC, Goldzieher JW, Paul SM (1982). Relative rates of 2- and 4-hydroxyestrogen synthesis are dependent on both substrate and tissue. FEBS Letters 138:40

Purdy RH, Goldzieher JW, Le Quesne PW, Abdel-Baky S, Durocher CK, Moore PH Jr, Rhim JS (1983). Active intermediates in carcinogenesis. In Merriam GR, Lipsett MB (eds): "Catechol Estrogens," New York: Raven Press, Chapt 13.

Raynaud J-P, Bouton M-M, Gallet-Bourquin D, Philibert D, Tournemine C, Azadian-Boulanger G (1973). Comparative study of estrogen action. Mol Pharmacol 9:520.

Richardson GS, MacLaughlin DT (eds) (1978). Hormonal biology of endometrial cancer. UICC (Union Int Centre Cancer) Tech Rep Ser 42:185.

Riggs BL, Seeman E, Hodgson SF, Taves DR, O'Fallon WM (1982). Effect of the fluoride/calcium regimen on vertebral fracture occurrence in postmenopausal osteoporosis. N Engl J Med 306:446.

Robyn C, Vekemans, M, Rozencweig M, Chigot D, Raynaud JP (1978). Double-blind corssover clinical pharmacology study comparing moxestrol (R 2858) and ethinyl estradiol in postmenopausal women. J Clin Pharmacol 18:29.

Salmon J, Coussediere D, Cousty C, Raynaud JP. Pharmacokinetics and metabolism in humans. J Steroid Biochem in press.

Sheffery JB, Wilson TA, Walsh JC (1969). Double-blind, cross-over study comparing chlordiazepoxide, conjugated estrogens, combined chlordiazepoxide and conjugated estrogens, and placebo in treatment of the menopause. Med Ann DC 38:433.

Silverberg SG (1978). Discussion. In Silverberg SG, Major FJ (eds): "Estrogens and Cancer," New York: John Wiley and Sons, p 177.

Smith DC, Prentice R, Thompson DJ, Herrmann WL (1975). Association of exogenous estrogen and endometrial carcinoma. N Engl J Med 293:1164.

Soloway AH, Le Quesne PW (1980). Potential endogenous mutagens/carcinogens. J Theor Biol 85:153.

Studd J (1976). Oestrogens as a cause of endometrial carcinoma. Br Med J 1:1144.

Tsang W-s, Griffin GW (1979). "Metabolic Activation of Polynuclear Aromatic Hydrocarbons." New York: Pergamon Press.

Wallach S, Henneman PH (1959). Prolonged estrogen therapy in postmenopausal women. JAMA 171:1637.

Weinstein MC (1980). Estrogen use in postmenopausal women - costs, risks, and benefits. N Engl J Med 303:308.

Weiss NS, Sayvetz TA (1980). Incidence of endometrial cancer in relation to the use of oral contraceptives. N Engl J Med 302:551.

Weiss NS, Ure CL, Ballard JH, Williams AR, Daling JR (1980). Decreased risk of fractures of the hip and lower forearm with postmenopausal use of estrogen. N Engl J Med 303:1195.

Intervention in the Aging Process, Part A: Quantitation, Epidemiology, and
Clinical Research, pages 267–278
© 1983 Alan R. Liss, Inc., 150 Fifth Avenue, New York, NY 10011

DEHYDROEPIANDROSTERONE:    AN ANTI-CANCER AND POSSIBLE ANTI-
AGING SUBSTANCE

ARTHUR G. SCHWARTZ, LAURA L. PASHKO AND ROBERT
H. TANNEN
FELS RESEARCH INSTITUTE, TEMPLE UNIVERSITY
MEDICAL SCHOOL
PHILADELPHIA, PA. 19140

Dehydroepiandrosterone (DHEA) and DHEA-sulfate are
major adrenal secretory products in humans (Vande Wiele et
al, 1963).  The plasma concentration of DHEA-sulfate, which,
next to cholesterol, is the most abundant steroid in
humans, undergoes the most marked age-related decline of any
known steroid (Migeon et al, 1957).  Although DHEA-sulfate
is the main precursor of placental estrogen (Baulieu and
Dray, 1963) and may be converted into active androgens in
peripheral tissue (Lebeau and Baulieu, 1973), there is no
obvious biological role for either DHEA or DHEA-sulfate in
the normal individual (Vande Wiele and Lieberman, 1960).

Retrospective studies have found that women with either
advanced or primary operable breast cancer have low plasma
levels of DHEA and DHEA-sulfate (Wang et al, 1974; Zumoff et
al, 1981) as well as low urinary excretory rates of
androsterone and etiocholanolone, the primary metabolites of
DHEA and DHEA-sulfate.  In order to determine whether this
steroidal abnormality preceded the clinical appearance of
the disease and was related to risk, Bulbrook et al (1971)
initiated a prospective study on the island of Guernsey.
Between 1961 and 1968, urine specimens were collected from
5,000 apparently healthy women aged 30 to 59 years.  The
excretion of 17-hydroxycorticosteroids and the DHEA metabolites androsterone and etiocholanolone was determined in
4,699 and 1,498 specimens, respectively.  An analysis of the
data in 1971, when 27 of the women had developed breast
cancer, showed that subnormal excretion of androsterone and
etiocholanolone was found up to nine years before diagnosis,
and that the highest risk was associated with the lowest

amounts of the steroid metabolites. By 1978, 48 cases had been reported, and the subnormal urinary levels of andros-terone and etiocholanolone were confirmed (Farwell et al, 1978).

In 1960 Marks and Banks demonstrated that DHEA is a potent inhibitor of mammalian glucose-6-phosphate dehydrogenase (G6PDH), the rate-controlling enzyme in the pentose-phosphate shunt. This pathway is a major source of extra-mitochondrial NADPH, a necessary co-factor for a variety of reductive biosyntheses, including the synthesis of fatty acids and ribo- and deoxyribonucleotides.


ANTI-OBESITY EFFECT

Yen et al (1977) reported that DHEA, when given p.o. at 450 mg/kg thrice weekly, produced a striking anti-obesity effect in VY-A$^{vy}$/a mice (genetically obese) without suppressing appetite. There was no apparent toxicity at the doses used, and the weight controlling effect was reversible upon withdrawal of treatment. The treated mice had reduced liver lipogenesis rates, which may have resulted from an inhibition of G6PDH by the steroid. This may have been the first demonstration of a compound that inhibits weight gain without suppressing appetite.

We have confirmed that DHEA, when administered either at 450mg/kg p.o. thrice weekly in sesame oil or in the diet (0.2% to 0.6%), inhibits weight gain without suppressing food consumption in C3H-A$^{vy}$/A, C3H-A/A, A/J, C57BL/6, and NZB mice, as well as in Sprague-Dawley and Zucker (obese) rats. The mechanism by which DHEA reduces weight gain is not clear. In part it may result from an inhibition in the rate of fatty acid synthesis through an inhibition of G6PDH and consequent NADPH production. We have found a 2.5 fold decrease in the specific activity of liver G6PDH in Zucker rats treated with 0.6% DHEA in their diet for 15 weeks. However, the specific activity of malic enzyme (which is not inhibited by DHEA) was increased twofold. Fatty acid synthetase activity, when measured in the presence of exogenous NADPH, was about threefold lower in the DHEA treated animals.

ANTI-CARCINOGENIC EFFECT

Reducing the weight gain of laboratory mice and rats by limiting their food intake produces what may be the most general anti-carcinogenic effect of any known treatment (Tannenbaum and Silverstone, 1953; Ross and Bras, 1971). Neoplasms as diverse as spontaneous breast (Tannenbaum, 1945) and liver tumors (Tannenbaum and Siverstone, 1949), spontaneous leukemia (Saxton et al, 1944), and benzo(a)-pyrene-induced skin carcinomas (Tannenbaum, 1944) and fibrosarcomas (Rusch et al, 1945) are all reduced in frequency by caloric restriction.

We speculated that DHEA, by virtue of its anti-obesity effect, might also have an anti-carcinogenic effect. We observed that long-term DHEA treatment of $C3H-A^{vy}/A$ and C3H-A/A mice, in addition to reducing weight gain without suppressing appetite, inhibited spontaneous breast cancer development (Schwartz, 1979; Schwartz et al, 1981)(Table 1). More recently, we have found that DHEA also inhibits DMBA- and urethan-induced lung adenoma formation in A/J mice (Schwartz and Tannen, 1981) (Table 2) and 1,2-dimethyl-hydrazine (DMH)- induced colon cancers in Balb/c mice (Nyce et al, 1982) (Table 3).

DHEA-SULFATIDE AND 16α-BR-EPIANDROSTERONE

In 1966 Oertel isolated a DHEA-sulfate conjugate from human plasma which he characterized as DHEA-sulfatide. He subsequently reported that DHEA-sulfatide, a labile substance that readily hydrolyzed to DHEA-sulfate and a diglyceride, was a more potent inhibitor of human red blood cell G6PDH activity than DHEA, whereas DHEA-sulfate was inactive. We have prepared DHEA-sulfatide (Fig. 1) and have found this compound to be a more effective inhibitor of mouse epidermal G6PDH activity than DHEA, and have also found DHEA-sulfate to have very little inhibitory effect (Pashko et al, 1981).

A still more active inhibitor of rat mammary gland G6PDH activity is 16α-Br-epiandrosterone (Epi-Br, Raineri and Levy, 1970). We observed this compound to be much more effective than DHEA against mouse epidermal and bovine adrenal G6PDH. Using purified bovine adrenal G6PDH, Epi-Br had a Ki of $0.3 \times 10^{-6}$M and DHEA a Ki of $17.6 \times 10^{-6}$M.

TABLE 1. Effect of Long-term DHEA Treatment on Breast Cancer Incidence in C3H-A/A and C3H-AVY/A mice

| Month | 4 | 5 | 6 | 7 | 8 | 9 | 10 | 11 | 12 | 13 | 14 | 15 | 16 | 17 | 18 |
|---|---|---|---|---|---|---|---|---|---|---|---|---|---|---|---|
| **C3H-A/A** | | | | | | | | | | | | | | | |
| Number controls living | 78 | 78 | 75 | 72 | 67 | 60 | 54 | 49 | 42 | 35 | 35 | 33 | 30 | 29 | 20 |
| Number controls with cancer (cumulative) | 0 | 0 | 1 | 3 | 4 | 6 | 6 | 7 | 8 | 13 | 13 | 13 | 13 | 14 | 21 |
| Number DHEA living | 77 | 76 | 75 | 75 | 75 | 73 | 63 | 54 | 52 | 48 | 44 | 42 | 38 | 32 | 29 |
| Number DHEA with cancer (cumulative) | 0 | 1 | 1 | 1 | 1 | 1 | 3 | 3 | 4 | 5 | 6 | 6 | 7 | 7 | 9 |
| **C3H-AVY/A** | | | | | | | | | | | | | | | |
| Number controls living | 27 | 26 | 26 | 24 | 21 | 17 | 15 | 12 | 11 | 9 | 7 | 7 | | | |
| Number controls with cancer (cumulative) | 0 | 0 | 0 | 2 | 5 | 9 | 11 | 14 | 15 | 17 | 19 | 19 | | | |
| Number DHEA living | 23 | 22 | 22 | 22 | 21 | 19 | 19 | 16 | 16 | 15 | 12 | 9 | | | |
| Number DHEA with cancer (cumulative) | 0 | 0 | 0 | 0 | 0 | 0 | 0 | 0 | 0 | 1 | 4 | 5 | | | |

TABLE 2. Effect of DHEA on DMBA- and Urethan-Induced Lung Tumorigenesis.

| Tumors per mouse | Number of mice having the indicated number of tumors | | | |
| --- | --- | --- | --- | --- |
| | DMBA alone | DMBA+ DHEA | Urethan alone | Urethan + DHEA |
| 0 | | 3 | | |
| 1 | | 5 | | |
| 2 | | 5 | | |
| 3 | 2 | 5 | | |
| 4 | 1 | 1 | | 1 |
| 5 | 1 | 1 | | |
| 6 | 2 | 2 | | |
| 8 | 3 | | 1 | 2 |
| 9 | 3 | | | 1 |
| 10 | 2 | | 1 | |
| 11 | 2 | 1 | | 1 |
| 12 | | | 1 | 3 |
| 13 | | | | 1 |
| 14 | 2 | | | 1 |
| 15 | 2 | | 4 | 1 |
| 16 | 1 | | 2 | 2 |
| 17 | 1 | | 2 | 2 |
| 18 | | | 1 | |
| 19 | 2 | | 3 | |
| 20 | | | 1 | 1 |
| 21 | | | 1 | |
| 22 | 1 | | 1 | 1 |
| 23 | | | 1 | 2 |
| 24 | 1 | | 2 | |
| 25 | | | 2 | |
| 26 | 1 | | 1 | |
| 28 | | | | 1 |
| 35 | 1 | | | |
| Number of mice per group | 28 | 23 | 24 | 20 |

TABLE 3.  Effect of Long-Term DHEA Treatment on Incidence of DMH-Induced Colon Tumors in Balb/c Mice

|  | Average number of tumors/animal | |
|---|---|---|
|  | 20 weeks | 26 weeks |
| DMH plus DHEA | 0.5 + 0.7 | 2.5 + 1.3 |
| DMH only | 8.3 + 6.2 | 13.2 + 6.4 |
| Control diet | 0 | 0 |
| DHEA only | 0 | 0 |

DHEA was effective in suppressing lung tumor formation in A/J mice when given 9 days after a single dose of a carcinogen, suggesting that the steroid may inhibit the promotion phase of tumor development.  Further evidence for this is the observation that DHEA blocks the stimulation of mouse epidermal DNA synthesis by 12-0-tetradecanoylphorbol-13-acetate (TPA) and also inhibits Epstein-Barr virus-induced morphologic stimulation of human lymphocytes in vitro (Pashko, et al, 1981; Henderson et al, 1981).

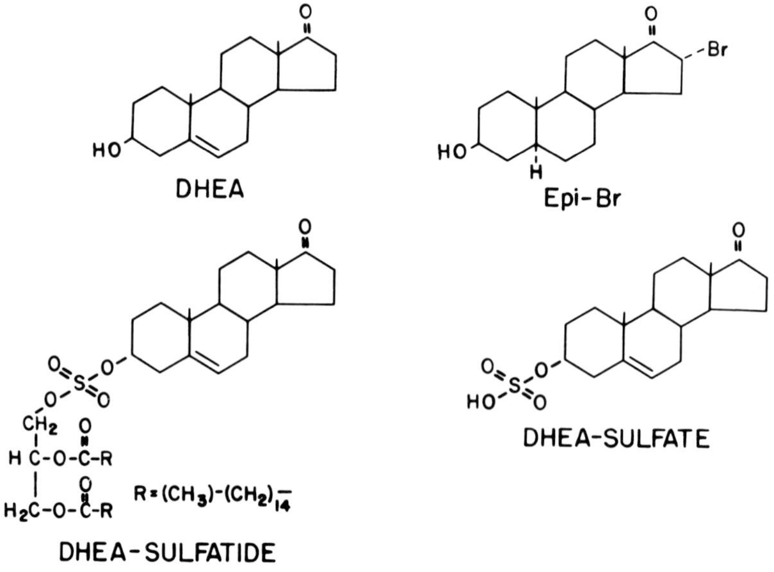

Fig. 1.  Structure of steroids

INHIBITION OF $^3$H-THYMIDINE INCORPORATION IN MOUSE EPIDERMIS

Chemically induced skin tumorigenesis in the mouse is a two-stage process involving initiation and promotion (Berenblum, 1978). Initiation refers to the events immediately following carcinogen application, i.e., carcinogen activation and binding of the activated carcinogen to DNA. If mice are initiated by a single topical application of a carcinogen to the skin and are then treated for prolonged periods with croton oil (or one of the active ingredients of croton oil, such as TPA) there is a marked enhancement in the rate of appearance of tumors. TPA alone is not carcinogenic and is referred to as a tumor promoter.

TPA stimulates cell proliferation and $^3$H-thymidine incorporation in the mouse epidermis (Hennings and Boutwell, 1970). It is currently believed that the stimulation of hyperplasia by tumor promotors is a necessary, but not sufficient, condition for tumor promotion (Marks et al, 1979). Experimentally induced liver (Peraino et al, 1973) and lung tumorigenesis (Witschi et al, 1977), as well as the transformation of normal mouse fibroblasts in culture (Mondal et al, 1976), occurs through a two-stage mechanism, and it may be a general phenomenon in carcinogenesis. Figure 2 shows that a single intraperitoneal injection of either DHEA or DHEA-sulfatide into ICR mice abolishes the TPA stimulation in the rate of epidermal $^3$H-thymidine incorporation over a 24-hr period, whereas DHEA-sulfate, at comparable dose, is without effect. In a dose-response experiment, Epi-Br was a much more effective inhibitor of $^3$H-thymidine incorporation than DHEA.

Of various sex steroids and a glucocortocoid that were tested, only corticosterone inhibited the rate of $^3$H-thymidine incorporation in TPA-stimulated epidermis. Glucocorticoids are known to inhibit epidermal DNA synthesis (Castor and Baker, 1950).

The much greater activity of Epi-Br as an inhibitor of DNA synthesis, along with its much greater efficacy as an inhibitor of G6PDH, suggests that inhibition of this enzyme and consequent pentose-phosphate shunt activity may account for the reduction in DNA synthesis rate. The pentose-phosphate shunt generates ribose-phosphate and the bulk of extra-mitochondrial NADPH, both of which are necessary for

deoxyribonucleotide synthesis. Further support for this
hypothesis is our observation that the addition of a
combination of four deoxyribonucleosides to cultured HeLa
cells reverses the growth inhibition produced by DHEA
treatment (Dworkin et al).

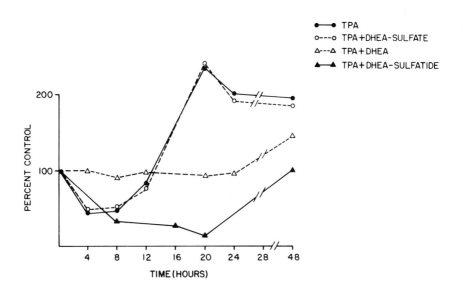

Fig. 2. Inhibition of TPA stimulation of [3]H-thymidine
incorporation in mouse epidermis by DHEA and DHEA-sulfatide.
Mice were injected with either DHEA (15 mg/kg), DHEA-
sulfate (20 mg/kg), or DHEA-sulfatide (48 mg/kg) 1 hr
before TPA application. The doses used are equivalent to 50
μmole of steroid per kg body weight. [3]H-thymidine was
administered at various time intervals, and the amount
incorporated per μg of DNA in the epidermis was determined.
Each point is the mean of the percent of control specific
incorporation for three separately treated mice with a SE of
<15%.

INHIBITION OF DEVELOPMENT OF AUTOIMMUNE HEMOLYTIC ANEMIA BY DHEA

DHEA treatment, like food restriction, inhibits the development of several types of tumors. This anti-carcinogenic effect of DHEA may result from both its anti-obesity action as well as from a probable direct inhibition of tumor promotion. Experiments are currently in progress in non-tumor prone long-lived strains of rodents to determine if DHEA treatment also retards aging.

Preliminary data are encouraging. The NZB mouse develops an autoimmune disease characterized by autoimmune hemolytic anemia, hepatosplenomegaly, anti-nuclear antibodies and renal dysfunction manifested as proteinuria and antigen-antibody type nephritis (Howie and Simpson, 1974). DHEA (0.4% of the diet) was administered chronically to 2 month old female NZB mice. By 6 months of age, control mice weighed $43.5 \pm 5.6$ gm (n=32) and treated animals, $30.0 \pm 2.5$ gm (n=33), $p < 0.001$. Food consumption was comparable in both groups, at 3.9 and 3.8 gm/mouse/day, respectively. Hematocrits of control mice were $46.9 \pm 3.6\%$ as compared to $49.3 \pm 2.1\%$ in DHEA treated mice, $p < 0.001$. Incidence of a positive Coomb's test was significantly reduced in DHEA treated mice (68% positive in controls vs 16% in treated, $p < 0.001$). At 9 months of age, differences were still apparent between control and DHEA treated mice with respect to weight ($50.9 \pm 6.5$ gm vs $30.3 \pm 3.1$ gm), hematocrits ($40.8 \pm 5.1\%$ vs $44.8 \pm 3.2\%$), and incidence of a positive Coomb's test (78% vs 48%).

Thus, long-term DHEA treatment does delay the rate of development of an important age-associated pathologic process.

REFERENCES

Baulieu EE, Dray F (1963): Conversion of $^3$H-dehydroisoandrosterone ($3\alpha$-hydroxy - $\Delta^5$- androsten-17-one) sulfate to $^3$H-estrogens in normal pregnant women. J Clin Endocrinol Metab 23: 1298-1301.
Berenblum I (1978): Historical perspective. In Slaga TJ, Sivak A, Boutwell RK (eds): "Carcinogenesis-A Comprehensive Survey." Vol 2. New York: Raven Press, pp 1-10.

Bulbrook, RD, Hayward JL, Spicer CC (1971): Relation between urinary androgen and corticoid excretion and subsequent breast cancer. Lancet 2:395-398.

Castor EW, Baker BL (1950): The local action of adrenocortical steroids on epidermis and connective tissue of skin. Endocrinology 47:234-241.

Dworkin CR, Gorman SD, Pashko LL, Nyce JW, Cristofallo VJ, Schwartz AG (1982): Inhibition of growth of HeLa and WI-38 cells by dehydroepiandrosterone and its reversal by ribo- and deoxyribonucleosides. Submitted.

Farwell VT, Bulbrook RD, Hayward JL (1978): Risk factors in breast cancer. A prospective study in the island of Guernsey. In Grundmann E, Beck L (eds): "Early Diagnosis of Breast Cancer: Methods and Results." Stuttgart: Gustav-Fischer Verlag, pp 43-51.

Henderson E, Schwartz A, Pashko L, Abou-Gharbia M, Swern D 1981): Dehydroepiandrosterone and 16$\alpha$-bromo-epiandrosterone: Inhibitors of Epstein-Barr virus-induced transformation of human lymphocytes. Carcinogenesis 2:683-686.

Hennings H, Boutwell RK (1970): Studies on the mechanism of skin tumor promotion. Cancer Res 30:312-320.

Howle JB, Simpson LP (1974): Autoimmune disease in NZB mice and their hybrids. In Dubois EL (ed): "Lupus Erythematosus." Los Angeles: University California Press, pp 124-141.

Lebeau MC, Baulieu EE (1973): On the significance of the metabolism of steroid hormone conjugates. In Fishman WH (ed): "Metabolic conjugation and Metabolic Hydrolysis." Vol. 3 New York: Academic Press, pp 151-187.

Marks PH, Banks J (1960): Inhibition of mammalian glucose-6-phosphate dehydrogenase by steroids. Proc Natl Acad Sci USA 46:447-452.

Marks F, Bertsch S, Furstenberger G (1979): Ornithine decarboxylase activity, cell proliferation, and tumor promotion in mouse epidermis in vivo. Cancer Res 39:4183-4188.

Migeon CJ, Keller AR, Lawrence B, Shephard TH (1957): Dehydroepiandrosterone and androsterone levels in human plasma. Effect of age and sex; day-to-day and diurnal variations. J Clin Endocrinol Metab 17:1051-1062.

Mondal S, Brankow DW, Heidelberger C (1976): Two-stage chemical oncogenesis in cultures of C3H/10T1/2 cells. Cancer Res 36:2254-2260.

Nyce JW, Magee PN, Schwartz AG (1982): Inhibition of 1,2-dimethylhydrazine induced colon cancer in balb/c mice by dehydroepiandrosterone. Proc Amer Assoc Cancer Res 23:91.

Oertel GW (1966): Uber steroid-konjugate in plasma. XVII. Isolieurung und charakterisiesung lipohiler steroid-konjugate aus nebennierenrindengewebe, plasma und liquor. Hoppe-Seylers Z Physiol Chem 343:276-281.

Pashko L, Schwartz A, Abou-Gharbia M, Swern D (1981): Inhibition of DNA synthesis in mouse epidermis and breast epithelium by dehydroepiandrosterone and related steroids. Carcinogenesis 2:717-721.

Peraino C, Fry RJM, Staffeldt E (1973): Enhancement of spontaneous hepatic tumorigenesis in C3H mice by dietary phenobarbital. J Natl Cancer Inst 51:1349-1350.

Raineri R, Levy HR (1970): On the specificity of steroid interaction with mammary glucose-6-phosphate dehydrogenases. Biochemistry 9:2233-2243.

Ross MH, Bras G (1971): Lasting influence of early caloric restriction on prevalence of neoplasms in the rat. J Natl Cancer Inst 47:1095-1113.

Rusch HP, Johnson RO, Kline BE (1945): The relationship of caloric intake and of blood sugar to sarcogenesis in mice. Cancer Res 5:705-711.

Saxton JA, Boon MC, Furth J (1944): Observations on the inhibition of spontaneous leukemia in mice by underfeeding. Cancer Res 4:401-409.

Schwartz AG (1979): Inhibition of spontaneous breast cancer formation in female C3H-A$^{vy}$/A mice by long-term treatment with dehydroepiandrosterone. Cancer Res 39:1129-1132.

Schwartz A, Hard G, Pashko L, Abou-Gharbia M, Swern D (1981): Dehydroepiandrosterone: An anti-obesity and anti-carcinogenic agent. Nutr Cancer 3:46-53.

Schwartz AG, Tannen RH (1981): Inhibition of 7,12-dimethyl-benz(a)anthracene and urethan-induced lung tumor formation in A/J mice by long-term treatment with dehydroepiandros-terone. Carcinogenesis 2:1335-1337.

Siiteri PK, MacDonald PC (1963): The utilization of circulating dehydroepiandrosterone sulfate for estrogen synthesis during human pregnancy. Steroids 2:713-730.

Tannen RH, Schwartz AG (1982): Reduced weight gain and delay of Coomb's positive hemolytic anemia in NZB mice treated with dehydroepiandrosterone (DHEA). Fed Proc 42:1131.

Tannenbaum A (1944): The dependence of the genesis of induced skin tumors on the caloric intake during different stages of carcinogenesis. Cancer Res 4:673-677.

Tannenbaum A (1945): The dependence of tumor formation on the degree of caloric restriction. Cancer Res 5:609-625.

Tannenbaum A, Silverstone H (1949): The influence of the degree of caloric restriction on the formation of skin

ion to, Strain GW,360-3363.

tumors and hepatomas in mice. Cancer Res 9:724-727.

Tannenbaum A, Silverstone H (1953): Nutrition in relation to cancer. Adv Cancer Res 1:451-501.

Vande Wiele R, Lieberman S (1960): The metabolism of dehydroisoandrosterone. In Pincus G, Vollmer E (eds): "Biological Activities of Steroids in Relation to Cancer." New York: Academic Press, pp 93-110.

Vande Wiele RL, MacDonald PC, Gurpide E (1963): Studies on the secretion and interconversion of the androgens. Recent Prog Horm Res 19: 275-310.

Wang DY, Bulbrook RD, Herian M, Hayward JL (1974): Studies on the sulphate esters of dehydroepiandrosterone and androsterone in the blood of women with breast cancer. Eur J Cancer 10:477-482.

Witschi H, Williamson D, Lock S (1977): Enhancement of urethan tumorigenesis in mouse lung by butylated hydroxytoluene. J Natl Cancer Inst 58:301-305.

Yen TT, Alan JV, Pearson DV, Acton JM, and Greenberg M (1977): Prevention of obesity in $A^{vy}/a$ mice by dehydroepian-drosterone. Lipids 12:409-413.

Zumoff B, Levin J, Rosenfeld RS, Markham M, Strain GW, Fukushima DK (1981): Abnormal 24-hr mean plasma concentrations of dehydroisoandrosterone and dehydroisoandrosterone sulfate in women with primary operable breast cancer. Cancer Res 41:3360-3363.

Intervention in the Aging Process, Part A: Quantitation, Epidemiology, and Clinical Research, pages 279–305

POSSIBLE ROLE OF MAGNESIUM IN DISORDERS OF THE AGED

MILDRED S. SEELIG, M.D., M.P.H., F.A.C.N.

GOLDWATER MEMORIAL HOSPITAL, MEDICAL DEPARTMENT
NEW YORK UNIVERSITY MEDICAL CENTER
ROOSEVELT ISLAND, NEW YORK, NEW YORK  10044

INTRODUCTION

Magnesium (Mg) is important in many reactions, and in prevention and treatment of functional and structural disorders of many tissues and systems.  There are numerous recent publications on its effects on enzymes, in subcellular and cellular preparations, and in plants and animals, including man.  However, relatively little has been done on MG in aging.  It is necessary to draw largely from studies that show changes in Mg deficiency that resemble those of old age, and relate Mg requirements to deficiencies of other nutrients particularly those with which Mg interacts.  It has been postulated that Mg deficiency early in life gives rise to chronic abnormalities that persist throughout life, increasing morbidity and mortality and shortening life (Seelig, 1977; 1977/1982; 1978; 1980).  Little attention has been paid to special Mg needs of old people, to whether Mg inadequacy might contribute to the aging process, or to whether Mg supplementation might have any beneficial effects in the aged.

MAGNESIUM REQUIREMENTS OF THE AGED

The general assumption that most Western diets are adequate in Mg has been questioned since analysis of metabolic balance studies disclosed that at intakes below 5 and 6 mg/kg/day in young women and men respectively, maintenance of Mg equilibrium is not consistent (Seelig, 1964).  Analysis of numerous typical sample meals of Americans of all ages has shown that the Mg intakes are usually below the Recommended Dietary Allowance (RDA) (U.S. Dept. Agr. 1980).  The RDA for

Mg has been estimated at 300–350 mg/day for young women and young men, (Food and Nutr. Board, 1980), providing about 4.5–5 mg/kg/day. The RDAs may not be optimal for everyday living, especially for the elderly, since they are derived from balance studies with young healthy adults under controlled stable conditions – usually protected from the vicissitudes of life (Seelig, 1981). Studies to assess the influence of age: (psycho-social, physical, chronic disease and therapy) on the Mg needs have not been done. It is probable that Mg requirements are elevated in the elderly, in view of the many factors in old age that increase nutritional needs and interfere with utilization (Figure 1).

Figure 1.

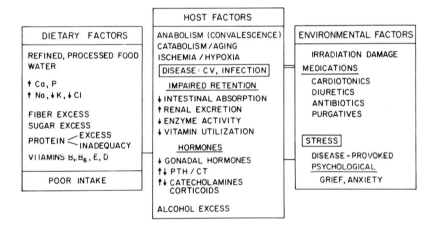

FACTORS AFFECTING MAGNESIUM REQUIREMENTS
— OF PARTICULAR SIGNIFICANCE IN THE AGED —

## Magnesium Intake, Absorption and Excretion

The Mg intake of old people tends to be low (U.S. Dept. Agr., 1980; Vir & Love, 1979), and their intestinal absorption of Mg declines gradually with increasing age (Mountokalakis et al, 1976); Johansson, 1979). Lower urinary Mg excretion has been reported by old than by young men. (Simpson et al, 1978). Young women excreted less Mg than did post menopausal women, a difference that was more marked in those taking oral contraceptives (Table 1, Goulding & McChesney, 1977).

Table 1.   *URINARY MAGNESIUM OF YOUNG WOMEN,*
*± ORAL CONTRACEPTIVES (O.C.), AND OF POST-MENOPAUSAL WOMEN*

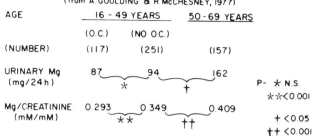

(from A. GOULDING & R. McCHESNEY, 1977)

| AGE | 16 - 49 YEARS | | 50 - 69 YEARS | |
|---|---|---|---|---|
| | (O.C.) | (NO O.C.) | | |
| (NUMBER) | (117) | (251) | (157) | |
| URINARY Mg (mg/24h) | 87 | 94 | 162 | P- ＊ N.S. ＊＊<0.001 |
| Mg/CREATININE (mM/mM) | 0.293 | 0.349 | 0.409 | + <0.05 ++ <0.001 |

## Serum and Tissue Levels of Magnesium

Serum Mg levels have been reported as quite constant in
healthy adults, regardless of age (Keating et al, 1969), and
as lower in old than young adults (Henrotte et al, 1976/1980).
In a study of circadian changes in serum Mg, young men exhibited lower peak (morning) levels than did old men (Touitou et al, 1978).  All subjects had their lowest serum Mg
levels during sleep hours at night.  The greatest circadian
amplitude was in old men.  In an on-going study of chronically hospitalized patients, most of whom are old, low Mg
levels and high Mg retention after parenteral loading are
being encountered (Seelig & Berger, unpublished).

Increased estrogen levels, or administration of estrogen, caused both reduced serum levels and urinary output of
Mg (Goldsmith et al, 1970; Goldsmith & Johnston, 1976/1981).
These effects are atrributed to estrogen-induced Mg shift to
tissues.  The bone loss of post-menopausal women has been
correlated with the loss of bone matrix Mg, as well as of
calcium (Ca); the higher incidence of thrombotic events in
young women and the increased incidence of cardiovascular
disease in old women might be due to the shift of Mg from
blood plasma in young and the loss of cardiac Mg in old women (Goldsmith & Goldsmith, 1966; Goldsmith & Johnston,
1976/1980; Seelig, 1980).

Mg is predominantly an intracellular cation, and serum
levels are an unreliable index of its status in the body
(Walser, 1967; Seelig, 1980; Wacker, 1980).  Cardiac integrity being particularly vulnerable to Mg loss (Seelig, 1972;

Seelig & Heggtveit, 1974), the drop in myocardial Mg seen
in aging rats may be germane to the high cardiac disease
rates in the aged. There were striking reductions in myocardial Mg levels of old versus young female rats. The
septum and ventricles of male rats lost the most Mg with
increasing age (Figure 2). The Mg reduction was accompanied by lesser falls in Ca and potassium (K), but not
in phosphate (P) levels. The cation changes were not
related to dilutional factors, as the oldest rats had

Figure 2.

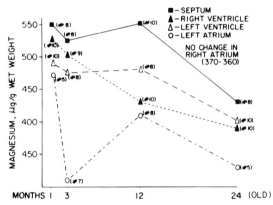

REGIONAL CARDIAC MAGNESIUM IN YOUNG, ADULT AND OLD RATS
(Derived from BASKIN & URICCHIO, 1979)

the lowest tissue water levels. There were significantly
lower Mg levels in aorta and liver of old rats than in
young, but little change in skeletal muscle or renal
Mg in a study in which renal Ca fell with age (Mori &
Duruisseau, 1960). In another study in which renal Ca
rose substantially with age, renal Mg fell (Baskin et al,
1981). Magnesium retention has been shown to decrease in
senescent mice (Draper, 1964).

NUTRIENT/MAGNESIUM INTERRELATIONS IN THE AGED

The intakes of most nutrients by the elderly decline
strikingly, especially in the seventh decade; the greatest decreases in the macronutrients are in fat and protein,
with only small carbohydrate decreases (Exton-Smith, 1970;

Crapo, 1982). Decreased physical activity is correlated
with reduced energy requirements of old age (McGandy et al,
1978). Protein needs, however, rise with increasing age
(Munro & Young, 1978; Uauy et al, 1978), which makes the
carbohydrate intake disproportionately high. Each of these
nutrients affect the Mg requirements, as do several of the
vitamins - low levels and poor utilization of which have
been found in the elderly (Oldham, 1962, Baker et al, 1979;
1980).

Fat, Sugar and Protein: Interrelations with Magnesium

Fat. Interference with Mg absorption by high intakes of
saturated fat was demonstrated long ago (Sawyer et al,
1918); high intestinal fat has contributed to hypomagnesemia
and resultant arrhythmia in patients with steatorrhea
(Chadda et al, 1973). Fats of different chain length and
degrees of saturation affect Mg absorption differently
(Rayssiguier, 1981). Experimental studies of the effects
of Mg on plasma lipids have yielded conflicting results,
depending on the dietary mix and the species used. Early
rat studies showed that Mg supplements exert a greater

Figure 3
EFFECT OF MAGNESIUM DEFICIENCY
ON PLASMA LIPOPROTEINS IN
RATS ON HIGH FAT DIET (CORN OIL)
(From Rayssiguier, 1981)

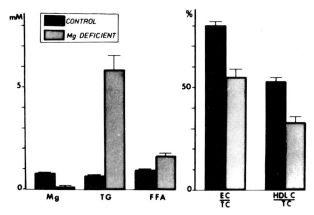

Dietary fat: 35% corn oil; Means ± SEM:

protective effect against fat deposition (in heart and arteries) than against hyperlipidemia, and lowered  lipoproteins
more than   liproproteins (Vitale et al, 1966; Hellerstein
et al, 1960). A more recent study has shown that rats fed
a Mg deficient diet that was rich in fat developed hypertrig-
lyceridemia and significantly lowered levels of high density
lipid cholesterol (HDL-C) (Figure 3, Gueux and Rayssiguier,
1981). The cholesterol-rich diet did not alter serum Mg
levels appreciably. Pigs fed a diet low in Mg developed
elevated serum triglycerides (Nuoranne et al, 1980). Young
women, who lost an average of 63 mg/day of Mg while on a diet
providing 4.2-5.4 mg/kg/day (the RDA), showed rising blood
lipids even though the dietary fat was low: 1g/day (Irwin
and Feeley, 1967). The authors recommended increasing the
RDA for Mg.

Even though serum Mg levels do not correlate reliably
with lipid levels in patients with atherosclerosis + hyperlipidemia, Mg treatment of patients with myocardial infarction has been reported to lower the LDL-C, to raise the
HDL-C, and to produce clinical improvement (Seelig, 1980:
chapter 5; Rayssiguier, 1981).

Sugar. High sugar intakes directly increase urinary
excretion of Mg (Lindeman et al, 1967; Lennon et al, 1974).
Perhaps the Mg loss caused by sugar contributed to the hyper-
triglyceridemia of Mg deficient rats fed a high sucrose diet
that was not rich in fat (Figure 4: Rayssiguier, 1981).

Figure 4.
EFFECT OF MAGNESIUM DEFICIENCY ON PLASMA TRIGLYCERIDES IN
RATS FED HIGH CARBOHYDRATE DIETS (FROM Y. RAYSSIGUIER, 1981)

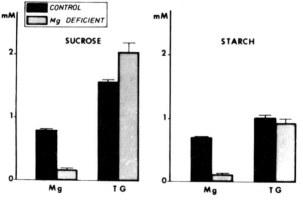

Means ± SEM for ten rats.

Diets disproportionately high in carbohydrate increase thiamin needs, which can increase Mg requirements (Infra vide).

Protein. Unduly low protein intakes have been shown to cause negative Mg balances in adolescent boys (Schwartz et al, 1973), and in young adults (Hunt and Schofield, 1969; McCance et al, 1942); increased protein intake improved the retention of Mg. However, protein loading has increased Mg loss (Lindeman et al, 1976/1980). Of importance for the elderly whose financial status often precludes increasing protein intakes substantially, is the finding that supplementing low to marginal protein diets with Mg (increasing the Mg to optimal or above) improved the retention of nitrogen of young people (McCance et al, 1942; Schwartz et al, 1973).

Vitamins with Interrelationships with Magnesium.

Thiamin. Mg deficiency interfers with responsiveness to thiamin in rats (Itokawa et al, 1974; Zieve et al, 1968). Correction of the Mg deficit has restored thiamin responsiveness in alcoholics with encephalopathy (Stendig-Lindberg, 1972). The Mg-dependence of thiamin utilization is a consequence of the role of Mg as a cofactor in enzymes requiring thiamin (Vallee, 1960). Additionally, evidence has been presented that Mg plays a role in binding thiamin with tissue protein (Itokawa et al, 1974). Thiamin deficiency also inhibits Mg utilization. It may be clinically important that Mg deficient rats with normal thiamin intake had lower plasma and tissue Mg levels than did those with double deficiency. (Figure 5, Itokawa, 1972).

It seems plausible that efforts to repair the $B_1$ deficiency in aged patients with or without alcoholism carry the risk, not only of a poor response to thiamin, but of intensifying Mg deficiency. The studies that show more vulnerability to thiamin deficiency in older than young subjects, and a need for higher intakes to correct the inadequacy (Oldham, 1962) did not provide data on the status of Mg. Studies of the effect of Mg supplements on the response of patients with vitamin $B_1$ deficiency are needed.

Pyridoxine. In early Mg deficiency studies, it was found that concimitant pyridoxine deficiency (sometimes with riboflavin deficiency) resulted in more rapid induction of the acute Mg deficiency syndrome (Greenberg, 1939). Experimental B6 deficiency causes loss of tissue Mg

Figure 5.   *EFFECT OF THIAMINE ON MAGNESIUM LEVELS IN RATS*

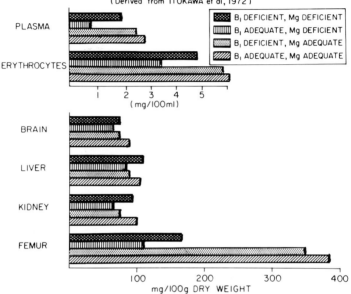

(Aikawa, 1960), and has been associated with transitory hyper-
magnesemia (Durlach, 1969), perhaps with egress of Mg from
tissues, and hypomagnesemia (Rigo et al, 1967), when tissue
Mg is depleted.   Several of the enzymes that require pyridoxal
phosphate also require Mg as a cofactor (Vallee, 1960).
The similarity of syndromes of experimental B6 and Mg deficiencies, and in the clinical disorders resulting from
their deficiencies (Seelig, 1981) are thus not surprising.
Included among disturbances in which both Mg and B6 deficiencies might play a role that are common in the aged
are chronic anemia and calcium urolithiasis.   B6 dependent
anemia (Frimpter et al, 1969) might also be dependent on Mg,
as Mg deficiency has been shown to cause damage to erythrocyte membranes (Elin, 1973, 1976/1980).   B6 and Mg have
been useful alone and in combination with calcium urolithiasis (Gershoff and Prien, 1967; Johansson et al, 1982).   Requiring further study is the possibility that Mg might
prove useful in B6-dependent disorders in which Mg-dependent
enzymes are involved.   Among explanations of B6 deficiency
in the aged, and the occasional failure to return to normal
after trypotophan-loading, is defective phosphorylation
of the vitamin by pyridoxal phosphokinase to its active form

(Hamfelt, 1964). This is one of the enzymes that requires Mg. Correction of pyridoxine deficiency should thus entail correction of Mg deficiency (Table 2).

Table 2.  *PYRIDOXINE-MAGNESIUM INTERRELATIONS*

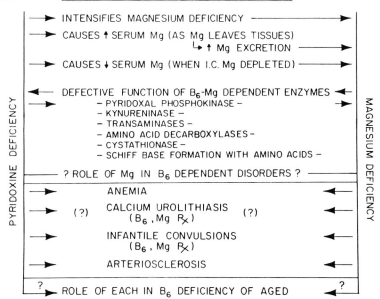

Interrelationships of zinc (Zn) with $B_6$ and Mg are also important. $B_6$ deficiency causes loss of tissue Zn (Hsu, 1965), as well as Mg. Both Mg and Zn are needed for nucleic acid synthesis and for the activity of many enzymes (Parisi and Vallee, 1969). Zn is necessary for energy-linked Mg accumulation by heart mitochondria (Brierley et al, 1967).

Vitamin E. Free radical damage to membranes and to immune surveillance is implicated in the aging process (Harman et al, 1977); both vitamin E as a free radical scavenger, and Mg (Elin, 1976/1981) are important in maintaining membrane stability. Interrelationships between the two are indicated by the lowered tissue Mg levels in vitamin E deficient animals (Blaxter and Wood, 1952) and manifestations of Mg deficiency in vitamin E deficiency in rats (Schwartz, 1962). It would be interesting to ascertain whether Mg administration can protect against

the free radical induced membrane damage associated with
lipid peroxides, and whether the postulated slowing of
the aging process by anti-oxidants (Tappel, 1968) might
be potentiated by Mg.

Vitamin D and Calcium. Experimental Mg deficiency
interfers with the utilization of vitamin D (Lifshitz et
al, 1967a), and vitamin D deficiency results in decreased
absorption of Mg and low serum Mg (Miller et al, 1964).
Clinical rickets has been associated with hypomagnesemia
(Breton et al, 1961). Correction of Mg deficiency has
corrected vitamin D refractoriness in children
(Rosler and Rabinowitz, 1973; Reddy and Sivakumar, 1974)
and adults (Medalle et al, 1976). On the other hand,
excess vitamin D has intensified Mg deficiency in animals
(Lifshitz et al, 1976b) and in clinical primary hypomagnesemia (Paunier et al, 1968). Vitamin D hyperre-
activity causes hypercalcemia (Seelig, 1969), and high
dietary Ca/Mg has been implicated in cardiovascular disease
(Karppanen et al, 1978). In the geriatric population,
vitamin D deficiency and hypocalcemia is more likely.
Mg deficiency can contribute to both by decreasing target
organ responsiveness (Wallach, 1976/1981).

Fiber and Phytates

Americans have been advised to increase their intake
of fiber because the incidence of several chronic diseases
is lower among population groups on a high fiber diet than
among those eating refined diets (U.S. Senate Comm., 1978).
Not generally realized is the interference by phytates with
the absorption of Mg (Seelig, 1981). Studies with natural
fiber-rich foods, or with artificial bulk substances added
to the diet, have shown production or increase of negative
balance (Reinhold et al, 1976; Slavin and Marlett, 1980).
Elderly people commonly use phytate or other bulk preparations to relieve their constipation. Their use, and
the abuse of purgatives other than Mg salts, may well interfere with Mg utilization.

RELATIONSHIPS OF SOME DISTURBANCES IN AGING TO MAGNESIUM

Among the changes prevalent in the old are some that
resemble abnormalities that are caused by Mg deficiency,
alone or in combination with other modalities. Diseases
to which the elderly are vulnerable, and some of the drugs

used in therapy, contribute to Mg loss. Although the evidence is insufficient to conclude that increasing Mg intake throughout life might delay changes in senescence, it is worth investigating whether prophylactic and therapeutic use of Mg might be beneficial.

## Cardiovascular Diseases, Cardiotonics, and Diuretics

Cardiovascular disorders are the major causes of morbidity and mortality in the population over 55. There is considerable evidence that long-term Mg inadequacy, of degrees not reflected by serum Mg levels considered subnormal, can contribute to functional and structural cardiovascular disease (Seelig, 1978, 1980; Seelig and Heggtveit, 1974; Seelig and Haddy, 1976/1981). Mg, rather than Ca, has been clearly demonstrated to be the critical protective water-factor in epidemiologic studies of the different cardiac mortality rates in hard and soft water areas (Anderson et al, 1975; Neri and Marier, 1977/1982). Magnesium deficiency or loss seems central to cardiovasomyopathy (Seelig, 1980: pages 135-264).

Figure 6. CENTRAL POSITION OF MAGNESIUM DEFICIENCY OR LOSS IN CARDIO-VASO-MYOPATHY

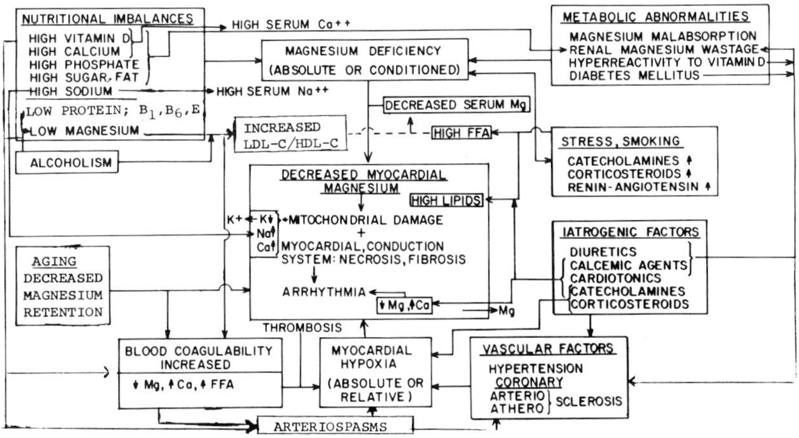

Coronary and peripheral vasopastic diseases have been attributed to high dietary (Karppanen et al, 1978) and blood and tissue Ca/Mg ratios (Altura et al, 1981; Altura, 1982). Numerous in vitro studies have shown the importance of Mg in regulating contractility of arterial smooth muscle, including coronary and cerebral arteries (Altura and Altura, 1980; 1981; Altura, 1982). Hormone and neurotransmitter-induced vasoconstriction, that is mediated by increased Ca,

is inhibited by increased Mg. Lowering Mg concentration
allows for more Ca uptake by blood vessels; raising Mg
levels to above the usual serum concentration decreases
the Ca influx. Mg, thus, is a natural "calcium blocker".
It potentiates pharmacologic Ca-blocking effects on
arteries (Altura, 1982; Turlapaty et al, 1981) and has
been found to have greater anti-spasmotic activity than
Verapamil in canine coronaries (Altura, p.c.).

Those with congestive heart failure and arrhythmia
can lose Mg as a result of hypoxia - which causes Mg egress
from tissues, including the myocardium (Hochrein et al,
1967; Seelig, 1972; 1980, p. 193). This has been shown
in hearts from animals with occluded coronaries (Cummings,
1960; Jennings and Shen, 1972). Since cardiotonics
stimulate Ca-inflow and Mg-outflow from the heart, and
inhibit Mg-dependent mitochondrial enzymes (Seelig, 1972),
it is not surprising that Mg deficiency and Ca treatment
intensify digitalis toxicity, whereas Mg treatment counter-
acts it (review: Seelig, 1980, pp 255-259). The long-
term use of diuretics in cardiac or hypertensive patients,
and in those being treated for calcific urolithiasis, is
the major drug-induced cause of Mg loss (Wacker, 1980).
Potassium loss is always sought and treated in diuretic-
treated patients; Mg loss is less often considered. Such
patients are prone to K-refractory hypokalemia, sometimes
with ectopic or premature ventricular contractions, that
are associated with decreased muscle K and Mg levels, and
that respond better when Mg is repleted than when K alone
is given. (Dyckner, 1980; Dyckner and Wester, 1981).

Transient ischemic attacks, that increase in prevalence with increasing age, are associated with increased
platelet aggregation and thromboembolic events. There is
in vitro evidence that high concentrations of Mg inhibit
platelet aggregation and release (reviews: Elin, 1976/1981,
Durlach, 1976/1981), and in vivo evidence that Mg administration before temporary arterial occlusion prevents
platelet deposition on the injured endothelium (Adams and
Mitchell, 1979).

The protective effect of Mg was demonstrated in
another study, in which arterial thickening, due to fibrosis and smooth muscle proliferation, was more marked in
vessels of Mg deficient rats than in controls (Rayssiguier,
1981).

Among the cardiovasopathic models that are protected
against by Mg, are the modified high fat diets that are
thrombogenic (Szelenyi et al, 1967; Savoie, 1972a;
Savoie and DeLorme, 1976/1981). In these studies, not
only were lipid blood levels increased, but Mg levels were
decreased. Mg has been effective in reducing the hyper-
coagulability of rats and dogs on thrombogenic diets
(Szelenyi et al, 1967; Savoie, 1972b).

The increased incidence of thromboembolic events in
women taking estrogen-containing oral contraceptives has
been blamed on the estrogen-lowering of plasma Mg
(Goldsmith and Goldsmith, 1976/1981; Goldsmith and Johnston,
1976/1981). Patients with latent tetany of marginal Mg
deficiency have exhibited phlebothrombosis (Durlach, 1967;
Seelig et al, 1976/1981). The data showing Mg reduction
of arteriospasm and of platelet aggregation seem directly
applicable to transient ischemic cerebral and cardiac
attacks; the data on Mg-protection against arterial and
cardiac damage seem relevant to the arteriosclerosis and
ischemic heart disease.

## Diabetes Mellitus; Decreased Glucose Tolerance

Diabetes mellitus, which contributes to hyperlipidemia
and cardiovascular disease, and has been termed a model
for aging (Eckel and Hoefeldt, 1982), has long been known
to be associated with Mg loss (Martin et al, 1952; Jackson
and Meier, 1968). A decline in glucose tolerance is
characteristic of aging. It has been reported in Mg
deficient rats (Rayssiguier, 1981). Insulin refractoriness
has improved with Mg therapy (Moles and McMullen, 1982;
Seelig, unpublished data). Diabetic retinopathy has been
correlated with hypomagnesemia (McNair et al, 1978), and
with increased platelet aggregation (Heath et al, 1971).
Since Mg inhibits platelet aggregation, its administration
to diabetics is worth trying.

## Collagen, Fibrosis and Aging

Collagen becomes more abundant, as well as more rigid,
with increasing age (Hall, 1969). Among the nutrients
that influence the metabolism of collagen are vitamins B6
and E, which have interrelationships with Mg (supra vide).
Mg deficiency increases the cardiac fibrosis that is
caused by noise stress-induced catecholamine release

Gunther, 1981; Ising et al, 1981). The arterial fibrosis and the delayed uterine involution and fibrosis of
Mg deficiency, has been attributed to the slowing of
collagen turnover (Larvor, 1981; Rayssiguier, 1981).

## Stress, Magnesium Loss and Cardiovascular Disease

Stress factors particularly likely to be encountered
by the aged include chronic anxiety and worry, and the
acute stress of bereavement. Regardless of the cause,
stress increases catecholamine and corticoid release, which
in turn cause Mg loss. Catecholamines also increase myocardial Ca uptake (Nayler, 1967). Since low Mg/Ca ratios
increase catecholamine secretion (Baker and Rink, 1975),
a vicious cycle is thus established when Mg deficiency pre-
exists. Well accepted is the contributory role of stress
to cardiovascular disease, including sudden unexpected
cardiac death. Less well known is the role of Mg loss in
the damage caused by stress (Figure 7). Long-term sub-
optimal Mg intake, to which adaptation had taken place,
so that signs of deficiency that were present early no
longer existed, resulted in decreased tolerance of stress
and shortened life expectancy (Heroux et al, 1973).

### Figure 7.

STRESS, MAGNESIUM DEFICIENCY/LOSS AND CARDIAC DISEASE

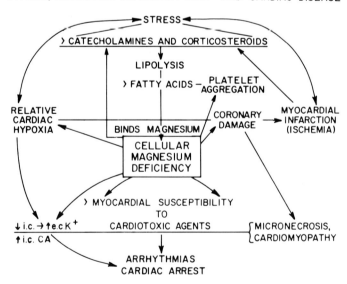

IMMUNOLOGY, ONCOLOGY AND INFECTION

With advancing age there are abnormalities in immune regulation, most of which involve altered T-cell function, such as lowered resistance to intracellular microbes, increased levels of autoantibodies, and reduced immuno-surveillance; i.e., against neoplasm (Makinodan and Yunis, 1980). It is thus provocative that Mg deficiency has been implicated in T-cell abnormalities and in impaired pro-tein synthesis (reviews: Seelig, 1979; 1980/1983). Young rats with acute Mg deficiency developed lymphoid and splenic hypertrophy (Hungerford and Karson, 1960), des-pite significant reduction of protein synthesis by spleen and thymus, little effect on RNA synthesis, but markedly increased splenic and thymic lymphocyte DNA synthesis (Zieve et al, 1977). The lowered lymphatic protein syn-thesis was correlated with impaired immune response of Mg deficient rats; the increase in DNA synthesis was con-sidered representative of an early lymphoproliferative process leading to neoplasia, as has been reported by others (Jasmin, 1963; Hass et al, 1976/1981). It is interesting that the neoplasms were seen only in rats deficient in Mg from early life, not in those made deficient when mature. The lymphomaproducing diets were very high in Ca, with Ca/Mg ratios of 140/1; diets that resulted in thymic hyperplasis, but not thymoma provided a ratio of 10/1 (Alcock et al, 1973). Very high Ca levels stimulate DNA synthesis and mitosis of cul-tured human lymphocytes (review: Seelig, 1979).

Mg deficiency suppresses levels of most immunoglob-ulins in rats and mice: IgG and IgA transiently, and antisheep red cell hemolysin substantially (Larvor, 76/81; Alcock and Shils, 1974; Elin, 1975; McCoy and Kenney, 1975). In contrast, IgE levels rose 3-4 fold (Prouvost-Danon et al, 1975). Fewer antibody-forming cells and markedly less rosette formation by lymphocytes of Mg-deficient mice suggest the dependence on Mg by helper T-cells and the impairment of T and B cell cooperation in Mg deficiency (Guenounou et al, 1978).

Mg's interrelationship with other nutrients that affect immunocompetence and immunosurveillance (reviews: Seelig, 1979; 1980/1983), such as interactions among Mg, Zn and B6, might influence reactions of the aged. Inter-relationships among agents that protect membrane stability,

such as Mg, vitamin E, Zn, and selenium might protect
against oncogenesis. It must be cautioned that Mg supplementation of patients with cancer is not recommended, in
view of the evidence that Mg depletion has inhibited the
growth of experimental and clinical advanced neoplasm
(Young and Parson, 1977).

Infectious diseases cause about a third of all deaths
in the aged, particularly those involving the urinary
tract, endocardium, lungs and skin (Mostow, 1982). Impaired host defenses make the facultative pathogens a
particular risk. Such microbes often require treatment
with antibiotics such as the tetracyclines and amino-
glycosides - both of which classes of drugs cause Mg loss.
The tetracyclines chelate Mg (Shils, 1962); the amino-
glycosides increase renal excretion of Mg as a result of
the tubular damage (Keating et al, 1977).

NEED FOR STUDY

To what extent intakes of Mg, insufficient to meet the
special needs of the aged, can increase susceptibility to
disorders with manifestations comparable to those produced
by Mg deficiency requires study. Complicating such studies
will be the many factors that affect Mg requirements, and
that are a particular problem in the elderly. In considering intervention studies that might lead to improved quality and possibly length of life, methods to evaluate long-
term Mg supplementation should be developed. Serum Mg determinations are unlikely to yield revealing data, usually
only profound deficiencies causing hypomagnesemia. Percentage retention of parenterally administered Mg is more
rewarding, but it is not appropriate for large scale screening tests. Simplified means to measure cellular Mg: i.e.
in white blood cells are under study (Ross et al, 1976/1981;
1982; Elin and Johnson, 1981; Ryan et al, 1981).

Other parameters, that should provide useful data on
Mg-induced changes, include changes in HDL-C/LDL-C ratios.
Electrocardiographic monitoring of patients on diuretics
for correction of occult EGG changes, in association with
Mg-correction of refractory hypokalemia, and in those whose
arrhythmias do not respond to K repletion, should be employed in high risk patients.

Important clues to the poor adaptation to stress of

the aged, might derive from extension of the important study that showed that young rats with Mg deficiency, adapted to sustained low Mg intake and ceased showing signs of deficiency (Heroux et al, 1973). The tolerance of stress by surviving old Mg deficient rats was significantly less than was that of control rats - in terms of cardiac necrosis and survival. (Figure 8). Also, their lives were shorter, even without stress.

Figure 8.

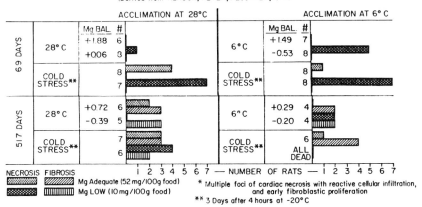

MYOCARDIAL LESIONS* IN ISOLATED COLD STRESSED ± COLD ADAPTATION
IN GNOTOBIOTIC RATS ± LIFE-LONG SUBOPTIMAL MAGNESIUM
(Derived from HEROUX, PETER, HEGGTVEIT, 1977)

It is not uncommon for infants with hypocalcemic convulsions, such as those shown to respond better to Mg therapy than to Ca or to barbiturates (Review: Seelig, 1978), to be treated with only Ca, Mg levels never having been obtained. Also, patients with mani-festations of Mg deficiency and recorded low Mg levels (i.e with alcoholism, cardiac disease, or recovering from surgery) have been treated conventionally, with-out Mg repletion. Adaptation to low Mg may explain the clinical tolerance of failing to correct Mg deficiency. Long-term follow-up of patients at risk, with and without Mg repletion, should yield important information. Inter-vention studies in older populations, selecting groups at risk of disorders to which Mg deficiency might be contri-butory: hypertensives or cardiacs receiving diuretics, those with family histories of IHD, and patients with diabetes mellitus, might provide clues more quickly.

REFERENCES

Adams JH, Mitchell JRA (1979). The effects of agents which modify platelet behavior and of magnesium ions on thrombus formation in vivo. Thrombos Haemostas (Stuttgart) 42: 603.
Aikawa JK (1960). Effects of pyridoxine and desoxypyrodixine on magnesium metabolism in the rabbit. Proc Soc Exp Biol Med 104:461.
Alcock NW, Shils ME (1974). Serum immunoglobulin G in the magnesium depleted rat. Proc Soc Exp Biol Med 145: 855.
Alcock NW, Shils ME, Lieberman PH, Erlandson RA (1973). Thymic changes in the magnesium-depleted rat. Cancer Res 33:2196.
Altura BM (1982). Magnesium and regulation of contractility of vascular smooth muscle. Adv Microcirc 11:77.
Altura BM, Altura BT (1981). Role of magnesium ions in contractility of blood vessels and skeletal muscles. Magnesium Bull 3:102.
Altura BT, Altura BM (1980). Withdrawal of magnesium causes vasospasm while elevated magnesium produces relaxation of tone in cerebral arteries. Neurosc Letters 20:323.
Altura BN, Altura BT, Carella A, (1981). Hypomagnesemia and vasoconstriction: possible relationship to etiology of sudden death ischemic heart disease and hypertensive vascular diseases. Artery 9:212.
Anderson TW, Neri LC, Schreiber GB, Talbot FDF, Zdrojewski A (1975). Ischemic heart disease, water hardness and myocardial magnesium. Canad Med Assoc J 113:199.
Baker H, Frank O, Jaslow SP (1980). Oral versus intramuscular vitamin supplementation for hypovitaminosis in the elderly. J Am Geriat Soc 28:42-45.
Baker H, Frank O, Thind IS, Jaslow SP, Louria D (1979). Vitamin profiles in elderly persons living at home or in nursing homes, versus profile in healthy young subjects, J Am Geriat Soc 27:444.
Baker PF, Rink TJ (1975). Catecholamine release from bovine adrenal medulla in response to maintained depolarization. J Physiol 253:593.
Baskin SI, Uricchio FJ, Kendrick ZV (1979). The effect of age on the regional distribution of four cations in the rat heart. Age 2:64.
Baskin SI, Kuhar KP, Uricchio FJ, Harper GR (1981). The effect of age on five ions of the kidney in the Fischer 344 rat. Reprod Nutr Develop 21:689.
Blaxter KL, Wood WA (1952). The nutrition of the young ayrshire calf. 9. Composition of the tissues of normal

and dystrophic calves. Brit J Nutr 6:144.

Breton A, Walbaum R, Raisnel M (1961). Dosage de la magnesemia chez l'enfant dans diver etats pathologiques. Pediatrie 16:445.

Brierley GP, Jacobus WE, Hunter GR (1967). Ion transport by heart mitochondria. VIII Activation of ATP supported accumulation of $Mg^{++}$ BY $Zn^{++}$. J Biol Chem 242:2192.

Chadda KD, Lichstein E, Gupta P (1973). Hypomagnesemia and refractory arrhythmia in a nondigitalized patient. Am J Card 31:98.

Crapo PA (1982). Nutrition in the aged. In Schreier RW (ed): "Clinical Internal Medicine in the Aged." Philadelphia: Saunders, p. 167.

Cummings JR (1960). Electrolyte changes in heart tissue and coronary arterial and venous plasma following coronary occlusion. Circ Res 8:865.

Draper HH (1964). Calcium and magnesium metabolism in senescent mice. J Nutr 83:65.

Durlach J (1981). Clinical aspects of chronic magnesium deficiency: In Cantin M, Seelig MS (eds): "Magnesium in Health and Disease." NY: SP Med Sc Books (2nd Intl Mg Symp 1976): p. 883.

Durlach J (1969). Donnees actuelles; les mecanismes de synergie entre vitamine $B_6$ et magnesium. J Med Besancon 5:349.

Durlach J (1967). Le role antithrombosique physiologique du magnesium. A propos d'une maladie phlebothrombosante par deficit magnesien. Coeur Med Interne 6:213.

Dyckner T (1980). Serum magnesium in acute myocardial infarction. Relation to arrhythmias. Acta Med Scan 207: 59.

Dyckner T, Wester PO (1978). Intracellular potassium after magnesium infusion. Brit Med J 1:822.

Dyckner T, Wester PO (1981). Relation between potassium, magnesium and cardiac arrhythmias. Acta Med Scand Suppl 647:163.

Eckel RH, Hoefeldt FD (1982). Endocrinology and metabolism in the elderly. In Schrier RW (ed). "Clinical Internal Medicine in the Aged." Philadelphia: Saunders, p 222.

Elin RJ (1973). Erythrocyte survival in magnesium-deficient rats. Proc Exp Biol & Med 142:1159.

Elin RJ (1976/1981). Role of magnesium in membranes; erythrocyte and platelet function and stability. In Cantin M, Seelig MS (eds): "Magnesium in Health and Disease." New York: SP Med Sci Books (Proc 2nd Intl Mg Symp), p 113.

Elin RJ, Johnson E (1882). The determination of the magnesium content of blood mononuclear cells. J Am Coll Nutr 1:117.

Exton-Smith AN (1972). Physiological aspects of aging; relationship to nutrition. Am J Clin Nutr 25:853.

Food & Nutr Board (1980). Recommended Dietary Allowances Ed. 9, Washington, D.C. National Acad Sci.

Gershoff SN, Prien EL (1967). Effect of daily MgO and vitamin $B_6$ administration to patients with recurring calcium oxalate kidney stones. Am J Clin Nutr 20:393.

Goldsmith LA (1967). Relative magnesium deficiency in the rat. J Nutr 93: 87.

Goldsmith NF, Goldsmith JR (1966). Epidemiological aspects of magnesium and calcium metabolism. Arch Env Health 12:607.

Goldsmith NF, Johnston JO (1976/1981): Magnesium-estrogen hypothesis: thromboembolic and mineralization ratios. In Cantin M, Seelig MS (eds). "Magnesium in Health & Disease." New York: Sp Med Sc Books (2nd Intl Mg Sympos) p. 313.

Goldsmith NF, Pace N, Baumberger JP, Ury H (1970). Magnesium and citrate during the menstrual cycle: Effect of an oral contraceptive on serum magnesium. Fertility Sterility 21:292.

Goulding A, McChesney R (1977). Oestrogen-progestogen oral contraceptives and urinary calcium excretion. Clin Endocr 6:449.

Greenberg DM (1939). Mineral metabolism: calcium magnesium and phosphorus. Ann Rev Biochem 8:269.

Geunounou M, Armier J, Gaudin-Harding F (1978). Effect of magnesium deficiency and food restriction on the immune response in young mice. Intl J Vit Nutr Res 48:290.

Gueux E, Rayssiguier Y (1981). The hypercholesterolaemic effect of magnesium deficiency following cholesterol feeding in the rat. Magnesium Bull 2:126.

Gunther T (1981). Biochemistry and pathochemistry of magnesium. Artery 9:167.

Hall DA (1969). Connective tissues. In Bakerman (ed): "Aging Life Processes." Springfield, CT Thomas, p. 79.

Hamfelt A (1969). Age Variation of vitamin $B_6$ metabolism in man. Clin Chim Acta 10:48.

Harman D, Heidrick ML, Eddy DE (1977). Free radical theory of aging: effect of free-radical-reaction inhibitors on the immune response. J Am Geriatr Soc 25:400.

Hass GM, McCreary PA, Laing GH (1976/1981). Lymphoproliferative and immunologic aspects of magnesium deficiency.

In Cantin M, Seelig MS (eds). "Magnesium in Health and Disease." NY: Sp Med Sci Books, P. 185 (2nd Intl Mg Symp, 1976).

Heath H (1971). Platelet adhesiveness and aggregation in relation to diabetic retinopathy. Diabetologia 7:308.

Hellerstein EE, Nakamura M, Hegsted DM, Vitale JJ (1960). Studies on the interrelationships between dietary magnesium, quality and quantity of fat, hypercholesterolemia and lipidosis. J Nutr 71:339.

Henrotte JG, Benech A, Pineau M (1976/1981). Relationships between blood magnesium content and age in a French population. In Cantin M, Seelig MS (eds): "Magnesium in Health and Disease." New York: SP Med Sci Books, (2nd Intl Mg Sympo). p 929.

Heroux O, Peter D, Heggtveit A (1977). Long-term effect of sub-optimal dietary magnesium and calcium contents of organs, on cold tolerance and on life span, and its pathological consequences in rats. J Nutr 107:1640.

Hochrein H, Kuschke HJ, Zaqqa Q, Fahl E (1967). Das Verhalten der Intracellularen Magnesium-konzentration in Myokard bei Insuffizienz, Hypoxie und Kammerflimmern. Klin Wschr 45:1093.

Hsu JM (1965). Zinc content in tissues of pyridoxine deficient rats. Proc Soc Exp Biol Med 119:177.

Hungerford GF, Karson EF (1960). Eosinophilia of magnesium deficiency. Blood 16:1642.

Hunt SM, Schofield FA (1969). Magnesium balance and protein intake level in adult human female. Am J Clin Nutr 22:367.

Irwin MI, Feeley RM (1967). Frequency and size of meals and serum lipids, nitrogen and mineral retention in young women. J Clin Nutr 20:816.

Ising H (1981). Interaction of noise-induced stress and Mg decrease. Artery 9:205.

Itokawa Y, Tseng LF, Fujiwara M (1974). Thiamine metabolism in magnesium-deficient rats. J Nutr Sci Vit 20:249.

Jackson CE, Meier DW (1968). Routine serum Mg analysis. Ann Intern Med 69:743.

Jasmin G (1969). Lymphoedeme, hyperplasie et tumefaction du tissu lymphatique chez le rat soumis a une diete deficiente en magnesium. Rev Can Biol 22:383.

Jennings RB, Shen AC (1972). Calcium in experimental myocardial ischemia. In Bajusz E, Rona G (eds): "Recent Advances in Studies on Cardiac Structure and Metabolism I." Myocardiology. p 639.

Johansson G (1979). Magnesium metabolism. Studies in health, primary hyperparathyroidism and renal stone disease. Scand J Urol Nephrol. Suppl 51:1

Karppanen H, Pennanen R, Passinen L (1978). Minerals and sudden coronary death. Adv Card 25:9.

Keating FR, Jr., Jones JD, Elveback LR, Randall RV (1969). The relation of age and sex to distribution of values in healthy adults of serum calcium, inorganic phosphorus, magnesium, alkaline phosphatase, total proteins, albumin, and blood urea. J Lab Clin Med 73:825.

Keating MJ, Sethi MR, Bodey GP, Samaan NA (1977). Hypocalcemia with hypoparathyroidism and renal tubular dysfunction associated with aminoglycoside therapy. Cancer 39:1410.

Larvor P. Magnesium, humoral immunity and allergy. In Cantin M, Seelig MS (eds). "Magnesium in Health and Disease." NY: Sp Med Sci Books, p 201 (2nd Intl Symp on Mg).

Lennon J, Lemann J, Jr., Piering WF, Larson L (1974). Effect of glucose on urinary cation excretion during chronic extracellular volume expansion in normal man. J Clin Inv 53:1424.

Lifshitz F, Harrison HC, Harrison HE (1967a). Response to vitamin D of magnesium deficient rats. Proc Soc Exp Biol Med 125:472.

Lifshitz F, Harrison HC, Harrison HE (1976b). Effects of vitamin D on magnesium metabolism in rats. Endocrinology 81:849.

Lindeman RD (1976/1981). Nutritional influences on magnesium homeostasis with emphasis on renal factors. In Cantin M, Seelig MS (eds). "Magnesium in Health and Disease." NY: SP Med and Sci Books, p 381 (Proc 2nd Intl Mg Symp).

Lindeman RD, Adler S, Yiengst MJ, Beard ES (1967). Influence of various nutrients on urinary divalent cation excretion. J Lab Clin Med 70:236.

Makinodan T, Yunis E (1977) (eds). "Immunology and Aging." New York: Plenum Medical Book Co.

Martin HE, Mehl J, Wertman M (1952). Clinical studies of magnesium metabolism. M Clin North America 36: 1157.

McCance RA, Widdowson EM, Lehmann H (1942). Effect of protein intake on absorption of calcium and magnesium. Biochem J 36:686.

McCoy JH, Kenney MA (1975). Depressed immune response in magnesium deficient rat. J Nutr 105:791.

McGandy RB, Barrows CH, Spanias A, Meredith A, Stone JL, Norris AH (1966). Nutrient intakes and energy expenditure in men of different ages. J Gerontol 21:581.

McNair P, Christiansen C (1978). Hypomagnesemia: risk factor in diabetic retinopathy. Diabetes 27:1075.

Medalle R, Waterhouse C, Hahn TJ (1976). Vitamin D resistance in magnesium deficiency. Am J Clin Nutr 29:854.

Melnick I, Landes RR, Hoffman AA, Burch JF (1971). Magnesium therapy for recurring calcium oxalate urinary calculi. J Urol 105:119.

Miller ER, Ullrey DE, Zutaut CL, Baltzer BV, Schmidt DA, Vincent BH, Hoefer JA, Luecke RW (1964). Vitamin $D_2$ requirement of the baby pig. J Nutr 83:140.

Moles KW, McMullen JK (1982). Insulin resistance and hypomagnesaemia: case report. Br Med J 285:262.

Mori K, Duruisseau J (1960). Water and electrolyte changes in aging process with special reference to calcium and magnesium in cardiac muscle. Can J Bioch Physiol 38:919.

Mostow SR (1982). Infectious diseases in the aged. In Schrier RW (ed). "Clinical Internal Medicine in the Aged." Philadelphia: Saunders, p 256.

Mountokalakis TH, Singhellakis PN, Alevizaki CC, Caramanakos E, Ikkos DG (1976). Absorption intestinale du magnesium chez des malades en insuffisance renale chronique. Rev Franc Endocr Clin Nutr Metab 17:229.

Munro HN, Young VR (1978). Protein metabolism in the elderly. Postgrad Med 63:143.

Nayler WG (1967). Calcium exchange in cardiac muscle: A basic mechanism of drug action. Am Heart J 73:379.

Neri LC, Marier JR (1978/1982). Epidemiology of sudden cardiac death - minerals and water story. In Naito HK (ed). "Nutrition and Heart Disease." New York: SP Med Sci Books, p 81.

Nuoranne PJ, Raunio RP, Saukko P, Karppanen H (1980). Metabolic effects of a low magnesium diet in pigs. Br J Nutr 44:53.

Oldham HG (1962). Thiamine requirements of women: Ann NY Acad Sci 98:542.

Parisi AF, Vallee BL (1969). Zinc metalloenzymes: characteristics and significance in biology and medicine. Am J Clin Nutr 22:1222.

Paunier L, Radde IC, Kooh SW, Conen PE, Fraser D (1968). Primary hypomagnesemia with secondary hypocalcemia in an infant. Pediatrics 41:385.

Prouvost-Danon A, Larvor P, Rayssiguier Y, Wyczolkowska J, Durlach J (1975). Taux serique d'anticorps reaginiques (IgE) chez la souris en carence magnesique. Rev Fr Allerg 15:147.

Rayssiguier Y (1981). Magnesium and lipid interrelationships

in the pathogenesis of vascular diseases. Magnesium Bull
3:165.
Rayssiguier Y, Badinand F, Kopp J (1979). Effects of magnesium deficiency on paturition and uterine involution in the
rat. J Nutr 109:2117.
Reddy V, Sivakumar B (1974). Magnesium-dependent vitamin D-
resistant rickets. Lancet 1:963.
Reinhold JG, Bahram F, Parichehr A, Ismail-Beigi F (1976).
Decreased absorption of calcium, magnesium, zinc and phosphorus consumption as wheat bread. J Nutr 106:493.
Rigo J, Szelenyi I, Sos J (1967). Connection between vitamine B6 and magnesium balance. Acta Physiol Acad Sc Hung
32:16.
Rosler I, Rabinowitz D (1973). Magnesium-induced reversal
of vitamin D resistance in hypoparathyroidism. Lancet I:
803.
Ross RS, Seelig MS, Berger AR (1976/1981). Isolation of leu-
kocytes for magnesium determination. In Cantin M, Seelig
MS (eds). "Magnesium in Health and Disease." New York: SP
Med Sc Books, p 7 (Proc 2nd Intl Mg Sympo).
Ross RS, Seelig MS, Berger AR (1982). Pilot studies of
mixed white cells and lymphocytes. J Am Coll Nutr 1:118.
Ryan MP, Ryan MF, Counihan TB, Thornton L (1981). The use
of lymphocytes to monitor cellular magnesium and potassium.
Magnesium Bull 2:113.
Savoie LL (1972). Production de necroses cardiaques non-
oclusives chez le rat par un regime thrombogene. Path Biol
20:117.
Savoie LL, DeLorme B (1976/1981). Magnesium inhibition of
cardiac lesions produced by sodium phosphate in hyperlipemic
rats. In Cantin M, Seelig MS (eds). "Magnesium in Health
and Disease." New York: SP Med Sci Books, p 537 (2nd Intl
Mg Symp).
Sawyer M, Baumann L, Stevens F (1918). Studies of acid
production. The mineral loss during acidosis. J Biol Chem
33:103.
Schwartz R, Walker G, Linz MD, MacKellar I (1973). Metabolic
responses of adolescent boys to two levels of dietary magnesium and protein. I. Magnesium and Nitrogen Retention.
Am J Clin Nutr 26:510.
Schwartz K (1962). Vitamin E trace elements and sulfhydryl
groups in respiratory decline. Vits Horm 20:463.
Seelig MS (1977/1982). Early nutritional roots of cardio-
vascular disease. In Naito HK (ed). "Nutrition and Heart
Disease." New York: SP Sci Med Books, p 31 (Proc 19th Ann
Mtg-Nutr).

Seelig MS (1979). Magnesium (and trace substance) deficiencies in the pathogenesis of cancer. Biol Tr Elem Res l: 273.

Seelig MS (1980). "Magnesium Deficiency in the Pathogenesis of Disease. Early Roots of Cardiovascular, Skeletal, and Renal Abnormalities." New York: Plenum Publishing Corp.

Seelig MS (1978). Magnesium deficiency with phosphate and vitamin D excesses: role in pediatric cardiovascular disease? Cardiovasc Med 3:637.

Seelig MS (1972). Myocardial loss of functional magnesium II . In Cardiomyopathies of Different Etiology. In Bajusz E, Rona G (eds). "Recent Advances in Studies on Cardiac Structure and Metabolism. I. Myocardiology." Baltimore, Univ Park Press, p 626.

Seelig MS (1981). Magnesium requirements in human nutrition. Magnesium Bull 3:26.

Seelig MS (1980/1983). Nutritional roots of combined systems disorders. In Lifshitz F (ed). New York: Marcel Dekker Inc. (in press).

Seelig MS (1964). The requirement of magnesium by the normal adult. Am J Clin Nutr 14:342.

Seelig MS (1969). Vitamin D and cardiovascular, renal and brain damage in infancy and child hood. Ann NY Acad Sci 147:537.

Seelig MS, Berger AR, Avioli LA (1976). Speculations on renal, hormonal and metabolic aberrations in a patient with marginal magnesium deficiency. In Cantin M, Seelig MS (eds). "Magnesium in Health and Disease." New York: SP Med Sci Books, p 459.

Seelig MS, Haddy FJ (1976/1981). Magnesium and the arteries I. Effects of magnesium deficiency on arteries and on the retention of sodium, potassium, and calcium. In Cantin M, Seelig MS (eds). "Magnesium in Health and Disease." New York: SP Med Sc Books, p 605 (Proc 2nd Intl Mg Symp).

Seelig MS, Heggtveit HA (1974). Magnesium interrelationships in ischemic heart disease: A review. Am J Clin Nutr 27:59.

Shils ME (1962). Metabolic aspects of tetracyclines. Clin Pharm and Ther 3:321.

Simpson FO, Nye ER, Bolli P, Waal-Manning HJ, Goulding AW et al (1978). The Milton survey: Part 1. General methods, height, weight and 24 hour excretion of sodium, calcium, magnesium, and cretinine. New Zeal Med J 87:379.

Slavin JL, Marlett JA (1980). Influence of refined cellulose on human bowel function and calcium and magnesium balance. Am J Clin Nutr 33:1932.

Stendig-Lindberg G (1972). Hypomagnesemi och uppkomst av

alkoholence-alopatier. Lakartingningon 69:1237.

Szelenyi I, Rigo R, Ahmen BO, Sos J (1967). The role of magnesium in blood coagulation. Thromb Diath Haemorrh 18: 626.

Tappel AL (1968). Will antioxidant nutrients slow aging processes? Geriatrics 23:97.

Touitou Y, Touitou C, Bogdan A, Beck H, Reinberg A (1978). Serum magnesium circadian rhythm in human adults with respect to age, sex, and mental status. Clin Chim Acta 87:35.

Turlapaty PDVM, Weiner R, Altura BM (1981). Interactions of magnesium and verapamil on tone and contractility of vascular smooth muscle. Europ J Pharmacol 74:263.

Uauy R, Scrimshaw N, Young V (1978). Human protein requirements: nitrogen balance response to graded levels of egg protein in elderly men and women. Am J Clin Nutr 31: 779.

US Dept Agric Nationwide Food Consumption Survey, 1977-1978 (1980). USDA Sci & Educ Adm.

US Senate Select Comm on Nutr & Human Needs (1978). Dietary goals for the U.S. Govt Printing Off. Washington, D.C.

Vallee BL (1960). Metal and Enzyme interactions: Correlation of Composition, Function and Structure. The Enzymes 3:225.

Vir SC, Love AHG (1979). Nutritional status of institutionalized aged in Belfast, Northern Ireland. Am J Clin Nutr 32:1934.

Vitale JJ, White PL, Nakamura M, Hegsted DM, Zamcheck N, Hellerstein EE (1957). Interrelationships between experimental hypercholesteremia, magnesium requirement, and experimental atherosclerosis. J Exp Med 106:757.

Wacker WEC (1980). "Magnesium and Life." Cambridge: Harvard Univ Press.

Wallach S (1976/1981). Physiologic and critical interrelations of hormones and magnesium. Consideration of thyroid, insulin, corticosteroids, sex steroids and catecholamines. In Cantin M, Seelig MS (eds). "Magnesium in Health and Disease." New York: SP Med Sc Books, p 241 (2nd Intl Mg Symp).

Walser M (1967). Magnesium metabolism. In Review Physiol Biochem Exp Pharm 59:185.

Young GA, Parsons FM (1977). Effects of dietary deficiencies of magnesium and potassium on growth and chemistry of transplanted tumors and host tissues in the rat. Europ J Cancer 13:103.

Zieve FJ, Freude KA, Zieve L (1977). Effects of magnesium deficiency on protein and nucleic acid synthesis in vivo.

J Nutr 107:2178.

Zieve L, Doizaki WM, Stenroos LE (1968). Effects of magnesium deficiency on growth response to thiamine of thiamine-deficient rats. J Lab Clin Med 72:261.

Zumkley H, Schmidt PF, Vetter H, Elies M (1982). Determination of magnesium concentrations in rbc by laser-micromass analysis (LAMMA). J Am Coll Nutr 1: (in press).

Intervention in the Aging Process, Part A: Quantitation, Epidemiology, and
Clinical Research, pages 307–323
© 1983 Alan R. Liss, Inc., 150 Fifth Avenue, New York, NY 10011

PHYSICAL CONDITIONING:   INTERVENTION IN AGING
CARDIOVASCULAR FUNCTION

JANET P. WALLACE, Ph.D.

ADULT FITNESS PROGRAM

SAN DIEGO STATE UNIVERSITY

Even though the mechanisms of aging will probably be
attributed to a cellular or molecular function, the study
of systems integration should remain an important topic in
the scientific investigation of aging (Shock, 1977; Shock,
1979).  The performance of most human physiological function
is dependent on the coordinated efforts of several organ
systems.  Shock has demonstrated greater aging decrements in
the performance of integrative systems than in the separate
variables themselves (Shock, 1972; Shock, 1979).  He further
states that functional aging, as we see it, may be more
a breakdown in the integration of systems than in specific
changes in molecules, cells, tissues, or organs.

One of the most rapidly declining and perhaps more
devastating functions with age is the perfomance of physical
activity (Shock, 1979).  Declines begin early in middle-age
and may be the limiting factor in the performance of simple
daily activities in old age.  In addition, similar declines
have been reported for disease processes associated with
premature aging (Bruce, 1973).  The most prominant of
these processes results in coronary artery disease which is
the major cause of morbidity and mortality in middle-aged men
(Kohn, 1977).  Recently, physical activity has been
considered to have a significant role in the prevention
(Paffenbarger, 1977) as well as the rehabilitation (Boyer and
Kasch, 1970; Kavanagh, 1979) of such diseases.

The quality of physical activity is measured by oxygen
uptake ($\dot{V}_{O_2}$) and expressed as a volume of oxygen used per
minute per kilogram of body weight ($ml \cdot min^{-1} \cdot kg^{-1}$).  The

process of oxygen uptake depends on the integration of the cardiovascular, respiratory, metabolic, neuro-muscular, and endocrine systems (Astrand and Rodahl, 1977). The function of a physiological system is often evaluated by its maximal capacity under stress. Thus, maximal oxygen uptake ($\dot{V}_{O_2}$max) is considered to be the criterion variable. It is measured during the final efforts of a dynamic exercise stimulus of progressive intensities. In normal function, maximal oxygen uptake is most often limited by the cardiovascular system. Therefore, $\dot{V}_{O_2}$max has been considered a measurement of cardiovascular function (Taylor et. al., 1955). This paper will address the longitudinal intervention of physical conditioning on aging cardiovascular function and associated diseases.

MAXIMAL OXYGEN UPTAKE AND AGE

Both cross-sectional (Robinson, 1938; Profant et. al., 1972; Dehn and Bruce, 1972; Drinkwater, 1975) and longitudinal studies (Dill et. al., 1964; Astrand et. al., 1973; Robinson et. al., 1975; Robinson et. al., 1976) report a decline in cardiovascular function throughout the life-span. Hodgson and Buskirk (1977) summarized these studies and constructed the aging curve for cardiovascular function which is illustrated in Figure 1. According to these studies, this decline begins around the third decade and progresses at a rate of 9% per decade into the ninth decade. Furthermore, this age related decline is independent of initial function which means that athletes as well as sedentary individuals appeared to decline at the same rate throughout the life-span. On the other hand, more recent and better controlled longitudinal studies (Gore, 1972; Robinson et. al., 1975; Kasch and Wallace, 1976; Pollock et. al., 1978; Kasch, 1980; Kasch and Kulberg, 1981) indicate that individuals who maintained conditioning patterns through middle-age do not conform to these aging curves for cardiovascular function or maximal oxygen uptake.

THE LONGITUDINAL STUDIES ON EXERCISE INTERVENTION AND AGING

The longest and most controlled of these longitudinal studies were initiated in the 1960's in the Adult Fitness Program at San Diego State University (SDSU) by Fred Kasch,

PhD and presently continues under the direction of Janet P. Wallace, PhD and Steven P. Van Camp, MD, FACC.  These studies have additional importance in terms of investigating the role of physical activity in the prevention and control of age-related diseases such as hypertension, hyperlipidemia, diabetes, and coronary artery disease.

Several groups of men and women have been observed for the past two decades.  Thus far, only two separate groups of men, observed for 10 and 15 years respectively, have been previously reported in the literature (Kasch and Wallace, 1976; Kasch, 1980; Kasch and Kulberg, 1981) specific to physical conditioning on cardiovascular function or maximal oxygen uptake.


Subjects

Demographics of these two groups plus an additional randomized control group are summarized in Table 1.  The men in the 15 year group were active prior to the initiation of the project in 1964 and have therefore been termed the previously active group.  In contrast, the 10 year group which consists of sedentary men who volunteered for a physical conditioning program between 1966 and 1968, has been called the previously sedentary group.  Since it is extremely difficult to keep sedentary controls involved in a longitudinal study of this nature, no control group has been observed longer than 2 years (Kasch et. al., 1973).

Of the 15 year group, one subject dropped out between the 10th and 15th reports.  On the other hand, the 10 year group recruited 150 sedentary men between 1966 and 1968.  The 24% that remains in this group after 10 years is higher than any exercise intervention study of this duration (Oldridge, 1979).


Methods

Variables measured on every subject throughout the entire project were 1) body weight and body height, 2) resting heart rate and blood pressure, 3) maximal oxygen uptake via a step bench, motordriven treadmill or a cycle ergometer, and 4) daily conditioning patterns.  Blood chemistries such as total cholesterol, triglycerides,

Table 1. Demographics of the subject groups.

GROUPS

| VARIABLE | 2 Year Sedentary Control | 10 Year Previously Sedentary | 15 Year Previously Active |
|---|---|---|---|
| Initial Measurements (year) | 1966 | 1966 - 1968 | 1964 |
| n | 6 | 36 | 15 |
| Age (years) | 48.2 * 6.0 @ | 47.3 NR | 44.6 6.9 |
| Height (cm) | 175.2 3.4 | 178.0 7.9 | 177.5 6.8 |
| Weight (kg) | 72.1 7.4 | 81.9 12.6 | 76.8 8.3 |
| $\dot{V}_{O_2}max$ ($ml \cdot min^{-1} \cdot kg^{-1}$) | 33.8 4.8 | 30.4 6.0 | 43.7 7.1 |

* = mean
@ =standard deviation
NR=not reported

glucose, and thyroid were first measured in 1968. HDLs
were added in 1978. However, blood results will be
reported elsewhere. Body composition was analyzed by
anthropometry (Yuhasz, 1974) beginning in 1972 and by
hydrostatic weighing (Brozek and Keys, 1974) beginning in
1975. This evaluation was administered at 0, 6, and 12
months of the first year of conditioning for the initially
sedentary subjects and yearly thereafter for all subjects.
Since the relative duration of the involvement of a control
group in these studies was short, limited comparisons between
the experimental and control groups were made. Instead,
population norms for the aging population were compared to

the two experimental groups.

Results

   Conditioning patterns. From 1964 to 1973, the men in
the 15 year group swam (n=2) or ran (n=13) or swam and ran
(n=1) at an average frequency of 3.0 per week for a duration
of 59 minutes and at an intensity of 86% of their maximal
capacity. In the following 5 years, conditioning frequency
increased 10%, but intensity and duration decreased 10% and
24% respectively. Two major injuries occurred in the group
in the last 5 years. The first was due to an automobile
accident and the second was due to severe knee joint
degeneration.

   In the 10 year group 7 men swam and 29 men ran.
Swimming frequency was 2.1 per week for a duration of 47
minutes whereas running frequency was 2.3 per week for a
duration of 37 minutes. Intensity for both groups was 70 -
80%. Attendence was 69% for the swimmers and 78% for the
runners.

   Maximal oxygen uptake. In 1964 the $\dot{V}_{O2}$max of the 15
year group was slightly higher than that of moderately active
men of the same age. In contrast to the previously
reported aging declines, this group of men maintained the
same $\dot{V}_{O2}$max for the next 10 years (Kasch and Wallace, 1976)
with typical aging declines in the following 5 years (Kasch
and Kulberg, 1981). The value for the 15 year $\dot{V}_{O2}$max was
higher than would be expected in normal aging. These changes
are illustrated in Figure 1.

   On the other hand, the $\dot{V}_{O2}$max of the 10 year group which
was sedentary prior to the study, was below that of sedentary
men of the same age. During the first 12 months of
conditioning the $\dot{V}_{O2}$max increased to slightly below that of
moderately active men of the same age. For the next 9
years the $\dot{V}_{O2}$max remained unchanged (Kasch, 1980). These
results are shown in Figure 2. The maximal oygen uptake of
the 2 year control group was similar to the appropriate
aging curve at the beginning of the study. During the
next 2 years this group continued to follow the normal aging
curve in cardiovascular function (Kasch et. al., 1973).

   Body weight. Figure 3 shows the changes in body weight

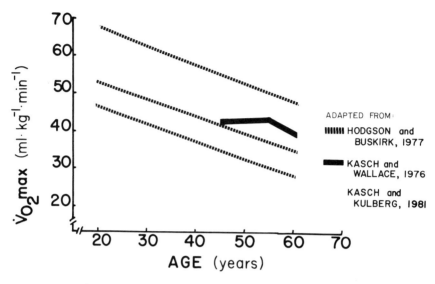

Figure 1.   15 years of conditioning vs. normal aging:
maximal oxygen uptake of previously active middle-aged men.

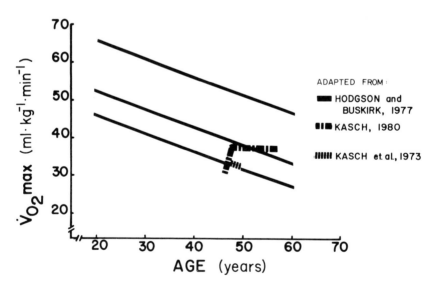

Figure 2.   10 years of conditioning vs. normal aging:   maximal
oxygen uptake of previously sedentary middle-aged men.

with physical conditioning vs. normal aging. Whereas the 10 and 15 year groups would have gained 1.3 kg and 3.0 kg respectively with normal aging (Brozek, 1952), they decreased 4.0 kg and 3.0 kg with conditioning. On the other hand, the 2 year control group followed the normal aging weight gains.

Resting blood pressure. Blood pressure changes are shown in Figure 4. At the beginning of the studies, both groups had slightly lower systolic and diastolic pressures than the population norms (Lasser and Master, 1959). However, 10 and 15 years later, pressures had decreased in contrast to the increasing pressures associated with aging. In the control group, systolic blood pressures were slightly higher and diastolic blood pressures were slightly lower than the normal corresponding age group, but both followed the normal aging changes.

Prevalence of exercise-induced ST segment depression. Figure 5 illustrates the prevalence of exercise-induced ST segment depression in an apparently healthy population (Cumming et. al., 1972) and in the 15 year group for the sixth decade. The prevalence of ST segment depression in the 15 year group was 6.3% by exercise ECG criterion. No angiography or radionucleid ventriculography was administered to this group at that time. In general, documented diseases included one Type I diabetic diagnosed in 1962, one hypertensive who had a cerebral vascular accident in 1977, one transient ischemic attack (TIA) in 1978, one hypertensive who had a myocardial infarction in 1977, and one obese subject. ECG abnormalities other than ST segment depression was demonstrated in one individual with occasional runs of paroxsymal atrial tachycardia and frequent PVC's during rest and exercise at 10 years, who later had the TIA at 14 years.

Discussion

The results of these longitudinal studies do not agree with the previous literature in terms of age changes in cardiovascular function (Hodgson and Buskirk, 1977), in body weight (Brozek, 1952), in resting blood pressure (Lasser and Master, 1959), or in disease prevalence (Cummings et. al., 1972). Most of these previous studies are based on cross-sectional data which are confounded by secular trends or cohort variation.

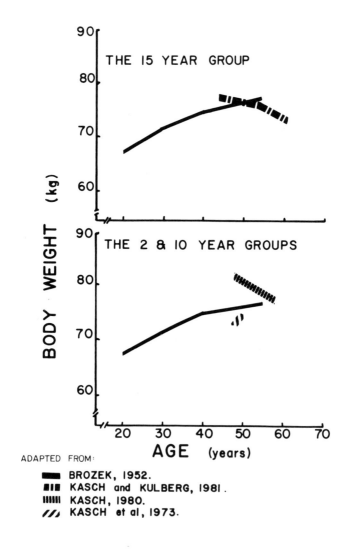

Figure 3.  10 and 15 years of conditioning vs. normal aging:
body weight of middle-aged men.

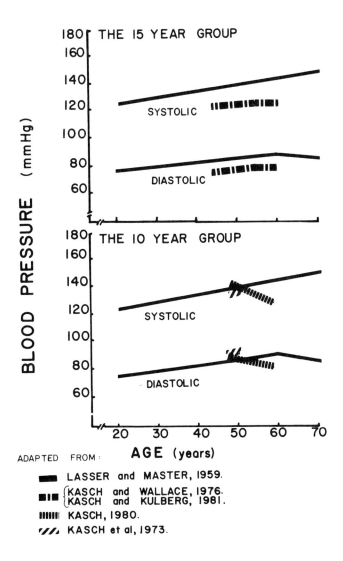

ADAPTED FROM:

▬▬ LASSER and MASTER, 1959.

▪■ {KASCH and WALLACE, 1976. / KASCH and KULBERG, 1981.}

ⅢⅢⅢ KASCH, 1980.

⁄⁄⁄ KASCH et al, 1973.

Figure 4.   10 and 15 years of conditioning vs. normal aging: resting blood pressures of middle-aged men.

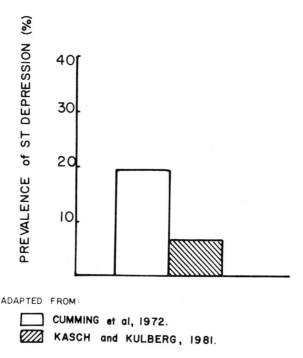

ADAPTED FROM:

☐ CUMMING et al, 1972.

▨ KASCH and KULBERG, 1981.

Figure 5. The prevalence of ST segment depression after 15 years of conditioning vs. normal aging in middle-aged men.


Perhaps the most relevant variable that would be responsible for such cohort variation is physical activity. According to the Specificity of Training and the Overload Principles, the quality of function is directly related to the exercise stimulus applied (Astrand and Rodahl, 1977). In Robinson's original 1938 work on cardiovascular function, he attributed the drop between the second and third decade cohorts to a difference in physical activity. Pollock and others illustrated that the changes in $\dot{V}_{O_2}$max among cohorts was directly related to the miles trained per week (Pollock et. al., 1978). Although it is unknown how conditioning patterns altered over the life-span, it is quite well known that each successive cohort had improved training methods (Lucas and Smith, 1978). Consequently, the application of the principles of training to a cross-sectional design should logically result in higher capacities for the younger cohorts. Therefore, longitudinal studies are a more valid approach to the construction of aging curves for cardiovascular function.

On the other hand, the early longitudinal studies supported the findings of the cross-sectional studies for active (Dill et. al., 1964; Dehn and Bruce, 1972; Astrand et. al., 1973; Robinson et. al., 1975) and athletic (Robinson et. al., 1976) populations. Just as in the cross-sectional studies, the design of the longitudinal studies which varied from 2 to 31 years in duration, failed to observe the influencing variable of physical activity. Only one of these studies attempted to relate conditioning patterns to maximal oxygen uptake (Robinson et. al., 1975). In this study, Robinson and others reported a deviant increase in maximal oxygen uptake during the last 10 years of the 31 year study for a subgroup of men who had increased their participation in vigorous activities.

Better controlled studies, ie; those which also observed physical conditoning, support the results reported by Kasch and others. In a review of Soviet literature on exercise and aging, Gore reports a 10 year longitudinal study on 25 men and women between the ages of 51 to 74 years who engaged in activity twice a week for 90 minutes. Modes of activity were walking, skiing, and rambling. After 10 years of conditioning the subjects had demonstrated no change in all the variables measured. Maximal oxygen uptake, however, was not measured directly (Gore, 1972).

Pollock and others measured maximal oxygen uptake and other related variables with training patterns in 8 champion masters runners for a period of 5 years. Neither training patterns or cardiovascular function changed over this 5 year period (Pollock et. al., 1978).

Future Directions

In conclusion, it seems possible that physical activity may appear to be able to delay the onset of aging and subsequent age-related diseases. However, two major issues should be addressed before this statement can be better substantiated. The first issue is to describe true aging. The second, then is to separate the integrative systems into their parts and observe the contribution of each to the aging decrements.

To accomplish this first task, aging researchers must first address the problem of separating the effects of sedenatry living from true aging. The human organism was designed for movement, yet in modern society experiences very little. This sedentary environment results in deconditioning. The physiological consequences of deconditioning are best illustrated by bed rest studies. Figure 6 compares the changes during 21 days of bed rest (Saltin et. al., 1968) to 30 years of aging (Astrand and Rodahl, 1977). The rate of these changes are remarkably similar.

The next step in addressing this problem is to identify the initiating variables. For example, the last 5 years of the 15 year study reported by Kasch and Kulberg showed declines in both maximal oxygen uptake and in conditioning patterns. Even though the changes in conditioning patterns could be associated with injuries and the occurence of disease, it remains difficult to ascertain which came first. In other words, in aging, do conditioning changes result in functional changes or do the functional changes of aging result in conditioning changes? Not until daily conditioning patterns are observed along with the functional changes can this issue be addressed. Presently, this is one of the tasks of the SDSU Adult Fitness Program in the next decade.

Once true aging changes have been established for such complex integrative functions, the separate systems should then be observed for their specific contributions to the aging decrements. For example, the observation of cardiac performance, blood volume, or capillary density should provide more information on the contribution of the cardiovascular system to integrative aging. Likewise, diffusion capacity, pulmonary functions and closing volumes

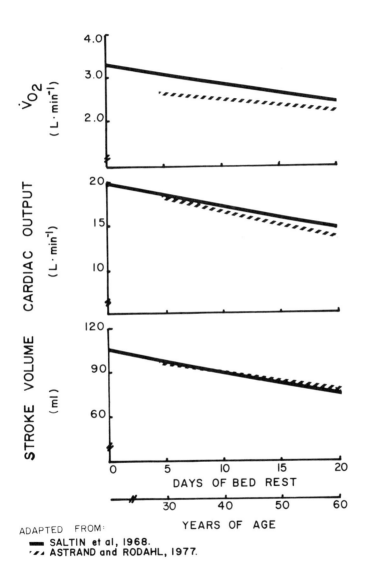

ADAPTED FROM:
— SALTIN et al, 1968.
⁄⁄⁄ ASTRAND and RODAHL, 1977.

Figure 6.  A comparison of the physiological changes
during 21 days of bed rest and 30 years of normal aging.

may provide more relevant information concerning the respiratory system. In terms of metabolic variables anaerobic threshold (the workrate at which the onset of metabolic acidosis occurs) and enzymes should also be observed. Neuro-muscular function can be examined in terms of reaction time variables, maximal strength and coordination. Finally, catecholamine, insulin, glucagon, growth hormone and cortisol response to stress with the accompanying dynamics of fuel availability and sympathetic control, should be the objective of endocrine focus. The observation of some of these variables is in the design of the Baltimore Longitudinal Study (US DHEW, 1980) which is the largest, longest, and most comprehensive investigation on aging. The SDSU Adult Fitness Program is also planning research in this direction with an emphasis on physical conditioning.

Identification and understanding of such variables most responsible for the clinical manifestations of aging may result in better management of the aging population. Exercise may have a significant role in this management; if not to forestall the onset or retard the rapid declines of aging, but to maintain the quality of life through the prevention and control of age-related diseases.

REFERENCES

Astrand I, Astrand PO, Hollback I, Kilbom A (1973). Reduction in maximal oxygen uptake with age. JAP 35(5):649-654.

Astrand PO, Rodahl K (1977). "Textbook of Work Physiology." McGraw-Hill.

Boyer J and Kasch FW (1970). Exercise therapy in hypertensive men. JAMA 211(10):1668-1671.

Brozek J (1952). Changes of body composition in man during maturity and their nutritional implications. Federation Proceedings 11:787.

Brozek J, Keys A (1951). The Evaluation of Leanness-Fattness in Man: Norms and Interrelationship. Brt J Nutr 5(2):194-206.

Bruce, Robert (1973). Principles of Exercise Testing, ed Naughton J, Hellenstein H. "Exercise Testing and Exercise Training in Coronary Heart Disease." Academic Press.

Cumming GR, Borysyk LM, Dufresne C (1972). The maximal exercise ECG in asymptomatic men. Canad Med Assoc J 106:649-53.

Dehn M, Bruce R (1972). Longitudinal variations in maximal oxygen intake with age and activity. JAP 33(6):805-807.

Dill DB, Robinson S, Balke B, Newton JL (1964). Work tolerance: age and altitude. JAP 19(3):483-488.

Drinkwater B, Horvath S, Wells C (1975). Aerobic power of females, ages 10-68. J Gerontology 30(4):385-394.

Gore I (1972). Physical activity and ageing-a survey of Soviet literature III: the character of physical activity; training and longitudinal results. Geron Clin 14:78-85.

Hodgson JL, Buskirk ER (1977). Physical fitness and age, with emphasis on cardiovascular function in the elderly. J Am Geriatrics Soc 25(9):385-392.

Kasch FW (1980). A ten year study of physiological changes in initially sedentary middle aged men. Proceedings XXXIII International Congress of Physiological Sciences, Prague.

Kasch FW, Kulburg J (1981). Physiological variables during 15 years of endurance exercise. Scand J Sports Sci 3(2):59-62.

Kasch FW, Phillips W, Carter L, Boyer J (1973). Cardiovascular changes in middle-aged men during two years of training. JAP 34(1).

Kasch FW, Wallace JP (1976). Physiological variables during 10 years of endurance exercise. Med Sci Sport 8(1):5-8.

Kavanagh T (1979). Intervention Studies in Canada: primary and secondary intervention. Pollock M, Schmidt D (eds): Heart Disease and Rehabilitation," Houghton Mifflin Professional Publishers.

Kohn R (1971). "Principles of Mamalian Aging." New
Jersey: Prentice-Hall.

Lasser RP, Master AM (1959). Observation of frequency
distribution curves of blood pressure in persons age 20-106.
Geriatrics 14:345.

Lucas J, Smith R (1978). "Saga of American Sport,"
Philadelphia: Lea & Febiger.

Oldridge N (1979). Compliance with exercise programs.
Pollock M, Schmidt D (eds): "Heart Disease and
Rehabilitation," Houghton Mifflin Professional Publishers.

Pollock M, Miller H, Ribisl P (1978). Effect of fitness on
aging. Phys Spts Med. August: 45-48.

Profant G, Early R, Nilson K, Kusumi F, Hofer V, Bruce R
(1972). Responses to maximal exercise in healthy middle-aged
women. JAP 33(5):595-599.

Robinson S (1938). Experimental studies of physical fitness
in relation to age. Arbeitsphysiologie 10:251-323.

Robinson S, Dill DB, Robinson D, Tzankoff SP, Wagner JA
(1976). Physiological aging of champion runners. JAP
41(1):46-51.

Robinson S, Dill DB, Tzankoff SP, Wagner JA, Robinson D
(1975). Longitudinal studies of aging in 37 men. JAP
38(2):263-267.

Saltin B, Blomquist G, Mitchell JH, Johnson RL, Wildenthal K,
Chapman CB (1968). Response to exercise after bed rest and
after training. Circ 37-38. Suppl (7):1-78.

Shock N, (1972). Energy metabolism, caloric intake and
physical activity of the aging. In Carlson CA (ed):
"Nutrition in Old Age," Uppsala: Almquist and Wiksell.

Shock N (1977). Systems integration. In Finch C, Hayflick L
(eds): "Handbook of the Biology of Aging," Van Nostrand
Reinhold Co. Pp. 639-664.

Shock N (1979). Systems physiology and aging. Fed Proc
38(2):161-162.

Taylor H, Buskirk E, Henschel A (1955). Maximal oxygen intake as an objective measure of cardiorespiratory performance. JAP 8:73-80.

US Department of HEW (1980). The Baltimore longitudinal study of the National Institute on aging. DHEW Publication No. (NIH) 78-134.

Yuhasz M (1974). Physical fitness and sports appraisal laboratory manual. University of Western Ontario.

# Index